DIVINE INSTITUTIONS

Uninscribed Black Gloss ware, Atelier des petites estampilles, third century BCE. Su concessione del Ministero per i beni e le attività culturali e per il turismo–Museo Nazionale Romano. (Photo credit: Author)

Divine Institutions

RELIGIONS AND COMMUNITY IN THE MIDDLE ROMAN REPUBLIC

DAN-EL PADILLA PERALTA

PRINCETON UNIVERSITY PRESS
PRINCETON & OXFORD

Published by Princeton University Press
41 William Street, Princeton, New Jersey 08540
99 Banbury Road, Oxford OX2 6JX

press.princeton.edu

First paperback printing, 2023
Paperback ISBN 978-0-691-24763-2
Cloth ISBN 978-0-691-16867-8
ISBN (e-book) 978-0-691-20082-8

British Library Cataloging-in-Publication Data is available

Editorial: Rob Tempio and Matt Rohal
Production Editorial: Brigitte Pelner
Production: Erin Suydam
Publicity: Alyssa Sanford (US) and Amy Stewart (UK)
Copyeditor: Dawn Hall

Jacket/Cover Design: Chris Ferrante

This book has been composed in Arno

Printed in the United States of America

CONTENTS

ABBREVIATIONS

ABBREVIATIONS OF ANCIENT AUTHORS generally orbit the format of the *Oxford Classical Dictionary*,[4] with some idiosyncratic variations. With the exception of authors included in *FGH* and *FRHist*—for which see below—I cite fragmentary authors from their standard or most recent editions, designating the edition used by supplying the name of the editor after the fragment number. (Thus, for example, Warmington = *Remains of Old Latin*; but I abbreviate Lindsay's 1913 edition of Festus simply as "L."). When citing fragments from books 14–20 of Dionysius of Halicarnassus's *Roman Antiquities*, I follow the alphanumeric scheme of Sylvie Pittia's 2002 edition. Please also note:

AE	*L'Année Épigraphique: Revue des Publications Épigraphiques Relatives à l'Antiquité Romaine*, 1888–.
AUSTIN	M. M. Austin, *The Hellenistic World from Alexander to the Roman Conquest*, 1981.
CIE	*Corpus Inscriptionum Etruscarum*, eds. C. Pauli et al., 1893–1996.
CIL	*Corpus Inscriptionum Latinarum*, eds. T. Mommsen et al., 1863–.
ERNOUT	*Recueil des Textes Latins Archaïques*², ed. A. Ernout, 1957.
ET	*Etruskische Texte*, ed. H. Rix, 1991.
FGH	*Die Fragmente der Griechischen Historiker*, eds. F. Jacoby et al., 1923–.
FRHIST	*The Fragments of the Roman Historians*, eds. T. J. Cornell et al., 2013.
IG	*Inscriptiones Graecae*, 1873–.
IGUR	*Inscriptiones Graecae Urbis Romae*, ed. L. Moretti, 1968–1990.
ILLRP	*Inscriptiones Latinae Liberae Rei Publicae*, ed. A. Degrassi, 1957–1963.

ILS	*Inscriptiones Latinae Selectae*, ed. H. Dessau, 1892–1916.
IMAG.	*Inscriptiones Latinae Liberae Rei Publicae: Imagines*, ed. A. Degrassi, 1965.
IMAGINES	*Imagines Italicae: A Corpus of Italic Inscriptions*, eds. M. H. Crawford et al., 2011. NB: Material *not* in commentary section is cited as Crawford et al., 2011.
INSCRITAL 13.3	*Inscriptiones Italiae*, vol. 13, fasc. 1, ed. A. Degrassi, 1947.
LTUR	*Lexicon Topographicum Urbis Romae*, ed. E. M. Steinby, 1993–2000.
MRR	T.R.S. Broughton, *The Magistrates of the Roman Republic*, 1951–1985.
ORF^4	*Oratorum Romanorum Fragmenta Liberae Rei Publicae*, ed. H. Malcovati, 4th ed., 1976.
RMR	*Roma Medio Repubblicana: Aspetti Culturali di Roma e del Lazio nei secoli IV e III a.C.*, 1977.
SIG	*Sylloge Inscriptionum Graecum*, eds. W. Dittenberger / F. Hiller von Gaertringen, 1917–1920.
SHERK	R. K. Sherk, *Roman Documents from the Greek East*, 1969.
SNG	*Sylloge Nummorum Graecorum*, 1930–.
TLE	*Testimonia Linguae Etruscae*, ed. M. Pallottino, 1968.
TLL	*Thesaurus Linguae Latinae*, 1900–.

FIGURES, COLOR PLATES, AND TABLES

Figures

Color Plates

Tables

ACKNOWLEDGMENTS

ON A WRETCHEDLY RAINY OXFORD DAY in January 2007, Martin Goodman set "Why did Greeks, Romans, and Jews build temples?" as the prompt for my second tutorial paper. Later that same year, when I encountered and devoured Anna Clark's *Divine Qualities* over coffee at Blackwell's, the seeds for this project were planted. (The title of this book is an expression of my debts to Clark's scholarship, and not just a nod to Lactantius.) At Stanford, these seeds began to germinate, and I renew my thanks both to the dissertation committee that nurtured some promising first growths while whacking the weeds—Walter Scheidel, Ian Morris, Josiah Ober, and Jennifer Trimble—and the Stanford Interdisciplinary Graduate Fellowship for its steady infusion of greenbacks. Since 2014, Walter Scheidel has continued to nudge and guide, not least of all by introducing me to the work of Seth Richardson when I was struggling to recast the manuscript. On a return trip to Stanford in February 2016 to present the project as it was sloughing off its old skin, Matthieu Abgrall and Josiah Ober peppered me with edifying questions, several of which took me in new directions.

The manuscript was refined and my frames of reference expanded during two delightful years at Columbia University's Society of Fellows. For conversation, encouragement, and lynx-eyed attention to work-in-progress, I thank Ben Breen, Christopher Brown, Maggie Cao, Eileen Gillooly, Brian Goldstone, María González Pendás, David Gutkin, Hidetaka Hirota, Murad Idris, Carmel Raz, Rebecca Woods, and Grant Wythoff. Columbia's Classics Department signed off on my designs to teach Roman religion and supported me in all sorts of ways: thanks to Marcus Folch, Joseph Howley, Deborah Steiner, Katharina Volk, Gareth Williams, and Jim Zetzel. During my time at the Society, friends at other institutions—Emilia Barbiero, Seth Bernard, and Amy Richlin—gave feedback on portions of the manuscript. Although I have not always been wise enough to heed their recommendations, the book would be much poorer without them.

Since I joined the Princeton faculty in fall 2016, the journey from rough manuscript to finished book has been made much more tolerable and enjoyable by colleagues who shared unstintingly of their time and good humor:

Yelena Baraz, Joshua Billings, Caroline Cheung, Marc Domingo Gygax, Denis Feeney, Andrew Feldherr, Harriet Flower, Michael Flower, Brooke Holmes, Bob Kaster, Daniela Mairhofer, and Brent Shaw. Participants in the SPQR reading group and the students who enrolled in the two graduate seminars I taught fall 2016 and 2017 opened my eyes to new ways of doing business; my warmest gratitude goes to Tyler Archer, Malina Buturovic, Katie Cruz, Katie Dennis, Brahm Kleinman, Maggie Kurkoski, Sarah Johnson, Caroline Mann, Carolyn Tobin, Keegan Valbuena, Thomas Wilson, and Elliot Wilson. At a 2017 Princeton conference that I co-organized with Amit Shilo (UCSB), Ashley Flavell (Auckland) gave a paper on temple construction in archaic Rome: I learned a great deal not only from drafting a response to the paper but also from the question-and-answer that followed.

At the invitation of Sandra Blakely and Megan Daniels, versions of chapters 2 and 5 were presented at the 148th SCS and AIA Joint Annual Meeting in Toronto (thanks 2x to Sandra and Megan for arranging the virtual presentation of my paper while the US immigration service took its sweet time processing my green card application) and at the 149th SCS and AIA Joint Annual Meeting in Boston (thanks to Cavan Concannon for incisive commentary and Sarah Murray and Annie Truetzel for discerning questions). Other audiences that vetted the book's contents in whole or in part include the Department of Classics at NYU in 2014 (thanks to Chris Parmenter and NYU's graduate students for the invitation, and Alessandro Barchiesi, Barbara Kowalzig, and David Levene for probing interventions); the Max-Weber-Center at Universität Erfurt in 2015 (thanks to Jörg Rüpke for co-organizing the workshop for which the paper was earmarked, Maik Patzelt for ensuring that I could deliver the paper over Skype, and Richard Gordon for articulating what I was hoping to do with the paper better than I could); and the School of Culture and Society at Aarhus University in 2018 (thanks to Anna Collar and Troels Myrup Kristensen for the invitation, Carsten Lange for an enriching response, and Birte Poulsen for educating me about Castor and Pollux). Anonymous referees for *PBSR*, *TAPA*, *AJP*, and *CA* have also been valuable interlocutors over the years: no matter how often I strenuously disagreed with their assessments of my work, I learned much from their reports.

On the march to submission, I came to rely increasingly on the company and inspiration of classicists and humanists of color to keep myself sane. Thanks to Shelley Haley, Patrice Rankine, and Emily Greenwood for modeling what it takes, Sasha-Mae Eccleston for many years of friendship and collaboration, and participants in the *Racing the Classics* initiative for comradeship in the struggle.

The interlibrary loan staff at Columbia and at Princeton fielded over four hundred requests for books and articles these past five years, allowing me to devote as much time as possible to reading and writing. The final manuscript came together thanks to Princeton's provision of sabbatical under the auspices of a bicentennial preceptorship, for which I'm incredibly grateful. At Princeton University Press, Rob Tempio, Matt Rohal, and Brigitte Pelner, as well as copyeditor Dawn Hall, have been very patient with an obsessive tinkerer. The press referees gave me generous and empowering feedback, all of which has left a deep mark on the book even in those instances when I remained obstinately glued to my position.

Three months before I submitted this book's first version to the press, my father died. It remains a source of acute regret that I did not finish *Divine Institutions* in time to present him with a hard copy, but I thank Domingo Padilla Rodríguez for everything he did over the years to make me trust in the power of books. My parents Maria Elena Peralta and Carlos José Peña and my parents-in-law Bob and Debbie Szladek have been bedrocks of support; Yando Padilla Peralta, Dorothy Kadar, Joe Szladek, Acadia Szladek, Stella Fiore, Jessica Szladek, and Zach Hazellief are perennial all-stars. But it is safe to say that without the vigilant prodding of Missy Padilla this book would never have been completed. Thanks for understanding that video-gaming deep into the night is "part of the process." To our little ones—Boots, canine companion through many rounds of revision, and his new human siblings Robinson and Lucia: I promise that the long walks will continue.

August 2019

DIVINE INSTITUTIONS

1

Introduction

ONE STATE, UNDER THE GODS

WRITING TO THE RESIDENTS of Teos in 193 BCE, the praetor M. Valerius Messalla boasted that the Romans "have wholly and constantly attached the highest importance to piety towards the gods . . . our own high respect for the godhead has become manifest to everyone."[1] Although it is not known what the Greeks of Teos made of Messalla's swagger, we know of at least one Greek who quite enthusiastically bought into the notion of Romans as peculiarly and uniquely pious: Polybius. In a famous and much-commented digression in the *Histories*, Polybius praised the Roman state as "distinguish[ing] itself best of all in observance towards the gods" and trumpeted "religious scrupulousness" (*deisidaimonia*) as the practice that "held the Roman state together" (*sunechein ta Romaion pragmata*). "Among the Romans," he added, "their magistrates handle large sums of money and diligently perform their duty because they have given their word on oath"; among the Greeks, by comparison, "men who hold public office cannot be trusted with the safekeeping of so much as a single talent."[2] Many centuries later, Niccolò Machiavelli and Thomas Hobbes separately mined this Polybian musing for insight into religion's efficacy for securing collective obedience.[3]

It is customary nowadays to gloss Polybius's remarks as a nakedly utilitarian reflection on the political and social utility of *Götterfurcht,* or what

1. *SIG*[3] 601 = Sherk no. 8. The cultural politics of the letter: Ma 2000, 101–2; Driediger-Murphy 2014. The "empiricist system" foregrounded in the boast: Ando 2010, 62.

2. Polyb. 6.56 (trans. Scott-Kilvert with modifications), to be read with Walbank ad loc.; Pédech 1965; van Hooff 1977; and Vaahtera 2000. A similar note is sounded by one of Polybius's intellectual heirs: Posidonius (fr. 266 Kidd = *apud* Athen. 6.107.274a). Religion in Polybius: Momigliano 1975a, 41 and 1975c, 73–77; Caygill 2011.

3. Machiavelli [1517] 1983, I.11–14; Hobbes [1651] 1994, I.12§§20–22.

Craige Champion in a recent monograph has pointedly branded "elite-instrumentalism."[4] One might also take these remarks, and late-republican and early Imperial glorifications of Roman piety, as the workings of a relatively straightforward ideological discourse for justifying Roman imperial domination. This book aims to show that there is substantive institutional content both to Messalla's brag and to Polybius's over-the-top praise. In separate but complementary ways, Messalla and Polybius were witnesses to a process: how the Roman state remade and retooled itself into a republic defined and organized around a specific brand of institutionalized ritual practices and commitments. This book argues that this process was a major driver of the Roman Republic's state formation during the years c. 400–200 BCE, conventionally designated as the "middle Republic." Periodization is important; I will come back in a moment to why these two centuries, which open with the ultimately successful siege of the Etruscan city-state of Veii at one end and conclude with the victorious resolution of the Second Punic War at the other, should be understood as a self-contained historical unit. The major focus of this book will be on the cultivation of religious mechanisms for soliciting and affirming internal cohesion, in ways that enabled and were in turn enabled by various forms of collective action. I will demonstrate that it was through these mechanisms that the middle Republic vaulted itself into a new kind of statehood.

At the outset, I should be forthright about what I mean by "state," "statehood," and "state formation," all terms that have launched a thousand ships of scholarly enterprise. Following in the footsteps of Michael Mann and Charles Tilly, I define the state as a coercion-wielding organization that is clearly differentiable from households or kinship groups and that projects authority from a center over all other organizations within a demarcated territory.[5] This definition is not without its critics,[6] but it has the virtue of clarity. By statehood, I mean the attributes that combine to form a state, decomposable according to the definition just provided: organization, the capacity to wield coercion, recognition as different from households and kinship groups, and centralizing preeminence over a describable expanse of geographic space. Finally, state formation is the process whereby entities with these characteristics are "made and remade."[7]

4. Döring 1978; Champion 2017; cf. Nelsestuen 2017, 233–34 on Polybian *deisidaimonia*'s socially coercive utilities.

5. Mann [1984] 1986, 112; Tilly 1990, 1. Survey and discussion of alternative definitions: Scheidel 2013; Davies 2018 on W. G. Runciman's state-formation scheme, which has received less traction than its Tillean counterpart.

6. Overview and dissection of the major definitional uncertainties: Abrams 1988.

7. Scheidel 2013, 9.

This terminology and its conceptual accessories have increasingly been brought to bear on the Roman Republic in recent decades, not without some dispute. Depending on the criteria used, the middle Roman Republic either does not make the cut as a full-fledged state, is a full-blown state with all the requisite appurtenances, or is too slippery to be shoehorned into taxonomies of statehood.[8] Perhaps unavoidably, it has been objected that even to ascribe statehood to Rome is to court oversimplification.[9] But while the notion of the "state" itself—with all its early modern Euro-American constructedness—does not necessarily correspond in whole or even in part to how premodern communities thought of themselves or their adventures in governmentality,[10] the absence of statehood as a conceptual or experiential category in the cognitive universe of the middle Republic by no means vitiates the usefulness of statehood as a heuristic device, provided one is explicit about the heuristic's fundamentally etic aspect.

Over the past two decades, some daylight has opened up between endorsers of Charles Tilly's precept that wars make states, for whom warfare is the foundational catalyst of state formation, and students of the discursive and ideologically enactive mechanisms of statehood, for whom the frictions and gaps between the rhetoric of power and its quotidian realities stand out as most in need of investigation.[11] This book engages with both parties, attending equally to the significance of war's dialogue with religious practice in the evolution of the mid-republican state and to the distance between the claims staked by this state and their material expression. At the same time, however, *Divine Institutions* contends that the payoffs of religious practice for the making of the Roman state should not be subsumed under those of constant

8. The papers collected in Eder 1990 for the most part shied away from explicit engagement with theories of statehood; for more theoretically versed treatments, Walter 1998 and the contributions to Lundgreen 2014; Bernard 2018c, 577–80 on the continuing dearth of engagement with statehood models in the study of archaic central Italy.

9. Purcell 2017, 113–14 for general comment on the propensity to oversimplify by appeals to "the state"; Capogrossi Colognesi 2014, xxii–xxiii, for objection to the terminology of the "state" on the grounds that it flattens "the notion of community" hardwired into the Roman res publica.

10. Thus Anderson 2018, following Quentin Skinner. I do not follow Anderson's leap from this argument to the claim that statehood is not a viable category for the analysis of premodern communities.

11. War making and state making: Tilly 1985 and 1992; but cf. Tilly 2005 and 2010 for a turn to the explanatory power of trust networks. Roman historians mining the Tillean vein: see, e.g., Eich and Eich 2005; Scheidel 2019, chap. 2, some aspects of which were anticipated in Scheidel 2006. The gap between rhetorics of state power and reality on the ground: the papers in Ando and Richardson 2017.

warfare. Although religion penetrated Roman warfare at every step of preparation and campaigning to such a degree as to hinder their decoupling from each other for analytic purposes,[12] it acted separately to bring about results that could not be realized through warfare alone—much as warfare brought about results that could not be secured through religion alone. On this book's reconstruction, the mid-republican state formation project is not fully reducible to a Tillean paradigm. Better-fitting models can be recovered from theorists of collective action and from anthropologists.

For many historians laboring in the shadow of Tilly, it made perfect sense to accord primacy to militarized coercion in studies of state formation and to assign ideological integration a secondary role, but the pendulum is now beginning to swing in the other direction as historical examples of "ritual polities" come to light or receive fresh consideration. In these states, religious mechanisms often shoulder the burden of social integration whenever states lack or, for whatever reason, cannot deploy capital- or coercion-intensive instruments.[13] Even though its affinity for near-constant military campaigning make it an obvious candidate for designation as a coercion-intensive state, the imperializing Roman Republic did not generally leverage fiscal tools or an internal monopoly on violence to engineer social cohesion.[14] What it did do, for the period under discussion in this book, was steadily direct resources toward the regularization of a complex system of ritual performances. *Divine Institutions* isolates this reliance on religious procedures for maintaining state unity—without having to press the lever on capital- or coercion-intensive procedures—as one of the middle Roman Republic's primary strategies for bootstrapping itself into statehood.[15]

12. Religious ritual on military campaign: Rüpke 1990.

13. See the treatment in Goldstone and Haldon 2009, 10–15.

14. Fiscality: Tan in progress on the interpersonal dynamics of *tributum* will likely rewrite the conventional wisdom here, but for now it remains hard to pick up a clear signal of early Roman taxation's socially integrative functions. Internal monopoly on violence as a stepping-stone to social cohesion: the obvious candidate here is the colonization program, whose violence is brought out powerfully in Jewell 2019; but cf. Pelgrom and Stek 2014 for new findings that call into question existing paradigms of colonization and Terrenato 2019, 219–26 for the argument that the colonies "were a far cry from a standardized imperial administrative tool."

15. The language of the bootstrap calls for brief comment. My use of the term gestures to the practice of computational bootstrapping (by which a program is loaded through the execution of a few basic instructions for uploading the program from another source) and to the statistical technique of bootstrapping (which designates procedures that apply random sampling, usually for hypothesis testing). These impinge metaphorically on my selection of the term *bootstrapping*—inasmuch as the book envisions a new form of statehood being downloaded by the

In elucidation of this claim, I argue that during the fourth and third centuries BCE, Roman religious practice comes to the forefront in negotiations of what Richard Blanton and Lane Fargher in their work on early state formation term "quasi-voluntary compliance," a conceptual instrument more sensitive to the gradations of statehood than Weberian models of domination.[16] The Roman state's effort to elicit and manage this compliance leaves a tangibly material footprint; much of this book therefore concentrates on what the material record of mid-republican Rome can be made to reveal about this strand of state formation and its distinctiveness relative to earlier and later periods of Roman history. However one classifies the states that flourished in Rome and Latium during the archaic and early-republican periods, not one of those predecessors is recognizable or legible as the classical Republic, for reasons to be detailed below. It is in the course of the fourth and third centuries that Rome develops the institutions and practices that would lend it coherence as a *res publica*—an entity held in common. This development is fostered by, and to a large degree dependent on, the adoption of public and high-visibility forms of religious experience. The aggregative effect of the sacred commitments under scrutiny in this book was the creation of two representations of statehood, each tightly welded to the evolving identity of the *res publica* during our period. The first, studied in the opening chapters, was prolific investment in monumental cult to the gods. The second, taken up in chapters 4 and 5, was the city of Rome's evolution into an enticing place to visit in order to offer cult to the gods. These two representations of statehood will be shown ultimately to align less with a Tillean scheme of war-making as state-making and more with a Geertzian account of statehood as ritual theater.

Before proceeding to a more detailed exposition of my project, I will first lay out its historiographical and methodological stakes. After a brief tour of trends in Republican and specifically mid-republican historiography, I will then offer some comment on recent developments in the study of Roman religion and outline the contents and objectives of this book.

I. The Middle Republic: Era of Transformations

The archaeological turn of early Roman history has made it possible to surmount the difficulties posed by the literary evidence and compose histories of

---

Roman state through the simple code of a core set of religious observances, and inasmuch as this new form is described with the help of basic statistics—but only metaphorically.

16. Blanton and Fargher 2008 on quasi-voluntary compliance; Kiser and Levi 2015 for its significance to tax-dependent states. The heuristic limits of Weberian domination: Ando 2000, 24–25.

institutional and political transformation that are grounded in the material record of the centuries preceding our period. There is perhaps no clearer and more compelling example of the rewards of an archaeologically focused approach than John North Hopkins's recent book, whose title, *The Genesis of Roman Architecture,* belies its far more ambitiously encompassing program of tracking the formation of the early Roman state.[17] In any case, the sheer abundance of material evidence unearthed in numerous excavations in Rome and its Latial environs from the 1800s onward has forced extensive interrogations—and on occasion outright dismissal—of the annalistic literary tradition around which modern historians such as H. H. Scullard, following in the footsteps of Niebuhr and other nineteenth-century historians, constructed their own Livian-style monolithic accounts. Unsurprisingly, however, the recourse to archaeology is not without its own controversies, chief among them the continuing and likely irresolvable debates about the appropriateness of reading material finds from the eighth through sixth centuries BCE through the testimony of those Roman historiographical and antiquarian traditions that crystallize centuries later.[18] The dogged pursuit of one-to-one correspondences between textual hint and archaeological "proof" in the study of Rome's beginnings has not been without a whiff of fetishism.

Revealingly, despite the generally agreed-on differentiation of the Republic's history into early, middle, and late phases (recently critiqued by Harriet Flower), it is not until the past few decades that single-author monographs have taken up the middle Republic as an object of study in its own right.[19] The most vibrant topic of conversation in recent years, "the beginnings of Latin literature" in or around 240, has been a major focus of disagreement among historians and philologists. Rome's turn to the adaptation and appropriation of a Hellenizing literature in the shadow of the First Punic War was a multicausal phenomenon, having as much to do with escalating aristocratic competition as with geopolitical signaling and (crucially) the arrival of large numbers of enslaved Carthaginians and Greeks in central Italy.[20] The distinctiveness

17. Hopkins 2016.

18. Defending the basic reliability of the historiographic tradition: Cornell 1995, chap. 1. Skepticism: Forsythe 2005, chap. 3. Cf. Holloway 1994 for an attempt at approaching the study of early Rome and Latium's historical trajectory from a strictly archaeological perspective.

19. Flower 2010 for the critique. Among single-author studies I have found most helpful: the underappreciated Starr 1980; Rosenstein 2004 and 2012; Bernard 2018a. Of non-Anglophone treatments, Humm 2005 is important if problematic. For collaborative volumes, note *RMR* 1977—a game-changer—and the collection of papers in Bruun 2000 and Jehne and Pfeilschifter 2006. Note also the review of scholarship on the third century in Roth 2013b, 102–4.

20. Gildenhard 2010, 158–59 helpfully groups explanations for the Hellenizing takeover into

of the mid-republican period as a stage in the city-state's development has also been asserted in accounts of the historical development of Roman political institutions, and in studies of the major magistracies in particular.[21] Representing a continuation of the Mommsenian tradition of constitutional history, these treatments are all to varying degrees concerned with the problems of the Republic's constitutional crisis and disintegration; the ghost of the first century BCE haunts them. Even the most significant recent contributions of German historical scholarship to the study of the middle Republic, for all their careful documentation of the mechanisms of consensus through which Rome's aristocracy and populace amassed the human, social, and economic capital that underwrote the city-state's successful expansion, are inf(l)ected by a consciousness of the republican system's eventual demise.[22] Nonetheless, the role granted to the enactment and promotion of consensus in this scholarship is relevant to the general program of this book. How and where this mid-republican formation of consensus took place—among aristocrats, within and through the *populus*, or somewhere in between—is a matter of ongoing and sometimes acrimonious debate, but it would not be a stretch to state that "locating the core of the consensus" is at the heart of contemporary historical work on the Republic.[23]

My book is partly indebted to this work on consensus but strives to take it a step further. To say that consensus was not generated solely by political actors or through political mechanisms, but by religious actors and through religious mechanisms as well, is not a terribly novel insight for any Roman historian; for any period of Rome's history, and especially for the middle Republic, religion and politics prove extremely difficult if not impossible to disentangle. Most other attempts to "locate the core of the consensus" have eyed religious matters warily, approaching a Claude Nicolet–style level of unwillingness to reflect critically on the productive contribution of religion to the ontology of Roman civic life.[24] Moving in a new direction, *Divine Institutions*

---

three main paradigms. Feeney 2005 mapped a program for historicizing this takeover as a "translation project," and Feeney 2016 realizes it; for the prominence of mass enslavement in this process see n. 34 below. But note Welsh 2011 on the ficticity of 240 as a "beginning."

21. See, e.g., Bleicken 1967 on the tribunate; Brennan 2000 on the praetorship; Pina Polo 2011 on the consulate; Beck 2005 on the *cursus honorums*.

22. Hölkeskamp [1987] 2011, with 1993 for a summary of some of the major ramifications and 2010 for a restatement and amplification of some of the major interpretive lines.

23. The phrase is the subtitle of Hölkeskamp 2010, chap. 8. Disagreement on whether to privilege the aristocracy or the *populus* as the arbiter of political and social power: cf. Millar 2002 and Hölkeskamp 2010. The theory, creation, and practice of consensus under the Empire: Ando 2000, chaps. 5–6.

24. Nicolet 1976a, 26: "la matiere . . . est étrangère à mes goûts comme à mes compétences."

explores how religious ritual and performance generated a consensus that was grounded in trust—with the prospect of force humming away in the background.

In its orientation toward the forging and maintenance of civic consensus, this book owes much to Karl-Joachim Hölkeskamp's publications on the rise of the patrician-plebeian *nobilitas*.[25] Exceptionally well aligned with the program of *Divine Institutions* are Hölkeskamp's descriptions of religious spectacle as acting on "the imperative of immediacy," through which "an intensified degree of visibility, personal presence, public performance and sheer physicality" all became staples of civic and institutional life at Rome.[26] However, even though *Divine Institutions* studies religious projects that are synergistic with and dependent on the formation of a consensus-driven and meritocratic elite culture, it does not endorse the idea that religion is defined by the same parameters of aristocratic presentation and communication as other aspects of political life.[27] That the same people could be and often were magistrates and priests does not justify conflating the two domains of their activity.[28] Conceding up front that religion and politics are for our period nested firmly within each other, I nonetheless hope to demonstrate why the demands and outcomes of religious practice in the fourth and third centuries amount to more than merely communication and discourse among elites themselves, or between elites and the *populus*. The meritocratic discourses whose lineaments Hölkeskamp has skillfully traced were never entirely self-sustaining; rather, these were constantly subject to external checks and critiques, of the sort that the action and intervention of the gods were held to supply. Far from simply being folded into the accumulation of honors and "lifelong dedication to the *res publica* alone,"[29] elite (and for that matter nonelite) commitments to reli-

25. Most influentially, Hölkeskamp [1987] 2011, whose new introduction offers a useful survey of scholarship on the "classical Republic" since the original publication.

26. Hölkeskamp 2011, 162 for the quoted phrases and discussion; I revisit this idea in chapter 4.

27. Religious practice through monumental temples and public rituals as one element of a "symbolischer Politik" (activated and replicated in the interactions of *nobilitas* and *populus*, patrons and clients, magistrates and assemblies, etc.): Hölkeskamp 2000, 224–25; cf. 1993, 28 for temple dedications as mirrors of the "new value system" in fourth- and third-century political culture. The theoretical backdrop to his notions of symbolic politics and political culture: citations collected at Hölkeskamp 1993, 16 n. 9a and 2000, 223 nn. 1–2; 2010, chap. 5 for the full exposition.

28. The tendency to conflate is not limited to Hölkeskamp: see, e.g., Mitchell 1973, 38–39, insisting that priestly activity "was made the instrument of the aristocrat's political appetite and the token of his dignity."

29. Hölkeskamp 1993, 30 for the quoted phrase.

gious practice maintained the fabric of the civic by gesturing to something beyond the civic.

This book's interest in exploring the consensus-weaving relations between the constitutional-political apparatus on one end and the social matrix of religious commitments and activities on the other did not arise solely from reflection on dominant trends in scholarship of recent vintage. Numa Denis Fustel de Coulanges's *La cité antique* (1864), a classic exploration of the interrelationships between religious and political institutions in ancient Greece and Rome, has been an inspiration for my methodological eclecticism. Rarely read or consulted nowadays, *La cité antique* left a lasting mark on the development of several modern disciplines that inform the design of this book—especially the sociology of religion, born with the publication in 1912 of *The Elementary Forms of Religious Life* by Fustel de Coulanges's most famous student.[30] For all its warts, *La cité antique*'s central idea—that the development of political institutions ought to be framed in relation to religious institutions and vice versa—has retained the capacity to inspire. In the 1970s, Sally Humphreys and Arnaldo Momigliano pursued a joint research program that sought to build on some of Fustel de Coulanges's main insights; more recently, his work has reentered the picture in comparative studies of ancient urbanism.[31] This latter-day reanimation of Fustel de Coulanges is one reason why this book concentrates on the transformation of Rome's urban texture through temple construction as both index and catalyst of state formation. Although cities and state formation are not in absolute lockstep throughout the premodern historical record, it is rare to find an imperial structure that does not have a city or set of cities as its home base or institutional and infrastructural pump.[32] Any history of state formation that does not center Rome's monumental urban transformation in the period under discussion would be incomplete. What I hope to underscore is why this transformation became so dependent on building religious structures, and how that dependence interfaced with the generation and maintenance of consensus.

Rome's ascent to peninsular and Mediterranean empire was the decisive factor behind this transformation. It is not for nothing that Polybius memorably opened his history by wondering aloud who would be so clueless as *not* to want to learn how Rome had attained its hegemonic status. The interplay be-

30. Fustel de Coulanges's influence on Émile Durkheim: Momigliano 1975b, 175–77. Usefully on the historian's work and legacy see Yoffee and Terrenato 2015, 6–10.

31. Momigliano 1980; Yoffee 2015.

32. Gutiérrez et al. 2015, 532–33. But the relationship is bidirectional: on empire's elevation of cities into infrastructural pumps—and the privileging of an urban political economy of religion in the process—see Ando 2017.

tween Roman bellicosity and its institutional formation has received a great deal of attention in the scholarly literature, from claims that militaristic aggression was built into Roman institutions and stoked through aristocratic rivalry to studies of conquest's role in the shaping of Rome's financial and economic morphology and of military service as a mechanism for integrating Italian allies into the city-state's ideological and cultural fabric.[33] Then there is the fraught question of how military conquest precipitated and structured that cultural process—or bundle of processes—traditionally characterized under the label "Romanization," both through the hard power of state-organized population transfers to colonies and through the soft power of cultural appropriation and emulation.[34] Whereas in the past this process was taken to be a device for Rome's intentional assertion of cultural as well as political dominance, lately more self-reflexive and self-interrogating models of recent vintage seek to understand the cultural nuances of Rome's relationship to its spear- and alliance-won conquests, especially in those centuries when "Romans encroached on Italy almost as much as Italians encroached on Rome and on each other."[35] However, despite the sophistication of these new models, some of which have called for abandoning the terminology of Romanization (as we shall see), the staging and orchestration of mid-republican Rome's cultural dialogues with the rest of Italy through urban religious spaces and ritualized activities remains in need of further study. This book proposes to remedy that deficit.

So far in this exposition of the scholarship, I have taken it more or less for granted that the middle Republic is a stable chronological target. In this respect I am reaffirming the conventional view that there is a "middle Republic"—different in kind from its "early" predecessor or "late" successor—to speak of. But the idea of a Republic that moves from youth to middle age to tottering senescence has come under fire. Harriet Flower has called for the replacement of this one Republic with several, each defined by a contingent

33. Bellicosity and the aggression of Rome's elite: Harris 1979, with North 1981 on the religious underpinnings; cf. Eckstein 2000 and 2006 on Hellenistic interstate relations. Warfare and Roman state formation: Eich and Eich 2005; Rosenstein 2009 and 2012; Scheidel 2019, chap. 2. Integration of the allies: Jehne 2006 and Scheidel 2006.

34. Colonization and (forced) migration: compare Scheidel 2004b and Jewell 2019; note also Isayev 2017b, 29 on private migration. Enslavement, migration, and appropriation: Richlin 2014 and 2017b.

35. Scopacasa 2016, 35 for the quotation. Besides David [1994] 1996a, notable treatments include Morel 1991; Lomas 1993; Dench 1995; Torelli 1995; Williams 2001; Curti 2001; Bispham 2007a; Bradley et al. 2007, especially the last chapter; Stek 2009; Scopacasa 2015a. Dench 2018 fuses synthesis and critique. The impact of archaeology on the study of Romanization: Curti et al. 1996; the essays in part 1 of Keay and Terrenato 2001; Stek 2018.

constellation of political innovations and practices.[36] In response to this summons, John North has put pressure on the traditional prioritization of politics and political history as the primary means of sorting out one incarnation of the Republic from another—an auspicious gesture for my own project, which sees in the originality and inventiveness of Roman religious practice during the middle Republic an important marker of difference.[37] I reference this back-and-forth not only because it has implications for the conventional formatting of Republican history, but also because it is my cue to outline the assumptions that are folded into my own practice of periodization more explicitly. It is to that subject that I turn next.

II. Periods and Periodicity

This book's starting point of 400 BCE looks to the resolution around that time of the siege of Veii and the tidal wave of agrarian, technological, and economic change that swept through Roman society in its aftermath.[38] Archaic central Italy and Rome have received their fair share of book-length studies recently, several of which are concerned with religious practice.[39] The early republican fifth century, on the other hand, continues to be a source of historiographic and archaeological vexation, although a number of recent publications suggest that the period is on the cusp of reappraisal.[40] Whatever the nature and scope of the "fifth-century crisis," a clear shift in Roman culture and politics occurs at the beginning of the fourth century, a period punctuated not only by the spectacular success at Veii but also by the immiseration of the Gallic Sack—an event of sufficiently seismic import to be registered by Aristotle and Theopompus several decades later.[41] One of the most conspicuous signals of this

36. Flower 2010, differentiating the period 400–180 BCE into three distinct Republics.

37. North 2010. For the middle Republic as a self-contained unit of Rome's religious history note also Curti 2000—which packs the punch of a monograph in a few pages.

38. Cornell 2000b for the main changes to the city itself in the decades after the siege; Bernard 2016 for a stimulating account of the economic impact. Acknowledgment of Veii as a watershed paired with caution against taking the siege's outcome as representative of mid-republican Rome's expansionist practice: Terrenato 2019, 114.

39. See, e.g., Hopkins 2016 and Potts 2016.

40. Talk of a fifth-century "crisis"—see the papers in *Crise et transformation* 1990—is now yielding to a more flexible assessment of the austerity regime that may have prevailed in Rome and central Italy during this era of warlords and *condottieri*: Armstrong 2016; Smith 2017; for warlords and *sodalitates* note also Maras 2018b. Artistic production in central Italy during the "crisis": Papini 2015, 99–100.

41. Aristotle fr. 568 Rose and Theopompus *FGH* 114 F 317; Cornell 1995, 312–14 and Humm 2016, 88-89 for analysis.

shift is a monumental investment in urban fortification, probably triggered by the Sack. The extant remains of the "Servian Wall" that was erected during these years convey an impression of the pools of labor available to the state in this period and are for that very reason significant as an index of state formation; with the wall's construction, Rome entered a new phase in its capacity to leverage both human muscle power and artistic and engineering skill, exploiting new sources of stone in the process.[42] Chapter 2 of this book will track the meaning of this newfound infrastructural capacity for temple construction, another major monumental undertaking of the fourth and third centuries. The mushrooming of temples across Rome's cityscape is tied to other region-wide shifts in material culture that accelerate in the years after 400, from alterations in the patterning of cult sites and urban settlement throughout Latium to the popularization of new types of votives; these changes form the focus of chapter 5.[43]

So much for the beginning of this book's story, but why does that story stop at the end of the third century? Although one could cite Roman awareness of an early to mid-third-century dividing line in the city's religious history as justification for backing up this book's *terminus* by some decades,[44] the arguments for extending the period under scrutiny to the middle of the second century or even later may seem even more compelling. A newly published survey of Roman republican history and the "making of a world state" takes 150 BCE as its point of departure.[45] One could even contend that the most consequential rupture occurs several decades later, as Rome moves from being "in a position of cultural receivership" to propagating a distinctive material culture that fuses Hellenizing practices with endogenous innovations such as concrete.[46] This book's determination to fasten onto the fourth and third centuries is prompted by several considerations. The overriding one is the significance of the Second Punic War and specifically Rome's victorious conclusion of it as a watershed moment without equal. The fact that most recently published accounts of the urban and rural demography and economy of Roman Italy commence with the state of affairs circa 200 discloses an aware-

42. Quaranta 2017 and (in detail) Bernard 2018a are necessary reading on this topic. Italian wall construction in the final centuries BCE: Gregori and Nonnis 2013.

43. The late fifth- and early fourth-century transformation of Latium's sacred landscape: Bouma and Lindenhout 1996.

44. Pliny *NH* 11.186 with Rüpke 2014b, 249 on the introduction of a new procedure for haruspicy during L. Postumius Albinus's tenure as *rex sacrorum* in 275 or 274.

45. Osgood 2018.

46. Terrenato 2015, 524 for ~100 BCE as the dividing line in the history of the city's urban infrastructure. The quotation is taken from Terrenato 2016.

ness of this bright line.[47] The wealth that flowed into Rome after the Second Punic War precipitated cultural, political, and demographic changes whose magnitude were difficult to appreciate at the time and remain controversial today.[48] Modifications to the institutional and fiscal morphology of the Roman state simply did not keep pace with the sheer volume of wealth pouring into the second- and first-century Republic—the corrosive effects of which became a commonplace in literary critiques of elite ostentatiousness in the decades after the Second Punic War.[49] One literary phase change in the years after 200 that is uniquely attuned to this influx is the emergence of historical narrative, whose "scripting of all of Roman history from a single point of view" Ingo Gildenhard has smartly contrasted "to the centrifugal *memoriae* of individual families" that had previously held sway over the commemorative routines of Roman culture.[50] Although the mythistorical and aetiological machinery for Rome's expansionist and multicultural designs was assembled during the fourth and third centuries,[51] it was not until the opening decades of the second century that its operations kicked into high gear—thanks in large part to Roman historiography's appearance on the literary scene. The impact of the post-Hannibalic dispensation is discernible in other cultural-cognitive domains as well; to mention only one, it is striking how quickly Roman notions of space and territoriality are retooled in the aftermath of the Second Punic War.[52]

Shifts in technology likewise justify a sharp differentiation of the fourth and third centuries from the second. Urban construction veered in new directions, as signaled not only by the cresting popularity of Hellenizing portico arrangements but also by the adaptation of the arch into a signature commemorative form.[53] Also proliferating during the early decades of the second

47. Morley 1996; Launaro 2011; Hin 2013.

48. Silver's influx into the second- and first-century Roman economy and its institutional reverberations: Rowan 2013b, to be supplemented with 2013a, 115–16 on the movement of silver away from the Greek East and toward Rome; Kay 2014 is comprehensive. Demography and mobility: Isayev 2017b.

49. See Tan 2017, chap. 3 on fiscal morphology. Early signs of "a counter-discourse that placed positive value on architectural refinement": Nichols 2010 on Plautus's *Mostellaria*.

50. Gildenhard 2003, 112 for the quotations.

51. Wiseman 1995 on Romulus and Remus is foundational; cf. Stucchi 2018 on one curious component of this machinery.

52. Carlà 2017, 120–21 for comment.

53. Pietilä-Castrén 1987 on these projects generally; Russell 2016, chap. 5 on porticos and Hrychuk Kontokosta 2013 on the arch (decoupled in her account from any votive or primarily religious function). To the evidence reviewed by the latter, add Tucci 2018 on the recent find of a false arch on the Arx datable to the fourth century.

century, both throughout Rome and other Italic cities, are *tabernae*—lead indicators of what Steven Ellis has arrestingly termed "the first retail revolution."[54] But it was one specific technological innovation that so decisively altered Rome's urban morphology in the final two centuries BCE as to render the city radically different from its mid-republican predecessor. Although the adoption of marble for decorative purposes marked a departure from centuries of reliance on easily weathered tufas, it is the introduction and popularization of concrete whose revolutionary repercussions cannot be emphasized enough.[55] Combined with the growing appetite (and resources) for requisitioning high-quality stone over long distances for decorative purposes,[56] the turn to concrete ushered in a new era in Roman monumentalism. Penelope Davies must be correct to insist on concrete as a catalyst not only of the "new language of political architecture" in the late Republic but also of the transgression of mid-republican building mores that this new language enabled. Interacting with this technological innovation and with the extraordinary infusion of wealth into second-century Rome was the decision of members of the Roman elite to initiate or underwrite sacred building projects outside of Rome, either in the communities from which their families hailed or at sanctuary locations whose interest to pilgrims ensured their monumental interventions a steady stream of admirers.[57]

A third reason more specific to the shape and rhythms of religious observance brings us back to this book's primary concern with cult practice as a means of grounding and perpetuating civic consensus. By the early third century, disputes over plebeian access to the *sacra* that had previously rested in the hands of the patriciate give way to a homeostatic equilibrium that proved remarkably accommodating of new divinities and their associated cultic practices. Even if this equilibrium is to some extent a mirage, the repeated recourse to exempla from the third century in later Roman tradition looks to be a function not only of the century's subsequent idealization, but also of a status quo

54. Ellis 2018, chap. 4, crediting this development to the post–Second Punic War "influx of wealth" streaming into Italy's urban centers.

55. Mogetta 2015 for the dating of this innovation to the mid-second century; Davies 2017c for the technology's sociocultural impact; Bernard 2018a, chap. 7 on the nature and extent of technological innovations prior to the advent of concrete.

56. To studies of imperial requisitioning, add now Russell 2017 on nonimperial demand for stone and the parameters of that demand's satisfaction.

57. For consular involvement in the monumentalization of a sacred complex outside of Rome see the work of M. Cornelius Cethegus, *cos.* 160, at Gabii: *CIL* I^2.3092d (heavily restored) with Ceccarelli and Marroni 2011, 184. Elite competition and the refurbishment of second- and first-century Italic sanctuaries: Carini 2016; Maschek 2016b for tabulation and explication of regional trends in monumental construction.

that appealed sufficiently enough to warrant idealization[58]—though I reserve the right to take this claim back if Livy's second decade finally reemerges from the rolls of Herculaneum or the dust mounds of Egypt. The more important issue, however, is that this status quo does not last. Domestically, the short-lived equilibrium yielded to an era of accelerated institutional innovation, peaking in the first two decades after the Second Punic War with a series of disputes over rules and norms that quickly attained exemplary status in their own right.[59] The long-term outcome of these disputes and their resolution was the late republican move toward systematization, practiced by an elite whose encounters with Mediterranean multicultural and ecological variety motivated an epistemic revolution and hastened the advent of a "market" for religious goods.[60] Significantly, the deployment of religious practice as a means of positioning the Roman state in relation to non-Romans shifted in the years after 200. Whether or not M. Valerius Messalla's boasting to the citizens of Teos conformed to Hellenistic standards of cultural self-fashioning or represented a uniquely Roman swagger, the decades after the Second Punic War saw the emergence of a variety of discursive and political tactics to differentiate more cleanly (and violently) between Romans and Others. This response to the rewards of empire and to the influx of free and enslaved people into the city of Rome appears to have checked the "accumulative civic polytheism" that had fueled the introduction of new gods to Rome in the two centuries prior.[61]

The increasing prominence of slavery at Rome during the middle Republic has other consequences for Roman religious practice, one of which will come to the fore in chapter 4: the urgency of devising a religious system that vindicated Roman conquest *and* Roman mass enslavement. The language of theodicy is present in Plautine comedy, whose performance in sacred spaces will

58. The core chapters of Roller 2018, the most focused treatment of Roman exemplarity to date, scrutinize the third-century lives and afterlives of Ap. Claudius Caecus, C. Duilius, and Q. Fabius Maximus Cunctator. That exempla were steeped in "exemplary timelessness" (thus M. Roller) does not preclude historicizing them as products of a specific sociocultural formation.

59. See Lundgreen 2011, chap. 5 on *Regelkonflikte* in the religious realm and chap. 8 for the concentration of these conflicts in the years 200–180; Arnhold and Rüpke 2017, 415–16 for a concise account of the highlights.

60. Late republican systematization and/as textualization: Rüpke 2012b; MacRae 2016, to be read with the generative critique of Mackey 2018. Ecological variety and its religious processing: Padilla Peralta 2018b. The rise of a market in religious goods: Bendlin 2000.

61. The phrase: Champion 2017. For the "sense of unease" among Rome's elite in the second century and its religious ramifications see Bendlin 2013, 472–73; on the emergence of a distinctive "slave religiosity" in this period, Padilla Peralta 2017c.

have resonated jarringly and harrowingly with the anguish of the enslaved. Within Roman religion, the drive to render slavery intelligible and apprehensible took on other features as well, and the co-optation of slave bodies into Roman elites' performance of ritual exactitude was among the most important. To my knowledge this observation has not been stressed nearly enough. The Roman elites whose actions and beliefs have been elaborated so painstakingly in Craige Champion's 2017 study of elite religiosity were not disembodied minds—but they were not the direct agents behind much of the ritual performance of Roman religion either. Their doing relied, not infrequently, on the labor of slave bodies. The move from a set of religious observances handled directly by members of an elite family *before* the era of mass enslavement to a system of state-managed cult entrusted to slaves *during* the era of mass enslavement receives recognition as an exemplary episode at the intersection of legend and annalistic history: the transfer of the oversight of the cult of Hercules at the Ara Maxima from the Potitii and Pinarii to public servants, the work of a censor whose activity in the sacred realm (chapter 3) came to be perceived as transgressive enough to have cost him his eyesight.

Having now introduced some of the major conceptual and historical perspectives behind the periodization of this book, I wish next to position this study within the landscape of scholarship on Roman religion before turning to the organization of the book's chapters and their anticipated interventions.

III. Mid-Republican Religion as Stand-Alone Category

The study of Roman religion has progressed considerably since the time of William Warde Fowler and Georg Wissowa, producing a bibliography far too vast to summarize here.[62] Religion's status in early Latin literature has been methodically probed over the past three decades, with striking results.[63] The workings of the mid- and late republican priesthoods, composed of both male and female religious actors, have been scrutinized intensively.[64] While much ink has been spilled on elite religiosity and elite ritual practice, nonelite obser-

62. For Forsythe 2005 to claim in a footnote that Fowler remains the best treatment of "archaic Roman religion" is impish. For coverage of trends and publications see the bibliographic essays in *Archiv für Religionsgeschichte*.

63. See, e.g., Feeney 1991 and 1998; Biggs 2017a.

64. Beard 1980 and 1990; DiLuzio 2016. For the prosopography of the major priestly colleges see now Rüpke 2008.

vances are finally receiving some consideration.[65] It is now impossible to overlook the importance of place to religious practice after the publication of the two-volume synthesis coauthored by Mary Beard, John North, and the late Simon Price.[66] The assumption, prevailing for much of the twentieth century, that Roman religious observance was strictly about ritual orthopraxis and only minimally about belief has been contested and sharply qualified.[67] Long in need of sustained critical engagement, issues of gender and gender politics in Roman religion are now at the forefront.[68] Finally, a sharpened focus on lived experience and communication, prominent themes in the writings of Jörg Rüpke, has played up very effectively the intersubjective and epistemic components of elite and nonelite religious sensibilities in Roman republican culture.[69]

My research draws on many of the new approaches flagged above, taking to heart their shared concern with conceiving of religious phenomena as broadly and flexibly as possible. But my book also seeks to improve on them by arguing for a new methodology that more cleanly and effectively sets apart mid-republican religious practice as an accelerant of state formation. This methodology is driven, first, by the conviction that we can tell a detailed and reasonably coherent story of change over time by looking at the archaeological and literary testimony available to us for the mid-republican city. One major dimension of this story is the unprecedented channeling of resources into temple construction at Rome; another is the reorganization of festival culture and sacred mobility that follows on the heels of this resource allocation. Mid-republican Rome is hardly the first or the last premodern state to resort to the intensification of certain types of religious practice in periods of imperial expansion; one need only turn to its great adversary Carthage to see a broadly analogous escalation at work.[70] The Roman case stands out because the Republic more or less stumbles into a bootstrapping formula that proves to be unusually felicitous: high-visibility monumental enterprises are paired with

65. Champion 2017 for elite practice; on nonelite observances see the bibliography cited in Padilla Peralta 2018a.

66. Beard et al. 1998.

67. Bendlin 2001; Davies 2004; Mackey 2009.

68. Kraemer 1992, chap. 5 on Roman matrons; Schultz 2006b and Carroll 2019 on women's religious lives in the middle and late Republic.

69. Strictly, e.g.,: Rüpke 1995a, 2012a and b, and 2018b.

70. Quinn 2018: chap. 5 on "the circle of the tophet," esp. 98 for the likelihood that child sacrifice crested in popularity as the pace of Carthage's conflicts with Greek *poleis* quickened; 106–12 for the prominence of its sanctuaries in the "tophet network" of the fourth and third centuries.

new incentives for human mobility in ways that dramatically and enduringly reorganize the rhythms of civic and communal experience.

While monumental religious commitments are certainly evident before and after the middle Republic, what is different for the years 400–200 BCE is the shape the commitment takes, the contexts in which it is processed, and the specific mechanisms through which its symbolic and ideological affordances are scaled. Temples and their anniversaries subsequently become focal points for festivals; through these festivals, Rome becomes integrated into a sacralized ecology of annual movements to and from sanctuaries, and this pulsating network begins the work of binding together the Italian peninsula more tightly. In the long term, at both the microlevel of person-to-person interactions and at the macrolevel of Rome's interactions with allied and nonallied states, mid-republican religion evolves into an important and efficacious means for negotiating and securing communal trust. To a large extent, this trust was elicited through the confidence game of persuading Romans and non-Romans that the *res publica* was more powerful than it actually was.

As Seth Richardson has argued with reference to early Mesopotamia, the expressly formulated claims of many premodern states to power and authority regularly outstripped state capacity to substantiate those claims; much of the brilliant sheen of premodern statehood turns on closer inspection to be a hallucination, successful in deceiving audiences under certain conditions of "strategic ambiguation."[71] In the world of the middle Republic, this ambiguation ensued directly from the collapsing of boundaries between the expectation of divine support for the Roman state—solicited and maintained through the construction of temples and the correct performance of ritual in their immediate proximity—and the practical realities of human support for the Roman state, with the latter being increasingly and purposefully assimilated to the former. "Trust" took the form of collective buy-in into the fiction that the social praxis of earning and maintaining human support was actually about earning and maintaining the backing of the gods. Styled as a literary fiction from the very beginnings of Latin literature, whose thematic and discursive parameters are configured in direct dialogue with questions of divine involvement and concern,[72] this fiction is apparent in Rome's monumental and architectural enterprises as well. The rise and consolidation of religiously mediated trust through the physical labor of engineering new temples and new circuits of mobility around them not only

71. Richardson 2017.

72. E.g., the *Bellum Punicum*'s characterization of the gods in/and Roman history: Feeney 1991, chap. 3; cf. Leigh 2010, 272–77 for the epic's encoding of the naval traumas of the First Punic War into its representations of Aeneas's struggles.

resolved a coordination problem in the short term—how to organize and discipline bodies in motion—but also promoted quasi-voluntary compliance in the long term.

Although cognitively premised research into religious awareness and experience undergirds some of this book's analysis,[73] I rely for the most part on methods harvested from the social sciences to pursue and refine my claims. Sociologists of religion have regularly documented religion's capacity to catalyze social and symbolic bonds.[74] These bonds have been studied either as they emerge within and work to define particular religious communities (intragroup) or as they structure the relationship of religious communities to the larger social entities of which they form part. Ultimately these bonds are predicated on social trust, but a small but significant fissure in the literature has opened up between scholars who would ascribe to religion a crucial role in the maintenance of this trust and scholars who see religious commitments as an alternative to mainstream social trust.[75] Michael Welch and his colleagues have scrutinized "the ambivalent role of religion in shaping dimensions of social trust";[76] the creation and reinforcement and bonds within the religious group may come at the expense of (or detract from) bonds between the group's members and members of other groups and/or society at large. The sociopsychological aspects of this trade-off have been most exhaustively researched in connection with modern cults. More germane to this book is work on the interrelationship of religious observance and social capital.[77] Almost without exception, these studies have tended to hone in primarily on contemporary religious practices—usually those of the United States or other first-world nations—and without much engagement with the record of premodern and early modern states, a rather far cry from the historical sweep and cross-cultural ambition of first-generation sociologists of religion such as Émile Durkheim.

Inspired in part by sociological inquiry, however, new research into the origins and evolution of social institutions and the rule of law has begun to engage more closely with the range of religion's social utilities as observable in

73. See Bendlin 2001, 193 for a call to embrace the cognitive study of religion; Mackey 2009 for a cognitive approach to Latin literature's representation of religiosity.

74. Welch et al. 2007, 26 for a concise overview; note also Uslaner 2002, 87–88.

75. Statement of the second position: Putnam 1993, 107.

76. The title and subject of Welch et al. 2004.

77. See, e.g., Wuthnow 2002 on the relationship between religious observance and "status-bridging" social capital; Beyerlein and Hipp 2005 on the link between religiously mediated social capital and neighborhood crime; Welch et al. 2005, 464–65 on the entwinement of "interpersonal trust, civic engagement, and confidence in governmental institutions."

the historical archive, foremost among them its ability to solve collective action problems "by presenting rewards and punishments that greatly reinforce the gains from cooperation in the here and now."[78] This line of research is especially pertinent to my book's concern with bringing into clearer focus mid-republican religion's success at promoting forms of consensus that held together the rapidly expanding Roman city-state.

Clarifying precisely how religious beliefs and activities incentivize coordination has been the task not only of sociologists and political scientists but of economists as well. Awareness of the economic dimensions and payoffs of religious practice is crucial to this book's exposition. The basic outline of an "economics of religion" was first sketched in Adam Smith's *The Wealth of Nations*, but only in the past two decades has the field truly come to life.[79] Broadly speaking, the study of the economics of religion has encompassed two research agendas: first, the interpretation of an individual or a communal choice for, or against, the espousal of a particular faith as a fundamentally economic phenomenon, with "competing" religious options understood as operating within a religious "marketplace" that is analyzable according to basic incentive and preference rubrics; second, the assessment of the impact that religion and religiosity have had and continue to have on economic behaviors of various kinds.[80] As was the case for the sociological study of religion, much of the research started along these lines has taken contemporary societies as its primary focus—hardly surprising given the wealth of modern data available to the enterprising economist.[81] But interest in the first of these topics is also gaining momentum among scholars working on the proliferation of cultic and religious choices available to inhabitants of the ancient Greco-Roman Mediterranean.[82] As for the second, ancient historians have come to recognize that religiously motivated or framed activities such as pilgrimage, festivals, and games have substantial economic implications; in the case of Rome, we even have one ancient writer speaking to this issue directly.[83] However, classical scholarship on the rhythms and patterns of religiously motivated economic

78. Fukuyama 2011, 50, building on Olson 1965.

79. For an outline of the discipline's history, see Witham 2010, chap. 6.

80. On the first of these, see Iannaccone 1991; Chaves and Cann 1992; Finke and Iannaccone 1993. On the second, and with exposition of the empirical and methodological distinctions separating these two subfields: Iannaccone 1998.

81. For the burgeoning literature, not all of it innocent of ideological or discriminatory taint, on certain kinds of religious preferences and economic growth note, e.g., Barro and McCleary 2003; Barro 2004; Brañas-Garza et al. 2004; McCleary and Barro 2019.

82. See, for example, Stark and Finke 2000 and Bendlin 2006, both mainly concerned with the Roman Empire.

83. Cassius Dio 52.30.4 and 7, to be read with Rüpke 2010a, 761–62. On the interaction of

consumption lacks systematic and methodologically explicit articulations of how religion and economics interact.[84]

This book will make use of quantification as one technique for visualizing and documenting the interaction of the mid-republican economy and mid-republican religion under the auspices of an imperialistic state. Since not all ancient historians have embraced the gospel of numbers, I should be clear here that my intention is not to succumb uncritically to what one modern anthropologist has charmingly termed the "seductions of quantification," but to exploit relatively simple quantitative and statistical models as a means of more crisply rendering the middle Republic's profile as a state in formation.[85] The contribution of religion to this phenomenon will be worked out over the course of four main chapters, the respective contents and objectives of which I survey next.

IV. The Road

To the end of demonstrating that religious activity structures and drives the middle Republic's social and economic transformation at several different tiers—from interpolity exchanges to person-to-person transactions—I concentrate on the materiality of cultivating and projecting trust. I argue through four interlocking chapter-long case studies that religious practice in mid-republican Rome promoted greater cohesion and trust through shared and repeated ritual practices, and that this cohesion underpinned both the rise of new collaborative cultural institutions and the authoritative coercion-wielding apparatus of the Roman state.

Religion's role in the imperializing middle Republic did not consist solely (or primarily) in greasing the wheels for more efficient rent extraction on the part of the elite, although that process would be firing on all cylinders by the late Republic.[86] In fact, as I will argue in the first two chapters, the quasi-voluntary compliance regime that emerges during the middle Republic is

religious tourism and economic activity during the Roman Empire see Koeppel and Künzl 2002, which I revisit in chapter 5.

84. Tackling this problem is one of the objectives of Collar and Kristensen 2020.

85. The phrase: Merry 2014, in a study of the use of quantitative indicators by modern human rights organizations; cf. the pointed comments of Smith 2018 on the perversities of "dataism." For the continuing aversion to quantitative models in some sectors of ancient history note Ober 2018, and Lerouxel 2017, 204–5 on Francophone Roman historians; cf. De Callataÿ 2014, 15–20 on the past and present of quantification in ancient history, and Morley 2014 on its prospects and limits.

86. Religion as a rent-extraction device in the "natural state": North, Wallis, and Weingast 2009, 38–39 and passim. For a fresh take on fiscality, rent extraction, and elites see Tan 2017.

rooted in (partial) redistribution of the proceeds of warfare through religious practices, which went a long way toward maintaining consensus. As part of my application of quasi-voluntary compliance to the study of mid-republican religion, I also document the success of ritual practice at bringing people together at Rome. I hope to show why it is not merely the fact that people came together but the fact that they came together *for the purposes of religious activity* that mattered. Trust was forged by coming and spending time together—over and over again, year after year after year, in the sacred spaces of Rome and through the mediation of Roman religious structures. It was this structured coming-together that enabled the social intervisibility through which communal self-recognition was augmented and enhanced, channeling the "common knowledge" that Michael Chwe and other theorists of collective action have examined.[87]

These interrelated arguments thread through the four main chapters of the book, which is organized into two parts. Part I, composed of chapters 2 and 3, opens with a quantitative reconstruction of temple building during the fourth and third centuries, evaluating the scale of the monumental intervention into the city's topography and the labor demands that it triggered. Chapter 3 describes and analyzes the secondary effects of temple construction, specifically the distribution of public goods and the consequences of that distribution for the production and reproduction of trust and quasi-voluntary compliance. In their emphasis on monumental construction and its cultural aftershocks, these chapters respond to the call of recent scholarship to attend more critically to world-historical trends in the interaction between state formation and infrastructural power.[88] Moreover, both chapters make heavy use of those encyclopedic publications that have digested and distilled centuries of archaeological investigation on the city of Rome. The peerless *Lexicon Topographicum Urbis Romae* is exploited often; my undertaking also taps the lusciously illustrated *Atlas of Ancient Rome* and numerous other works.[89]

The second part of this book takes up Rome's festival culture and the phenomenon of pilgrimage, as two interactive and synergistic developments that follow on the heels of the mid-republican city's monumental improvements. Chapter 4 concentrates on the forms this festival and pilgrimage culture took as mirrored in the literary tradition, while chapter 5 shifts gears to concentrate on the far more abundant archaeological and votive material. Much like chapter 2, chapter 5 makes much of its argument through quantitative models and closes with a test run of social network analysis in order to generate new ques-

87. Chwe 2001.

88. Note, e.g., the essays in Ando and Richardson 2017; Scheidel 2018.

89. Carandini 2017.

tions and posit some provisional answers about the relationship between religiously motivated mobility and the exchange of knowledge and information. Common to both chapters 4 and 5 is an emphasis on those feelings of trust and cooperation that were elicited in the course of many decades of ritualized cultic observance. One consistent theme in both parts I and II is the importance of defamiliarizing those generally recognized components of mid-republican religion and those conceptual and pragmatic binding agents that held it together. The institutional morphology of the Greco-Roman city in its period of monumental transformation and expansion should not be taken for granted or as self-evident. Comparative research has brought to light numerous examples of civilizational complexes whose urban designs and sacro-monumental interfaces were plotted along entirely different axes; Emma Dench has encouraged us to keep our eye on the other end of Eurasia if we need a reminder of the paths toward scalable performance and ceremonial that Rome did not take.[90] A second consistent theme is the commitment to reading the material record not as a transparent record of institution-building—or as an assortment of "static props of ceremonial dramas through which Romans . . . endlessly enacted their roles in the cultural script"—but as a dynamic participant in the enactment of those processes that held the res publica together.[91]

Unifying all of these chapters is a vision of the pluripotency of ritual experience in engendering the collective buy-in at the core of state formation. This book subscribes to the notion that Roman religious activity was simultaneously infused by and stimulative of psychological states. Ritual activity marks and communicates intentionality, as Jacob Mackey has stressed in a recent (2017) call for reclaiming belief as a feature of Roman religion. Taking a page from Richard Blanton, we might interpret the intentional religious practices under study in this book as "rites of governmentality" that actively contributed to disseminating a broader understanding of the governance—divine and aristocratic—of the *res publica*: "rites of inclusion," those collective acts of worship (and the historical memory of collective acts of worship) that brought members of the urban community from all walks of life into more regular contact with one another; "discursive rites" such as the *ludi scaenici* that not only incentivized physical co-presence but also supplied an interpretive scaffolding for it; and "morality rites" that in ludic and nonludic contexts

90. See Lewis 2015 for a study of public space in Han China and ancient Rome; Dench 2018, 32 for a snapshot of major divergences in public ritual. For more on religion and state formation in Qin and Han China see Robinson 2016 and Marsili 2018.

91. The quotation is from Ando 2000, 210–11. On reading artifacts as enactive and not simply as mirrors of institutional processes see the comments of Knappett 2011, 26–27.

exalted a certain set of virtues for the appreciation and edification of the *populus Romanus*.[92] The conclusion to this book, in addition to recapitulating my findings and outlining directions for future investigation into the interplay between religion and state formation, demonstrates the cumulative weight of religious rites on Roman social life by quantifying the amount of civic time consumed by them. Centuries before any official text formulated an "absolute link between the realization of the *sacra* and membership in the Roman community,"[93] Rome's mid-republican transformation impressed on Romans and non-Romans alike the vitality of the relationship between religious practice and political identity by embarking on a species of temporal colonization.

Each of the book's chapters keeps an eye on considerations of robustness and proper inference. In the preference for a case-study arrangement, I have aimed for something like a wigwam, to borrow Tim Cornell's metaphor: even if "each strut is relatively weak and can barely stand on its own,"[94] in the aggregate the case studies bolster one another to a degree that make the cumulative argument for religious practices as institutionally productive and consensus-building behaviors that much more compelling. By opting for a case-study format, I have elected against incorporating a narrative emplotment of the kind that normally features in historical analyses of the Republic. One of the reasons for this decision is that there are excellent narrative and thematic histories of the middle Republic now in print.[95] Even though, as Josiah Ober affirms in concurrence with Deirdre McCloskey, "there is no inherent conflict between social scientific and narrative approaches to history,"[96] I have also chosen to avoid narrativizing emplotments in order to register a measure of exasperation with how religious change is normally integrated into narrative histories of the Roman state. Works that are nimble when it comes to political or economic matters resort to curiously awkward or ham-handed expedients when religious issues roll around—losing the thread of religious history after an initial discussion and picking it up only intermittently as the narrative lurches forward, or shoving much of the religious material into a chapter-length unit that is artificially severed from politics or economics. The loss of faith in the old sweeping narratives of steady religious decline followed by an Augustan rejuvenation may have something

92. The taxonomy and its justification: Blanton 2016.

93. Moatti 2018, 394 on Caracalla's Edict: "le premier texte officiel à formuler le lien absolu entre l'accomplissement des *sacra* et l'appartenance à la communauté romaine."

94. Cornell 2000b, 224, gleaning from Hopkins 1978, 20.

95. Rosenstein 2012 is an invigorating read.

96. Ober 2018, 9.

to do with this habit.[97] More in line with historical-sociological investigations into Roman history, I have eschewed a narrative frame to focus primarily on social structures.

The disavowal of continuous historical narrative as an organizing structure for this book has its roots in another choice that calls for comment here. Although *Divine Institutions* selectively taps literary evidence to model the birth and evolution of institutions (chapters 2 and 3) and to describe the messages that these institutions propelled into general circulation (chapters 4 and 5), its primary preoccupation is with the testimony of material culture, for two reasons. The first is that literary sources contemporaneous with the structural transformations of interest to this book are few and far between. Overreliance on the testimony of the annalistic tradition that is preserved in Livy and Dionysius of Halicarnassus—or refracted in other authors who wrote two or more centuries after the middle Republic's heyday—carries with it the obvious risk of distorting anachronism.[98] Those Roman and Greek works that line up chronologically with these transformations do receive attention below, though given their usually fragmentary nature I have tried not to make a mountain out of a molehill. Second, it is worthwhile to center the material evidence, not so much to avoid having to take sides in the conflict between Cornell-style optimism and Forsythe-style pessimism regarding the merits of the literary tradition,[99] but to clear a space for a rethink of mid-republican institutions that does not answer exclusively or primarily to the expectations and demands of late republican and early Imperial Roman writers. It is quite possible that Romans of later periods only dimly grasped the middle Republic's institutional patterning; it is less possible though not completely implausible that Romans of later periods got much of that patterning wrong in those retrospective historical and antiquarian accounts that have long driven and continue to drive scholarship on Roman religion. If "Rome after Plautus fades into something rich and strange,"[100] then a fortiori the Rome of Plautus would have been profoundly strange to the Rome(s) that succeeded it.

I round off this introduction to the book's scope and ambition with three closing remarks on methodology and terminology. First, I will not be terribly concerned in what follows with drawing a bright line between Roman Italy on the one hand and the Hellenistic Greek poleis and kingdoms on the other.

97. Writing the religious history of the Republic after the debunking of this old emplotment: North 1986.

98. Further on problems and issues in the historiography of Hellenistic Italy: Dench 2003, 295–96.

99. Compare Cornell 1995, chap. 1 and Forsythe 2005, chap. 3.

100. Richlin 2017b, 193.

Whatever the merits of Heraclides Ponticus's designation of Rome as a *polis hellenis*, it is obvious that by the end of the fourth century at the latest the mid-republican city-state was actively seeking a place in the greater world of Greek and Hellenizing Mediterranean communities.[101] I will not, therefore, invoke or belabor essentializing distinctions between Romans and Greeks—though I will duly note, beginning with the next chapter, instances where Romans appear to depart self-consciously from or innovate on contemporaneous Hellenistic practices.

Second, I have characterized this book as concerned with cohesion and consensus, in the process steering clear of the lexicon of unity. An emphasis on cohesion is in my view more faithfully responsive to the connectivity that came to define Roman ritual practice. Whether we can speak of cultural unity in any meaningful sense before the Social War is not a question this book will attempt to answer. That Romans fashioned and projected a discourse of *religious* unity is evident enough, but one should not confuse discourse with reality.[102] As Filippo Marsili's comparative study of Roman and early Chinese religious observances crystallizes quite effectively, premodern imperial systems could and did embark on projects of unification without having recourse to a "shared religion" that organized and actualized itself in exactly the same ways in the mind of every individual practitioner.[103] *Divine Institutions* capitalizes instead on the proposition that the repetition of communally orchestrated religious practices—temple construction, festival celebration, and regular pilgrimage—conduced to greater cultural cohesion over time. On my reconstruction, the fastidiousness of cult that Marcus Valerius Messala and Polybius (and, a century later, Cicero) trumpeted as distinctively Roman is best understood as the end outcome of a repetitive dynamic through which Roman identity became increasingly entwined with a specific bundle of group-forming religious technologies.

The maintenance of social cohesion through the cultivation of trust does not presuppose or mandate a blanket cultural unity or homogeneity. What the type of trust under investigation in this book simply requires is a willingness to place "valued outcomes at risk to others' malfeasance, mistakes, or failures"—a willingness conspicuously showcased in the Roman state's long-term adherence to the collective action of military expansion.[104] My use of the term *consensus* should not be taken to signal or imply agreement, unity, or

101. *FGH* 840 F 23 with Momigliano 1975a, 13; Curti 2000, 77–78 on incipient Roman awareness of Greek civic institutions and practices.

102. Cf. De Cazanove 2007 on "the impossible religious unity of the Italian peninsula."

103. Marsili 2018.

104. See Tilly 2005, 12 for this quoted definition.

unanimity; I have in mind a mode of coming together that valorizes and routinizes "assent, consent, and collaboration" even while accommodating disagreement.[105] Without attempting to minimize the occasionally frictive and fractious outcomes of the middle Republic's religious practices,[106] I will outline at the end of chapter 2 and again at the beginning of chapter 4 some reasons why the religious apparatus for holding the Roman state together maintained public trust and consensus while keeping explosive social crises to a minimum during our period. Where and as appropriate, I will also gesture to those incentives for cultic systematization that culminated (after our period) in the game-changing works of Varro, whose attention to local Italic religious variety was mediated at least in part by his lived experiences during and after the Social War.[107]

Finally, the alert reader will have noticed my studious avoidance of definitions for the term *religion*. Having recently chastised a fellow traveler in mid-republican history for failing to engage the prodigious amount of critical scrutiny expended on this term,[108] I will seem the very embodiment of hypocrisy if I do not make clear what I mean by the word. I take religion to consist of a set of ritual practices by which humans acknowledge, honor, and negotiate with superhuman agents. Purely in the interests of argumentative economy, this book will sidestep the question of when and how Roman culture develops an understanding of and a lexicon for religion as a discrete social category, although it seems to me more probable than not that the epistemic revolution (or rupture) responsible for the conceptualization of Roman ritual practices and their attendant affective components as a "religion" had as one of its prerequisites the monumentalization of the city during the middle Republic.[109] Again in the interests of argumentative economy, this book privileges public or public-facing religious activity, not out of a desire to slight the force of private ritual observance but out of recognition that full justice to the (mostly)

105. I quote from and follow the suggestion of Flower 2013b, 9.

106. Cf. Dench 2018, 34–35 criticizing belief/consensus models of Roman imperial rule for falling into this habit.

107. Cf. Rüpke 2014b, 264 on Varro and "the problem of the unification of Italy."

108. Padilla Peralta 2018a, xxxix–xl; to the bibliography cited therein, add M. Flower 2017, 425–26. Cf. Marsili 2018 for a confrontation with the epistemological limits of "religion" in comparative religious studies; Anderson 2018, 63 on "religion" in the wake of the ontological turn; Driediger-Murphy 2019, 47–50 on the value of keeping the term *religion* in histories of Roman cultic practice.

109. On the nature of this epistemic and cognitive revolution compare Ando 2008 and Rüpke 2012b; specifically on temple construction and *ludi* as mediating agents, Rüpke 2010b, 35–38 = 2012b, 28–31; on Varro's isolation of a "religious" sphere as innovative, North 2014; chap. 3 n. 140 for additional bibliography.

obscure dynamics of familial and gentilician *sacra* in the fourth and third centuries would necessitate another monograph.[110] At the same time, and once again in the interests of argumentative economy, my book will glide past the religious personhood and authority of individual Roman priests and of the major priesthoods—topics that have benefited from ample treatments lately—to concentrate instead on the built structures that gave tangible expression to that authority.[111] Lastly, my attention to public religion as a group-centered activity will preclude meaningful engagement with the brewing controversy over Roman religion's capacity to foster individualization—although it should be noted that none of the positions advanced in this book is necessarily incompatible with capacity-building of this kind.[112]

110. Private *sacra*: Cic. *De leg.* 2.46-53, to be read with North 2014, 229–31. Important studies: De Marchi [1896–1903] 1975; Fiorentini 1988 and 2008. For private cult and/as "domestic medical practice" in mid-republican Italy—a development taken up in chapter 3—note now Draycott 2019.

111. The evolution of the major priesthoods: Beard 1990. Differentiation between priests and magistrates in Republican Rome: Scheid 1984.

112. The controversy: see Scheid 2018, reviewing Rüpke 2013. Chap. 4 below comments on the rejection of the ritual individuality of the enslaved; on assertions of religious personhood triggered in response see Padilla Peralta 2017c.

PART I

Build

2

Temple Construction

FROM VOWS TO NUMBERS

> The material aspect of temple founding would be of great interest, especially in the context of that other crucial question of financing temples' construction; unfortunately, the scantiness of archaeological evidence makes it absolutely impossible to try assessing the outlay of work and money required for even those few Mid-Republican temples about whose original architecture we can still form some hazy ideas.[1]

WHILE THE FOURTH- AND THIRD-CENTURY EXPLOSION of temple construction at Rome has not escaped the attention of Roman historians, its historical significance extends well beyond its status as a marker of mid-republican imperialism. At first glance, the state of the evidence for this period in the Republican city's topographical history presents some daunting obstacles. Our knowledge of a boom in temple construction at Rome has been mostly culled from fragmentary or incomplete literary sources. Although the loss of Livy's second decade leaves us mostly in the dark for much of the third century, enough survives from the annalistic and antiquarian traditions to afford a rough sense of the cultural and political ferment set in motion by the introduction of new sacred structures to the urban landscape, and by the introduction of the new or hitherto low-visibility gods who came to be housed in these structures. In recent decades archaeological investigation has broadened and deepened our understanding of Rome's temple-construction habit, by chronicling in increasingly vivid detail previous stages in Roman sacred construction and by attempting to trace (where

1. Ziolkowski 1992, 193–94.

and as possible) the cultural and technological conduits of this monumental escalation.[2]

Even in the wake of new archaeological findings, certain fundamental questions about the Roman polity's investment in sacred structures prove challenging to answer. Prominent among them are the issues pertaining to the "material aspect of temple founding," as Adam Ziolkowski raised in the epigraph to this chapter. Confronted with Ziolkowski's pessimism, one could state that the Romans built many temples and leave things at that. Yet yielding to this counsel of despair is to deny ourselves a golden opportunity for developing and refining a set of theories about how Roman society worked in the centuries under discussion. It is the objective of this chapter to demonstrate how, with the aid of a few relatively simple assumptions, a new cultural history of the fourth and third centuries can be plotted, with temple building supplying the major orientation points. At the center of this cultural history is a reckoning of the labor and capital inputs that temple construction entailed. To arrive at such a reckoning, I will construct a series of models, which will in the first instance be of interest to students of Rome's architectural and economic history. What will ideally become apparent over the course of this chapter is that a refined approach to scales and magnitudes can improve our grasp of the middle Republic's institutional and state-formation arc.

Since the most complicated and arguably most intriguing element of this chapter's exposition will be not so much the conclusions themselves but the paths taken to reach them, the suspense will not be spoiled if I set out the conclusions at the beginning. The models elaborated in these pages open up a space for imagining a Roman monumentality—and with it a Roman conception of statehood—that did not fixate on sheer bigness. It has become almost de rigueur to speak of Rome's commitment to temple construction during the middle Republic as grand or extravagant in scale.[3] However, in contrast to the dedication of the Capitoline temple at the end of the archaic period, or (to fast-forward several centuries) the Empire's massive urban structures with their "timeless and universal attraction,"[4] the temple constructions of the middle Republic exemplify a social commitment to smallness—*repetitive* smallness. The contrast with earlier construction vogues is striking. Scrupulously sifting through the archaeological record, Charlotte Potts has cataloged how sixth-century central Italian communities made the decision "to invest

2. For sharp comment on the formalist tendencies of this research into Rome's urban fabric, see Bernard 2018a, 3–4.

3. E.g., Harris 2016, 50, writing of the "great resources [that] were devoted to temple-building."

4. DeLaine 2002, 207.

great resources in building monumental temples rather than maintaining relatively modest shrines"; John North Hopkins has placed the study of this process in archaic and early republican Rome on an admirably firm footing.[5] However one chooses to interpret early fifth-century trends in monumental construction, lavish expenditure on and investment in the construction of a few temples give way—after the troubles of the middle and late fifth century—to a regime of regular but (relatively) inexpensive projects by the fourth and third centuries. When it comes to size, no temple that was erected during the middle Republic compares to the Capitoline Temple of Jupiter Optimus Maximus. Yet what the middle Republic lacks in the size of its temple foundations it makes up for in their sheer number, and in the rhythms that the regularity of their construction imposed on Roman civic life.

If, according to Rem Koolhaas's enticingly and memorably rebarbative formulation, the subtext of bigness is "fuck context,"[6] the subtext of repetitive smallness is what needs further parsing in mid-republican Italy. That responsibility is the driver of chapters 3 and 4, which explore in greater detail how and why the commitment to build small but frequently propelled the realization of a very specific brand of civic-religious power. The guiding ambition of this chapter, by contrast, is to lay the foundation for a better appreciation of what Seth Richardson in the context of ancient Mesopotamia characterizes as the "shell game of ancient agricultural states": "to privilege attention to the monumental, to imply its political and social importance in (false) economic terms, and to re-valorize the community labor it marshalled."[7] This is not, of course, to say that premodern agrarian societies did not strive to satisfy their hunger for compelling myriads of women and men into monumental labor, often under brutal conditions; among those societies, the Rome that emerges from the mid-republican moment would prove to be nearly without peer in its capitalization and exploitation of human muscle.[8] But the shell game, as Richardson and others have interpreted it, consisted partly in veiling the costs of certain kinds of infrastructural commitments so as to create a mystified projection of the state's power.

In order to recreate the operations of that shell game in the middle Republic, we will need to be as clear as possible about the political and economic

5. Potts 2015; Hopkins 2016; note also the assessment of archaic central Italian monumentalism in Lulof 2014.

6. Koolhaas 1995, 502.

7. Richardson 2015, 298; cf. Xie et al. 2015, 67–68 for pithy recapitulation of the "common conclusions" of the major studies on premodern monumentalism: "the labor required to build monuments is less than previously thought." A similar note is sounded at Scheidel 2018, 239.

8. See the survey of Morris 2015, chap. 3, indexing agrarian state formation to social values.

inputs that had to be coordinated for temples to rise from the ground. We will also have to attend to the possibility that the relatively minimal upfront costs of temple construction were a means of veiling the far greater costs of secular monumental projects: the aqueducts and roads that from the period of the Samnite Wars engineered a profound and lasting revolution in how Romans and non-Romans interacted with and conceived the *res publica*.

I. Why and How Were Temples Built?

We begin with the primary agents for temple construction, and their motivations. At an institutional level, we are reasonably well informed about the procedures for the vowing and dedication of a temple in mid-republican Rome. The decision to build usually followed one of three channels: either a Roman general, usually in the heat of battle, made a vow of a temple to a god or goddess in exchange or in gratitude for their assistance; or the Senate, in its handling of a particular communal crisis, decreed the building of a temple to a particular divinity after a consultation of the Sibylline Books; or, somewhat less frequently, aediles vowed a temple in the course of carrying out some corrective and (potentially) controversial measure.[9] By Eric Orlin's calculations, four-fifths of the temple vows attested from the foundation of the Republic to the first century BCE were undertaken "as a response to an external, military situation involving a foreign enemy."[10] For the majority of temple foundations, then, the initial vow was directly related to the military activity of senior magistrates with *imperium* or the religious oversight responsibilities of the Senate. Which factors compelled commanders in the battlefield to make a vow to a specific deity are not entirely clear, though for a few cases we know of the immediate ecological or environmental contexts that prompted the vow.[11] In instances when the Senate took the lead in vowing a new temple,

9. See Orlin 1997 on temple construction. Broadly on the evolution of the aedileship see Becker 2017; for aedilician fines and temple foundations, Piacentin 2018 (with Estienne and De Cazanove 2009, 29–34 on the uses of *pecunia multaticia*); for a case study of one aedilician foundation, Padilla Peralta 2018c. The distribution of responsibilities for construction: Daguet-Gagey 1997, 27.

10. Orlin 1997, 20; see table 2.1. Further on these vows, Rüpke 1990, 155–56; Aberson 2010 on the "théâtralité" of the ritual's performance on the field; Rüpke 2018b, 92–95 on the genesis of the vow as a strategy for communicating with the gods.

11. In 268, P. Sempronius Sophus vowed a temple to Tellus when the earth shook in mid-battle (Flor. 1.14); in 259, L. Cornelius Scipio vowed a temple to Tempestates when his fleet was buffeted by storms off the Corsican coast (*ILLRP* 310; Ovid *Fast.* 6.193–94). Ecological shocks and innovation in mid-republican religion: Von Domaszewski [1909] 1975, 22–24 and Palmer

the choice of deity was determined by the recommendation of the Sibylline Books.[12] That magistrates and Senate alike chose by and large to vow *temples* is not as obvious a choice as one might think; the second and first centuries witnessed a decisive move in the direction of commissioning and dedicating other types of structures.[13] In the next chapter I will discuss what may have made temples exceptionally appealing subjects of a vow during the middle Republic.

As a stipulation that the temple would be built if a successful outcome materialized—for the general and his army, or for the polity as a whole—the vow was contractual: there was no obligation to build if the gods did not deliver.[14] The complexities did not end with the vow. Adam Ziolkowski is right to characterize the founding of a public temple as "a long and complex, many-sided process" involving among other matters the multiplayer procedures of financing, *locatio*, *inauguratio*, and *dedicatio*.[15] Labor and materials had to be requisitioned (or commandeered) for the temple's building; a site for the new construction had to be chosen and demarcated, subject to the availability and suitability of space within or outside of the *pomerium*;[16] and finally, once the temple had been completed, select magistrates—who may or may not have been the original parties to the vow—had to oversee the official dedication. For each of these different stages, different technologies (from the legal and documentary formulas of the vow, the contract, and the augury to the engineering skills of the quarry and the work site) were mobilized, and a progressive thrust toward standardization and systematization steadily reaffirmed.[17] Moreover, from the moment that augurs departed the Arx to perform their

---

1997, 54–57 on cult to the Tempestates; Padilla Peralta 2018b on divination and ecology; cf. Leigh 2010 on maritime traumas and early Roman literature.

12. Expiatory vows undertaken after consultation of the Sibylline Books: Satterfield 2008, 75–82 and 2012.

13. The rationale for this move: Orlin 1997, 68–70; Russell 2016, 116–17; chapter 1 n. 53 for more bibliography. Construction vows in the western Roman Empire: Ehmig 2016.

14. Exhaustive discussion of the vow: Orlin 1997, chap. 1.

15. Ziolkowski 1992, 193, but incorrectly insisting that individuals could vow and dedicate without consulting the Senate or people; see Orlin 1997, 4; for continuing strife between Senate and *populus* over temple dedications, note Varro *ARD* frr. 45 and 46c Cardauns with Rüpke 2014b, 258–59. The protocols: Mommsen 1887–88, II.621–24; Orlin 1997, chaps. 4–5; Humm 2014, 319–21 for lucid treatment of *inauguratio*. Stambaugh 1978, 557–68 glosses over important details. Further on the gridding of urban space: chapter 3 n. 4.

16. The long-standard claim that temples to "foreign" cults had to be placed outside of the *pomerium* has been conclusively debunked: see Orlin 2002, 5–8 and Mignone 2016, 210 on "Ambrosch's rule."

17. Cf. Rüpke 2010b = 2012b, chap. 2 on writing as spur to institutionalization.

inaugurationes to the final ritual act of dedication, the procedure of temple building was studded with spectacles. While elites vied for the public attention that these spectacles offered, "fervency of devotion" will have mattered to some extent as well.[18] At each step, then, temple building brought together organs of the political system and bodies of citizens in ritually scripted and socially constitutive ways.

This activity did not occur in some timeless institutional vacuum, nor did the procedural channels outlined above emerge fully formed from the head of Jupiter. Rather, these channels came into being and received their juridical and legal shape through the demands that were imposed by the large-scale commitment to temple building. In other words, temple building and its proceduralization were codependent and coemergent phenomena: the more temple building that took place, the more clearly elucidated and refined the system that evolved to handle it. The "first" first-order effect of the commitment to temple construction was therefore the formation of an institutional apparatus that was designed to fulfill that commitment. The annalistic tradition's relative lack of interest in institutional change over time is not a decisive impediment to visualizing the contours of this institutionalization. On three levels, this institutionalization's effects on mid-republican society were acutely felt for generations.

1. Rome's cultural Hellenization. In the selection of deities for temple honors, the Roman state and its magistrates evince awareness of and interest in cultic developments in the wider Mediterranean world, as has long been recognized.[19] But such Hellenization was undertaken with a high degree of selectivity and rigor; there was no freewheeling adoption of *sacra peregrina*, and it would be incorrect to brand the process as uncritically emulative.
2. Elite political competition. Although elite competition in general and in the field of religious practice in particular has been the focus of much recent scholarship, the extent to which the commitment to monumental building over several generations redefines relationships both within the hybrid patrician-plebeian entity that emerged

18. For instances of jostling for the dedicatory limelight see Jenkyns 2013, 47–48, though his aprioristic dismissal of the quoted emotion strikes me as misguided. On the transit of *augurs* from the Arx and down the Sacra Via to conduct the *caerimoniae* of inauguration, see Varro *LL* 5.47, with Tucci 2018, 33–36 for topographical clarification.

19. E.g., Rome's investment in cults to "divine qualities": Clark 2007. For "accumulative civic polytheism" in Hellenistic Rome, see Champion 2017, 143–63 and *passim*. Against the presumption that Hellenization lay behind the selection of deities in the late fourth and early third centuries: Wallace 1990, 285–86.

in the aftermath of the Licinian-Sextian Rogations and between this elite and the nonaristocratic citizens of the res publica awaits further clarification.[20]

3. Peer polity interaction and power projection. Anthony Snodgrass persuasively argued three decades ago that monumental temple construction in archaic and early classical Greece reflected inter-*polis* rivalry.[21] The middle Republic's investment in temple construction similarly represented a form of "costly signaling" to other polities; the question to answer is, which polities were the intended (and unintended) recipients of the message.

Although there are other interpretive avenues that one might explore, it is primarily for these three areas that the extant literary and archaeological evidence allows us to spin a story, albeit one that is fragmentary and incomplete. In the remainder of this section, I will examine each area in turn, on the premise that what temples did to alter and rewrite relations among Roman citizens and between Rome and the greater Hellenistic world matters to the arc of Roman state formation. But this story is incomplete without a focused analysis of the scales at which these relations were being modified and the costs thus incurred—one reason why the next section of this chapter attends to the quantitative aspects of the political economy of temple-building.

1. *Choice and Selectivity in a Hellenistic Context*

The selectivity and discrimination at work in the apportioning of temples to new and old gods were direct outcomes of a system whose procedural channels entailed multiple (and sometimes conflicting) degrees of choice: individual generals responding to crisis on the battlefield, aediles hoovering up fines, and the Senate acting on the recommendation of the priestly *collegia* and the Sibylline Books. The evolution of this system testifies to the tense but generative coexistence of individual initiative alongside pluralized or "corporatized" decision-making. Meanwhile, the variety of mechanisms in place for the vowing and dedication of a temple interacted with other considerations, among them the social trajectory of individual divinities at Rome and the imprint of multigenerational continuities on the city's sacred topography.[22]

20. Cf. Padilla Peralta 2018a on Champion 2017.

21. Snodgrass 1986. Outlines of a counterargument, with reference to the great Panhellenic sanctuaries: Scott 2010, 255–56.

22. Cf. the transition from altar worship to monumental temple construction as a marker of state formation in archaic Greek contexts: De Polignac 1984, chap. 1; Whitley 2001, 137–40. The essential continuities of sacred "place" in the ancient Mediterranean: Horden and Purcell 2000,

If, as has been strongly suspected, many of the temples vowed and dedicated in the middle Republic were likely vowed to gods who were already receiving worship at altars or rudimentary *aedicula* at Rome, one relevant issue from a state-formation angle is why specific divinities earned or were deemed worthy of monumentalization at this particular historical conjuncture. Another issue that calls for comment is why the three major pathways to building a temple did not yield outcomes of equal magnitude; temples built in fulfillment of a general's vow outnumber those built in compliance with a Sibylline oracle or on the initiative of the aediles (table 2.1).[23] We should be wary of reading too much into the preponderance of individually initiated vows. A general's *votum* was usually subject to senatorial oversight and approval. Even if the vow itself could not be contested, the Senate and *populus* had other means at their disposal to prevent the temple from being built. Ultimately, then, the "principle of joint action" firmly undergirding the processes of *locatio, inauguratio,* and *dedicatio* meant that even individual vows ultimately depended for their fulfillment on the compliance and support of other institutional actors.[24]

As noted earlier, not just the lead-up to but the act of dedication itself was a virtuoso showcase of intersecting agencies. Although no mid-republican foundation will have been nearly as grand as the Imperial rededication of the temple of Capitoline Jupiter,[25] dedications were theatrical performances, literally and metaphorically. Individually initiated temple vows thus played into a broader game of aristocratic jockeying for status and prestige, governed by

chap. 10; cf. Woolf 2005 for a skeptical corrective. For spatial continuities of cult at Rome, see n. 67 below and chapter 3 n. 188.

23. Sources: Ziolkowski 1992, 200; Orlin 1997, Appendix 1. Cf. Rüpke 2018b, 126–27 for a full list of foundations from the fourth century to Caesar's death; Varro *ARD* frr. 35–39 Cardauns with Rüpke 2014b, 253–59 for the late republican pedigree of temple-foundation lists. Temples are listed from earliest to latest date of dedication except for the last five under the first column and the antepenultimate and penultimate for the third, for which we have no secure dedication dates owing to the loss of Livy for the years 292–219. The Aventine temple of Luna is not included; see Pedroni 2009 on its possible third-century foundation.

24. This principle and the *duumviri aedi locandae*: Ziolkowski 1992, 204; cf. Orlin 1997, 172–78. Obstruction of Cn. Flavius's temple vow to Concordia: Liv. 9.46.6–7 with Ziolkowski 1992, 21–22 and 219–20. A *vetus decretum* requiring senatorial approval for the dedication of a shrine vowed in battle: Tertullian *Ad nat.* 1.10.14 and *Apol.* 5.1 = Varro *ARD* fr. 44 Cardauns with Hölkeskamp [1987] 2011, 153–54. Doubts about this notice: Ziolkowski 1992, 201–2, following Mommsen 1887–88, II.619 and III.1050–51 and Wissowa 1912, 406. *Dedicatio*: Cic. *Dom.* 127 with Cornell 1995, 375 n. 17 for a *lex Papiria* forbidding consecrations without the permission of the *plebs*; cf. Schultz 2018 on *consecratio/dedicatio* and *sacrificium*. Temples and the taxonomy of urban space: chapter 3 n. 4; for a fresh take on the imperial juristic evidence, Estienne 2017.

25. For this episode see Tac. *Hist.* 4.53 with Scheid 2017.

Table 2.1. Temple Vows according to Vowing Entity, c. 400–200 BCE

General with *imperium*	Aediles	Senate on rec. of *collegia*/ consultation of Sibylline Books
Iuno Regina	Concordia	Mars
Iuno Moneta	Venus Obsequens	Aesculapius
Quirinus	Iuppiter Libertas	Summanus
Salus	Flora	Honos *extra Portam Collinam*
Bellona		Iuppiter Fulgur
Victoria[1]		Magna Mater
Iuppiter Victor		
Iuppiter Stator		
Fors Fortuna		
Hercules Invictus		
Consus		
Tellus		
Pales		
Vortumnus		
Minerva		
Ianus		
Tempestates		
Fides + Spes		
Neptunus		
Volcanus		
Ops Opifera		
Iuturna		
Iuno Curritis		
Fortuna Publica		
Honos		
Fons		
Feronia		
Hercules Magnus Custos		
Honos et Virtus		
Fortuna Publica *citerior*		
Hercules *ad Portam Collinam*		
Lares		
Penates		
Vica Pota		

1. On whether this temple was the work of aediles or of L. Postumius Megellus see Ziolkowski 1992, 172–79.

rules and arbitrated by the *populus*; truly outré vows would have been frowned on. Even so, the weight of individual choices in the temple-building institutional apparatus should not be overlooked, nor the trend that is perceptible once we aggregate them. Rome's magistrates shared a taste for the abstraction-oriented, victory-themed, and Herculean cults that became popular throughout the Mediterranean world after the death of Alexander.[26] It is this apparent hankering after the deities of the Hellenistic world that an earlier generation of scholars cited in justification of the charge that mid-republican religion consigned indigenous "archaic" cults to a slow death in its full-throttle pursuit of Hellenization. It is unlikely that so-called archaic cults were autochthonous ur-Italic creations, though debates on this front cannot be resolved here.[27] My interest lies more in ascertaining how religious decision-making came to be implicated in the program of choices through which Roman elite and nonelite identities were made and remade in this period.

These choices were given expression in a monumentalizing form whose broad parameters and architectural specifics trended in a Hellenizing direction, although the decision-making process behind these cultic adoptions diverged in some important respects from that attested for classical and Hellenistic Greek poleis and kingdoms. The most pronounced divergence is one that we have already remarked: the "republicanization" of the process by which deities received new temples. *Summi viri* could and did exercise extraordinary influence over the process, but their choices were mediated and funneled through other institutional actors. We are dealing here neither with a democratically endorsed sanctioning of any one particular cult nor with any one autocratic ruler promoting his cultic preferences.[28] What I will suggest later in this chapter is that the mid-republican institutional quirk of balancing competing agencies in the vowing and dedication of temples has much to do with the *scale* of Rome's building, as dictated by highly contingent labor and economic parameters. In this respect, temple building provided a convenient

26. Weinstock 1957 on the introduction of victory cults at Rome; Fears 1981 on the theology of victory, and Ando 2000, 278–92 on the afterlife of Victoria's worship; Spannagel 2000, Clark 2007, and Miano 2015 on abstract deities and "divine qualities," and Hölkeskamp 2000 for the special case of *fides*; Miano 2018, 99–122 on the Hellenizing faces of Republican Fortuna, esp. 104–5 on the divinity's appeal to the third-century plebeian nobility. Obscure Vica Pota's victory-cult connection: Mommsen *ad CIL* I^1.58. Cf. Hellenizing motifs on Roman coinage: Burnett 1989.

27. For one divinity that seems to have toggled between Italic indigeneity and Hellenization see Padilla Peralta 2018c, 287 on Flora.

28. Cf. the case of Athens: Garland 1992; Evans 2010, chap. 2. Sacred construction in Hellenistic *poleis*: Migeotte 1995. Royal patronage of Hellenistic sacred foundations: Winter 1993 and 2006.

testing ground for practicing and refining the balancing of individual agency against and in dialogue with collective decision-making. This dynamic would leave its mark on many fronts, above all in those political and commemorative discourses through which exemplary attributes came to be ascribed to Rome's senatorial elite and to its leading members. I have more to say on this subject in the next chapter.

2. *Intraelite Competition and Display*

Temple building and dedication swiftly became pillars of the competitive self-definition of Rome's aristocratic elite. Since honoring the gods with temples was understood to ensure their continued support and protection, magistrates who vowed and dedicated temples stood to earn some reputational credit in the eyes of the Roman public for securing divine good will (*pax deorum*). But this was by no means the only motivation behind a temple vow. The vowing and dedication of a temple were clearly reckoned among the signature achievements of an individual magistrate's career, as is reflected by the practice of listing the building of a temple among the *res gestae* recorded in *elogia*.[29] Which other (more ostensibly "secular") benefits were reaped by these individual magistrates, or by the Senate as a body, whenever a temple's construction was authorized?

Most conspicuously in the case of those structures that clustered in the vicinity of the Circus Flaminius, the positioning of temples alongside or in the immediate vicinity of the route(s) taken by triumphs exemplifies how temples came to be linked to a magistrate's triumph (if he had earned one) and of the *res gestae* for which it had been awarded. The sacred edifice, headlined by an inscription recording the name of its dedicator, inscribed the *memoria* of the general's attainments onto the topography of the city.[30] Temples built in fulfillment of a magistrate's battlefield vow were thus polyvalent: at once signifier

29. See, e.g., *ILLRP* 310 (L. Cornelius Scipio, son of Barbatus, *dedet Tempestatebus aide mereto[d]*), which dates to our period. Mentions of temple construction in the Augustan *elogia* for Republican *summi viri*: *InscrItal* 13.3.10 (A. Postumius Regillensis and the fifth-century temple of Castor and Pollux), 13.3.12 (restored on the basis of its Arretine copy, 13.3.79: Ap. Claudius Caecus and the third-century temple of Bellona), 13.3.17 (C. Marius and the late second-century temple to Honos and Virtus *de manubieis*). Augustus's pride in his temple building and renovation: *RG* 19–23 with North 2000, 42–43.

30. On the Republican triumph compare Itgenshorst 2005 and Beard 2007; on the *pompa triumphalis* as one element of the "Republic of processions," see Hölkeskamp 2017, chap. 7; on the variability of the route, Köstner 2019. Republican construction and individual and gentilician *memoria*: Blösel 2003; Kuttner [2004] 2014; Walter 2004; Flower 2009. Manubial temples and triumphal memory: Popkin 2016, chap. 2.

and signified, intended both as achievements in themselves and as reminders of the magistrate's other achievements. Yet this dialectic of embedded *memoria* is in turn implicated in a more sweeping development, which we can only sketch here: the rise of a new aristocratic elite in the decades after the Licinian-Sextian Rogations of 367, and the relationship of its members to the nonaristocratic citizen body.

I noted in the introduction that the concept of "consensus" has been mobilized to explain how this aristocracy got business done. As outlined in the preceding subsection, the practice of temple building evolved within a system of aristocratic competition that was governed by a particular set of rules (*mos*). That consensual agreement shaped the behavior of Republican magistrates when it came to temple construction seems a reasonable enough claim on its face, if in need of some sharpening. Karl-Joachim Hölkeskamp has deftly applied the concept of "symbolic capital" to the analysis of the Republican elite's habits of self-promotion, proposing that the maintenance and replenishment of this capital required regular "deposits" of *honos*, primarily in the form of magistracies and priesthoods.[31] One specific feature of the temple-building regime that plugs right into Hölkeskamp's scheme is that a magistrate's decision to direct spoils into temple construction also worked to tame and focus the "conspicuous consumption" of the elite. If not purely an artifact of our source limitations for the fourth and third centuries or later Roman glorifications of the austerity of the *maiores*,[32] it is noteworthy that members of the new patrician-plebeian elite do not for the most part appear to have been redirecting military proceeds into economically self-enriching activities. As one component of this self-regulating performance of abstemiousness, temple vowing and construction operated within a matrix of aristocratic behaviors that were designed to maintain consensus relationships: with the gods, through the solicitation of the *pax deorum*; and within the *nobiles* and their families, through the soft "requirement" that the most militarily accomplished among them set aside the fruits of their victory to religious infrastructure.

This last point will be examined in the next chapter. For now, let me simply stress that the tendency of mid-republican temples to fall more or less within the same band of scale is no accident. No one magistrate attempted (as best we can tell) to dwarf the constructions of his predecessors by commissioning a monstrously large temple; none of Rome's constructions in the fourth and third centuries come anywhere close to the size of the massive temples erected in the archaic and early classical Greek world—or the Capitoline temple dedi-

31. Hölkeskamp 2010, chap. 8.

32. "Tales about the modest means" of the Republican *maiores*: Harris 1979, 264–65.

cated after the expulsion of the Tarquins.[33] The internalization of a code of restrained conspicuous consumption among the mid-republican elite did encompass monumental construction, as Cato the Elder's inclusion of "excessive building" in a rhetorical list of character warts seems to confirm.[34] Interacting with and acting further to entrench the commitment to monumental self-restraint were the difficulties that stood in the way of any one magistrate's attempt to secure enough funds and materials for truly extravagant temples. It was not until the concrete revolution took off in the second half of the second century that aristocrats moved toward bending and then shattering the mid-republican monumental consensus.[35] All in all, then, the construction of "middling" temples mirrored and reified a distribution of religious power that was deliberately calibrated so as to prevent any one individual or family from monopolizing the sacro-monumental apparatus.

Unsurprisingly, mid-republican temple construction was republican in scope and form.[36] The outlay for many small temples was integral to the game through which the aristocracy simultaneously sought validation and reaffirmation from the two constituencies most empowered to supply them—the *populus* and the gods—and policed its own consumption and display. The cultural imperatives that drove an elite "learning to work within constitutional limitations" to promote temple architecture within Republican Rome also incentivized the rise of new patterns in office holding; as Richard Weigel has demonstrated, the fulfillment of temple vows seems to have been put off until the maker of the vow attained another high office, usually the censorship.[37] In the long run, then, temple construction in the measured

33. I will cycle back to the "soft" rule of Stamper 2005 below. Greek comparanda: Pedley 2007, 153–63; Whitley 2001, 294–313.

34. Cato *ORF*[4] 8.133 = fr. 97 Cugusi-Sblendorio Cugusi (*Qui ventrem suum non pro hoste habet, qui pro re publica non pro sua obsonat, qui stulte spondet, qui cupide aedificat*), with Nichols 2010, 43–44, who would read this fragment as primarily concerned with private building (on which note also Dubois-Pelerin 2016); cf. Dutsch 2014, 17–18 and Nichols 2017, 92 on the place of architectural taste in the constellation of Catonian virtues.

35. Davies 2017c, 77–83 on the "delicate balance" of mid-republican monumentalism, 83–99 on the concrete-fueled upheaval that followed.

36. Here I paraphrase the comments of North 1986, 257 on the prodigy system.

37. Davies 2014, 28, commenting on this elite's adoption of "powerful Greek forms"; Weigel 1998, 140–44 for office-holding; the argument is developed further in Davies 2017c, 78–79. The pursuit of office-holding to commission and then to complete construction projects is documented elsewhere in Roman Italy (see, purely e.g., *Imagines* Abella 3 [c. 100 BCE]; Terventum 4 [c. 175 BCE]; Potentia 1 [c. 125]); the timing of this pattern in relation to the Roman conquest requires further study. The diverging tracks of censorial and manubial construction in the second and first centuries: Tan 2017, 28–34.

form that became characteristic of the middle Republic fanned the flames of elite competition but did not douse them in gasoline. When passions did run high, this circumscribed monumentalizing habit even developed a safety valve: the dedication of a temple to Concordia, the abstract quality that best exemplified the harmony of Hellenizing innovation and cultural conservatism.[38]

3. *Peer-Polity Games and Interstate Communication*

Although I have already drawn attention to the orientation of mid-republican Rome's constructions toward the Greek world, it will be helpful to put that connection on firmer ground and to think through some of the signaling and communicative possibilities that were facilitated as a result. Despite its limitations, peer-polity theory is a convenient instrument of analysis here. In its simplest form, this conceptual framework attempts to clarify the (often competitive) exchanges taking place among multiple autonomous political entities in close geographical proximity to one another.[39] The foundational contribution of peer-polity theory is its move away from a vision of any one political unit as self-contained in its cultural and socioeconomic development; such development is understood as continuously in dialogue with parallel processes in neighboring regions. At the heart of the theory's conceptual configuration is the term *peer*; political and cultural relations of straightforward domination in which one polity holds undisputed sway and/or the capacity to impose anything resembling a program of sociocultural standardization or uniformity are removed from consideration. It may at first glance seem implausible to find peer polities for Rome since, as explained in the book's introduction, the mid-republican state was throughout our period hard at work overwhelming the peninsula before applying its energies to Carthage and the western Mediterranean. With some tweaks, however, the theory can be tapped for insight into the impressions the middle Republic's constructions might have left on other urbanizing allies and adversaries, and their bearing on the lengths to which fourth- and third-century Rome went in the effort to establish relationships (often asymmetrical in nature) with city-states both in and beyond peninsular Italy.[40] The communicative con-

38. Cn. Flavius's temple, n. 24 above; Curti 2000, 80–81; Hardie 2016, 66–70 on the relationship of Concordia and the Camenae to Hellenizing Pythagoreanism at Rome.

39. For fuller definitions and specific criteria see Renfrew 1986; cf. Ma 2003 on peer-polity dynamics in the Hellenistic world.

40. On these asymmetrical alliances, Badian 1958 was pioneering; for a recent take see Terrenato 2015, 518.

tent of those impressions will be taken up in more detail over the next several chapters.

An important preliminary step is to compare Roman sacred building practice with previous and contemporary trends in Mediterranean monumentalism.[41] Rome's investments in temple construction are hardly unprecedented in the western Mediterranean (figure 2.1).[42] The sixth- and fifth-century spike in temple building throughout the Greek city-states of the West has led students of Magna Graecia to speak of an "Age of Sanctuaries," whose substantial social and intercultural impacts are especially well documented for Sicily.[43] It is precisely the conspicuousness of this buildup in the archaeological record that inspired Snodgrass's application of peer-polity theory. With recent work on non-Greek Sicilians bringing to light the degree to which indigenous elites bought into this practice of monumentalization, large-scale temple construction has come to be appreciated as one more element of "Mediterraneanization," the process of integration—yielding both winners and losers—that knitted together the political and commercial units of the Mediterranean into ever-tighter networks over the course of the first millennium BCE.[44] In light of the many other indices for its exposure to the greater Greek world of the archaic and early classical period, it is no surprise that Rome also committed to monumental temple building in that same interval, exemplified not only by the Capitoline Temple but also by the temples of Castor and Pollux in the Forum Romanum, the temple to the plebeian triad Ceres-Liber-Libera on the Aventine, the temple of Apollo Medicus in the Campus Martius, and the two-phase temples of Fortuna and Mater Matuta in the Forum Boarium.[45]

After this initial flurry, the early Roman state moved away from monumental sacred architecture for nearly a century, for reasons still contested in the

41. In what follows I limit myself to the first millennium BCE, although comparisons of even more ambitious chronological sweep are possible; for a multimillennial approach to Mediterranean monumental construction see, e.g., Vella 2016.

42. Data on 174 temple and sanctuary constructions, tabulated from entries for forty-three poleis in Spain/France, Sicily, and Italia/Campania in Hansen and Nielsen 2004. *Poleis* for which no temple or sanctuary structure is documented have been excluded; also excluded are structures commissioned by *poleis* at the Panhellenic sanctuaries. For data-mining and statistical manipulation of Hansen and Nielsen 2004 cf. Fleck and Hanssen 2018.

43. The scope of this investment: Urquhart 2010, 225–40; De Angelis 2016, chap. 3.

44. Morris 2003, 49 on temples.

45. On these constructions see now the succinct exposition of Lulof 2014 and the synthesis of Hopkins 2016, both emphasizing (to differing degrees) their significance as markers of state formation; for monumental precedents in archaic central Italy, see Potts 2015, esp. chap. 7 for peer-polity networks of interaction and competition.

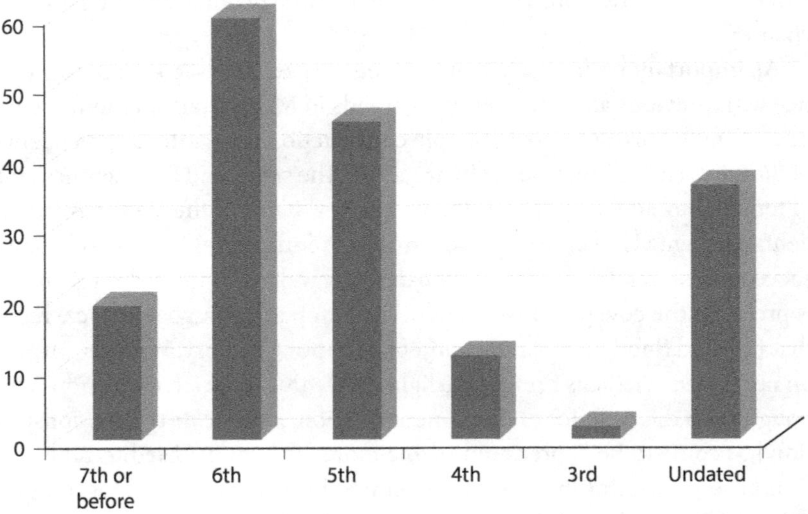

FIGURE 2.1. Construction of temples and sanctuaries in Magna Graecia, seventh–third centuries BCE.

scholarship.[46] Once this lag was in its rearview mirror, however, the mid-republican state scaled up the frequency of its construction at the same time that the scope of temple construction shifted downward in Magna Graecia, in a curious divergence that may nonetheless be an early sign of peer-polity exchange in action: for lags to be followed by an accelerated "catch-up" is typical of state formation processes at other times and places in the ancient Mediterranean.[47]

On the one hand, Rome's march to peninsular domination following the overhaul of its alliance system in the 340s and the initiation of a large-scale colonization scheme pitted the middle Republic against formidable opponents whose trajectories of state formation were also guiding them toward monumentalizing projects.[48] Contemporaneous with Rome's scaling up of

46. See chapter 1 n. 40.

47. Cf. the archaeological markers for ancient Greek state formation: Morris 2009, 134–36.

48. Usefully on fourth-century state formation in the Italian peninsula: Terrenato 2014; cf. Lippolis 2016, 204–5 for the takeoff in urbanization and population growth in the 340s and 330s. Sewell 2010, 50–53 applies peer-polity theory to town planning and architecture in the middle Republic's colonies but does not take into consideration their sacred architecture (for which now see Bertrand 2015, 99–187 and bibliography cited in chapter 5 n. 47). For the special case of walls, "symbols of community and labor identity" (Smith 2003, 280), see Bernard 2018a for fourth-century Rome; Gregori and Nonnis 2013, 494–95 for third-century wall constructions elsewhere in central Italy.

temple construction are upticks in monumental construction in Etruria—whose city-states were steadily incorporated into the imperial Republic over the course of the fourth and third centuries—as well as throughout the Hellenistic world, from the Greater Greek poleis of Neapolis, Tarentum, and Syracuse to the kingdom of the Ptolemies.[49] In terms of the frequency and scale of monumental construction, Ptolemaic Alexandria is arguably the only one of these cities to rival (if not surpass) mid-republican Rome, and not only because it was built virtually from scratch; the Ptolemies could draw on a more centralized and revenue-extractive fiscal regime to underwrite the costs of construction.[50] We remain mostly in the dark about Rome's great adversary Carthage, though it would not be unreasonable to posit a similar arc of monumental transformation.[51]

These parallel surges in construction activity did not, however, distribute themselves equally across the same monumental forms. In much of the Hellenistic Greek world, the resource investment into theater far outpaced expenditures on temples, as theatrical performance came to assume a leading role in the fashioning of an international Greek identity in the age of Alexander and his successors.[52] In Roman central Italy, by contrast, it was the temple that became the node for civic euergetism—although the middle Republic did find a way of marrying temple dedications to theatrical displays, as I will detail in chapter 4.

Rome's urban transformation is best understood by reference to civic metamorphoses closer to home. Archaeological and epigraphic testimonies confirm not only an uptick in monumental sacred construction for multiple re-

49. Etruscan urban and suburban sanctuaries in the fourth and third centuries: Colonna 1985, 67–115. Neapolis: Lepore 1952, 306–13 on its economy; Greco 1986 on the urban core's monumentalization during the fourth and third centuries; Giangiulio 1986 on cult. Tarentum: Lippolis 2011 on mausolea, *naiskoi*, and decorative artisanal production; cf. Battiloro and Osanna 2011, de Cazanove 2011, and Battiloro 2018 on developments in non-Greek Lucania. Syracuse: Lehmler 2005; Wilson 2013, 80–99.

50. See McKenzie 2007, chap. 3 on Ptolemaic Alexandria; on temple and chapel construction across Ptolemaic Egypt, Huss 1994, 26–39 and Arnold 1999, 320–33. Ptolemaic fiscality in comparative Mediterranean perspective: Monson 2015.

51. Carthaginian temples: Lancel 1995, 212–15; Melliti 2016, chap. 5 for monumental temple construction at Carthage in the context of changes to the urban fabric; Melliti 2006 and 2010 on Hellenization and religious practice. State formation in Carthaginian North Africa in "the context of Roman expansion": Terrenato 2019, 86–93.

52. For the shift away from temple and toward theater construction in late classical and Hellenistic Magna Graecia, see Marconi 2012. In the Greek East, however, synoikism-fueled urbanization propels continuing financial investments in monumental cult: Meier 2012; Boehm 2018, chaps. 2–3.

gions of Italy during the fourth and third centuries but also the tightening interarticulation of this construction with local office holding and the centralized management of contracts—heralding the advent of a new political economy.[53] It would be presumptuous to credit the Roman expansion as the primary motor for this construction and for the administrative forms in which it came to be encased; urbanization was on the rise up and down the peninsula, and especially in eastern central Italy, in the decades before the conquest.[54] But with the expansion creating excellent conditions for competition between Rome on the one hand and its Etruscan and Campanian peer polities on the other, investments in sacred monumental architecture became inseparable from the contest for regional preeminence. Roman and Etruscan religious monumentalisms in particular entered into closer dialogue with each other, as disclosed not only by those literary traditions that assigned an Etruscan origin to the rise of monumental sacred architecture in Rome but also by the evidence for Roman-Etruscan interactions in the religious realm during the fourth and third centuries.[55]

Despite their progression away from an earlier fixation on monumental temples and toward the embrace of theaters, the city-states of Magna Graecia did exert influence on the architectural transformation of the mid-republican city. It has long been appreciated—beginning with the Romans themselves—that the region was home to the specialized artists and dramaturges whose talents were put to work at Rome during the second half of the third century and after. Only recently, however, has the extent to which Roman architectural innovations of the third century and early second centuries relied on and in some cases directly appropriated Hellenistic technical expertise come to light. From the Greek-influenced design of the mid-republican Comitium to the adaptation of Syracusan engineering methods, signs of an intensifying appetite for early Hellenistic civic architecture multiplied across fourth- and third-century Rome.[56]

53. See *ILLRP* 483 = *Imagines* Falernus Ager 1 for one example: the inscription names four individuals as responsible for the letting out of a contract for *cippi*.

54. Terrenato 2019, 140–41 with figure 4.8.

55. See, e.g., Pliny *NH* 35.157, crediting the Capitoline Temple's cult statue of Jupiter and acroterial terra-cotta quadriga to a Vulca from Veii. Artistic mobility in archaic central Italy: Smith 1998; Bourdin 2012, 527–32; Hopkins 2016; see chapter 5 n. 101. Artistic mobility and the Hellenizing contents of temple decorative programs in central Italy: Jannot 2005, chap. 6. Religiously inflected exchanges between Rome and Etruria: Torelli 1997 on the testimony of the Appius Alce gem; Padilla Peralta 2018c on the intercultural semiotics of hammers and nails.

56. Coarelli 1985, 22–27 on the Comitium; Bernard 2018a, 215 on Archimedean lifting technology at Rome. Note also Tucci 2018 on the possibility that a conspicuous mid-republican funerary monument on the Arx was the work of Greek masons at least in part.

In these contexts of transfer and incorporation, it is hardly surprising that a sense of rivalry with Syracuse and other Hellenistic states is hinted at in an extant fragment of the Roman epic poet and playwright Naevius.[57] The visits of a Ptolemaic embassy to Rome in the 270s and of Hieron II of Syracuse a few decades later provided still more incentive for decking out the Republican city in a manner befitting a major Hellenistic *polis*.[58] To be sure, monumental urban expenditure was not a priority for all of Rome's rivals, some of whom opted against binding themselves to this species of costly signaling. Samnium, home to a coalition of Oscan communities that emerged as Rome's most intractable foe in the period prior to the Pyrrhic Wars, did not pursue urbanized monumentalization at the time of its fourth- and third-century entanglements with Rome; instead, rural sanctuaries became the most prominent staging grounds for communal organization and self-definition.[59] In other regions of the peninsula, monumental sacred architecture did not precede but rather followed the tread of Roman conquest.[60] But this development takes us beyond the peer-polity dynamics most relevant to my line of argument in this section, which can be summarized simply as follows: Rome's temple-building habit was rounding into shape as Etruria to the north and the Hellenistic world in south Italy and beyond also embraced different types of monumental construction.

Rome's mobilization and usurpation of resources to make its own monumentalization a reality participated in a Hellenistic conversation. As Caroline Lehmler has registered in her analysis of Syracuse's architectural and artistic accomplishments under Agathocles and Hieron II, monumental construction

57. *Tarentilla* fr. 1 Ribbeck^2 = *com. pall.* frr. 69–71 Warmington: *Quae ego in theatro hic meis probaui plausibus / ea non audere quemquam regem rumpere / quanto libertatem hanc hic superat seruitus*. I circle back to this fragment in chapter 4.

58. The Ptolemaic embassy of 273 and its aftermath: Dionysius of Halicarnassus *AR* 20.14.1–2; Val. Max. 4.3.9; Just. *Epit.* 18.2.9; Dio Cassius fr. 41 (= Zon. 8.6.11), to be read with Gruen 1984, II.673–76. Hieron II's visit *ad ludos spectandos*: Eutr. 3.2.1 with Lehmler 2005, 205–6; cf. Feeney 2016, 127–28.

59. The arc of Samnium's transformation: Stek 2009, chap. 3; Scopacasa 2015a, chap. 4.3, esp. 190–92 on the temple buildup beginning c. 250 and 205–7 on the monumentalization of Pietrabbondante; Hoyer 2012 and Scopacasa 2016: 46–47 on the economic and state-formation background. Site-specific studies (purely e.g.): Pelgrom and Stek 2010 and Stek 2018.

60. Survey archaeology in other parts of Italy is changing (and complicating) the picture: see de Haas 2011 on the Pontine sector; for Lucania, Battiloro 2018 nuances and supplements the interpretations of Osanna 2011, Fracchia 2015, and Battiloro and Osanna 2015. Monumental construction in Latium and Campania after the Second Punic War as fueled by the proceeds of empire: Bodei Giglioni 1977; Coarelli 1983 and 1987; cf. Maschek 2016b on the significance of different rates of monumentalization in Latium/Campania and Samnium/Picenum.

formed part of a complex of institutional behaviors for communicating a city-state's power to residents and foreigners alike.[61] Pertinent to any assessment of the peer-polity and communicative effects of Roman temple construction is Rome's funding of much of its sacred building with wealth extracted from the battlefield, an issue to be explored further in chapter 3. Over time, Rome's encroachments on Etruscan and Greater Greek polities would result in commodity flows from war that enabled the imperial Republic to sustain a level of construction activity unparalleled elsewhere in the peninsula; peninsular preeminence in matters monumental came to be interdependent on preeminence in matters military. In this respect, the intensification of monumental cult at Rome was in itself a species of imperialism, taking the form of "systematic acquisition of the goods belonging to the conquered, among them those of a religious character";[62] how Roman appropriation of deities and cults acted to cement the city's status as a religious metropole will occupy us in the second half of this book.

These temples became, in time, part of Rome's self-branding as a polity that took its relationship with the gods seriously. Already in the Pyrrhic era there appear numismatic indications of Rome's efforts to market its own *fides*. Then, in connection with the Punic Wars, a confrontational discourse about Roman piety that adduced Rome's public performances of piety for legitimation and vindication rapidly emerged, as the evolution of a polemic about Carthaginian impiety and as M. Valerius Messalla's letter to the citizens of Teos both serve to convey.[63] That a counterdiscourse to the Roman brand surfaces in the second century is perhaps the clearest sign of this brand's consolidation—and indirectly bears out the viability of peer-polity theory as "not merely a modern intellectual concept imposed on its unsuspecting subjects, but something which those subjects were themselves practising, with some acumen and deliberation of purpose."[64]

Let me now recap the arguments laid out in the preceding three subsections. I understand temple construction, an activity overseen by Rome's aris-

61. Lehmler 2005, chap. 6 on the cultural ambitions of Syracuse's kings; Wilson 2013, 86–97 with updated details on the Hieronian building program.

62. Coarelli 2017, 173: "Si tratta in effetti di un fenomeno caratteristico dell'imperialismo romano, che si manifestò non solo attraverso l'espansionismo militare e la conquista, ma anche nell'acquisizione sistematica dei beni appartenuti ai vinti, inclusi quelli di carattere religioso."

63. Miles 2011 on the discursive formulation of Hannibal's impiety.

64. I quote Snodgrass 1986, 58. The counterdiscourse: see, e.g., the report of a Roman general raving at the sanctuary of Naupactus and delivering an unprompted oracle of Rome's imminent destruction: Antisthenes of Rhodes *FGH* 257 F 35, with Momigliano 1975a, 40–42 and Caygill 2011.

tocratic elite but moderated by the *populus*, as setting in motion a number of transformations in Roman politics and society. First, even though considerable latitude was afforded to the generals in the field whose vows were responsible for the majority of temple foundations in our period, the practice of temple building evolved into a strategy for honoring old and new gods that operated along systematized and institutionalized lines. This systematization and institutionalization came about through the repetitive demands of temple building, which interacted dynamically with the formation and social reproduction of the hybrid patrician-plebeian *nobilitas*. Second, temple construction was incorporated into the competitive repertoire of the Roman aristocracy; the steering of battlefield wealth into monumental building acted to sustain the symbolic capital that kept the behavioral-ritualistic economy of consensus afloat. Finally, temple construction positioned Rome at the intersection of a multipolity dialogue that was mediated through monumental construction, with the result that this sacred monumentality could come to be wielded as a weapon of "soft" cultural power.

But none of these outcomes came without cost, and it would not be meaningful to set these down as outcomes without attending more rigorously to questions of cost. Earlier I described temple construction as a species of "conspicuous consumption," making note of the use of wealth extracted through military campaigns and (less frequently) fines, yet with no elaboration of the financial and human outlays. It is now time to consider the scale and the costs of mid-republican temple construction in more detail. Although the political rewards of elite investment in the monumental fabric of the city have commanded no small amount of attention in recent scholarship, the differential texture of this monumental fabric eludes characterization until and unless the specifics of temple construction as a social practice receive careful scrutiny. It is primarily to this task that the arguments and models of this chapter's remaining sections are directed.

II. The Human Investment in Temples: Scale and Inputs

As a necessary preliminary to quantifying costs, we will need to be as precise as the sources allow in plotting the overall scale and trajectory of temple building at Rome. Collating the ancient source testimony, figure 2.2 graphs the distribution of temple dedications at Rome during the fourth and third centuries.[65] The upward swing in dedications is, unsurprisingly, more or less in

65. Catalogs of temple construction: Aust 1889; Wissowa 1912, 594–95; Popkin 2016, 50–57. For a comprehensive account and full citations see Ziolkowski 1992, Part I.II; the appendixes of Aberson 1994 and Bernard 2018a supply additional information. Excluded from the graph are

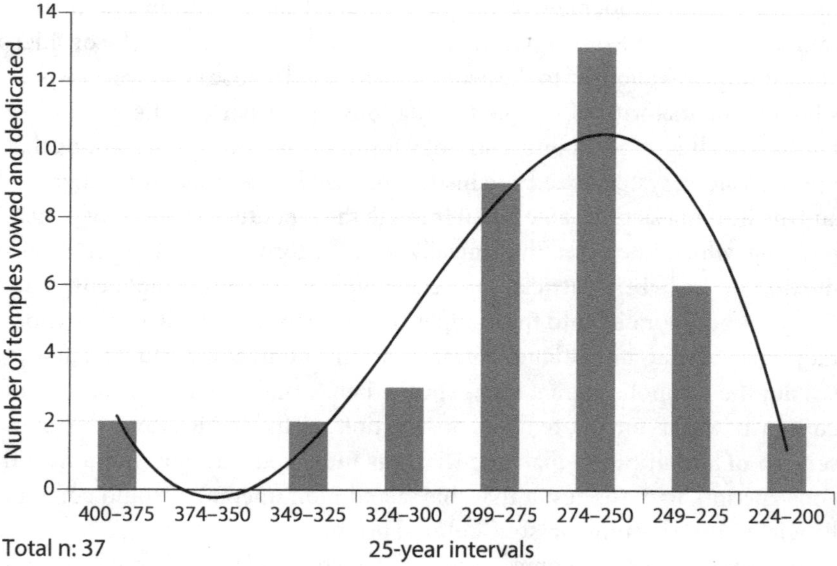

FIGURE 2.2. Temple construction in mid-republican Rome (with trend line).

lockstep with the intensification of Roman military expansion during this period. Two temples were vowed and built in the first quarter of the fourth century; none in the second quarter, as the patrician-plebeian conflicts reported in the literary tradition came to a head with the Licinian-Sextian Rogations; another two more were erected in the third.

In the final quarter of the fourth century, however, the pace of construction activity dramatically accelerated, reaching new levels: twelve new temples were erected in the fifty-year period from the Caudine Forks to the Pyrrhic Wars, and another nineteen from the era of Pyrrhus to the Gallic invasion and the Battle of Telamon. Predictably, the years of Hannibalic duress saw the numbers decrease, but by that point Rome's urban landscape was saturated with temples, with the ones clustered along the triumphal route in particular beginning to exert their formidable and enduring pull on civic memory and commemoration.[66]

temples that cannot be confidently dated within any of the twenty-five-year intervals as well as structures that are likely to have been open-air shrines; Bernard 2018a, 63 with figure 3.1 follows a similar protocol. For the terminological distinctions between different kinds of built sacred space in Roman sources see Castagnoli 1984, 3–6.

66. Temple construction as "symptom" of economic and demographic transformation in early third century: Cornell 1995, 381–85; cf. Lomas 2018, 314–16. The boom in temple construction after the Second Punic War: Orlin 1997, 127 n. 32; contrary to the insistence of Davies 2014,

The most striking aspect of this temple-building habit comes into clearer focus with the aid of cross-temporal comparison. For those readers accustomed to thinking of ancient Rome as a city ceaselessly renewing its monumental face, the mere fact of an efflorescence in temple construction will not come across as novel; it is more productive to scrutinize how this burst relates to other periods in Roman monumental construction, and whether there is anything unusual about the middle Republic's allocation of energy and capital to *temple* construction in particular. Distilling the more abundant literary and archaeological documentation for the monumental projects of the late Republic and Empire, figure 2.3 tracks construction activity at Rome from the archaic period to late antiquity.[67] The overall wax and wane—a peak of construction at Rome in the first centuries BCE and CE—is no surprise in view of the numerous other indicators for the Roman Mediterranean's economic boom during this period.

What does stand out, however, is the shift in the ratio of sacred to secular constructions over time. In the middle Republic, sacred building predominated; secularizing projects took precedence by the late Republic and remained in the lead well into the High Empire; then, in the era of Constantine after, the pendulum swung back. Of course, characterizing this shift in such broad-brush terms oversimplifies complicated sociocultural and economic dynamics, and it masks the degree to which rebuilding (and reappropriation) dictated urban monumental rhythms in all periods of the city's history.[68] For all its crudity as an instrument, the graph does at least have the benefit of

32 on an "economic depression" in the early second century, see the evidence gathered in Kay 2014 and Bernard 2018a, 239–41 with figure A2.1; note also the calculations for expenditures on public works in Taylor 2017. Tracking temple construction in Rome after 167: Crawford and Coarelli 1977 and Maschek 2016b, 69–70; purely for example, note Goldberg 1998, 5–9 on the rebuilding of the Palatine temple of Magna Mater and Nielsen and Poulsen 1992 on the rebuilds of the temple of Castor and Pollux.

67. Data for this graph were generated from the "Chronological list of dated monuments" in Richardson 1992, supplemented with Krautheimer 1983 for the number of Christian churches; on the scope of the shift toward Christian church foundations beginning with Constantine, see also Moralee 2018, 49–51). Excluded from the graph: catacombs, on whose construction note Rutgers 2019. Rome's urban and monumental rhythms in late antiquity: Mulryan 2011; after late antiquity, Maskarinec 2018. Impressive if faux-precise tabulation of the number of buildings in the city "that can be dated to the period between the ninth century BC and the sixth century AD": Bossi in Carandini 2017, I.129.

68. Thanks to *LTUR* and Carandini 2017, a *longue durée* analytic study of the city's monumentality is now possible; ideally it would complement recent treatments of "power" (e.g., Harris 2016, to be read with the criticisms of Hölkeskamp 2018). One neighborhood's shifting urban profile from the archaic period to late antiquity: Andrews and Bernard 2017. On trends

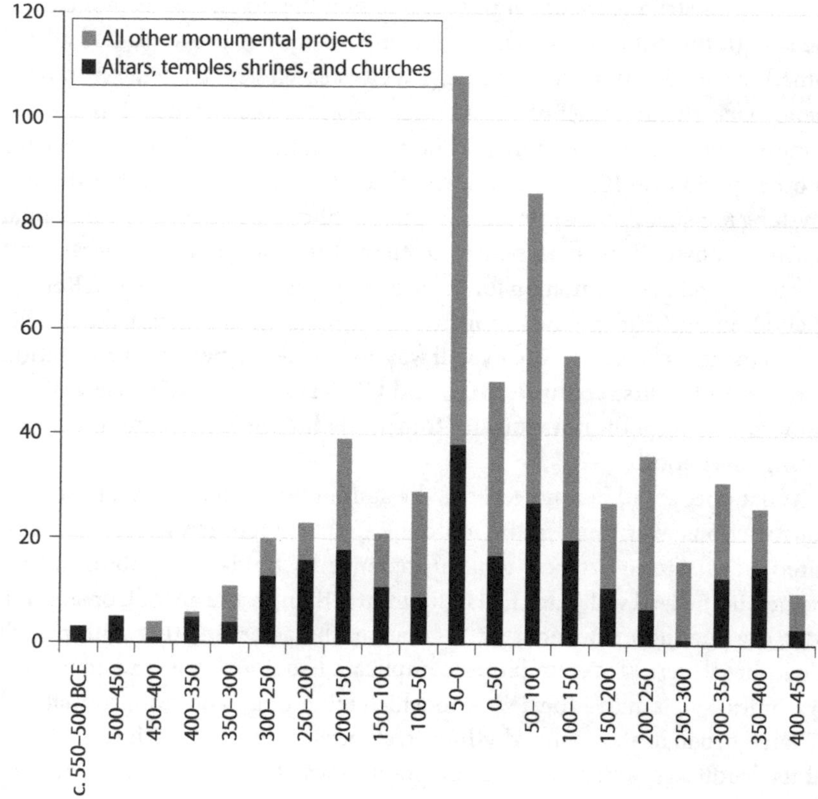

FIGURE 2.3. Construction at Rome in the *longue durée*, c. 550 BCE–CE 540.

bringing out the distinctiveness of the mid-republican construction regime in comparison to what came before and after. Where this representation is manifestly deficient is in capturing how monumental construction interfaced with the lives of Rome's population. To the end of reanimating that interface, we will need to employ a different conceptual frame.

In periodizing the distribution of temple construction in the middle Republic by explicit reference to which wars were being fought, my intention was to underline that monumental activity was taking place even as the Roman state fielded large armies. If construction of this sort was in fact possible even in the teeth of significant manpower commitments on the battlefield, one obvious implication is that the middle Republic had sufficient manpower reserves at its disposal to field armies and carry out monumental

in monumental urbanism throughout the Roman Empire see Hanson 2016, 75–80 and 122–24, figures 18–23.

projects while maintaining the economic productivity required for population subsistence and commercial activity.[69] Yet how did these domains of civic and communal enterprise interact with and shape one another? To answer this question, we will need to determine the labor inputs that were required to sustain the mid-republican spike in temple construction. The best means of establishing some general parameters for these labor demands—the human costs of monumental building—is to devise a simple and testable model.

1. *The Basics*

I pursue modeling as a means of testing the general hypothesis that mid-republican temple building consumed a significant amount of Roman state resources. The specifics of the model's design are intended to assist in calibrating the extent of this consumption, as are the comparative exercises that follow the introduction of the model. Neither the model nor the exercises that build on it propose anything approaching a "real answer" to the questions that orbit mid-republican temple construction; their primary objective is to establish a more or less plausible range of possibilities.[70] With this range in mind, we will be better positioned not only to assess the merits of the claim introduced at the beginning of this chapter—that Republican monumentalism had some of the characteristics of a shell game—but also to gauge temple construction's contribution to the rhythms of Republican urban life. The ulterior objective of this chapter's modeling, then, is re-creating the social web of relations that linked activity around temples to other domains of Roman life. Because this book works up to this re-creation partly through the cumulative force of other models proposed and tested in chapters 3 to 5, the full scope of Rome's monumental rhythms and of temple construction's standing in relation to them will not become apparent until chapter 6.

À propos of this chapter's aims in particular, modeling also offers a means of maneuvering around some of the limitations of the evidence at our disposal. Throughout the fourth and third centuries, Rome was in the incipient stages of monetization, making tricky any effort to assign currency-based costs to particular projects.[71] Moreover, only a fraction of the temples that were dedicated at Rome in the fourth and third centuries have been excavated in decent enough condition to enable podium measurements (in some cases

69. To Morel 2007 on the economy of mid-republican Italy add now Kay 2014, chap. 1.

70. Cf. the useful comments of Goodchild 2013 on the stakes and rewards of modeling; Davies 2018, 52 n. 1 for bibliography on historical modeling.

71. Coinage production and monetization: Burnett 1989; Kay 2014, chaps. 5–6.

conjectural) of the original foundation.[72] Our knowledge of building practice in the middle Republic remains fairly incomplete, in comparison to the wealth of evidence for construction procedures from the Empire; in view of the substantial transformations in materials employed and technologies harnessed in the last two centuries BCE, it would be methodologically unsound to project backward.[73] Still another hurdle to clear is that, with rare exceptions, studies of Roman architecture do not often dwell on labor costs.[74] To compensate for this deficit, one could follow in the footsteps of Janet DeLaine and devise a model that scaled up from some reasonable assumptions about the length of time it took to work and dress specific types of building materials.[75] A less winding path exists for arriving at the same final destination: a schematized model that proceeds from a few simple propositions to a global reconstruction of the cumulative bio power that underwrote temple construction. This subsection will develop such a model, proceeding from the following premises:

a. Work on temples was carried out only circa seventy-five days a year, with laborers averaging twelve hours per workday. The demands of yearlong military campaigning—a reality no later than the first quarter of the third century—and the agricultural cycle will have combined to make temple construction a seasonal activity. The concentration of temple dedication and anniversary dates in the summertime points in the direction of some seasonal constraints on monumental activity, as does the existence of impediments to mobility during the winter.[76]

72. Five to be exact: the temples of Victoria in Palatio, Portunus in Portu, Iuturna (?) in Martio (= Largo Argentina Temple A), Feronia, and Iuppiter in Insula; if the earliest recoverable platform for the temple of Apollo Medicus is classed as mid-republican, the number rises to six. Stamper 2005, 43, table 3.1 offers podium measurements of select major Etrusco-Roman temples from the sixth to the third centuries; for the dating of the first podium of the temple to Portunus, see Del Buono 2009.

73. Primer on the "technica edilizia" of Republican Rome: Cairoli Giuliani 1982. Construction practice and oversight in the Empire: Kolb 1993; Daguet-Gaguey 1997; note also chapter 1 n. 56.

74. See, e.g., Wilson Jones 2000 and Taylor 2003—both concerned with architectural principles and process.

75. DeLaine 1997 and 2001. Illustrative and clarifying extensions of DeLaine's methods: Pakkanen 2013 on the shipsheds of the Zea harbor in the Piraeus; Maschek 2016a on the Marble Stoa at Hierapolis; Bernard 2018a on the Servian Wall; Rutgers 2019 on early Christian catacombs. The energetics of trench digging in the Roman world need further exploration; for some pointers on method see Xie et al. 2015.

76. A twelve-hour workday is adopted as the baseline in Pegoretti 1986, the manual em-

b. On average, it took three years to build a temple. Undeniably, some temples will have been built and dedicated more quickly, others more sluggishly; however, in terms of the amount of continuous work that went into an "average" mid-republican temple, three years at seventy-five working days per annum would have sufficed to get the job done.[77]

c. The labor force required to build a temple came in one of three sizes:

n = 500 laborers (small)

n = 1,000 (medium)

n = 2,000 (large)

This n will be taken to represent the sum total of all the laborers involved in the temple's construction: the gangs that worked tufa and limestone quarries and logged forests in order to supply raw material for the temple; the individuals who were responsible for the material's transport to Rome; the architects, artists, and unskilled laborers who were charged with the erection and decoration of the temple itself and with the construction of architectural embellishments within or immediately abutting the temple precinct.[78] For various reasons, it is unlikely that any mid-republican temple required two thousand laborers;

ployed by DeLaine 1997, 103–7 and 2001, 232–34. Bernard 2018a, 78–79 calls for five to six hours per day as a more realistic expectation, whereas Maschek 2016a, 398 opts for ten hours; see the sensitivity graph below for adjustments to the length of the workday. Yearlong campaigning: Rosenstein 2004, chaps. 1–2. Comparative evidence for seasonal limits on monumental construction: Redfield and Villa Rojas 1964 (Maya); Vogt 1969 (Mesoamerica); Bierbrier 1982 (dynastic Egypt); Osborne 1987, 13–16 (classical Greece); further on seasonality, see chapter 3 nn. 151–55.

77. See Weigel 1998 for the political considerations that dictated the time from vow to dedication. Of the eighteen Republican temples for which we have reliable (i.e., annalistic) sources for year of vow and year of dedication, the interval between the two ranges from one year to seventeen—the latter being the exceptional case of M. Claudius Marcellus's temple to Honos and Virtus. Cf. the time-to-completion of Hellenistic projects, "étendues sur des périodes relativement longues": Migeotte 1995, 80.

78. The economics of tufa extraction are unclear, though exploitation by members of the landowning aristocracy is likely (cf. Arizza and Rossi 2018 on archaic precedents); for the seasonality of tufa extraction, see chapter 3 n. 157. The indispensability of wood and wood transport to public construction at Rome: Liv. 35.41.10 with Veal 2017, 331–32. Architectural embellishments: note, e.g., the vaulted cryptoporticus in *tufo giallo* from the early phase of the temple of Portunus: Del Buono 2009 and Bernard 2018a, 201–2.

I offer this size only to generate some pressure on the model, as will become clearer below.[79]

d. An "available labor" constant, generated from what best we can glean about the demography of fourth- and third-century Rome. For my model to be heuristically useful, person-hour figures in a vacuum would be useless; such figures attain their full significance only through comparison to the total amount of disposable labor that was available to be extracted from the population—through some combination of free hire, corvée, and enslavement.[80] The last of these is unquestionably one of the most decisive catalysts for changes to Roman labor practices during our period, although the extent of its demographic and economic impingement on preexisting systems of free and corvée labor is difficult to gauge.[81] Unsurprisingly in view of this complexity, Republican demography is a notorious minefield, with many questions about fluctuations in the urban and rural population over time still nowhere close to being resolved. With no pretense to authoritative intervention in any of the most disputed issues,[82] I will proceed down the path of least resistance in choosing some round numbers on which to base the generation of an "available labor" constant:

79. I do not differentiate between on- and off-site labor, since the quasi-industrialized organization of off-site labor in the Empire (Taylor 2014, 194–95 on brick production) is unlikely to have obtained in mid-republican central Italy, or between skilled and unskilled (see Pakkanen 2013 for how one might go about modeling the distinction; cf. Lancaster and Ulrich 2014, 158 on Imperial ratios of skilled to unskilled workers). Five hundred (500) as the magic number: cf. Welch 2007, 56–57 on the number of carpenters required to assemble and take down temporary seating in the Forum Romanum; beyond Rome, Randall 1953 on the Erechtheum accounts (117 workers for end of second and third phases of construction; perhaps ~500 total); Abrams 1987 on 411 workers for a palace-temple in Mayan Copán (cf. Carrelli 2004).

80. A parchment fragment of Livy Book 11 found in 1986 appears to reference an episode of compulsory labor in 291 that is reported by the *Periochae* and by Dionysius of Halicarnassus: Bravo and Griffin 1986; Gabrielli 2003, 253–59; Pittia et al. 2005, 244–49. On *corvée* in the early and middle Republic, see Brunt 1980, 82; Duncan-Jones 1990, 175–76; and Bernard 2018a, 109–13. Imperial corvée: Taylor 2014, 200 and Bruun 2003, 319–20 for citations. Military labor and temple construction: cf. Fischer-Bovet 2014, 329-62 for Ptolemaic Egypt.

81. Labor flows, debt-bondage, and the growing appetite for slavery in fourth-century Rome: Bernard 2016; cf. Scheidel 2018 for a global overview of corvée in premodern societies and its (possible) coupling to stages of monetization. The scale of mid-republican mass enslavements: Harris 1979, 59 on figures for the first decade of the third century; Volkmann 1990 for compilation of notices of mass enslavement in the Hellenistic world; Welwei 2000 for a source-critical approach to literary notices for Roman mass enslavement; Scheidel 2011, 294–95 on the path from Sentinum to Pydna.

82. On the high/low count controversy, see Morley 1996, 46–50; Scheidel 2004a, 2–9.

i. The census for 393/2 returned slightly over 150,000 citizens.[83] Taking this return as trustworthy, I will assume that the absolute maximum number of citizen adult men between the ages of seventeen and forty-five who were available for work at Rome and its environs at any point during the first three quarters of the fourth century fell somewhere in the neighborhood of 32,000.[84]

ii. In 294/3, the census returned 262,321—a substantial leap from 323, when the figure sat at 150,000.[85] Whatever the reason for this increase, it is probably safe to presume given Rome's colonial foundations during this time that the population was in fact expanding.[86] Splitting the difference between the 294/3 census and its predecessor in or around 323 would leave us with a ballpark estimate of 200,000 for the population, which is not prima facie implausible. On the assumption that the ratio of men ages seventeen to forty-five to the overall population remained the same as in (i) above, the maximum male labor force available will have stood at approximately 43,000.

iii. Census returns from the mid-third century indicate that at this stage the population had cleared the 250,000 threshold and was approaching 300,000. If we take the lower figure as our baseline, the maximum available labor number from this point forward (until the end of the third century) rises to around 55,000.

iv. My three benchmarks will therefore be an available male citizen labor pool of 32,000 for the first three quarters of the fourth century; 43,000 for the next three quarters, from the late fourth to the middle of the third; and 55,000 for the last two quarters of the third.[87] Despite the middle Republic's increasing commitment to enslavement (especially over the course of the third century) and

83. This census: Pliny *NH* 33.16. On the credibility of early republican census returns see Ward 1990. Beloch 1926, 209 set 20,000–25,000 as the fourth-century population of the city, but this is too pessimistic; cf. Frank [1933] 1975, 34, who proposed 100,000; for a hypothetical growth curve of the urban population in the fourth and third centuries see Scheidel 2004a, 6, figure 3.

84. Coale and Demeny 1983 West level 3 stipulate that men in this age range composed 43.5 percent of the male half of the population. I follow Bernard 2018a, 103, which relies on Hin 2008, 198–99.

85. Liv. 10.47 for the former; Eutr. 5.9 and Oros. 5.22.2 (and Liv. 9.19 with the emendation of Brunt 1971, 13) for the latter.

86. Colonization and population displacements during this period: Scheidel 2004b.

87. Cf. Morley 1996, 33–39, who works toward a total urban population of 200,000 at the beginning of the second century.

the obvious fact that so much of the Roman state's urban and rural labor regimes rested on the shoulders of women and children,[88] I concentrate on male citizens as provisioners of labor partly to eliminate the complexity of incorporating multipliers into my analysis and partly to test the hypothesis that temple labor demands could be met by the male citizen population. Confirmation would mean that temple construction did not trigger labor demands that had to be satisfied by drawing on other pools of labor, such as free women or children or slaves. My decision to limit myself to the male citizen should not be taken to imply that other pools of labor were not being exploited for temple construction.

v. The final task under this heading is to settle on a percentage of the available labor pool that could be hired or distrained at any given time. With agricultural and military demands taken into consideration, it would be reasonable to propose that at the very most *half* of the pool could be tapped for temple construction, under the work conditions specified in (a) and (b) above.[89]

e. I will account for the construction of *new* temples only. To be sure, there is strong archaeological evidence for the renovation and reconstruction of archaic and early republican foundations at various points during the fourth and third centuries, partly as a result of the destructive fires and floods that are mentioned in the literary sources.[90] In the interests of devising as streamlined a model as possible, however, I refrain from taking this repair work into consideration.

f. I will not attempt to parcel out or otherwise segregate the resource outlays for the fine artwork that was commissioned or appropriated for these temples. Details of the decorative schemes for mid-republican temples are hard to recover, though the costs would not have been prohibitive.[91] As for statues, Roman armies and their

88. See Scheidel 1995 and 1996b for a blow to the Greco-Roman literary representation of women as working primarily at home and not in the fields; Rosenstein 2004 for models of their potential and expected labor contributions; and Medina Quintana 2017 for later (epigraphic) evidence of women's occupational diversification.

89. Cf. Acton 2014, 302–7 for a model of "manufacturing participation by adult males" in classical Athens that returns a total full-time equivalent of 49.8 percent.

90. Floods: Aldrete 2006. Repair and renovation of at least four temple structures and complexes is archaeologically verifiable for our period: see Bernard 2018a, Appendix 2 on Fortuna and Mater Matuta, Apollo Medicus, Vesta, and Spes. Cf. Davies 2001 on the costliness of temple repair and renovation in the Greek Mediterranean.

91. For attested decorative schemes and their cultural significance see chapter 3 n. 174.

> commanders became exceptionally proficient at plundering and relocating them during our period.[92] What we know about the extraordinary costs for commissioning and erecting cult statues and accompanying decorative programs elsewhere in the classical and Hellenistic Mediterranean may not be applicable to fourth- and third-century Rome.[93]

With these premises established, we can proceed to the model's basic equation. The total labor required in person-hours for temple construction in any given period can be obtained through a simple formula:

A (total # of temples built in 25-yr period) × n (# of laborers)
× ([75 × 12] × 3) = **LR** (person-hours)

The total *available labor* that could be tapped in any given period can be derived through another simple formula:

0.5 × (males ages 17–45 at any given point in 25-yr period)
× ([75 × 12] × 3) = **AL** (person-hours)

Dividing the labor required by the total available labor provides us with the percentage of how much labor *relative to the overall disposable* total was needed for temple construction ([LR/AL] / 100). It should be emphasized that these equations result in point estimates whose main benefit consists of furnishing a sense of orders of magnitude; their accuracy does not extend beyond that. A probabilistic model that employed a Monte Carlo simulation would be even better,[94] but for the purposes of this chapter a point-estimate model with easily adjustable numbers will suffice.

92. Looting of a statue of Jupiter from Praeneste in the early fourth century: Liv. 6.29.9 and Festus 498 L. with Russell 2016, 106–7. Cf. Pliny *NH* 34.16.34 on the two thousand statues removed from Volsinii after Rome's intervention there in 264; a statue base unearthed in the area of S. Omobono and inscribed *M. Folv[io(s) Q.f. cos]ol [dede]d Volsi[nio] cap[to]* (*CIL* I^2.2836) may have pertained to an installation of these statues. Reuse of a Sicilian statue of Aphrodite (the so-called Ludovisi Acrolith) as the cult image for the temple of Venus Erycina: Cirucci 2013, 137–39, with nn. 26–27 for earlier bibliography; La Rocca 2010, 97–100 on the art-historical context of mid-republican cultic statuary.

93. Cf. the itemized costs for the decorative program of the Epidaurian Asklepieion: Burford 1969. The economics of statuary in classical Athens: Acton 2014, 215–25. Synthesis of the available evidence for Hellenistic temple construction: Migeotte 1995. For more on these projects, see the end of this subsection and the conclusion to this chapter.

94. For comment and demonstration of Monte Carlo's utilities for ancient history, see Lavan 2016 and Jew in progress.

My next objective is to cycle through the basic model's various permutations in order to concretize the labor regimes that can be derived by application of the two formulas. Table 2.2 takes the equations on a ride through the labor benchmarks set out in (c) and (d). Under the scenario in which $n = 500$, the demands of temple construction on the Roman state's available supply of labor would have been very manageable. Even at the high point of temple construction in the years 274–250, a quarter century that encompassed the Pyrrhic War and the first fourteen years of the First Punic War, only 30 percent of the disposable adult male workforce would have been required for temple construction. Seeing as we had stipulated for the model that at the most 50 percent of the adult male population was "free" for hire or corvée, the 30 percent of AL translates to 15 percent of the entire male workforce; and the average allocation per twenty-five-year interval for the fourth and third centuries comes to 11 percent of AL, or 5.5 percent of all men between the ages of seventeen and forty-five. Doubling n to 1,000 does not impinge substantially on the labor capacities of the mid-republican state: at the high-water mark, 60 percent of available labor would have been distrained, or 30 percent of adult men; the average across all periods of the fourth and third centuries comes out to 21 percent of available labor, or 10.5 percent of all adult men. Only under a scenario in which n equals 2,000 would the requirements of 274–250 have surpassed the amount of available labor, with the preceding twenty-five-year interval not far behind. In all other periods, meeting temple labor demands would not have caused much difficulty: the average throughout the fourth and third centuries is 43 percent of available labor, or a shade under 22 percent of the overall male workforce.

On an initial run of the model, then, the burdens of temple construction were hardly onerous at all. In order to refine and sharpen this conclusion, I wish to conclude this subsection by examining how sensitive this model is to alterations of several of its core premises: what if, instead of varying the number of laborers required for each temple, we modify the number of days spent in temple work a year, or the number of hours worked per day, or the number of years that were required on average for each temple's construction? Color plate 1 presents a simple sensitivity graph, the purpose of which is to gauge the model's range by plotting three modifications: (1) the number of days spent on temple work is raised to 100, or lowered to 50; (2) the number of hours per workday is raised to 14, or lowered to 6; (3) the average number of years-to-completion is raised to 6, or lowered to 1.5. I have computed the modifications for a labor-pool of $n = 500$, holding other model parameters constant.[95]

95. Modeling at $n = 500$ suffices for heuristic purposes, since recalibrating with a $n = 1{,}000$ or $n = 2{,}000$ simply moves the Condition outcomes up, closer to and eventually past the avail-

Table 2.2. Labor Requirements of Temple Construction, Three Conditions

Period	Temples built	Labor required (LR)		Available labor (AL)	LR/AL
$n = 500$					
400–375	2	2,700,000		43,200,000	6%
374–350	0	0		43,200,000	0%
349–325	2	2,700,000		43,200,000	6%
324–300	3	4,050,000		58,050,000	7%
299–275	9	12,150,000		58,050,000	21%
274–250	13	17,550,000		58,050,000	30%
249–225	6	8,100,000		74,250,000	11%
224–200	2	2,700,000		74,250,000	4%
Total	**37**	**49,950,000**	**Average**	**56,531,000**	11%
$n = 1{,}000$					
400–375	2	5,400,000		43,200,000	13%
374–350	0	0		43,200,000	0%
349–325	2	5,400,000		43,200,000	13%
324–300	3	8,100,000		58,050,000	14%
299–275	9	24,300,000		58,050,000	42%
274–250	13	35,100,000		58,050,000	60%
249–225	6	16,200,000		74,250,000	22%
224–200	2	5,400,000		74,250,000	7%
Total	**37**	**99,900,000**	**Average**	**56,531,000**	21%
$n = 2{,}000$					
400–375	2	10,800,000		43,200,000	25%
374–350	0	0		43,200,000	0%
349–325	2	10,800,000		43,200,000	25%
324–300	3	16,200,000		58,050,000	28%
299–275	9	48,600,000		58,050,000	84%
274–250	13	70,200,000		58,050,000	121%
249–225	6	32,400,000		74,250,000	44%
224–200	2	10,800,000		74,250,000	15%
Totals	**37**	**199,800,000**	**Average**	**56,531,000**	43%

The resulting outputs have been juxtaposed against the original model (calculated at $n = 500$) and the amount of available labor for each twenty-five-year period.

able labor threshold. One outcome is double-tagged ("1.5 years to temple completion" and "6 hours per work-day") because it reflects two arithmetically identical results.

Not a single one of the tweaks to the basic conditions would bring us anywhere close to the available labor threshold. If laborers were spending on average one hundred days a year at twelve hours of work per day on temples, construction would have climaxed in 274–250 at 31,500,000 total person-hours—still only 54 percent of available labor for this period. Halving the total time required for the average temple or halving the hours per workday for its construction would bring the peak-period tally down to 8,775,000 person-hours, or a mere 15 percent of available labor. How substantially the realia of temple construction differed from or converged on any one of these scenarios is ultimately beyond definitive corroboration, but there are other means at our disposal for further refinement both of the model and of the conclusions to be derived from it. I turn now to a more systematic reckoning of the sense and significance of the model's outputs, by comparison to what we know or can reconstruct about person-power investments in other domains of Roman life and in other corners of the Hellenistic Mediterranean.

III. Testing the Model: Internal and External Comparanda

In subjecting the model to the stress test of comparison, this section will seek to confirm the small-but-repetitive pattern through which the middle Republic's temple construction habit left its mark on the city. I will first line up temple building's demands against those of other construction programs that contribute to the molding of Rome's urban space during the fourth, third, and second centuries (1); then I will look to the labor demands of the military (2); finally, ranging beyond central Italy, I will conclude by evaluating the mid-republican temple regime against the evidence for labor inputs that can be gleaned from Hellenistic construction accounts (3). On one level, this section seeks to validate comparison as a tool for firming up not only the specific model at the core of this chapter but also the various secondary models that will be required to gauge its merits and tease out its ramifications. The more sweeping ambition behind this species of iterative comparisons, however, is to make as compelling a case as possible for the benefits of quantitative focalization—as a strategy not only for redescribing the religious history of the middle Republic but also for querying Tillean schemes of state formation and development. As the conclusion to this chapter will emphasize, the middle Republic's allocations of labor to the construction of many small temples fell in a Goldilocks zone of state (trans)formation: enough to yield a monumentally impressive and socially meaningful outcome without obstructing military mobilization or triggering significant political unrest. The virtues of remaining within this Goldilocks zone will receive a more careful work-over in chapters 3 to 5; for now, I concentrate on demonstrating what this zone looked like.

1. *The Servian Wall*

Measuring about 11 kilometers in length, the fourth-century circuit wall—certainly not "Servian" in date, as archaeological study has conclusively established—was completed within a few decades of the Gallic Sack, and by the middle of the fourth century at the latest. Although the Servian Wall is by no means the only major nonreligious construction of the fourth and third centuries,[96] it is the first to benefit from comprehensive quantitative modeling. Seth Bernard has formulated a scheme for tabulating the labor inputs that were required to build the circuit wall; his model accounts for the extraction costs of quarrying stone, the processing costs of shaping the stone, riverine and intraurban movement of finished stone to its destination, the excavation of the wall's foundations, the laying of the ashlar masonry, and the erection of the *agger*. The aggregate cost of the wall comes out, by Bernard's calculations, to 6,803,059 person-days.[97]

To compare this figure to mine, we simply need to convert person-days to person-hours. On the assumption of twelve hours per person-day, Bernard's costing of the Wall translates to 81,636,708 person-hours of labor. This is a breathtaking figure, though not out of line with other recent quantifications of labor expenditure on wall-building in the ancient Mediterranean.[98] In the context of the demographic regime for labor availability that I proposed above, such an investment represents nearly double the amount of available labor, or almost 95 percent of the entire adult male labor force for the period under discussion.[99] The building of an 11-kilometer circuit wall, then, did impose extremely burdensome demands on the labor pool of the mid-republican state, and it is for this reason that Bernard has claimed that the wall's construction stifled economic productivity for a number of years; plebeian resentment

96. Aqueducts (the pioneering Aqua Claudia and the Anio Vetus): Hodge 2002. Roads (the Viae Appia and Aurelia, with a grid of at least four other roads coming into being by the end of the First Punic War): Chevallier 1997, chap. 13; Laurence 1999, chap. 2; for more on roads, see the end of this subsection.

97. Bernard 2018a, chap. 4 with tables 4.1–2. Cf. Starr 1980, 18–19 for some back-of-envelope calculations of the number of people required to defend the wall.

98. Cf. the labor projection for Megara Hyblaia's walls in De Angelis 2016, 93; these are estimated to have required the movement of more than double the amount of stone and earth that was required for the construction of Selinous's seven large temples (on which see n. 121 below).

99. I have divided the aggregate figure into the AL calculated for 400–375 (table 2.2).

of the wall's labor demands is explicitly affirmed by the annalistic tradition.[100] By comparison, temple construction was nothing to write home about. Setting n for the average temple at 500, each temple will have entailed 1,350,000 person-hours of work, or a little under 2 percent of the wall's cost; with a n of 1,000, the final cost rises to 2,700,000 person-hours, or around 3.3 percent of the wall's cost; and with a n of 2,000, the final cost reaches 5,400,000 person-hours, or about 6.6 percent of the wall's cost. Notably, although with n set at 500 the cumulative labor cost of temple construction in the fourth and third centuries falls well short of the commitment necessitated by the Servian Wall, once n is set to 1,000 or 2,000 the overall labor expenses of sacred construction would have surpassed the amount consumed by the fortification.

In order to check Bernard's model for the Servian Wall as well as my manipulation of it, we will need to interrogate briefly the skimpy evidence preserved in the literary sources for the cost of other large-scale building projects in the middle and late Republic.[101] An inscribed copy of an early first-century contract for repairs to the Via Caecilia lists several figures, although the restoration of one of these is too uncertain to allow for a comprehensive tabulation of the repair's overall cost. To remedy this problem, historians of Rome's road network have exploited epigraphic evidence from the Empire to derive an approximate cost of 500,000 sesterces (HS) per mile of road construction; however, assuming that such a figure corresponded in order-of-magnitude terms to the realities of road construction in the third and second centuries BCE would not bring us all of the way to a costing of mid-republican construction, as we remain in the dark about the precise extent of road building during this period.[102] One might also turn to a notice preserved in the annalistic tradition that on one occasion 1,000 talents (≈ 24 million HS) were set aside for the cleaning and repair of Rome's sewers, although here the difficulty is that we lack not only a date but even a temporal window for the cleaning and refurbishment.[103] Better luck has attended the preservation of details concerning Q. Marcius Rex's renovation of the Aqua Appia and Anio Vetus and construction of the Aqua Marcia in the 140s: the Senate allocated 180,000,000

100. Bernard 2017; I discuss this resentment at the end of this chapter.

101. Our knowledge of building costs during the Empire is more comprehensive because better epigraphically documented: see the citations gathered at Maschek 2016a, 401.

102. For the figure see Pekáry 1968, followed closely in Chevallier 1997, 275 and others.

103. Via Caecilia: 150,000 HS to 600,000 (?) HS as recorded in *CIL* I^2.808, to be read with Guidobaldi 1999. Sewers: Acilius fr. 8 Chassignet = *FRHist* F 6 with commentary ad loc. for arguments over the dating and credibility of this report. For the possibility that this sewer project was contracted during the consulship of Cato the Elder and M. Valerius Flaccus in 184, see Bruun 2003, 308.

HS for the full project, which took four years from start to finish.[104] This initiative, "the single most expensive building project undertaken during the Republic," was greeted with religious obstruction that may have occasioned some delays, but in the end the then-praetor Q. Marcius Rex prevailed, and the aqueduct program was allowed to continue.[105] The allocation will have covered both compensation for on-site skilled and unskilled labor and the capital required for the requisitioning and transporting of materials to sites; since we are in the dark about the percentage of the overall disbursement that was apportioned to each, in what follows I will take the figure simply as representative of aggregate labor cost.[106] With numbers for aggregate cost and for time to completion, two of the three items necessary for reconstructing the labor expenditure that underwrote the aqueduct program are at our fingertips. The third and unfortunately irrecoverable one is average wage per person-day of work. To avoid bogging down in a debate whose final resolution awaits the clarity of a felicitous textual or epigraphic find, I will assume that the average wage for one day's work was either 4 or 6 HS.[107] Finally, to facilitate comparison, I will assume that the work year for the aqueducts was seventy-five days long, the same as that for temple construction.

Venturing from these premises to the calculation of the labor force required for the Marcian aqueduct program is not complicated (table 2.3). By comparison to this massive outlay of labor, both Bernard's figures for the manpower investment in the Servian Wall and mine for temple construction in the fourth and third centuries take a back seat. The higher estimate for the manpower required for the Marcian program (Condition I) is approximately six times greater than Bernard's estimate for the Servian Wall. As for how temple construction compares to the Marcian enterprise, it is noteworthy that, even under the $n = 2{,}000$ scenario, the sum total of person-hours expended on temple work (199,800,000) amounts to a little more than half of the lower estimate of the manpower required for the Marcian program (Condition II).

104. Front. *Aq.* 7.4–5, with the annalist Fenestella (*FRHist* F 12) as his source; Pliny *NH* 36.121 for more information on the Marcian aqueduct program.

105. I quote Kay 2014, 24. Religious obstruction: see Liv. *Ox. Per.* 54 (*Aqua [Marcia in Capit] olium contra Sibyllae carmina [perducta]*) with Morgan 1978 and Rodgers 1982; cf. Osgood 2018, 25–28.

106. An uptick in Roman minting in this period may reflect the need to pay workers: Crawford 1974, 2.697–797 with table LVIII.

107. On the wage history of the Republic, see Scheidel 2010a, 442–44. In what follows I lump unskilled and skilled labor together purely for simplicity's sake; for skilled laborers being paid by unit produced and not by hours worked see Cato *De agri cultura* 4.1–5 and Cic. *Q Fr.* 2.4.2 with Taylor 2014, 202.

Table 2.3. Labor for Rome's Aqueducts, 140s BCE

Parameters	**Condition 1:** 4 HS Daily Wage	**Condition 2:** 6 HS Daily Wage
Cost	180,000,000 HS	180,000,000 HS
Total person-days of labor [Final cost/wage per person-day]	180,000,000 HS / 4 = 45,000,000 person-days = 540,000,000 person-hours	180,000,000 HS / 6 = 30,000,000 person-days = 360,000,000 person-hours
Labor force [Total person-days of work/ total days of work]	45,000,000/(75 days a year x 4 years) = 150,000 laborers	30,000,000/(75 days a year x 4 years) = 100,000 laborers

Even if the labor costs for the aqueduct work of the 140s only accounted for 60 percent or 70 percent of the disbursement—with the remainder of the 180,000,000 HS being set aside for materials and transport—the manpower siphoned off by the aqueducts would still outstrip the quantity of labor that propelled mid-republican temple construction at the n = 2,000 level. But this finding is exactly as it should be and lends additional support to Bernard's and my respective models. Aqueduct construction in general and the unusually long and high-volume Aqua Marcia in particular will have entailed a prodigious and unrivaled labor allocation, made possible only in the context of the second-century economic and demographic transformation that benefited equally from natural population increase and the importation of slaves from all corners of the Mediterranean.

The mid-republican state that oversaw the building of the Servian Wall and directed manpower resources to temple construction could not compete with the monumental capacity of second-century Rome, which by the time of the Aqua Marcia's contracting was firmly entrenched in its place as Mediterranean hegemon. However, the middle Republic's capabilities were hardly negligible, as attested by Rome's investments in road construction beginning with the censorship of Ap. Claudius Caecus in 312. Returning to the procedure by which we reverse-engineered the labor inputs for the Aqua Marcia can clarify, if only in a very approximate sense, the extent of the middle Republic's infrastructural capacity. If we apply Pekáry's figure of 500,000 HS per mile to the 125-mile segment of the Via Appia from Rome to Capua that was contracted out by the censor, and assume a five-year construction window for laborers who were being compensated at the mid-republican equivalent of 4 HS per workday under the conditions outlined in table 2.3, the road will have required over 40,000 laborers to build—reason enough to agree with Ray Laurence that the road's construction "would have made a considerable number of people obliged to" the censor.[108]

2. *The Military-Industrial Complex*

For an even starker illustration of the relative insignificance of temple construction's labor demands, we turn next to the manpower allocations for military campaigning during the middle Republic. At first blush, the obviousness of this exercise will be apparent not only to any Roman historian but also to anyone who has spent time in the company of Charles Tilly's writings on state formation. If war-making makes states, it should come as no revelation that the Roman state's primary labor allocations were directed toward warfare. Beyond simply confirming this fact, the historical arrangement of mid-republican Rome's alliance system, with its structural commitment to siphoning not regular tribute but bodies for war-making, slots neatly into Tilly's rubric of coercion-intensive revenue extraction.[109] As mentioned earlier, however, the purpose of modeling is to establish a range of possibilities for contextualizing this species of extraction, in the anticipation of a payoff several chapters down the road.

In the case of military commitments, our primary source of data is the annalistic tradition, with one catch: prior to 218, the annalistic record preserves little detail on year-to-year legionary deployments, let alone whether legions were manned at full or at partial strength. For the years 218–167, however, Livy offers enough information to allow for judicious conjecture. Following G. De Sanctis and A. Afzelius, Peter Brunt collected military enrollment notices in the literary sources in order to recreate the annual legionary numbers (with corresponding manpower figures) for the Second Punic War. Table 2.4 reproduces these manpower figures in simplified form and with their person-hour equivalents, the person-hour equivalents derived by multiplying the first row by 12 hours (per workday) and 200 days (per campaign year).[110]

108. Laurence 1999, 15, with pp. 16–18 for evocative description of the tasks and time involved in the first segment's construction; despite the suggestion of the ancient sources that the road paving was started and completed in 312, I side with Laurence's stance that the building "was probably undertaken over a period of five years down to 308 BC." The labor required: 500,000 HS × 125 miles (Rome-Capua) = 62,500,00 HS total cost, to be divided by 4 HS for a total of 15,625,000 man-days of labor; dividing this last figure by 375 (75 days per work-year × 5 years) yields 41,666 workers.

109. Tilly 1992, 17–20 on the difference between capital- and coercion-intensive forms of extraction; Eich and Eich 2005, 15–16 and Scheidel 2019: chap. 2 for application to Rome.

110. Brunt 1971, 418, table X. I follow without any modification Brunt's extrapolation from legions to men; for defense of this see Brunt 1971, 419–20. But I omit Brunt's scenarios for

Table 2.4. Roman Manpower in the Legions, 218–201 BCE

Year	Number of legionaries enrolled (and number of legions)	Person-hour equivalent
218	27,000 (6)	64,800,000
217	50,000 (11)	120,000,000
216	65,000 (13)	156,000,000
215	60,000 (15)	144,000,000
214	75,000 (20)	180,000,000
213	75,000 (22)	180,000,000
212	80,000 (25)	192,000,000
211	75,000 (25)	180,000,000
210	65,000 (21)	156,000,000
209	65,000 (21)	156,000,000
208	60,000 (21)	144,000,000
207	65,000 (23)	156,000,000
206	55,000 (20)	132,000,000
205	50,000 (18)	120,000,000
204	55,000 (19)	132,000,000
203	60,000 (20)	144,000,000
202	50,000 (16)	120,000,000
201	45,000 (14)	108,000,000
Total		2,584,800,000
Average		143,600,000

A full accounting of Roman military deployments would take stock of allied commitments, as Brunt recognized, but because the primary focus of this section is the citizen labor regime, I will not attempt to calculate manpower figures for Rome's allies.[111] In any case, the totals in table 2.4 only apply for the Second Punic War and do not offer any insight into the manpower investments of the middle Republic before Hannibal's appearance on the scene. To rectify that shortcoming, another model is needed.

In order to align these figures with the twenty-five-year periodization of the temple construction scheme, the first step is to derive a military manpower allocation for the years 225 to 200 from Brunt's numbers. If the annual average of 143,600,000 person-hours—the equivalent of a shade under 60,000 men,

before/after Trasimene and before/after Cannae for the years 217–16; see the notes to table X for comment on the reshuffling of and *supplementa* to legions in the aftermath of military defeats. On demographic extrapolations from Polyb. 2.23–34—the roll of Roman and allied forces in 225—before and after Brunt, see Lanauro 2011, 38–44.

111. Brunt 1971, 420–22, which also differentiates between terrestrial and naval commitments.

or about 13 legions of 4,500 men each—held true for the entire twenty-five-year period, the cumulative manpower allocation will have been 3.59 billion person-hours. Obviously, this era's mobilization rates were exceptional, and not just in the annals of Roman history.[112] For the preceding decades it will be necessary to carry out some kind of downward adjustment and to lean on judicious conjecture once again. For the years 400–375 and 375–350, let us assume that on average the Roman state annually mobilized 10,000 men (about two legions) and had them campaigning for 100 days each year (with 12 hours of active duty per day), for a total of 300 million person-hours of military commitment in each twenty-five-year window. For the second half of the fourth century, let us assume an average annual mobilization of 15,000 men—with spikes in conscription during the Romano-Latin and Samnite Wars partially offset by periods of relative inactivity—while holding hours per day and days per year from the previous half-century constant, for a total of 450 million person-hours for the periods 350–325 and 325–300. For the first quarter of the third century, let us assume an increase in the average number of Romans annually enrolled to 20,000 and an increase in number of campaign days to 150, for a total of 900 million person-hours. Since the Pyrrhic War and the First Punic War will have seen yet another surge in average annual conscription as military commitments stretched across the sea for the first time, let us raise the enrollment number to 25,000 and bump up the number of days in the field, for a total of 1.5 billion person-hours for the years 275–250. The following period will have seen a drop-off in manpower commitments after the resolution of the First Punic War, then a slow rise as Roman armies were dispatched to fight in Sardinia, Corsica, and Illyria; therefore, we may revise the annual average of Roman citizens serving downward to 20,000 but hold the remaining variables from the preceding period constant, for an aggregate of 1.2 billion person-hours in the years 250–225. As the end point of this progression, the figure of 3.59 billion person-hours for 225–200 now seems somewhat more credible. With this scaffold in place, we are now in position to evaluate temple construction's demands against the backdrop of mid-republican military campaigning.

Color plate 2 visualizes the contrast. If not already apparent from the preceding paragraph's orders of magnitude, the diminutive scale of temple construction's manpower requirements comes into crystal-clear perspective when lined up against the middle Republic's military motor. At the n = 2,000 scenario for the years 275–250, the temple building model calls for an aggregate

112. In global history, Rome's mobilization of manpower in the heat of the Second Punic War was perhaps equaled only by the Confederacy during the US Civil War: Scheidel 2004b, 6 with n. 29.

person-hour investment equivalent to 5 percent of the amount of manpower required for battlefield activity. Besides the virtue of clarifying juxtaposition, plate 2 enhances the credibility of the temple construction model in two related but distinct ways. First, if the model had called for manpower investments that were on a par with or in excess of those that were channeled into military service, either the political history of the middle Republic would have had to be comprehensively reconceived or the temple building model would have to be ditched as heuristically useless.

Second, the sheer differential in scales between military campaigning on the one hand and temple construction on the other invites renewed consideration of the possibility entertained at the outset of this chapter: that temple building is effectively a "shell game" that relies on one impressive-seeming but relatively low-cost social enterprise to paper over the costs of a far costlier one. This second point will be queried in the conclusion to this chapter and in the final chapter of this book. At this stage, however, it is time to introduce some external comparanda that, in addition to acting as checks for the model, position mid-republican temple building within the general history of classical Greek and Hellenistic sacred monumentalism.

3. Apples to Apples: Mediterranean Parallels

As noted earlier, epigraphic dossiers of temple building and repair survive from the classical and Hellenistic Greek world and list figures for expenditures on different components of construction and decoration. With some arithmetic dexterity, these figures can be rendered into person-hour equivalents for comparison with the numbers obtained from the temple building model. As proof of concept, let us first consider the epigraphic account for the building of the Asklepieion at Epidauros, the subject of intensive study first by Alison Burford and more recently by John Salmon.[113] The latter's calculations for the quarrying, transport, and construction costs for each of the Asklepieion's structural components put the final aggregate cost at 54,280.91 drachmas.

The pivotal next step in converting this sum into a person-hour equivalent is to settle on the average wage in drachmas per workday for those charged with the construction. Here the fifth-century Athenian Erechtheum accounts and the fourth-century Eleusinian complex records come to our rescue, since they supply the crucial datum that an average wage of 1.5 drachmas for work on structures of this sort was not atypical.[114] The Asklepieion's total cost of

113. *IG* IV I^2 102 with Burford 1969 and Salmon 2001; note also Mathé 2017, 144–45.

114. Randall 1953; Loomis 1998, 104–20. Unskilled labor was compensated at one drachma

54,280.91 dr. therefore translates to 81,421 man-days of labor, or 977,056 person-hours if we assume a 12-hour workday. This figure is not all that far off from the average cost of a temple at Rome under the n = 500 scenario (1,350,000 person-hours); the difference effectively disappears when we posit an average wage of 2 dr. per workday, in which case the Asklepieion's cost in labor equivalent will have been 1,302,741 person-hours. It would not have been unreasonable for the Asklepieion to cost less in labor equivalent than the standard mid-republican temple: measuring 11.76 x 23.06 m at the stylobate, the Epidaurian structure was smaller than four of the six mid-republican temple foundations whose dimensions have been confirmed.[115] In any event, if we hold the average wage figure steady at 1.5 dr. for Epidauros and a n = 500 labor scenario for Rome, the conclusion that emerges is that the middle Republic built the equivalent of fifty-one Asklepieia during the fourth and third century—no trivial feat.

One secondary benefit of this comparison is that we now have at our disposal a means of reverse-engineering currency equivalents for the mid-republican temple construction regime. These will serve as the basis for a final round of adventurous comparisons. Earlier I had refrained from converting person-hours to wage equivalents because of the dearth of information for daily wages in Italy in the middle Republic; extrapolating from the indirect evidence of the late Republic and Empire is hazardous given the shifts in monetization, economic production, and demography that took place in the last two centuries BCE.[116] Nonetheless, there are some advantages to proceeding down this route, chief among them the prospect of arriving at an apples-to-apples comparison of Rome's construction investments to those of other polities in the classical and Hellenistic Mediterranean. Recall that, under the n = 500 condition, an average temple cost 1,350,000 person-hours, the equivalent of 112,500 workdays. If we presume that each workday of labor in mid-republican Rome was compensated at the purchasing-power equivalent of 1.5 Athenian drachmas, the typical Roman temple will have cost 168,750 dr. Should we adjust this conversion substantially downward, out of deference to the possibility that the average wage for construction work in classical and early Hellenistic Athens was in purchasing-power terms double that of its

or slightly less, skilled at around two drachmas or more; I split the difference. High real wages in classical Greece: Ober 2010, 262–66; Scheidel 2010a, 441–42.

115. For references to the dimensions see n. 72 above. The Asklepieion as a "comparatively modest" structure: Burford 1969, 56.

116. The indirect evidence is collected and assessed in Scheidel 2010a, 444–46. Modeling the variables that interacted to drive real wages in the last few centuries BCE: Scheidel 2007, 341–43 with table 2.

mid-republican counterpart, each Roman temple built under the $n = 500$ scenario will have instead cost on average 84,375 dr., or about 14 Attic talents (1 talent = 6,000 dr.). At the high scenario of $n = 2{,}000$, each temple will have cost 337,500 dr. If the compensation baseline of a purchasing-power equivalent to 0.75 dr. per workday of labor held true for the entirety of the middle Republic, Rome will have expended anywhere between 3,121,875 dr. ($n = 500$ scenario; 520 talents) and 12,487,500 dr. ($n = 2{,}000$ scenario; 2,081 talents) to build thirty-seven temples over the course of the fourth and third centuries. While these are not trifling figures by any means, what stands out especially under the $n = 500$ scenario (with compensation set at the Roman equivalent to 0.75 dr. per workday) is the relative affordability of a mid-republican Roman temple. By the second century, Roman infantry were earning around 120 *denarii* a year in *stipendium*, or about a third of a *denarius* daily; if the average price of construction labor on a temple fell somewhere in this compensation range, one temple under the $n = 500$ scenario will have cost approximately 37,000 *denarii*—hardly an overwhelming figure.[117] Even a general who brought back a meager amount of booty from campaign would have had the resources to cover its cost.[118]

Several other data points bring the moderation of Roman temple building into clearer focus.[119] Periclean Athens poured 460 talents into the Parthenon and 300 on the Propylaia; from 447/6 to 432/1, 51 talents were allotted annually to the Acropolis's monumentalization. This resource investment, as spread out across two decades, gives the two centuries of mid-republican construction a run for their money. At the zenith of its construction spree in the seventy-five-year period from 300 to 225, Rome dedicated anywhere between the equivalent of 392 talents (at an average of 5 talents per year) and 1,512 talents (at an average of 20 a year) to temples. It should of course be noted that the lavishness of the Periclean Acropolis program was made possible by the existence of an alliance system that funneled monetized tribute to Athens, a situation that did not obtain for mid-republican Rome; and that a budget of this kind ceased to be a possibility in the years after the Peloponnesian War, with only half a talent a year on average being earmarked for sacred construction by the time Alexander the Great and his successors appeared on the scene. Extending our gaze beyond classical Athens, we might cite as another comparison the Epidauros complex whose Asklepieion we have already dis-

117. Polyb. 6.39.12 for military compensation; Scheidel 2007, 330–31 for contextualization against the longer history of income growth in Roman Italy.

118. *Pace* Orlin 1997, 129.

119. The figures that follow are culled from Spawforth 2006; Migeotte 2014; Pritchard 2015; and De Angelis 2016. On the economics of monumental construction in classical Athens note also Acton 2014, 202–15.

cussed, the final cost for which fell somewhere between 240 and 290 talents to build—well below the aggregate cost of Rome's constructions under the $n = 500$ condition. A worthier rival is late archaic and classical Delphi's monumentalization: the first stages in the late sixth century cost somewhere in the vicinity of 300 talents, while the fourth-century renovations entailed between 320 and 400 talents. That the outlay for Rome's temple constructions compare favorably to the expenditures at a Panhellenic sanctuary whose renovations were underwritten to varying degrees by poleis throughout the Greek world is another testament to the significance of the middle Republic's enterprise.

One final candidate for suggestive contrast are those monumental initiatives in the western Mediterranean whose place in the trajectory of peer-polity dynamics I had referenced in this chapter's opening section. Approximate costs have been calculated for the great archaic and early classical monumental programs of Magna Graecia, with Paestum's four temples priced at 420 talents (or 105 talents per temple); Selinous's five temples at 1,300 talents (260 talents per temple); and Agrigentum's four temples at 1,900 talents (475 talents per temple). Under the $n = 2{,}000$ condition, Rome's expenditures on sacred construction barely clear the example set by Agrigentum, one of whose temple complexes may have left a deep impression on Roman eyes during the First Punic War.[120] Likewise, only under the $n = 2{,}000$ condition will the labor costs of mid-republican Rome's thirty-seven temples have outpaced those incurred by Selinous in the course of building seven large peripteral temples from circa 550 to 460 BCE.[121] Of course, Agrigentum's unfinished Olympieion, which measured 110.09 by 52.74 m, will have dwarfed any one of Rome's mid-republican structures, such as the temple of Apollo Medicus whose platform after renovation in the fourth century measured 38.20 x 21.45 m. One obvious takeaway from this comparison is that, whereas Agrigentum and its late archaic/early classical Greek peers concentrated their wealth in a few truly (and overwhelmingly) spectacular exhibitions of monumentalism, the middle Republic distributed its wealth across many small structures. How that wealth was secured and recycled into temple building is a process that will be examined at greater length in the next chapter. Another, somewhat less obvious, takeaway is that an Agrigentum-style commitment to monumentalism could have nonetheless been accommodated under Rome's labor regime; as explained earlier, even an investment in temple labor under the $n = 2{,}000$ sce-

120. Naevius *Bellum Punicum* fr. 8 Blänsdorf = 7 Flores as an ekphrasis of the Gigantomachy that formed part of the decorative program of Agrigentum's Olympieion: Feeney 1991, 118–20; Ridgway 1999, 30 n. 32; Flores 2011, xxiii; and Giusti 2018, 58–63 for an exceptionally nimble reading.

121. A minimum estimate of 7.3 million person-hours for their construction: De Angelis 2016, 89–91.

nario would have been a drop in the bucket relative to the prolific manpower deposits that sustained the middle Republic's military campaigns.

The question to address now is why Rome went in the direction of distributing wealth across a flurry of small temple constructions instead of emulating polities such as early classical Agrigentum (or classical Athens) by channeling wealth into several large ones. The first answer that presents itself is a path-dependent one: for reasons laid out in the chapter's first section, the mid-republican state evolved in a direction that privileged these bounded and comparatively humble buildings. Conversely, a veer in the Agrigentine direction would have thrown the mid-republican system into disarray. Translating wealth into a multitude of small temples was a more efficacious way of setting up and perpetuating the "shell game" through which the middle Republic ensured the continuing commitment of its population to the one enterprise that did consume bodies and time: nearly ceaseless belligerence. The details of this proposition will be elucidated over the next two chapters; for now, let us put a bow on temple construction and models for clarifying its scope.

IV. Conclusion

A quantitatively focused approach to religious practice enables comparison, which can in turn work to develop a more richly textured understanding of change over time not only within the Roman world of the middle Republic but also within the Hellenistic Mediterranean more broadly. In this chapter, I have been concerned primarily with explaining how the scales and rhythms of Rome's temple construction habit interface with the trajectory of the mid-republican state. Other applications of this chapter's models are of course possible and to be welcomed. There is far more to be said about the monumental religious history of the Hellenistic Mediterranean, suspended as it was between dynamics of globalization and "glocalization."[122] While this chapter has been propelled by the conviction that quantification can afford a new perspective on historical issues hitherto approached from more qualitative angles, it would be foolish to assert that I have offered anything remotely close to a fully worked-out rubric for how to deploy quantification in the service of mid-republican history. What this chapter has offered instead is the following:

1. An introductory and predominantly qualitative assessment of the institutional pathways to temple construction in mid-republican Rome, with the focus firmly on the elite actors responsible for the surge in

122. The second term's utility for Rome's religious history: Rüpke 2014a, 23–24.

and regularization of the process—and on the Hellenizing backdrop against which their commitment to monumental sacred architecture flowered.

2. A simple and easily adjustable quantitative model that relies on a few basic premises to reconstruct the labor costs of the thirty-seven temples built at Rome over the course of the fourth and third centuries. As calculated under three different scenarios, the aggregate labor costs could be handled by Rome's citizen population, with no need of any supplemental labor to remedy any manpower deficits.
3. Contextualization of the model's findings against what we know or can plausibly re-create about labor demands both in mid-republican Rome and elsewhere in the classical and Hellenistic Mediterranean.

Part of the genius of the middle Republic's construction shell game lay in the selection of a species of monumentalization that did not incur high opportunity or enforcement costs. As the exposition and testing of the model will have clarified, the prioritization of small-temple building did not substantially encroach on other collective endeavors yet still enabled the Roman state to reap the signaling effects of sacred construction—the best of all worlds. The same would not have been true for the erection of supersized structures, which in addition to siphoning significant labor from other undertakings will have required the surveillance and management of a much larger and potentially far more restive pool of workers. Plebeian resistance to large-scale labor demands is discernible in the annalistic tradition, which preserves notices of brewing discontent during the construction of the Capitoline Temple and during the refurbishment of the city following the Gallic Sack several centuries later.[123] And even though the Roman state would follow in the footsteps of its Hellenistic peer states in exploiting captive and slave labor for monumental projects, there were serious downsides to this exploitation—chief among the prospect of large-scale insurrection among the enslaved, which did occur during the second and first centuries.[124] In any case, for a cautionary tale about the diminishing marginal returns to extravagantly sized temples, the Roman state had only to turn to its city-state peers in southern Italy and Sicily, whose supersized temples were in several cases never completed.

123. The Capitoline Temple: Cassius Hemina *FRHist* F 17 and Livy 1.56 with Ogilvie *ad loc.* Construction-related social frictions after the Gallic Sack: Bernard 2017.

124. Captive labor in Ptolemaic construction: see, e.g., *P. Petrie Kleon* 52 with Van Beek 2017 *ad loc.* The composition of the unskilled and skilled labor pools for the massive extraurban infrastructural projects of the late fourth and early third centuries is uncertain: on the scope of the Pontine reclamation see now Attema 2018, 155–56; for a tightly stitched presentation of the economic and political dimensions of these projects, Bernard 2018a, chap. 5.

Besides its relevance to the Mediterranean and global history of premodern urban monumentalization, the comparisons set out in the third section of this chapter also offer some insight into the institutional and demographic patterns that coalesced around a commitment to religiously oriented building. With most work on political economy and the premodern state training its sights on military expenditures, the institutional morphology of those states that steered a significant amount of time and resources toward ritual religious activity remains understudied.[125] One option available to us is to integrate these comparisons—which in their present form gesture obliquely toward the efficaciousness of the sacred monumentalism by which Rome bootstrapped itself into statehood—into a more wide-ranging account of the middle Republic's political economy. Not only do the labor patterns underpinning temple construction provide evidence for this political economy, accumulative sacred monumentalization also equipped the city of Rome with the power to project its religious system beyond its walls and thereby summon into existence a new political economy.[126] Although the city's tessellation into islands of temple building during the fourth and third centuries was certainly expressive of "Rome's nature as a factionalized oligarchy,"[127] the development more immediately relevant to the objectives of this book is whether and under what circumstances temple building became attached to the delivery of those public goods that held the elite and nonelite members of the *res publica* together. That temple building will have furnished skilled and unskilled laborers with the opportunity to forge social connections should not be doubted; modeling the scale and ripple effects of these interactions poses some conceptual challenges that will be taken up in chapter 5.[128] The public goods that I will examine in the next chapter stem from the evolution of Rome's temples into markers and nodes of infrastructural capacity. It was the storage of this capacity within temples that ultimately made their projection of "distributed power" both appealing and durable.[129]

125. See the comments of Hoffman 2017, 1563–64, on Monson and Scheidel 2015.

126. Cf. Ando 2017 on religion and the political economy of cities under the early Empire.

127. Terrenato 2015, 524.

128. Note Cline 2018 for the application of a *chaîne opératoire* model for the reconstruction of the social networks of laborers in classical Athens; chapter 5 n. 148 for additional bibliography.

129. "Distributed power" and premodern cities: Sinopoli et al. 2015, 390–93.

3

Temples and the Civic Order

FROM NUMBERS TO RHYTHMS

THE POLITICAL MACHINERY BEHIND MID-REPUBLICAN temple vows and dedications has benefited from the attention of scholarship, as we saw in the opening section of the last chapter. Still in need of meticulous exposition, however, are the institutional and infrastructural outcomes of temple building and their role in promoting and consolidating the quasi-voluntary social compliance that bound the *res publica* together. Forged in the crucible of traditional gentilician rivalries and face-offs between new "interest groups," Rome's "precarious statehood" during the middle Republic came increasingly to depend on multifunctional temples to mediate the execution of civic responsibilities that in later centuries would be tackled by a differentiated bureaucracy.[1] These responsibilities assumed their shape not only in time but in space; in topographical terms alone, the surge in temple construction altered the urban fabric of Rome by the mere fact of the quantity of land being claimed for and apportioned to cult, even as the steady rise in the city's population necessitated the claiming of additional space for residential building. If the dimensions of the thirty-seven temples that were built in the fourth and third centuries on average mirrored those of the temple of Apollo Medicus, a minimum of 30,000 square meters of urban territory will have been redefined as sacred, at a time when the shape and texture of Roman savoir-faire about the delineation and demarcation of land were undergoing a dramatic transformation.[2] In conjunction with these changes to the residential patterning of the city that ensued from demographic increase, this spike in

1. "Precarious statehood": Walter 2014, 105, elaborated in Rüpke 2018b, 111–12. Multifunctionality of Rome's sacred structures: Lacam 2010, 88–90.

2. The cityscape's alteration: Taylor et al. 2016, 19–31 with figure 12; Popkin 2016, plate 4. This quantification of reclaimed land is the product of multiplying 38.20 × 21.45 m (the platform

monumental construction was responsible in the long run for the ramshackle impression the mid- and late republican city left (or was imagined to leave) on visitors.[3]

How the warping of Rome's urban landscape molded Roman experiences of sacred and nonsacred space, with cultural and phenomenological outcomes of lasting consequence, has been elegantly surveyed by Amy Russell.[4] It is tempting to credit temple construction as a major catalyst of Roman religion's intensifying preoccupation with the materiality of space and place, the fruits of which come into clearer view by the late Republic.[5] Throughout our period, the accelerated gridding of space interacted with the paving of new streets and the orchestration of human and animal movement to create a new cartographic imaginary for the city; shrines and temples attained greater visibility as nodes for spatial orientation and neighborhood organization and remained so, in some cases well into late antiquity.[6] But the repercussions did not stop there. Rome's temples were also a conspicuous expression of the state's growing infrastructural capabilities, a fact that studies of statehood and infrastructure in ancient Rome sometimes overlook.[7] And despite the relative flimsiness of Rome's bureaucratic apparatus during our period, the city would have truly been an anomaly among its Hellenistic peers if its monumental metamorphosis had not relied on a regime of documentation and record-keeping to keep the predecessors of the Empire's paper-pushers busy.[8] The first section of this chapter will present several rather straightforward testimo-

---

dimensions for the temple of Apollo Medicus) by 37 and is intended purely as an order-of-magnitude estimate; it does not account for the space around temples.

3. On this impression see Hartnett 2017, 27–28 and Russell 2017, 72–73, both citing and commenting on Cic. *leg. agr.* 2.95–96. Residential zoning in republican Rome: Mignone 2016, chap. 5 and 2017.

4. Russell 2016, chap. 5. For Roman taxonomies of urban space note also Taylor 2000, 79–91; Humm 2014 for augury's role in the constitution of mid- and late republican political space; Gargola 2017, 119–53 on relevant refinements to Roman augural science; and Festus 474 L. with Glinister 2015 for the spatial demarcation of *fana* in colonies. The differentiation of *sacrum*, *publicum*, and *privatum*: Crawford 1989.

5. The historical and conceptual significance of Rome's "gods of place": Beerden 2018, 887–90 on Flower 2017.

6. For spoofing of this imaginary see Ter. *Adel* 572–83 with Hartnett 2017, 298–302; cf. p. 33 for "a walk up the Clivus Salutis to reach the early [*sic*] republican Temple of Salus." The durability of this imaginary in the case of one mid-republican temple foundation: Mulryan 2011.

7. See, e.g., Schneider 2014, where the emphasis is primarily on roads and aqueducts; cf. the omission of temples from the coverage of infrastructure in Carandini 2017.

8. Cf. Jones 1940, chap. 16 for urban public works and administration in the Greek East.

nies of exactly the sort of record-keeping that presupposes *some* degree of bureaucratization.

The caretaking of temples for centuries after their dedication mirrored and amplified the original infrastructural commitment that drove their construction. Refurbishment and renovation created new opportunities—religious, economic, political—for elites and nonelites alike.[9] In what follows, however, I will assess the infrastructural goods that mid-republican temples delivered within the first several generations of their mushrooming across the city. The innovativeness of mid-republican temples did not stop with their addition of architectural novelty and variety to the *urbs*.[10] The proliferation of multifunctional sacred buildings provided new opportunities for small- and large-scale collective coordination and action, whose multiplier effects further propelled Rome's evolution into a ritual polity. Notwithstanding its designation as a "consumer city" in the works of some modern scholars,[11] Rome from the middle Republic on became increasingly adept at providing tangible services, both to residents and out-of-town visitors. These religious services closed the gap between the Roman state's rapidly expanding capacity to project power abroad and its rather more muted bureaucratic initiatives at home.

I. *Praeda* and the Genesis of Infrastructural Power

In their fiscal and economic impacts, Rome's temples were not radically dissimilar from their Hellenistic counterparts,[12] with the partial exception of their financing—and the positive and negative externalities associated with it. This section will situate temples more centrally within the story of ancient Rome's "fiscal regime," normally emplotted as an evolution from the capture of booty on the battlefield to the imposition of taxes.[13] As James Tan and others have shown, the truth of the matter is somewhat more complicated, but even the most probing interventions in the ongoing debates over republican and imperial Rome's fiscality take little to no cognizance of the specific attri-

9. The regular allocation of funds for temple maintenance is confirmed by Liv. 24.18.10. For material evidence of repair in mid-republican Rome see Bernard 2018a, Appendix 2; for caretaking and enhancement of mid-republican temples and sanctuaries outside of Rome see Moser 2017 on Ostia and 2019, chap. 1 on Ostia and Ardea. The *custodia templorum*: Ménard 2006, esp. 236–37 on the *aedituus* of Plautus *Curc.* 203–4.

10. Temples as sites for architectural experimentation: Popkin 2016, 63–74.

11. See Morley 1996 for a thorough critique of this paradigm's application to ancient Rome.

12. Temples and cults as fiscal and economic entities in the Greek Mediterranean: Von Reden 2010, chap. 7; Chankowski 2011.

13. Beginning with Max Weber; for recent perspectives see Scheidel 2015, Tan 2015, and Bowman 2017.

butes of sacred monumental building. I will contend in this section that temples emerged as mechanisms for the redistribution of the wealth obtained from military activity, and that this species of redistribution slotted quite neatly into a quasi-voluntary compliance scheme that was tethered to the delivery of public goods.

As we saw in chapter 2, not all temples built during the middle Republic were funded through booty. The father of the Ti. Sempronius Gracchus who secured a resounding victory at Beneventum during the Second Punic War oversaw the building of the temple of Iuppiter Libertas on the Aventine "out of fine-money" (*ex multaticia pecunia*), one of at least two aedilician foundations in the third quarter of the third century.[14] By and large, however, most of the temples built during the fourth to early second centuries were paid for with war spoils or with the proceeds obtained through their sale. Carmine Ampolo has attributed the dearth of temple constructions in early republican Rome to the ineffectual nature of Roman military engagements prior to the beginning of the fourth century.[15] While correlation does not imply causation, it is no accident that temple construction surged just as the Roman state began to enjoy a string of military successes. Beyond the fact that it was usually magistrates with *imperium* who took the lead in vowing and dedicating temples, another and more economically relevant consideration to keep in view is that war booty represented the single most substantial supply of capital for the Roman state during the middle Republic. The determination to put that spear-earned booty to work, both to fund temple complexes and to decorate them, bore fruit in a host of economic and infrastructural contexts.

The annalistic tradition preserves several notices of the quantities of *praeda* and *manubiae* seized on campaign. Before gauging the credibility of these notices, we should be forthright about the semantic uncertainties that cluster around these two terms. By the second century CE, Romans themselves seem to have been confused about the exact meanings of *praeda* and *manubiae*.[16] Modern efforts to clarify the lexical and juridical range of each term during the Republic have valiantly struggled against the inconsistent usages of later

14. Liv. 24.16.19 with Coarelli 1997, 215 and *LTUR* s.v. Iuppiter Libertas. Ti. Sempronius Gracchus *père* was *aed.* 246 and *cos.* 238 (*MRR* I.216–217, 221), a contemporary of the Publicii Malleoli who as aediles dedicated a temple to Flora from fine-money. Bibliography on *pecunia multaticia*: chapter 2 n. 9.

15. Ampolo 1990; cf. Bernard 2018a, 64 for questioning of the traditional consensus regarding early republican monumentalism.

16. Gell. *NA* 13.25.3–4: the definition *manubiae enim dicuntur praeda, quae manu capta est* is swiftly rejected by Favorinus, who argues that *manubiae* applies to the *pecunia a quaestore ex uenditione praedae redacta* (13.25.25–26). The interpretation of this passage put forward in Tarpin 2009 muddies the waters: see the comments of Rich 2011.

authors. As Eric Orlin has remarked, "we do not know how the spoils were divided into the categories of *manubiae* and *praeda*, or how much booty fell into each category. The victorious commander's role is murky; did he make the division? Did he keep a portion for himself?"[17] Recognizing that airtight definitions for either term will prove elusive, I will accept for the time being the Mommsenian verdict that *praeda* was the umbrella term, with *manubiae* referring to a subset of *praeda*.[18]

Terminological wrangles notwithstanding, we are on better footing when it comes to enumerating what actually counted as booty for the Romans: not just physical goods (humans, weapons, jewelry) captured on the battlefield, but precious artifacts and more mundane objects looted from conquered territories. As Favorinus's clarification regarding *praeda* and *manubiae* seems to suggest, one important intermediating agent in the process of converting booty seized through conquest into expendable assets was monetization. Possibly by the late fourth century and no later than the early third, bullion and currency appear to have been obtained through the sale of these goods and artifacts in the course of or immediately after the conclusion of campaigning. Relevant both to the terminological haziness of *praeda* and *manubiae* and to the disposition of assets for monumental undertakings is the bifurcation of options available to the enterprising commander who settled on building a temple. He could either hand over all the booty in liquidated form to the state treasury and seek a subvention from the Senate for the purposes of construction—in which case the Senate would take an active role in the final disposition—or rely solely on his portion of the booty to underwrite the costs. Each option came with its benefits and drawbacks.[19]

The exact role monetization played in this process is not easy to determine. The introduction of coinage in mid-republican Rome is a complicated phenomenon that admits of many potential explanations, not all of them mutually reconcilable.[20] What is beyond doubt, however, is that monetization gained

17. Orlin 1997, 117. Tentative answers: Shatzman 1972, 177–205; Orlin 1997, 117–27; Tarpin 2000, 366–68; Coudry 2009; Rosenstein 2011, 134–36 and 143–44.

18. See Mommsen 1879, II.443 n. 62 on *manubiae* as specifically and only referring to the proceeds obtained from the sale of booty; cf. Kay 2014, 22–23 on *manubiae* as the general's portion and *praeda* as the remainder. Division of booty into four categories: Coudry 2009, 23–24, followed by Chemain 2016, 40–41.

19. Thus Russell 2016, 115–17, echoing Orlin. The regulation of access to the public treasury: Fabius Pictor *FRHist* 26.

20. Monetization in the Greco-Roman Mediterranean: Von Reden 2010, chaps. 1–2, esp. pp. 47–55 for developments in republican and imperial Rome. "The social history of early Roman coinage" and the destabilizing effects of monetization among the Roman elite: Bernard 2018a, 136–53 and 2018c. The shift from gift-exchange to monetization at Rome: Coffee 2016, with the criticisms of Rosenstein.

in significance as one means of turning sometimes illiquid booty into more liquid assets. Annalistic reports of the spoils carried in triumphs give a sense of the scale of the wealth that was extracted through military campaigning and then converted into expendable form. To cite only one example, here is Livy's report of the triumph of L. Papirius Cursor after the battle of Aquilonia in 293:

> *Aeris grauis trauecta uiciens centum milia et quingenta triginta tria milia; id aes redactum ex captiuis dicebatur; argenti, quod captum ex urbibus erat, pondo mille octingenta triginta.*
>
> Carried along were two million five hundred thirty-three thousand pounds of bronze—the bronze said to have been obtained (*redactum*) from the (sale of) captives—and one thousand eight hundred thirty pounds of silver captured from the cities.[21]

While numbers of this kind were liable to distortion in the hands of ancient historians and could well have been corrupted in the course of textual transmission, the annalistic tradition seems to have drawn on *elogia* or on family archival records that contained itemized lists of battlefield proceeds. After the Second Punic War, increasing vigilance about the use or abuse of booty may have motivated the institutionalization of reporting requirements for *praeda* and *manubiae*, if such requirements were not in place already.[22] Not only do the figures reported by the annalists "show a degree of interest in measuring and recording that was not typical of that time," they also gesture to the possibility that such methodical recording evolved in part as a means of facilitating the conversion of booty into assets that could be expended domestically.[23]

Indirect evidence for precisely such a dynamic can be gleaned from one surviving mid-republican *elogium*, the inscription that was installed to commemorate Gaius Duilius's victory over the Carthaginians at Mylae in 260 and his subsequent celebration of the first naval triumph awarded to a Roman general. This text, first erected in the lifetime of Duilius, appears to have been

21. Liv. 10.46.4–5, with Oakley ad loc. for discussion of the figures. On revenue-generating sales of captives see n. 42 below.

22. Full tally of Livy's notices: Frank [1933] 1975, 43 n. 3. Cautions about the stylization of numbers: Scheidel 1996a and Duncan-Jones 1997; Scheidel 2016 for an important qualification. Ancient skepticism regarding transmitted figures for booty: Liv. 1.55.7–9 on L. Calpurnius Piso Frugi (*FRHist* F 19). Republican historiography's penchant for numbers: Chassignet 2017, 256–57. Accountability for misappropriation: Rosenstein 2011, 134–35 on the famous episodes; the monograph version of Kleinman 2018 will greatly advance our understanding of accountability in Republican Rome.

23. Quotation and discussion: Harris 1979, 59.

restored (with multiple incorrect archaisms) in the early Principate.[24] Whether or not the manner in which it lists the monetized *praeda* that were paraded in Duilius's triumph was the norm for inscriptions of this type, the coexistence of *nummi* and *asses* in the text's recapitulation of booty invites some speculation as to the types of economic differentiation that were facilitated or mediated by the turn to currency in general and access to silver in particular.[25] I quote lines 13 to 16 of the *elogium*, with Attilio Degrassi's restorations:

> [AVRO]M CAPTOM NVMEI ϕϕϕDCC (?) [*vacat*]
> [ARCEN]TOM CAPTOM PRAEDA NVMEI m[. . . . ?]
> [OMNE] CAPTOM AES mmmmmmmm[mmmmmm]
> [mm]mmmmmmmmmmmmm[mmmmm?]
> [TRIVMP]OQVE NAVALED PRAEDAD POPLOM [DONAVET]

> Gold captured, coins: 3,700 (?)
> Silver captured, *praeda*, coins: 100,000 (++?)
> All captured bronze: 1.4 million
> 1.5 million (or more?)[26]

Left ambiguous is whether the phrase *omne captom aes* is meant to give a total tally for all the booty (in *asses*) or simply a reckoning of the amount of bronze captured (in Roman pounds). Following Michael Crawford, Kondratieff adduces the quantities that Livy lists for the amount of bronze displayed at Papirius Cursor's triumph to resolve the issue.[27] On his reading, the inscription will have tabulated at least 2.9 million—and possibly 3.4 million, if the symbol *m* [= 100,000] is carried to the end of line 16—pounds of bronze, each pound weighing approximately 324 grams, that were carried in Duilius's triumph; this amount of bronze will have yielded anywhere between 3.4 to 4.1 million coined asses.[28] Arguably more important than the exact amount of metal wealth that is detailed on the *elogium* are the uses to which this wealth was put—and it is here that the differentiation between *nummi* and *asses* may be particularly relevant, since it points us in the direction of a specializing

24. *CIL* I^2.1.25 = *ILS* 65 = *InscrItal* 13.3.69 = *ILLRP* 319. On the dating of the original and its restoration see now Kondratieff 2004, 10–14 with Rosenstein 2011, 138 n. 18 for further comment; for the cultural charge of the Duilius *elogium* and monument in Augustan Rome, Biggs 2017b and Roller 2018, 147–62.

25. Thus Rowan 2013b, 372.

26. Kondratieff 2004, 14–15, whose translation I follow except for line 14, which he translates as "Silver coins captured and from the sale of booty."

27. But contrast Crawford 1974, 626 with Crawford 1985, 59 n. 14.

28. Kondratieff 2004, 20–21 for the math.

economy in which multiple forms of currency and proto-currency emerged in conjunction with the imperatives of liquidation and expenditure.

Among the expenditures that Duilius himself oversaw was the construction of one of Rome's thirty-seven mid-republican temples: that of Janus near the Forum Holitorium, likely funded at least in part by the *praeda* of Mylae.[29] On one level, to offer a temple out of *praeda* was simply a scaled-up variant of offering a dedication to one's preferred divinity out of spoils.[30] Perhaps even more significantly, however, the increasing turn to manubial temples during our period as a means of translating booty into monumental form argues strongly for the coupling of the two—for what Clare Rowan has aptly characterized as "earmarking."[31] The entrenchment of the norm that at least some of the proceeds of the battlefield had to be set aside for temple construction represents an important step in conceiving and delivering on the expectation that warfare would yield public benefits, not merely private ones. By channeling at least some of battle's proceeds into sacred construction, the Roman aristocracy supplied tangible proof of a commitment to the public weal, improving in the process the likelihood of securing the quasi-voluntary compliance that was needed for the military engine to keep firing on all cylinders.

To see why this may have been the case, let us probe the middle Republic's fiscal regime more carefully. *Praeda* represented a much-needed infusion of capital for a state that, for virtually all of the fourth and third centuries, did not have a streamlined and centralized taxation and revenue-extraction protocol in place. We are mostly in the dark about the origins and early development of the interface between warfare and the economy. *Tributum*, a form of direct contribution that subsidized the payment of soldiers' wages (*stipendium*), played by far the largest role; although we have a general sense of the rate(s) at which it was assessed and of the work of the *tribuni aerarii* responsible for its management, details of the institutional apparatus that evolved to coordinate its administration and collection remain shrouded in mystery, as does the precise machinery for paying soldiers.[32] Nonetheless, at least one piece of evidence at our disposal appears to link *praeda* and *stipendium*. According to

29. Tac. *Ann.* 2.49: *Iisdem temporibus deum aedes uetustate aut igni abolitas coeptasque ab Augusto dedicauit* [sc. Tiberius] . . . *Iano templum, quod apud forum Holitorium C. Duilius struxerat, qui primus rem Romanam prospere mare gessit triumphumque naualem de Poenis meruit.* For more on this structure see *LTUR* s.v. "Ianus, Aedes (apud Forum Holitorium)."

30. See, e.g., the dedication of a certain M. Furius, recovered at Tusculum: *M. Fourio C. f. tribunos / militare de praidad Maurte dedet* (*CIL* XIV.2578 = *ILS* 3142). Further on dedications to the gods from spoils see n. 42 below.

31. Rowan 2013b, 373–74.

32. Nicolet 1976b, 19–26 and 1980, 149–69 for discussion, to be supplemented with Northwood 2008, 265–69; Rosenstein 2011, 137–38; and Tan 2017.

Livy's account of the events of 293, the plebs chafed at Papirius Cursor's decision to deposit all of his *praeda* in the *aerarium* because there would have been no need for *tributum* to be exacted for the *stipendia* of the soldiers if he had spurned the glory of making such a deposit and distributed the *praeda* among his soldiers instead. By contrast, his co-consul Sp. Carvilius, who had held a triumph of his own, earned the gratitude of the plebs by issuing donatives to his soldiers out of the *praeda*: 102 asses for every soldier and 204 asses for centurions and cavalrymen. Not content with distributing donatives, Sp. Carvilius deposited 380,000 pounds of *aes graue* in the *aerarium* and still had enough *praeda* left over to fund the building of a temple to Fors Fortuna *ex manubiis*.[33]

A mid-republican culture preoccupied with asserting the prerogatives of an aristocratic elite could have stigmatized the handling of booty by common Roman soldiers and their allies prior to their disposition by commanders,[34] though unequivocal evidence of such a norm is lacking. In any event, the more important point is that, separate from *direct* distribution of booty acquired on the field in the form of donatives, several indirect means of redistributing wealth did exist, among which monumental construction is a standout. Polybius, our most celebrated non-Roman witness to Roman piety, does not mince words when it comes to another Roman attribute: a tightfistedness and miserliness about money that approached almost comic levels.[35] The two are not disconnected, as Polybius himself recognized. I will have more to say on temple building as a species of resource distribution that sustained and justified elite miserliness and frugality in other domains at the conclusion of this chapter.

The rudimentary nature of the middle Republic's rent-extraction system was matched by the relatively few channels for procuring and regulating those rents. *Tributum* was raised to cover the *stipendia* of soldiers, but any surplus

33. Liv. 10.46.5 and 14–15 with Rosenstein 2011, 142–43; Bernard 2018a, 143–45 for what the episode discloses about "different views of the metallic income of military conquest and its relationship to political power." On the identification of this temple see, in addition to the *LTUR* entry, Biddau 2005 and Miano 2018, 100–104. Although Kondratieff 2004, 22–23 reads the Duilius *elogium*'s claim of a donative to the *populus* as a departure from the usual practice of presenting soldiers with donatives, *populus* could here mean "the people in arms" (i.e., the army); on this archaic meaning see the citations gathered at Cornell 1995, 257 n. 60. For distribution of *praeda* to individual soldiers (*viritim*) see Cato the Elder *FRHist* F 140 with accompanying commentary; for other non-Livian testimonies of donatives to soldiers out of booty see Dionysius of Halicarnassus *AR* 14H and 15J with Pittia et al. 2005, 199.

34. Thus Tarpin 2000, 369 argues that *normally* "la coutume, et les intérêts de l'État aristocratique, excluent les soldats du partage immédiat des objets précieux."

35. Polyb. 32.12.9 with Hands 1968, 26–48.

appears not to have been retained in the state's coffers. As for other revenue streams, our knowledge of the rents collected from the use of the *ager publicus* at this time is hazy, save for those fines that were pooled toward monumental enterprises, and much the same could be said for other types of *vectigalia* such as harbor dues and tolls—unambiguous evidence for which does not come into view until the second century.[36] How effective state officials were at collecting these revenues is an unanswerable question given the state of the evidence; the second-century indications of administrative overreach cast at best a slanting light on third-century precedents.[37] The Roman state did in time refine its mechanisms for exploiting metal resources, but only after access to these expanded beyond all previous precedent in the decades after the Second Punic War, with Rome's consolidation of control over the Iberian Peninsula.[38] That the middle Republic did not have to turn to intensive forms of rent extraction may be one proxy of the relative stability of its ruling class; peer Hellenistic states resorted to higher levels of taxation in part because of their internal instability.[39] In any case, the main pump for the Roman economy of the fourth and third centuries was booty and the economic transactions that its capture and circulation incentivized, conversion into liquid wealth foremost among them.[40]

Once we think beyond the booty itself, to the multiplier economic transactions that ensued from its capture and redistribution, the magnitude of the economic stimulus generated through Roman military predation becomes apparent. It was through these transactions that constant warfare may have become "economically self-perpetuating," although it would be more accurate to describe the revenue stream harnessed by Roman bellicosity as boom or bust, with occasional looting windfalls offsetting years (if not decades) of striking out. Most of Rome's conflicts during the fourth and third centuries may not have paid for themselves, let alone resulted in a meaningful surplus.[41]

36. Summary and discussion of the notices for *vectigalia*: Taylor 2017, 167–69; on Rome's exploitation and commodification of salt beds, Purcell 1996, 190–93, and Walsh et al. 2014 on the ecological signatures of wetland reclamation; for the leasing and sale of *ager publicus* by the mid-republican state, Siculus Flaccus 103.34–104.4 Campbell with the comments of Pelgrom 2018.

37. Discussion of these indications: Tan 2017, 21–24.

38. On the institutional and economic consequences of silver's increasing availability in the second century see Rowan 2013b, 362–66.

39. For this argument and "instability indices" of the major Hellenistic states see Monson 2015.

40. Cf. the comments of Harris 1979, 59 and Tarpin 2000, 365.

41. Rosenstein 2011, 146–52 with table 1 for the profit-loss profile of mid-republican warfare beginning with the Second Samnite War; Kay 2014, 27 for quotation and discussion, to

Among the major multiplier mechanisms was transacting in captives, through the setting of ransom prices and through the sale of the unransomed into slavery; it is no surprise that Livy characterizes the *aes graue* paraded by Papirius Cursor as *aes redactum ex captiuis*.[42] One immediate consequence of Rome's militarized integration into the slave networks of the Hellenistic Mediterranean was the abolition of debt slavery (*nexum*) during our period. Also moving around and generating additional value within the mid-republican wartime economy of convertible assets were captured weapons and other valuables, many of which were decorated with and sometimes hammered out of gold and silver. Even though *spolia* were often employed as monumental ornaments and as decorations in private homes, they circulated within commercial networks as well.[43]

The need to transact in these items was probably one of the catalysts for the development of Roman contract and sale law.[44] It was not so much that a gift-giving economy of redistributing booty to soldiers was succeeded or came to be supplanted by a market-oriented one, but that the traffic in booty made equal use of gift-giving and market dynamics as it gained increasing prominence in mid-republican cultural and religious life. The aspect of market dynamics is especially noteworthy: sales of humans and nonhumans both on and beyond the battlefield were ritually structured, with a religious air lingering over the proceedings; the sacralization of sale interacted with and served to enhance those forms of cultural memory that worked to affix the legacy of conquest and enslavement to those manubial temples where *spolia*

---

be read with the criticisms of Taylor 2017, 170–71. Not all spoils entered economic circulation, since commanders could opt to dedicate battlefield items to a divinity by incinerating them: see, e.g., Fabius Pictor *FRHist* F 17 with commentary ad loc. on Q. Fabius Rullianus's decision in 325.

42. Evidence for ransom tariffs in the third century: Scheidel 2005, 15 with n. 51. The differential treatment and commodification of war captives (with captured elites ransomed, as opposed to the already-enslaved who were more likely to be sold off): Auliard 2002, 61–64; Welwei 2000, chaps. 3–4 for a more critical assessment.

43. Gold- and silver-gilded weaponry: see, e.g., Liv. 9.40.4–7 and 16–17 on the Samnite panoply; Rouveret 2000, 85–86 and passim on booty display in Magna Graecia. Monumental ornamentation: Hope 2003, 83; Rawson 1991a, 583–86 and 595; cf. Köster 2013 on the "religious life" of plunder. Parallels in archaic and classical Greece: Pritchett 1979, 240–95. Private decoration: Flower 1998, 230 on the Falerii Veteres breastplate. Romans exhibiting *spolia* that they had not acquired themselves while on campaign: Cato *ORF*^{3} fr. 97. The Novios Bannios cuirass (*SEG* 29.1026): Colonna 1984.

44. *Emptio venditio* and *spolia*: Mommsen 1885, 262, commenting specifically on the role of quaestors in the process; for the evolution of this magistracy in the third century see now Prag 2014, 195–201.

were deposited.[45] The cultural slippage between *spolia* as immobilized repositories of *memoria* and as circulating and exploitable commodities is strikingly evoked in a fragment of Ennius's *Sabinae*, a *fabula praetexta* composed and performed not long after the Second Punic War: "Since you have taken us as *spolia* from our bridegrooms," the Sabine women exclaim, "what inscription will you give us?"[46]

As an expanding state that succeeded in applying its monopoly over violence into the acquisition of wealth on the battlefield and subsequently leveraging that wealth, mid-republican Rome was no trailblazer; the trajectory outlined in the preceding pages has a great deal in common with ancient and early modern state-building processes, as Armin and Peter Eich have demonstrated.[47] Throughout our period, more regular access to larger quantities of booty not only enhanced the appeal of war to Rome's belligerent aristocracy but also subsidized the temple foundations and other monumental constructions undertaken by that aristocracy; simultaneously, the increasing amounts of booty and the elaboration of mechanisms for its disposal gave rise to a new infrastructural regime. On a first impression, one might even speculate that the Roman state's dependence on booty as an important source of capital throughout our period has something in common with the tendency of more autocratic premodern polities to capitalize on externally sourced revenues as a means of emancipating their leaders from conciliating or humoring their taxpayer base. However, James Tan's description of the taxation-as-representation dynamics of the third century undercuts this link and points us instead to the possibility that monumental structures such as temples functioned as public goods for eliciting and securing the quasi-voluntary compliance of an occasionally recalcitrant taxpayer base. As outlined by Richard Blanton and Lane Fargher and more recently reiterated by Gary Feinman, societies with distributed power and "higher degrees of commoner leverage" exhibit higher investments in public goods and infrastructure, which operate together with restrictions on elite conspicuous consumption "to develop higher degrees of trust and credibility with the general population."[48] This

45. Sales of goods acquired on the battlefield: Rüpke 1990, 210–14. The properties of sale qua religious rite in the Roman world: Purcell 2012, citing Mauss 1923–24, 96–97.

46. Ennius *Sabinae* 370–71 Vahlen^3 = 379–80 Warmington: *cum spolia generis detraxeritis / quam inscriptionem dabitis?* (trans. Warmington with modifications). Discussion: Rawson 1991a; La Penna 2000. The language of *spolia* in Plautus: Fraenkel [1922] 2007, 164–65; further on Roman drama's refraction of the anguish of battlefield enslavement see Richlin 2017a and chapter 4 below.

47. Eich and Eich 2005.

48. Feinman 2016, 6 for the quotations; Blanton and Fargher 2008, 250–52 for background.

state of affairs certainly seems to have held true for mid-republican Rome, especially during the First Punic War.

Coming into the war without a rent-extraction surplus and lacking an ingrained culture of regular public borrowing from wealthy elites, the third-century Roman state confronted novel fiscal demands—in the form of an accelerated buildup of naval capacity—that could not be met except through the consent of the citizen taxpayer.[49] It was this consent that would ultimately dictate the rhythms of the conflict with Carthage, and elites became well aware of what could happen if such consent were to be withheld.[50] The clearest indicator of the role of temple building in securing this consent is the decision of multiple First Punic War commanders—Duilius among them—to direct the proceeds of battle into monumental sacred construction. As documented in chapter 2, temple construction reached its high-water mark in the era of Rome's first truly traumatic maritime moment,[51] and the alignment was not a coincidence. Funneling booty toward the monumental upgrade of the city communicated to the urban population at large and the taxpayer base in particular that the war represented a worthwhile investment, and that the proceeds of war would continue to be earmarked for the glorification of the gods. While this messaging did not enjoy uninterrupted success,[52] the rise in the number of temple vows and dedications during the First Punic War is one sign of its perceived efficacy. Although the mid-republican state did not wield the same fiscal tools as other Hellenistic polities when it came to underwriting the costs of monumental construction,[53] it could have resorted to other mechanisms to fund temple building. For the most part, however, it did not—an earmarking preference that speaks volumes.

The euergetistic drive toward temple construction could be read as an expression of altruistic generosity on the part of the Roman elite, in line with Neil Coffee's recent exposition of gift exchange's wax and wane during and after our period.[54] Yet this section has sought to demonstrate that it may be

49. For public borrowing in the Hellenistic world see the epigraphic dossier compiled by Migeotte 1984.

50. Tan 2015 for synopsis of the argument; 2017 for its full-length exposition and chaps. 5–6 for the First and Second Punic Wars.

51. The refraction and processing of this trauma at the dawn of Latin literature: Leigh 2010.

52. See Tan 2017, 108–13 on taxpayer "revolts" during the First Punic War.

53. For an overview of these tools and their deployment by Hellenistic poleis see Meier 2012, chsap. 3–6.

54. Coffee 2016. For an account of the transition from gift exchange to euergetism in the Greek world that is similarly well versed in anthropological literature and sophisticated in its handling of historical questions see Domingo Gygax 2016.

more fruitful to interpret temple construction as a social practice geared toward securing and maintaining popular backing for the Roman state's war effort through the redistribution of wealth. Notably, in light of the relative affordability of a moderately sized temple,[55] it was not so much the lavishness but the gesture of redistribution that seems to have mattered most. That this redistribution was understood to function best through the apportionment of some (but not all) booty to the soldiery and some (but not all) booty to monumental civic enterprise is perhaps best encapsulated by the negative *exemplum* of the transgressive consul L. Postumius Megellus, who—indignant at not being tapped to lead the foundation of several colonies after his victories in 291—liquidated his entire store of booty in donatives to his troops.[56] In any case, the homeostatic equilibrium of *tributum*-temple construction-taxpayer consent would be irreversibly altered in the years after the Second Punic War, when the surge in external revenues that culminated with the cancellation of *tributum* after Pydna effectively disenfranchised the Roman taxpayer base. During our period, however, monumental sacred construction took center stage as a high-profile expression of the state's commitment to locking in the consent of the Roman citizen body. What now calls for review is how temples themselves, besides signaling the return of the proceeds of war to the Roman people, functioned as vehicles for the distribution of other public goods in the course of the middle Republic's bootstrap into statehood. I examine this process next.

II. Public Goods A: Civic Upkeep

That temple construction brought about a variety of changes in the structure of the Roman polity should be obvious by now. The real challenge is formulating an account of this transformation that directly relates the presence of these temples to the middle Republic's institutional morphology. While the fragmentary nature of our evidence impedes anything approaching a full reconstruction, there are a number of options at our disposal. One might, for example, consider how the temple backdrops for speeches delivered from *podia* conditioned late republican oratorical performance and audience reception; or how the cluster of temples in the Campus Martius interacted with the deployment of public rituals to promote a kind of sacred "ecological signaling" for those citizens gathered in the Saepta to vote and those summoned

55. Affordability and expense: see chapter 2.

56. Dionysius of Halicarnassus *AR* 18B, who adds that the consul spitefully disbanded his army before the arrival of his successor. For another episode in this figure's checkered consulship see chapter 2 n. 80.

closer to the Capitoline in the event of a levy; or how temples in different sectors of the city increasingly came to define and sustain a diverse array of commercial, residential, and familial activities.[57] The archival responsibilities shouldered by several major temples interacted continuously not only with patterns of state formation but also with literary disciplines and epistemes, as Varro's writings would make clear a century and a half after our period.[58] In the interests of analytic brevity, and in order to remain close to the mid-republican evidence, I will single out for special treatment below three domains where the contours of temple construction's interface with institutional innovation and infrastructure transformation can be traced. The first case study in this section will approach the theme of civic upkeep indirectly, by examining the contribution of temple construction to the physical repositioning of the Senate; the second will scrutinize the role of temple construction in the management and provisioning of firefighting and water distribution; the third will investigate the role of temples as organizing nodes for the delivery of medicine and healing.

1. *New Shelter for the New Senate*

The dual-purposing of the Campus Martius's temple of Bellona, vowed by Appius Claudius Caecus in 296 and dedicated sometime afterward, provides a convenient point of departure.[59] At Bellona's shrine, the Roman Senate convened to receive embassies from enemy or nonallied peoples, deliberated the granting or refusal of a triumph, and sent off or welcomed magistrates who

57. Temple backdrops for oratory: Taylor 1966, 20; Ulrich 1994, but note the criticisms of David 1996b and Bendlin 1997; cf. Morstein-Marx 2004, 57–59. The interarticulation of gods and civic space in late republican oratory: Hölkeskamp 2015, 192–93; Clark 2018. "Ecological signaling": Bulbulia et al. 2013 for the concept; Cic. *De off.* 3.104 for a historical example. Voting in the Saepta: Taylor 1966. The likely location(s) of the levy: Brunt 1971: Appendix 19. The sacral dimensions of assemblies and of the locations in which they were held: Pina Polo 1996, 19–20; Linke 2000, 293–94. Commerce, cult, and family in Rome's neighborhoods: Palmer 1980; Morel 1987; Marcattili 2012 for the special case of the Aventine; Bendlin 2013, 475–76 on temples and shrines as "respectable micro-economic systems in their own right."

58. Padilla Peralta 2019 for the importance of temple contents to Varronian antiquarianism. For archiving at Roman temples see n. 68 below.

59. Liv. 10.19.17 with *InscrItal* 13.3.10 (as restored on the basis of 13.3.79 = *CIL* XI.1827, the Arretine *elogium* that explicitly names the temple); on this temple's significance to the exemplary fashioning of Ap. Claudius Caecus see Roller 2018, 113–19 and n. 90 below. The decisive breakthrough in identifying the temple's location: Coarelli 1968. For other sources and bibliography see Viscogliosi *LTUR* s.v. "Bellona, aedes in Circo"; De Nuccio 2011, which details the scope of the Augustan-era renovation; and Bernard 2018a, 246.

were departing to or returning from their *provinciae*.[60] In the decades after our period, at least one *senatus consultum* was passed following a special session of the Senate *apud aedem Duelonai*: the *SC de Bacchanalibus*.[61] Given the evidence for the Senate's deliberative and administrative undertakings at the temple of Bellona, it is germane to consider whether the sanctuary itself informed or molded deliberations in any way. The claim to be fleshed out over the next few pages is that the building of Bellona's temple was integral to the mid-republican Senate's constitution as a corporate body. Meeting in the temple of Bellona defined the Senate in new and institutionally innovative ways, establishing such an important precedent that by the late Republic senatorial meetings were not only held within temples but also were run according to detailed religious protocols.[62] But to pave the way for this argument, I need first to address a few historical preliminaries.

The Republican Senate met in consecrated spaces, and usually in a consecrated building; the Curia, the main location for those meetings that were not held in temples, was itself an inaugurated *templum*. Although the practice is best attested during the late Republic, the *SC de Bacchanalibus* and other annalistic and antiquarian notices make it clear that the convening of the Senate in sacred structures was a feature of mid-republican life.[63] Also employed as a regular meeting place for the Senate was the temple of Apollo Medicus immediately adjacent to Bellona, first vowed and dedicated in the first century of the Republic and then rebuilt in 353.[64] For meetings *intra pomerium*, candidates included the temple of Jupiter Optimus Maximus on the Capitoline and the temples of Castor and Pollux and of Concordia in the Roman Forum.[65] After our period, the renovation and diversification of the city's sacred topography in the second and early first centuries increased the number of available

60. The temple's placement outside the *pomerium* made it convenient for holders of *imperium*; see Von Ungern-Sternberg 2006, 291–92 for additional commentary on the location. It is not clear whether the so-called *senaculum* was located right next to the temple (Festus 347 L.; on other *senacula* in the city see Kaster 2011 *ad* Macr. *Sat*. 1.8.2); senators will have met there for informal deliberation before proceeding to the inaugurated space of the temple. Debates over the awarding of triumphs, most of which were held in the *aedes Bellonae*: Pittenger 2008.

61. *CIL* I.196 = I^2.1.581 = X.104 = *ILS* I.18.

62. Protocols: Gellius *NA* 14.7 on the Varronian *commentarium de officio senatus habendi*.

63. A catalog of all Senate meetings with known locations from the Hannibalic War to Augustus: Bonnefond-Coudry 1989, 32–47, and 146–47 for meetings *extra pomerium*; Stambaugh 1978, 580–81 for a more skeletal account.

64. For this temple's archaeological imprint see Bernard 2018a, Appendix 2.

65. The Senate met in the temple of Castor to pass the *SC de Tiburtibus*, probably in 159: *CIL* $I.2^2$.586 = *ILS* 19; for the temple's history prior to its renovation in 119 see Nielsen and Poulsen 1992.

options; one mid-republican construction that hosted the Senate in the second century was the temple of Fides, where the fateful meeting immediately prior to the ritualized murder of Tiberius Gracchus was held.[66] Other temple structures, built during our time or in the century after, were eventually integrated into the senatorial circuit.[67] There were, to be sure, nonsenatorial analogues for the use of temples as centers for magistrate activity and political administration. Already in the first century of the Republic, the plebeian organization installed the office of the tribune of the plebs near the Aventine temple of Ceres and used the temple itself to store *senatus consulta*, possibly in emulation of then-standard practices in the greater Greek world. Whether or not the Senate established a precedent for other official groups to make use of temples, its members would in time take the lead in repurposing temples for a variety of purposes, from the dialogic to the gustatory.[68]

Beyond simple convenience, what might have encouraged the Senate to make a regular habit of meeting in temples? Three factors warrant additional scrutiny here. The first is that senatorial meetings in temples, and in particular those held at the temple of Bellona, tended to focus on the most serious and sensitive dilemmas facing the *res publica* and (mainly for this reason) were very well attended. It is noteworthy that the ancient sources repeatedly use the phrase *frequens senatus* when referring to meetings at the temple of Bellona.[69] The term's association over time with a "quorate" threshold of two hundred senators has implications not only "for our estimates of the average level of attendance in the senate" but for how we conceive of the relationship between the Senate as a body and the spaces in which it was convened, since even the large *cellae* of the Capitoline temple will have become cramped once the two-hundred-person threshold had been crossed.[70] I draw attention to this packing

66. Appian *B Civ* 1.16.1 for the meeting; on this temple's vowing and dedication by A. Atilius Calatinus (*cos.* 258 and 254) see Cic. *ND* 2.23.61 with Spannagel 2000, 242.

67. The *SC de Thasiis* of 80 BCE (Sherk no. 20) may attest the use of another temple: for restoration of the fragmentary [..]μητηρίωι to [τι]μητηρίωι with a view to the (Marian) temple of Honos and Virtus see Taylor 1960, 268 n. 3; cf. Bonnefond-Coudry 1979, 601–22 and 1989, 115–21, for identification of the τιμητήριον as the *Atrium Libertatis*.

68. Archiving at the temple of Ceres: Liv. 3.55.13 with Cornell 1995, 263–65; cf. Sickinger 1999 on the Athenian Metroon. (Critique of) the notion of a plebeian Aventine: Mignone 2016. Official groups meeting in Roman temples: Stambaugh 1978, 581–82, with Beard 1998 on their (epigraphic) archival flair. Temple dialogues: Varro *RR* 1 with Padilla Peralta 2017b. *Cenae sacerdotales* were held not only in private homes (Macr. *Sat.* 3.13.10–12 with Rüpke 1999, 46–62) but also inside temples: for the case of the Salii, see Suet. *Claud.* 33 with Nielsen 2014, 232; cf. Varro LL 5.162 for *cenacula* in Latial temples.

69. Ryan 1998, 19–20.

70. Quotation: Ryan 1998, 46.

of senators within the less-than-luxurious interiors of temples to tease out a simple point: the dynamics of senatorial interaction were structured around a divinely policed physical proximity, with the possibility of discomfort for a significant portion of the Senate's members who may have had to stand.[71] If recent research into the ergonomics of dishonesty is any indication, the packing of bodies may have promoted more prosocial behavior among senators, at least for the period under discussion. On this reading, enforced proximity was integral to the small-group and small-network interactions that contributed to the forging and maintenance of social bonds within the senatorial elite, "strengthen[ing] the rest of the aristocracy by forcing the magistrates to operate in the company of their peers."[72] The need for a space and structure of homosocial bonding will have been all the more pronounced if the Senate of this period was in fact composed of individuals who were looking out primarily for the interests of their clans and their home towns in Latium and central Italy, as Nicola Terrenato has contended. During the decades of military conflict that bracketed the temple's dedication and construction, a period defined less by coordinated and centralized war-making than by heterogenous and not always easily reconciled individual and gentilician initiatives, the Senate was only starting to assume the corporate identity that would characterize it in later eras.[73]

The second consideration is more compactly stated. Many of the temples in which the Senate met were themselves products of senatorial agency. These structures commemorated the activity and achievements of members of the Senate or of their ancestors as magistrates, and in many if not all cases their construction and dedication had been authorized by the Senate. Senatorial decision-making was thus embedded within physical vessels of *memoria* that had been molded to monumentalize individual, familial, and corporate achievement.[74] As the aristocratic home furnished constant reminders of the family's glorious past to its inhabitants in the form of the *imagines* and their corresponding *tituli*,[75] so too did the Senate's various meeting places supply reminders of the governing aristocracy's attainments. Of these attainments,

71. Taylor and Scott 1969 argued that the *senatores pedarii* were so named because they had to stand on account of the limited space for seating; but cf. Ryan 1998, 54 for an alternative stance. I am not persuaded by Taylor and Scott's argument that meetings at the Capitoline Temple took place not in the *cellae* but in the colonnaded porch (1969, 559–69).

72. Tan 2017, 24. The spatial ergonomics of (dis)honesty: Yap et al. 2013.

73. Terrenato 2013, 2014, and now 2019 on gentilician activities and priorities as the motor for fourth- and early third-century Roman state formation; cf. Cornell 2004 for a reappraisal of the Samnite Wars along compatible lines.

74. Budesheim 2006, 74, following Flaig 2003.

75. Ancestral *imagines* in the home: Flower 1996, chap. 7.

one held a special place in the Senate's self-definition: the oversight and management of the *res publica*'s relationship with the gods.

Hence the third and most intriguing aspect of the Senate's practice of meeting in temples, which is that it enacted a species of sacralization through which the Senate's primary responsibility for the cultivation of the city's relationship with the gods was repeatedly and publicly justified. At the level of the behavior and conduct of its individual members and at the level of the cultic managerial expertise expected from it as a corporate body,[76] the Senate positioned itself as acting from within temples to order the *res publica*'s communication with the gods, in a continuous dialogue that would result time and time again in the construction of even more temples. Far from being a static, unchanging aspect of the Senate's place in Roman life, this third aspect was the outgrowth of a historical process that, accelerating in the decades immediately before and after the Licinian-Sextian Rogations, reached a decisive turning point in the lifetime of Appius Claudius Caecus. Although we remain mostly in the dark about the earliest stages of the Senate's development—with the body's transition from an essentially ad hoc advisory council in the regal and early Republican period to its mid-republican incarnation as the preeminent decision-maker on religious and political matters enveloped in fog—two developments seem reasonably certain: that the classical republican Senate of interest to Polybius and later sources emerged during the late fourth and early third centuries; and that its transformation was masterminded at least in part by the peculiar and institutionally groundbreaking career of Appius Claudius Caecus, credited with the first or first-to-be-recorded *lectio senatus*.[77] Appius Claudius Caecus's success in wresting control of Hercules's worship at the Ara Maxima from the *gens Potitia* and entrusting it to public slaves, and his scribe-turned-aedile's tempestuous back-and-forth with the *pontifices* over the publication of the *Fasti* and the dedication of a temple to Concordia, are important markers in the move away from gentilician and privatized control over the *sacra* to a more centralized management of cult.[78] But for such a move to have

76. Budesheim 2006, 77: "Die Stellung des republikanischen Senates war auch bedingt durch seine Verantwortung, die *pax deorum* sowohl durch das Verhalten des Einzelnen als auch durch das gemeinsame Aufrechterhalten überlieferter Kultmaßnahmen zu garantieren."

77. The early stages of the transition: Richard 2005. Rules for curule iteration and alternation: Beck 2005, part II; Rilinger 2007. The *lectio senatus*: Cornell 1995, 369–70 and 2000a; Humm 2005, chap. 3 for an alternative account; Jehne 2011, 217–19 and 2013, 25–26. The Senate and Roman law: Capogrossi Colognesi 2014, 81–84.

78. Liv. 9.29.9–11 and 9.46.6–7, Festus 270 L., Serv. *ad Aen.* 8.179 and 8.269, with North 1989, 622–23; Rüpke 1995a, 248; Muccigrosso 1998, 118; Rüpke 2011, 45. Further on the slave *familia* charged with the Ara Maxima: Palmer 1990, 237–38 on Festus 282 L.; Padilla Peralta 2017c, 334 n. 84 for additional bibliography.

been maximally effective and durable in the long term, it was not enough for one magistrate to lead the way; the state's core administrative institutions—the hierarchy of magistrates, acting as individuals during their terms in office and in the senatorial body after their terms were concluded—had to be repositioned as religiously efficacious agents in the eyes of the citizen body. One legitimizing tactic readily at hand for doing so was convening the Senate in sacred structures.

The legitimation sought after and obtained by locating senatorial deliberation within the shrine to Bellona derived its force from a powerful feedback loop: it was successful war-making that had enabled the temple's vowing and dedication in the first place; it was the need to approve and make provisions for continued war-making that consumed the time and attention of the Senate whenever it met at this temple; and it was the outcome of war-making itself that furnished decisive proof of whether Bellona really did stand behind individual members of the senatorial elite, the Senate as a corporate body, and the res publica as a whole. Both the integration of senatorial deliberation into the physical structure of Bellona's cult and the discourses that flowed from this integration would subsequently accrue another layer of meanings when a plot of land in the neighboring Circus Flaminius was metaphorized into a *hostilis locus* for the fetial casting of spears.[79] Whether or not Appius Claudius Caecus himself ordered the Senate to meet in the temple of Bellona that he had dedicated, the institutionalization of holding meetings at an *aedes* such as Bellona's lent a distinctive air to senatorial proceedings. As they deliberated in the presence of the gods, senators would be expected to carry themselves in a matter befitting *ex omni ordine optimi*.[80] The practice thus functioned to ensure that the Senate's members, invested with responsibility for the oversight of public cult, were imbued with an appropriate awe for the sanctity of their own deliberations. For nonelite Romans, meanwhile, the sight of senators entering and exiting temples to deliberate matters of state importance in the company of the gods will have offered reassurance that senators were guided by a higher power, thereby locking in the trust necessary to maintain social harmony in times of crisis. In the midst of changing expectations for individ-

79. Ovid *Fast.* 6.203–8; Suet. *Claud.* 25.5; Serv. *ad Aen.* 9.52; Paulus-Festus 30 L.; Rüpke 1990, 105–9 on the fetial *Speerwurf* and Ando 2008, 116–17 on its epistemological dimensions. The transference of this "suggestive homology" to theater performances in the area: Germany 2016.

80. Cf. the installation of a statue and altar to Victoria in the Curia Iulia at some point during the early Principate for an analogous effort to focus and structure behavior: on Victoria's cult under the Principate see Ando 2000, 278–92; for the polemics this altar would later inspire, Thompson 2005; for the *longue durée* history of the senatorial Curia as a site for sacralizing legitimation, Bond 2015.

ual members of the Senate and shifting procedures for senatorial *lectiones*, it was the repetitive signaling of meeting in temples that justified and optimized the Senate's claim to be the "Best."[81] In addition to being steeped in those abstract values that came to be literally enshrined in the city's monumental landscape, the senatorial ethos taking shape during and after Appius Claudius Caecus's lifetime articulated itself through structures such as the temple to Bellona.

Seeing as the Senate increasingly tied its corporate identity to cult structures in the decades after the tribune-won concessions of the Licinian-Sextian Rogations, it is tempting to speculate that senatorial auto-sacralization ran on a parallel track (or perhaps even evolved in response) to tribunician sacrosanctity.[82] Be that as it may, understanding the practice of convening sessions in temples as a strategy for sacralizing the Senate clarifies how changes to the sacred landscape of the Republican city moved in tandem with the transformation of this corporate decision-making body. It will not come as news to students of the Republic that meetings in public spaces and venues afforded opportunities for ritualized assertions of legitimacy. Egon Flaig has described the Republican political environment as blanketed in "ritualisierte Politik," and there is no question that public gatherings carefully choreographed verbal and visual communications between magistrates and the Roman *populus*. Attention has lately been drawn to the ways and mechanisms through which popular assemblies such as the *contio* and the electoral *comitia* operated as "rituals of integration."[83] Yet despite their incorporation of anthropologically and sociologically informed approaches to ritual, most recent discussions of Republican political culture acknowledge the explicitly religious contexts and circumstances of these political meetings only in passing, if at all. If voting rituals interacted with the sights and soundscapes of temples and prayers to effectuate "la sacralisation du peuple comme instance de légitimation,"[84] we should be prepared to identify much the same process at work in the ritualization of the senate's meetings. Richard Weigel has argued that a magistrate's decision to convene a Senate meeting on the Capitoline relayed "the message that something special was happening," and Jerzy Linderski has painstakingly reconstructed the immediate sequence of events preceding Tiberius Gracchus's murder in order to underline how the tribune's assassination was

81. For this formulation and senatorial virtue signaling more generally, see Hölkeskamp [1987] 2011, chap. 5; Hölkeskamp 1993, 33–37; and now Clemente 2018.

82. Whether tribunician sacrosanctity is an invention of the late Republic and early Principate is a matter I cannot take up here; see Walter 2017.

83. Fundamental: Jehne 2001; Flaig 2003, chaps. 8–9.

84. Hollard 2010, 57–63.

framed and staged as a fundamentally religious act that ensued after a meeting of the Senate on the Capitoline.[85] Even after these case studies, however, a fuller explanation of the historical and institutional consequences of convening the Senate *in aedibus deorum* has been lacking.

The explanation will hopefully be apparent by now. The habit of calling the Senate to meet not only within an inaugurated *templum* but also specifically within a built temple tightened the association between the political rituals of the Senate and the quasi-sacred status that it would believe itself to hold and see as its duty to publicize. That the temple of Bellona was one of the first sacred structures in which we know Senate meetings to have taken place is no accident. Nor is it accidental that a temple built by one of the individuals most responsible for overhauling the mid-republican Senate became the home for its meetings. The temple was vowed and built at an important juncture in Republican institutional history, when the Senate, coming into its own as the main port of call for matters political and religious, sought to clothe itself in the garments of sanctity. The Senate's use of the *aedes Bellonae* and of the neighboring temple of Apollo is therefore evidence for the catalytic spur of temple construction to the form and direction of institutional transformation at Rome. Through their second life as meeting places, these temples were active agents the legitimation by which the Senate backstopped its claim to rightful precedence in the management of the *res publica*'s relationship with its gods, particularly (though not exclusively) in the waging of war and—starting around 249—oversight of the prodigy expiation system. Legitimation through documentation was only part of the story; the transformation of the Senate into "the custodian of public spirit" during our period would not have been possible without the performance of meeting at temples, the structures that most palpably and publicly exemplified the senatorial elite's care for the *salus* of the community.[86] One secondary outgrowth of this performance was the late republican and early Imperial literary figuration of the council of the gods as a meeting of the Senate,[87] a feat of cognitive association that may well have taken its cue from the cloaking of senatorial identity in sacred monumental garb.

85. Weigel 1986; Linderski 2002 = 2007, 88–114. Scipio Nasica led his band in pursuit of Tiberius Gracchus out from the temple of Fides: sources at n. 66 above, with Rodríguez-Almeida 1993 on this temple's location and Connors 2016 for the interaction of the structure with the messaging of Plautine drama (on which see chapter 4).

86. Documentation as a cornerstone of senatorial authority: Rüpke 2010b, 33–34 = 2012b, 25–27. The Senate's evolution as "Hüter des Gemeinsinns": Jehne 2013, esp. 25–27 on developments in the century after the *lex Ovinia*.

87. On this topos see Barchiesi 2008.

Another consequence of this structured association between the Senate as institution and the sacred landscapes of Rome was the aura of senatorial majesty that left such a deep impression on Greek visitors. Although Pyrrhus's ambassador Cineas was bowled over by "the council of many kings," it was Prusias II of Bithynia with his veneration of the senators as "savior gods" who registered with his extravagant flattery the intended force of the Senate's self-projection as a sacred elite.[88] While mid-republican Rome was hardly unique among Hellenistic states in having a major organ of government perform its functions at a temple, a sustained interaction of this kind between sacred meeting site and aristocratic self-definition does not appear to have an obvious counterpart elsewhere in the Mediterranean.[89] In this domain, as in many others, Ap. Claudius Caecus was an institutional and infrastructural trendsetter; the anchoring of his legacy and that of the *gens Claudia* to the "mixed-use" structure of the temple of Bellona would persist for centuries.[90]

2. *Fire and Water*

The administrative innovations that were hitched to the construction of several temples in the Campus Martius during the last few decades of the third century offer the most poignant testimony to the multifunctional capabilities of Rome's sacred buildings. As with most discussions of mid-republican topography, we will occasionally be skating on thin ice in what follows, though the overarching argument about the infrastructural pliability of temple structures should remain true or at the very least plausible regardless of possible cavils with the details. This subsection will zero in on the degree to which a

88. Cineas's description of the Senate to Pyrrhus (ἡ σύγκλητος αὐτῷ βασιλέων πολλῶν συνέδριον φανείη): Plut. *Pyrr.* 19.5; cf. Florus 1.18.20, which has Pyrrhus's embassy report back to him that "the city had seemed to them a temple, the senate an assembly of kings" (*urbem templum sibi visam, senatum regum esse concessum*). Prusias II's behavior: Polyb. 30.18.1–7; for differing readings of this episode cf. Padilla Peralta 2017c, 351–52 and Champion 2018a, 288.

89. With the possible exception of the Carthaginian Senate, which held meetings in the temple of Asklepios-Eschmoun: see Liv. 41.22.3 and 42.24.3 with Melliti 2006, 385–86 and 2010, 94.

90. The censor as innovator: Schneider 2014, 213–14 (infrastructure); Capogrossi Colognesi 2014, 120–25 (law and institutions); Roller 2018, chap. 3 (exemplary discourse). Bellona and the *gens Claudia*: Von Ungern-Sternberg 2006 passim and Russell 2016, 117–20. The *imagines clipeatae* of the *gens*, installed in the temple: Pliny *NH* 35.12 with Flower 1996, 40–41 and De Nuccio 2011, 196. Cf. Russell 2016, 130–39 on the Claudii Marcelli's complex outside the Porta Capena; Biddau 2005, 445–46 on the *gens Carvilia*'s association with the Fors Fortuna precinct at the sixth milestone.

specific grouping of temples in the Campus Martius blended the sacred and the "secular" through the lodging of administrative headquarters and services in close proximity to the temples themselves. As part of the argument, I will propose an explanation for why particular administrative functions were allocated to this grouping and why the answer to that question has implications for this chapter's premise that the distribution of public goods under the auspices of religious infrastructure is another distinctive aspect of Roman state formation in the fourth and third centuries.

Filippo Coarelli's study of the central Campus Martius expounds with great vigor and erudition the topographical reconstruction on which I will rely.[91] Combining the testimony of the Severan Marble Plan with epigraphic, historical, and antiquarian sources, Coarelli has contended that several of the temple structures in the area of the Largo Argentina were erected in the course of a "unico, grandioso progetto di sistemazione del Campo Marzio" executed over the course of the 230s.[92] The temple whose corner butts up against the *crypta Balbi* on the Severan Marble Plan, and which can be reasonably identified on the testimony of the calendrical *fasti* and Imperial dedications as a shrine to Volcanus, became at some point home to the *triumviri capitales* (or *nocturni*).[93] This band of men, charged with nighttime watch-keeping and firefighting and involved in at least two incidents that can be dated to the third century, evolved into the *praefectura vigilum* of the Imperial period whose presence is documented epigraphically.[94] In close topographical proximity to this temple of Volcanus was an *aedes Nympharum*, where cult was offered to a group of divinities that were patron goddesses of water and of water's rapport with fire.[95] Either this sanctuary or the nearby temple of Iuturna, nowadays identi-

91. Coarelli 1997, part II, esp. 210–50, followed by (among others) Torelli 2006, 92–93; but cf. Bernard 2018a, 5–11 on the limits and shortcomings of this species of topographical reconstruction. Historical survey of construction in the Largo Argentina: De Stefano in Carandini 2017, I.542–48.

92. Coarelli 1997, 244.

93. Testimonia for the housing of an *officium/statio* of magistrates within or adjacent to other temples: Wissowa 1912, 57–58; Stambaugh 1978, 582–83; n. 68 above on the plebeian organization at the Aventine temple of Ceres-Liber-Libera and chapter 4 n. 58 for the guild of actors at the Aventine temple of Minerva. For this temple to Volcanus see Manacorda in *LTUR* 5.211–213 s.v. "Volcanus, aedes."

94. The *triumviri capitales* and their responsibilities: Festus 468 L. on the *lex Papiria* that arranged for their election (236 or 235?); Val. Max. 8.1.*damn*. 5 on the prosecution of the *collegium* for arriving late to a fire. Imperial *praefectus vigilum* in the area: *CIL* VI.798 = *ILS* 1448. History and responsibilities of the *capitales* and *vigiles*: Lintott 1999, 141–42; Rucinski 2003; Robinson 1977 on the logistics of fire prevention.

95. Identified with the remains of the republican-era temple on the modern Via delle Bot-

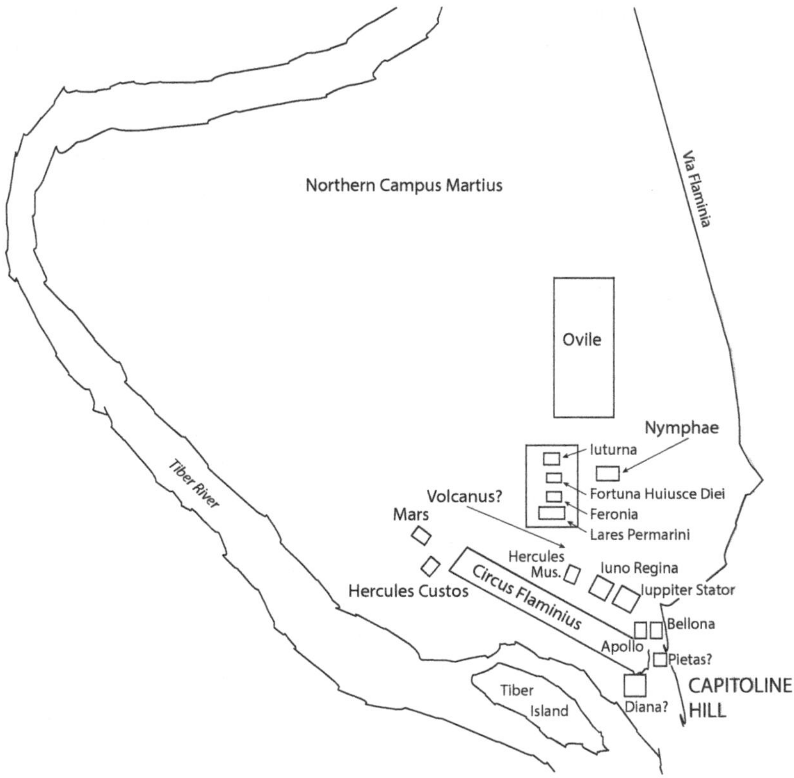

FIGURE 3.1. Schematic reconstruction of third- and second-century structures in the Campus Martius. (Drawing: Author, after Coarelli 2007, 268 fig. 25; Jacobs and Conlin 2014, xiv)

fied as Temple A in the Largo Argentina, was linked to the *statio aquarum* whose placement in the vicinity is strongly suggested by literary and (Imperial) epigraphic testimony.[96] Sensibly enough, the firefighting watch was positioned next door to the administrative hub for water distribution and aqueduct oversight.[97] The reconfiguration of this area into an organizational

teghe Oscure: Coarelli 2007, 281 with figure 68.3. *Nymphae* and *lymphae*: Varro *RR* 1.1.6 with Deschamps 1983. Nymphs and healing: Bendlin 2000, 130–31; n. 112 below.

96. Some prefer Temple C: see, e.g., Ziolkowski 1986; additional discussion in Coarelli *LTUR* s.v. "Iuturna, templum" and Coarelli 2007, 279–80.

97. As confirmed by a late republican testimonium: Cic. *Har. resp.* 57 disparages the Clodiani for incinerating the temple of those goddesses *quarum ope etiam aliis incendiis subuenitur*. Refinement of Coarelli's thesis: Bruun 2007, 9–11.

node would incentivize the later development of other administrative structures nearby: the first incarnation of the *Porticus Minucia Frumentaria* that was built during the late second century rose to the immediate east of the Largo Argentina.[98]

The large-scale overhaul of this sector of the Campus Martius that occurred in the immediate aftermath of the First Punic War is attributable in the first instance to an infusion of *praeda*: the proceeds of war underwrote infrastructural refurbishment. But one specific domestic incident likely accounts for why these temples were dedicated to these particular divinities of fire and water and why a network of firefighting and water distribution would subsequently emerge with these temples as the network's core nodes. Some months after the finalization of the peace treaty with Carthage in 241, a sequence of flooding and fire ravaged the city with such force and devastation as to prompt a consultation of the Sibylline Books.[99] Although no source explicitly affirms the result of the consultation to have been vows of temples to gods of water and fire, what we know of the targeted vows that were made at other times of social crisis make such a possibility not hard to envision. And despite our limited evidence, guesses as to the identities of two leading members of the senatorial aristocracy who were involved in the monumentalization of the Campus Martius can be hazarded. The legendary hero of the fire in 241 was L. Caecilius Metellus—twice consul and distinguished First Punic War commander, *pontifex maximus*, and honorand of the earliest preserved Republican *laudatio*—who famously rescued the *sacra* from the burning temple of Vesta and in doing so lost his eyesight.[100] This same Caecilius Metellus probably vowed and dedicated the temple of Ops Opifera on the Capitoline that shared a feast day with the temples of Volcanus and of the Nymphs in the Campus Martius. The celebration of this temple's anniversary on the same day as that of these two other temples broadcast their association with him, and by extension with the events of 241 that made him into a legend.[101] Meanwhile, a contemporary of this Caecilius Metellus, the C. Lutatius Catulus who triumphed over the Carthaginians in 241, is generally believed to have dedicated Temple A.[102]

98. Discussion of the *porticus* and the administration of *frumentationes*: Virlouvet 1987.

99. Oros. 4.11.5–9, drawing on Livy (cf. Liv. *Per.* 19); Aug. *De civ. D.* 3.18. Naevius may be our earliest source for the fire: see *BP* fr. 64 Flores (= fr. 60 Blänsdorf) with Flores 2011, xlvii–viii.

100. L. Caecilius Metellus (*cos.* 251, 247) and Ops Opifera: Coarelli 1997, 228–34. The *laudatio*: Flower 1996, 136–42.

101. On anniversary days and the Roman calendar see the next subsection.

102. One of his descendants dedicated the neighboring Temple B to Fortuna Huisce Dei a century and a half later: Leach 2010. An alternative candidate for the dedication of Temple A

FIGURE 3.2. Temples A–C, Largo Argentina, Rome. (Photo credit: Author)

The interweaving of military (and specifically naval) prowess with cult to water divinities and the construction of temples in the Campus Martius had a clear precedent, if the Largo Argentina's Temple C has been correctly identified as the shrine to the water goddess Feronia whose construction M.' Curius Dentatus oversaw in the same period that the Anio Vetus was being built. It received a further boost with the erection of a temple to Neptune in the vicinity of the Circus Flaminius.[103] This network of associations continued to be strengthened after our period with the monumentalization of the cult of the Lares Permarini, as the representative of another illustrious *gens* applied his energies and resources to the insertion of a mixed-use complex into the urban fabric of the region.[104] All in all, by the late Republic there would be "at least five temples in the Campus Martius related to divinities associated with water," a circumstance that invites more intensive examination of water management's centrality to Roman aristocratic self-representation and power projection.[105] However, my sights in the next few pages will be trained on one feature of Coarelli's reconstruction as it pertains to this chapter's guiding argument and the remit of this section. Instead of simply reacting to episodes of crisis, these temple dedications in the Campus Martius also implemented an institutionally embedded program of response to future calamities of flood and fire, "speaking into being" an infrastructural power that had not previously existed. This program harmonized cult to the gods deemed responsible for the

would be Catulus's brother Q. Lutatius Cerco, subjugator of Falerii Veteres; on these brothers see Padilla Peralta 2018c.

103. On the latter structure see Viscogliosi in *LTUR* 3.341–342 s.v. "Neptunus, aedes" and Tucci 1997.

104. Feronia and M.' Curius Dentatus: Coarelli 1997, 197; 2007, 279–80. The cult of Feronia: Di Fazio 2012. The temple to the Lares Permarini, commemorating L. Aemilius Regillus's naval victory and triumph over Antiochus III: Liv. 40.52.4–7 with Flower 2017, 91–103; Russell 2016, 113–14 for the scope of the Aemilian construction program.

105. Thus Stamper 2005, 44–45; further on hydrology and Roman power see Purcell 1996.

control of water and fire with the "novità amministrative" through which water distribution and firefighting were centralized.[106] In this instance, it is important *not* to dissociate the sacred (the enterprise of cult) from the ostensibly more pragmatic (firefighting and water management); the two were in lockstep with each other.

Earlier I referenced the concept of "quasi-voluntary compliance" in explaining how states work to sustain social cohesion between rulers and ruled. As has historically been the case for other premodern states with a simple administrative machinery, the middle Republic would have resorted to securing quasi-voluntary compliance through cost-effective infrastructural arrangements. As Richard Blanton, Lane Fargher, and other collective action theorists have argued, one core element of any program to strengthen quasi-voluntary compliance bonds between a state's citizens and its leadership is the promotion of trust and credibility; another is the distribution of public goods.[107] In the case of the Campus Martius building program, it is straightforward enough to assign "cult to the gods" to the category of strategies for promoting trust and "firefighting and water management" to the category of public goods. What made the "novità amministrative" of the Campus Martius institutionally creative and cost effective was the pairing of a trust-generative device with a specific public good, with synergistic outcomes. If the area's infrastructural overhaul represented a commitment on the part of the state to the physical well-being of its citizens, the cultic investment represented a commitment on the part of individual magistrates, acting both on their own individual initiative and as representatives of the state, to the physical well-being of its citizens as maintained through the beneficent care of the gods—itself a species of public good, inasmuch as its successful monitoring ensured the state's success on all other fronts. With the renovation of the Campus Martius following the catastrophic fire of 241, these two investments were integrated so as to operate in harmony.

By linking the offer of cult to the gods to the provisioning of a public good, the Republican state earned more bang for its buck. For one, the avoidance or timely mitigation of fires in the future would be credited to the state's continuous appeasement of the appropriate gods through cult and to its provisioning of the public good necessary for keeping them at bay. Fires and floods were a fixture of urban life, especially as the population grew, but catastrophes of the kind that leveled the city in 241 were once-in-a-generation events;[108] the gen-

106. The quoted phrase: Coarelli 1997, 237.

107. Blanton and Fargher 2008, 20–21, modifying and adapting Levi 1988, chap. 3; cf. Fukuyama 2011, 49–51 on religion and collective action.

108. Patterns of fire and flood, especially after deforestation of the upper Tiber shifted the

eral public will have thus interpreted a conflagration-free status quo as a direct result of the *res publica*'s dual investment in cult and infrastructure. On the other hand, in the case of disastrous outbreaks, the first culprit to be flagged will have been not run-of-the-mill human incompetence or malfeasance but the disequilibration of the *res publica*'s relationship with the gods. Although on at least one occasion *nocturni* were prosecuted for negligence,[109] by and large the decision to couple the administration of firefighting and water distribution with the management of the *pax deorum* will have motivated the Roman community to endorse (and be satisfied with) additional investment in cult as a hedge against urban calamities. In another variation on the "shell game" of monumentalism introduced in chapter 2, the *res publica* transacted in what it could control—the provisioning of cult to the gods—to assert a measure of control over what in the end defied the infrastructural capabilities of most urbanizing premodern states: the vulnerability of densely crowded cities to fires. This sleight of hand tips off the existence of a quasi-voluntary compliance regime. Without hastening to the conclusion that this system of quasi-voluntary compliance was recognized as such by Roman elites of the third century, it is not a stretch to venture that those individuals who came to offer dedications at the Largo Argentina did so out of a sense of gratitude at the brand of communal commitment that was embodied in the area's gleaming new temples and their infrastructural capabilities.[110]

To summarize, then, the building up of the Campus Martius in the 230s created new structures and a new topography for religious and secular uses. The distinctive institutional efficacy of an arrangement that embedded the "practical" within the sacred resided in its ability to generate confidence among those affected by the fire of 241 that the state was doing everything it could to ensure such a calamity would never take place again, by reorganizing in one fell swoop the divine as well as human networks that were viewed as indispensable to effective fire management. Disaster was traumatic; in the dedication of temples to the appropriate gods and in the multifunctional utility of these new structures, the Roman state's leadership showed its sensitivity to the importance of managing this trauma. It was not merely a matter of "turning to" religion in the face of collective trauma,[111] but of routing through

region's hydrology: Aldrete 2006, chap. 2, esp. 74–77. Generally on the environmental consequences of Roman Italy's deforestation: Harris 2013, 181–83.

109. See Val. Max. 7.1 *damn.* 5. Coordinated arson gave rise to a different set of issues: for a remarkable episode in 210 see Liv. 26.27.1–9 with Briquel 2002.

110. For one third-century dedication discovered in front of Temple B's steps see *AE* 1948.89 = *ILLRP* 294 = Coarelli in *RMR*: 122 no. 130 = Kajanto et al. 1981, 87–88.

111. For a recapitulation of this line see Toner 2013, 42–43, 59, and 73.

the frame of the religious new organizational technologies that brought the practices of cult in line with the practicalities of civic upkeep. In the processes, these technologies conduced to the affirmation of a statehood that bundled nonritual public goods into the spaces and structures of divine cult. Even though it is difficult to establish with precision how access to and worship of water divinities interacted with other features of ritual life at the Largo Argentina complex, the recovery of more than 550 small ointment jars from the site—many of them in the immediate vicinity of Temple A—has supplied powerful circumstantial evidence for the region's association with practices of bathing and purification, and potentially even of healing.[112] For more conspicuous evidence of a civic commitment to healing, we next turn to a neighboring sector of the mid-republican city.

3. *Civic Health: Healing and Medicine*

I indicated at the beginning of the previous section that my appraisal of the public goods at stake in the repurposing of temples as firefighting and water-distribution infrastructure rested on a compelling but by no means secure reconstruction of the third-century Campus Martius. Should the Coarellian reconstruction's sturdiness be a source of concern, there is still another opening for the kind of institutional analysis essayed above: the dedication of sanctuaries to healing divinities, best exemplified by the vowing and dedication of a temple to Aesculapius on the Tiber Island during the late 290s. The introduction of the cult of Aesculapius and the delivery of healing services under the auspices of his worship are broadly analogous to the systematization of crisis management that we have been discussing in connection with the Campus Martius. Modern discussions of the importation of Aesculapius and other healing divinities to Rome tend to concentrate primarily on the immediate sociohistorical contexts of their appearance and on the significance of these divinities for the Hellenization of Roman religion.[113] Although these interpretive directions have proven fertile, an approach centered on the institutional

112. The excavation of these *balsamari* and their cultic significance: Andreani et al. 2005; Moser 2019a, 74–75. Water, nymphs, and healing: bibliography cited at n. 95 above. The presence of these items strengthens the case for identifying Temple A's divinity as Feronia (*pace* Coarelli), if Hor. *Sat.* 1.5.24 (*ora manusque tua lavimus, Feronia, lympha*) credibly alludes to face and hand washing as features of Feronia's cult.

113. Purely for example, Orlin 1997, 107 for the claim that the cult's introduction marked a turning point in Rome's desire to partake of the religious culture of Magna Graecia, elaborated in Orlin 2010, 63–66; for a similar argument see Scheid 1985b, 97–98. Critique: Satterfield 2008, 107–8. On the spread of the cult throughout central Italy either concurrently with or after its introduction in Rome see now van der Ploeg 2018, 64–72; for evidence that other divinities

logic of healing sanctuaries in their urban context may serve us better. This subsection will work toward demonstrating that the cumulative effect of these sanctuaries' integration into the sacred topography of Rome was the emergence of a sacralized "public health ministry," oriented toward the safeguarding of *salus publica*.

The tendency of modern scholarship to oversimplify the interaction of religious ritual and public health in ancient urban settings has inhibited attention to the complexities of this entanglement. Building on A. M. Hocart's observation that "temples are just as utilitarian as dams and canals," Peregrine Horden has sounded the call for a more probing engagement with ancient conceptions of the medical efficacy of religious ritual.[114] To view religious rituals that were aimed at bringing disease episodes to a close as materially ineffective or counterproductive ignores the capacity of ritual to effect transformation not only at an individual or collective level but also at an *institutional* level. In the spirit of Horden's admonition, and in keeping with recent scholarship's engagement with the active agency involved in securing the healing intercession of the gods, I propose that we understand the Roman state's turn to temple vowing and dedication in the course of disease episodes as utilitarian and efficacious because institutions charged with providing for the public good of *salus* were thereby created and consolidated, as backstop for the quasi-voluntary compliance that prevented the *res publica* from flying off the rails.

In mid-republican Rome, the conceptualization of communal health as a public concern that demanded the state's attention is apparent on multiple fronts. Whether or not in direct response to a disease episode, the installation of the eventually infamous Greek medic Archagathus in quarters near the *compitum Acilium* in 219, under the oversight if not the behest of the Roman Senate, aligns well with the practice of soliciting and installing doctors at public expense and in high-visibility urban areas that is attested for other regions of the Hellenistic Mediterranean.[115] While the subsequent zoning of the neighborhood around the *compitum Acilium* into a local and regional hub for

besides Aesculapius were credited with the power to heal, Carroll 2019, 18–19 and chapter 5 below.

114. Hocart [1936] 1970, 217; Horden 2000 = 2008, chap. 3, esp. 33–38. The point is stressed in Wazer 2016, 128–29.

115. Cassius Hemina *FRHist* F 27 with Kudlien 1986, 53 and Von Staden 1996; for additional bibliography see *FRHist* III.74. On the exceptionality of "delineating public space for specific actors" in Rome see Tan 2017, 24. Public doctors in the Hellenistic world: Jones 1940, 219 for a succinct overview; Kudlien 1979, chaps. 2 and 4 for the details. Archagathus, the *compitum Acilium*, and the philhellenic senatorial Acilii Glabriones: Dondin-Payre 1987.

medical expertise has all the trappings of a path-dependent outcome,[116] it would be misguided to characterize the association as accidental or incidental; the linking of medical practice with the sacrality of the *compitum* mutually enhanced and enriched each. Even if Archagathus's stint at Rome was "a failed experiment" in senatorial sponsorship of public physicians, it matters that the Senate saw arrangements for the management of civic health as a responsibility that fell on its shoulders.[117] Where the Senate's intentions can be most clearly discerned, and their ramifications more capably mapped, is in the process through which healing divinities were installed at Rome, best documented in the case of Aesculapius's appearance on the scene.[118]

According to the annalistic tradition, an epidemic in 293 prompted the Senate to order a consultation of the Sibylline Books, on the recommendation of which a delegation was dispatched to Epidauros.[119] The envoys came back from the Epidaurian Asklepion with a sacred snake believed to embody the god; later legend would have it that, once disembarked from the ship on which it had been transported up to Rome, the snake went of its own accord to the Tiber Island to mark the site of its future cult. The plague soon abated, and a temple to the god was dedicated in or around 291.[120] It should be stressed that, although the literary sources and the scholarship committed to their interpretation have taken the god's introduction to mark a turning point in Roman religious life, the archaeological record has given rise to the suspicion that the god Aesculapius and the incubatory healing practices linked to his worship were known at Rome before the official inauguration of his cult.[121] Whatever the case may be, the novelty of his cult's monumentalization in mid-republican Rome is not up for dispute. The vowing and dedica-

116. The history of this neighborhood: Palombi 1997–98; the urban toponym Velia for the area around the *compitum* may be a reminiscence of the famous school of Greek medics that flourished in Hellenistic Velia.

117. Wazer 2016, 127 for the quotation, and the essay as a whole for other senatorially monitored rituals of civic healing—such as *lectisternia* and other expiations recommended by the *decemuiri sacris faciundis*.

118. Other healing-oriented divinities that received cult before or during our period were also implicated in state-mediated interventions, though the specifics of their introduction and/or monumentalization are not as well known: see Edlund-Berry 2006 for a list.

119. Liv. 10.47.6–7; Val. Max. 1.8.2; [Aur. Vict.] *De vir. ill.* 22; Oros. 3.22.5. Ovid's poeticization of the event: *Met.* 15.622–44. Citations of the secondary literature on this episode are collected at Beard et al. 1998, I.68 nn. 217–22.

120. For this structure see D. Degrassi in *LTUR* 1.21–22 s.v. "Aesculapius, aedes" and the bibliography cited at Bernard 2018a, 247.

121. Discussion: Beard et al. 1998, I.69–70. Onomastic evidence seems to point in the same direction: see the Appendix for the *pocolom* that names the god.

tion of a temple to this divinity were in fact transformative, but not for the reasons that are usually cited.

Students of the material culture of the Tiber Island have long recognized that Aesculapius's temple installation spurred a substantial rise in inscribed and uninscribed votive dedications to the god.[122] In the second half of this book, I will propose a technique for quantifying these dedications and the human dedicators who were responsible for them. For now, the emergence of a votive economy that revolved around the cult of Aesculapius is relevant primarily as evidence for the *moyenne* and *longue durée* aftermaths of erecting a temple and demarcating a sacred precinct for a healing god in Rome. In the case of Aesculapius, the material evidence for the continuation of his cult at the site of a mid-republican temple foundation has bearing on how we anatomize the interaction between "official" and "personal" (or "experiential") modes of religious practice in mid-republican Rome. The erection of a sacred structure for the healing god not only provided a space for this interaction but also gave structural expression to the state's pursuit of and provisioning for civic health and hygiene. Although we cannot be certain that the Roman Senate and its agents had the cycles of the votive and healing cult economy explicitly in mind when relocating a manifestation of the god to Rome or when vowing and dedicating a temple to him, the signs of Aesculapius's familiarity to Romans prior to his solicitation and arrival gesture toward a plausible theory of intent. As the popularity of healing cults among both elites and non-elites resonated throughout the Greek world in general and southern Italy in particular during the fourth and early third centuries,[123] Roman magistrates would have been exposed, at the very least through hearsay and quite possibly through personal experience, to some of the practices and movements the cult set in motion. In other words, it is conceivable that Roman magistrates acted not only with the short-term resolution of the epidemic (pressing as it was) in mind when they dispatched an embassy to entice the god to Rome but also with an eye on social developments elsewhere in the Hellenistic world—in conformity with what one might expect from a peer-polity system.[124] Even if Roman magistrates did not have a finely elaborated understanding of the likely institutional consequences, they would have had some inkling of how

122. Catalog and analysis of the epigraphic material: Renberg 2006–7. I take up the explosion of anatomical votive dedications in chapter 5.

123. Asklepios's healing cult in the Greek world: Edelstein and Edelstein 1998, I: nos. 337–481 for testimonia; II.139–80 for medical and therapeutic practice at Asklepian sanctuaries. For healing cult as a form of "alternative medicine" in pre-Roman and Republican Italy cf. Edlund-Berry 2006 and Griffith 2015.

124. See Orlin 2010, 62–66 on the introduction of the god as an "overture to Magna Graecia."

the god's presence in Rome might bring about changes in the patterning of individual and communal life.

By framing the temple installation of Aesculapius and the vast economy of primarily anatomical terracotta votives as a unified phenomenon of civic health management, we can improve on the customary differentiation between "official" and "personal" modes of religious experience that has long been a staple of studies of Republican religion. For Patrizio Pensabene, the mid-republican votive deposits from the city and especially those clustered in the vicinity of the Tiber were evidence for "la ricerca di un'esperienza religiosa valida da contrapporre a quella tradizionale e ufficiale"—a hankering for religious experience that was then manipulated by the "classi dirigenti" at particular moments of social tension.[125] According to this reading, "personal" religious experience and "official" religious dispensations converged only episodically, at moments of general societal crisis and only when it was in the best interests of the state hierarchy. Once again, however, it is imperative that we imagine the other varieties of religious experience whose fullest instantiation came not at historically salient instances of community-wide panic but through daily and yearly repetition. In the aftermath of Aesculapius's installation at Rome, the religious *esperienza* of an individual seeking a cure at the hands of the god came to be embedded quite felicitously in longer-term institutional arrangements. By supplying a space for rituals of healing, the installation of the god's cult in monumental form delivered a public good whose impact would be felt well after any one episode of hygienic crisis.

To erect a temple for the healing god Aesculapius was not only to pay him immediate honor and offer him thanks for the *sedata pestilentia*, it was also to facilitate his worship among future generations, with the expectation that such worship would avert or mitigate any maladies to which the individual worshipper or the community at large might be susceptible. The public interest of the Roman state in the maintenance of Aesculapius's temple is apparent within the first few decades of the structure's foundation, if an inscription on travertine recovered from the Tiber Island that credits two curule aediles with the consecration of an altar and a repair of the sacred precinct is datable to later in the third century.[126] But in the context of the "public health ministry" that

125. Pensabene 1982, 78. Cf. Champion 2017 for a takedown of elite-instrumentalist approaches.

126. Nunziata in *AE* 2008 no. 199 = Panciera 2016, 367–71. The restoration of this inscription and its dating are uncertain, with Nunziata and Panciera differing on several important details. If Panciera is correct to restore the name of one of the aediles as Valerius, the identification of this *gens* with public-health-oriented cultic activity would receive an added boost: see *ILLRP* 39 for the late republican scion of the family who carries out repair work on the Island *de stipe*

came to be shaped around the cult of Aesculapius, a distinction between official intervention and private or personal religious experience of the sort Pensabene proposes is rather inert. It would be better to say that official intervention in the form of vowing and dedicating a temple to Aesculapius incentivized private religious practices whose continued performance was perceived to be conducive not only to the health of any one individual but also to the health of the community as a whole. The placement of the temple on the Tiber Island might even speak to a desire to maximize the cult's accessibility and its perceived efficacy.[127]

The institutionalization of this cult as an instrument for and caretaker of communal health would not have been geared toward curtailing or hemming in informal and domestic healing practices. After all, the exercise of medicine was not necessarily and invariably embedded in the postures of public worship; the scripturalization of self-consciously "folksy" medical wisdom in Cato the Elder is sometimes indexed to the performance of rituals with public analogues, but often not.[128] That said, it would not be shocking if private cultic attention to matters of individual and familial health—*sacra privata* of the kind Jane Draycott recently studied—gained a new conceptual and directional orientation in conjunction with the state's monumentalizing intervention.[129] We observed in our earlier analysis of fire and water management that the cumulative institutional effect of providing a public good was the promotion of trust among the citizen body. There, I had invoked Blanton and Fargher to argue that this trust underwrote the quasi-voluntary compliance regime through which the Roman state maintained social cohesion. The virtue of creating a permanent built structure and sacred precinct where prayers could be offered and dedications made for individual and communal *salus* was that such a structure, and the steady stream of individuals it drew annually, gave material expression to the Roman state's commitment to the hygienic well-being of its citizens—the importance of which was recognized by the decision to celebrate a festival in honor of the god and of his cult on the Kalends of

Aesculapi; generally on the health-centered mythistory and politics of the Valerii note Padilla Peralta 2018c, 298–301 (to whose bibliography on the Valerii add J. W. Rich's *FRHist* commentary on Valerius Antias and Richardson 2018).

127. Placement on the Tiber Island as reflecting a desire to site the structure within a "salubrious environment": Vitr. *De arch.* 1.2.7 with Baker 2013, 133–34.

128. For Cato the Elder's literary self-fashioning as practitioner of home remedies—in response to increasing Roman interest in Hellenistic medicine—see Draycott 2016, 436–38, with nn. 20–23 for citations to the relevant passages in *De agri cultura*; cf. Padilla Peralta 2017c, 347 on the religious significance of Catonian healing incantation as a "Hellenizing technology."

129. For these *sacra* and especially their focus on dietary regimen note Draycott 2017.

January each year.[130] Thus, the monumentalization of the cult of Aesculapius, far from merely commemorating the resolution of a pestilential episode, contributed in its own specific way to mid-republican Rome's civic upkeep—the sacro-political enterprise whose institutional webbing we have been tracing in this chapter. The building of a temple to this divinity is also important as a marker of a coordinated state response to the cresting popularization of healing cult, not only in central Italy but also throughout the Hellenistic Mediterranean.[131] Finally, the arrival of the god's cult to the Tiber Island stimulated the cross-fertilization of topography and healing that secured the area's enduring association with miracle-working.[132]

III. Public Goods B: The Regularization of Festival Culture

For Romans of the middle Republic, the festivals that emerged in conjunction with the surge in temple construction were vital to the project of "structur[ing] time as a means of elucidating numerous aspects of their collective religious experience."[133] Prefiguring the bread and circuses of the Empire, the Republican state's escalating investment in the celebration of *ludi* attest to an awareness of mass entertainment's potential. With their intoxicating medley of ritual and song, the *ludi* over time became a public good whose payoffs far exceeded their upfront costs. At least seven major *ludi* were introduced for the first time or regularized as components of the annual calendar during the fourth and third centuries, and minor *ludi* were regularly offered whenever a temple was dedicated.[134] Increasingly central to these games were theatrical performances, which became a fixture of the major *ludi* that were vowed and celebrated over the fourth and third centuries.[135] Later tradition held that the *scaenici* that were staged in conjunction with the *ludi Romani* of 240 gave birth

130. The festival's calendrical alignment with other celebrations "concerned with the wellbeing of the state": van der Ploeg 2018, 66.

131. Hellenistic healing sanctuaries and medical specialization: Oberhelman 2014.

132. "Miraculous charity" and the Christian saints of the Tiber: Maskarinec 2018, chap. 4; note also Isid. *Etym.* 13.13.1 on the therapeutic qualities ascribed to the waters of the Tiber.

133. The quotation: Forsythe 2012, xii, introducing a monograph on Roman time.

134. Full discussion of the mid-republican games in Bernstein 1998, 119–226; synthesis in Lacam 2010, 130–36. The seven: the *ludi maximi/Romani, Tarentini, magni, plebeii/Ceriales, Apollinares, Megalenses,* and the *Florales*; I pass over as irresolvable the debates over the dating of their first iterations; see, e.g., Wiseman 2008, 171–74 contra Bernstein 1998, 157–58 on the *Ceriales*. Minor *ludi* to accompany temple dedications: Liv. 36.36.7 for the temple of Iuventas in 191; Lactantius *Div. inst.* 6.20.34 implies that the practice was standard.

135. Feeney 2016 for a fresh treatment.

to Latin literature.[136] Both the games and the theatrical shows put on in conjunction with them were believed to involve the gods. Late republican evidence paints a vibrant picture of gods not only watching the proceedings from their temples but even participating in processions and sharing in meals.[137] The extent of this involvement will have been all the more pronounced if, as Inge Nielsen has speculated, the performances encompassed not only plays and mimes but also "ritual dramas" of the kind best known and studied in connection with ancient Near Eastern temple complexes.[138]

As a preliminary to the analysis of the public goods disseminated through dramatic festival culture that will occupy us for much of the next chapter, I offer in this section an account of how modifications to the Roman calendar operated in tandem with the introduction of new festivals to restructure civic time. Although the feedback loop linking civic and political temporal rhythms with shifts in religious practice has been on the radar of modern scholarship,[139] the precise contribution of temples themselves to the shaping of these rhythms remains underexplored. Much as temple construction and dedication marked the reassignment of civic space as divine property, so too did the calendar come to embody and signify the reassignment of civic time to Rome's deities.[140] My main objective will therefore be to tease out how the incorporation of temple anniversaries into the mid-republican calendar revolutionized the experience of civic time at Rome, and thereby to counteract the lingering tendency to underestimate "the important role religious festivals played in the organisation of time in the yearly life of a community."[141] However, in order to bring out the full force of this transformation, some comment on the overarching principles behind the republican calendrical regime is in order.

The previous chapter referenced the activities of Cn. Flavius, the shadowy figure behind the inaugural publication of the calendrical *Fasti* and the first aedilician dedication of a temple (to Concordia). Pliny preserves an intriguing detail from this temple's dedicatory inscription, whose text apparently specified that the *aedes Concordiae* had been built "204 years after the dedication of the Capitoline temple (of Jupiter)."[142] This evidence for a "Capitoline time" is

136. The testimonia: Suerbaum 2002, 93–94; for historicization see Feeney 2016, chap. 5.

137. Critiquing Latte's skepticism regarding the religious content of the *ludi publici*: Brelich 1961, 328. Participation of the gods at the *ludi*: Beard et al. 1998, 40 with n. 119. Roman gods in procession: chap. 4 n. 16.

138. Nielsen 2007.

139. See, e.g., the concise and illuminating discussion in Salzman 2013.

140. I paraphrase the pithy formulation of Rüpke 2014c, 224.

141. Thus Curti 2000, 79.

142. Pliny *NH* 33.19: *factam eam aedem CCIIII annis post Capitolinam dedicatam.*

striking for what it suggests about the chronographic consciousness of the Republic, and it is meaningful for us in its association of a monumental sacred structure with communal temporal awareness.[143] However, Pliny's unadorned presentation of the inscription's contents may indicate that at the time of the inscription's composition temporal calibration by reference to the dedication year of the Capitoline temple was an unremarkable aspect of mid-republican life. Flavius's act of reckoning time from the towering sacred structure on the Capitoline was probably not in itself surprising to his contemporaries, even if its encapsulation in epigraphic form was memorable enough for Pliny to preserve it. At least by comparison to the upwardly mobile *scriba*'s better known and far more antagonizing innovations, the dedicatory text itself seems not to have triggered anything close to a social crisis; it was just one more epigraphic embellishment for a rapidly diversifying monumental landscape. But the Concordia temple's dedication is emblematic of a process whose imprint on the temporal perceptions of Romans, while subtler than the year-to-year calculation of elapsed time, was in some respects even more profound: the interweaving of new temples into the organization of civic time as their foundation dates secured a place in the religious calendar.

Modern scholarship has labored hard over the surviving late Republican and Imperial *fasti* to reconstruct the history of the Roman calendar's development.[144] Energy was initially expended on extrapolating backward from these late epigraphic exemplars to the original calendar as introduced in the archaic period, and which the ancient sources credited to King Numa. In his reexamination of the sources, Jörg Rüpke has shown that the parameters of the Republican calendar (to the extent that these can be recovered from later epigraphic and literary testimonies) were established by Flavius and refined by a *lex Hortensia*, passed sometime around 287.[145] The gridding of days into *fasti* and *nefasti*, the aspects and conventions of the abbreviations employed on the calendar, and the sociocultural rationales responsible for the calendar's form all, in Rüpke's opinion, point rather unequivocally to a "birth" for

143. Purcell 2003, 27–33a, followed by Feeney 2007, 141–42; note also Carlà 2017, 146 on the Capitoline as center not only of Roman space but also of Roman time. For the keeping of "Capitoline time" through the ritual of the so-called *clavus annalis* see now Padilla Peralta 2018c. The plurality of time-keeping devices in this period: Pliny *NH* 7.212–15 with Ando 2015, 81–84.

144. The classic treatments: Mommsen 1859; Degrassi 1963, which remains the authoritative edition of the epigraphic evidence; Michels 1967; Scullard 1981. Of more recent vintage: Feeney 2007 and Rüpke 1995a (revision and translation: Rüpke 2011), both of which I lean on below.

145. Rüpke 1995a, chap. 7; 2011, chap. 5. For a more sanguine contemporary perspective on recovering the contents of the "archaic" calendar see Coarelli 2017.

the calendrical *Fasti* in the lifetime (and through the agency) of Flavius. In short, then, there was no "calendar" of the kind known to us from late republican and early Imperial epigraphic evidence prior to Flavius; although techniques for tracking and marking time certainly existed, the knowledge to deploy them rested in the hands of the priestly elite that was not terribly interested in redacting this information into a transmissible and publicized written format.

In its initial Flavian iteration, it is more likely than not that the calendrical *Fasti* did not include temple anniversaries. The first publication probably set out the basic texture of the year, which featured the F/N structure and those important traditional public festivals such as the Lupercalia and Parilia that were marked in capital letters. A tweak subsequently introduced through the *lex Hortensia* helped to resolve the issue of whether market days (*nundinae*) could be *dies fasti*, a crucial matter in the creation of incentives for out-of-towners to travel toward Rome.[146] But what about the temple anniversaries designated so scrupulously on the late republican and Imperial calendars? Since the temple anniversary dates preserved in the late republican *Fasti Antiates maiores* all seem to refer to temple constructions prior to the 170s, Rüpke has claimed that these *dies natales templorum* were aggregated for incorporation into the second attested "publication" of the calendrical *Fasti*: M. Fulvius Nobilior's exhibition in his temple to Hercules Musarum, built sometime in the 170s.[147] By displaying this "new and improved" calendar in his temple—whether in painted or book form and possibly both—Fulvius Nobilior, one of the great political figures of the post–Second Punic War generation, sought to certify his structure as representing in some sense the culmination of Roman time. The monumentalization of the city, now memorialized through its integration into the calendar and this calendar's integration into Fulvius's temple project, will have thus been reformatted into living proof of the Ennian aphorism *moribus antiquis res stat Romana virisque*.[148] Crucially, the organizing framework for the calendar's intervention in the spatial and temporal rhythms

146. *Nundinae*: Liv. *Per.* 11.11 with Rüpke 1995a, 274–83 = 2011, 59–63 and 1996 for the details; Ker 2010 for the multiplicity of functions and meanings ascribed to *nundinae*. The *nundinae* and farmers' trips to Rome: Rutilius (Rufus?) *apud* Macr. *Sat.* 1.16.34 = Bremer 1896, 45. The economic scale and impact of *nundinae* in later periods: Morley 1996, 166–74.

147. Rüpke 1995a, chap. 9.2 = 2011, chap. 7.2, followed and supplemented by Gildenhard 2003, 95–97. Further on the symmetry and symbolic power of the consular *fasti*'s installation in the temple see Gildenhard 2007, 84–86. I am unpersuaded by Rüpke's argument that the consular *fasti* on display at the temple *began* with the consuls for 179; see Feeney 2007, 287 n. 25.

148. Ennius *Ann.* 156 Skutsch with Rüpke 1995a, 324 = 2011, 100. The Fulvian *fasti* as a "data bank" for the *Annales*: Feeney 2007, 170.

of the city was supplied yet again by a temple complex, one whose blurring of the distinction between public and private was integral to its heterotopic program.[149]

In any event, on the assumption that the installation of a comprehensive set of *fasti* within the temple of Hercules Musarum served to codify knowledge of the expanding calendar, it will have taken at least until the third decade of the second century for the impact of fourth- and third-century temple foundations to register on a public or semipublic display of the Roman calendar. That these temple foundations were deemed worthy of inclusion is, however, indicative of the significance the foundations and the festivals linked with them had accrued in the preceding decades, and especially in that "creative half-century from 220 to 173 [that] crystallized the distinctive games-rich religious calendar."[150] But how precisely had temple anniversaries changed the rhythms of Roman life in the years prior to Fulvius Nobilior's self-aggrandizing intervention? Answering this question will require first taking stock of these anniversary dates as a whole and their relation to the agricultural year, then outlining their interplay with the timing of military triumphs and their capacity to generate social utilities that extended well beyond the day of celebration itself. We may begin with one intriguing feature of the calendrical distribution of temple anniversaries: their clustering in June and August (figure 3.3).[151]

Chapter 2 demonstrated that, even taking account of the amount of Roman manpower that was tied up in the increasingly lengthy campaigns that the imperial Republic waged against its enemies, the Roman state had enough labor muscle at its disposal to handle the diversion of some of it to monumental construction. However, in a labor regime already juggling the double pressures of yearlong warring and agricultural production, labor flows toward monumental projects were likeliest during medium- to low-activity months of the agricultural cycle—in other words, outside of the two-month band for harvesting in late spring and early summer and the two-month band for sow-

149. For details of the complex of Hercules Musarum see Russell 2016, 139–45, though her claim that the artwork and ornamentation "were more successful a monument to their patron's name than the temple" (p. 141) elides the question of what would have constituted "success" for different components of the monumental program.

150. Purcell 2013, 448.

151. Source: Scullard 1981, cross-checked against the reconstruction and discussion of fragmentary late republican calendars in Degrassi 1963 and Ziolkowski 1992, part II.2; note also Curti 2000, 82–83. Total number of anniversaries: sixty-three, the sum of the thirty-seven temples of chapter 2 and the *aediculae*, open-air shrines, and other structures that were excluded from chapter 2's models. The mid-republican calendar is in lunisolar alignment for most of our period: see Rosenstein 2004, 34–35 with 208 n. 44.

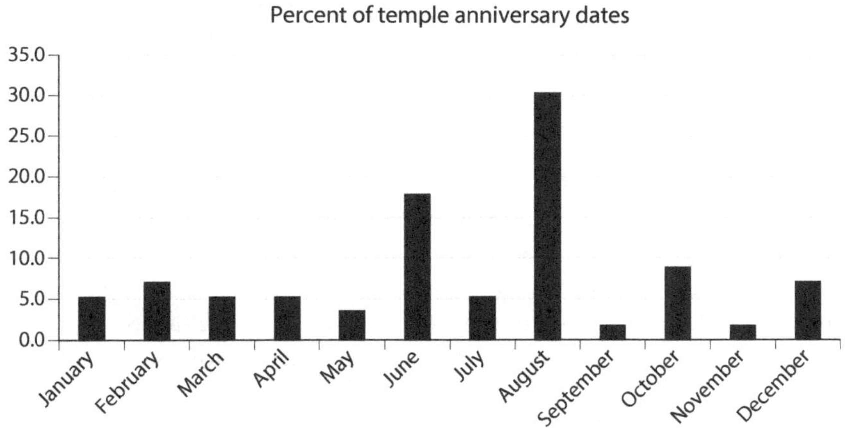

FIGURE 3.3. Anniversary dates for temple foundations, 400–186 BCE.

ing in the early fall. Seasonal construction patterns of this sort are attested both within and beyond the premodern Mediterranean.[152]

If temples were dedicated immediately upon or shortly after completion, the double peak of temple anniversaries in June and August would seem to confirm the existence of a seasonal construction pattern at Rome. Manual labor in the high summer to complete work on temples will have exposed laborers to the ravages of the urban pathogen cycle, whose spike during estival heat is confirmed by evidence for mortality trends from later periods in Rome's urban history.[153] In a particularly cruel epidemiological conjuncture, many of the temples dedicated during the fourth and third centuries were built on or in the immediate vicinity of what was effectively marshland, the choicest breeding grounds for malaria-transmitting mosquitos.[154] Partly in the hope of shielding themselves from the worst of this disease cycle, generations of Roman elites fled the city during the summer.[155] How the urban-rural toggle of Roman aristocrats affected or dictated the delegated supervision of those work gangs that bore the brunt of temple construction can only be speculated. Regardless of whether such movements were in full bloom during

152. See chapter 2 n. 76 and Hawkins 2016, 26–32; for seasonal corvée, Scheidel 2018, 241 and 244.

153. Calendrical rhythms of infectious disease in Rome: Shaw 1996, 115, figure 5; Scheidel 2012, 120, figure 6.6.

154. See Sallares 2002, 214–15 with table 8 on the distribution of bodies of water in different sectors of the city; although taken from the late antique *Curiosum*, this information shines some light on the state of affairs several centuries earlier.

155. The survival of this ancient rhythm into the modern period: Lanciani 1897, 6–7.

our period, if mid-republican Rome was beginning to swell with economically distressed individuals in search of employment or with underemployed slaves brought home from the battlefield, hard labor during the high summer months will have been a reality for those not already occupied with the work of harvesting and reaping.

It could be that the bunching of temple dedications into these calendrical slots is more reflective of a culturally evolved taste than of the rhythms of the agrarian economy per se; since in that case we would still be left with the question of determining what may have conditioned this taste in the first place, this appeal to taste yields at best only a partial answer. But invoking the agrarian labor cycle is not on its own a sufficient explanation for the calendrical rhythms of temple dedication. In light of the sheer amount of collective human energy that had to be set aside for the grim work of the summer harvest, it is curious to see so few anniversaries clustered in the winter months, the down period for Rome's agrarian economy. One possible explanation is that the winter months were, precisely by virtue of being unencumbered by agricultural demands, optimized for family-making.[156] Other factors besides the demographic and economic pacing of subsistence agriculture should also be borne in mind: the friability and limited durability of the tufa stone that was exploited for mid-republican temple building would have steered construction work away from Italy's rainy season and toward the summer, the same season that the riverine network employed to transport blocks of Grotta Oscura tufa was at its most navigable.[157]

These, then, were the structural and material parameters that dictated why temple anniversaries congregated at specific times of year.[158] What, if any, were the sociocultural repercussions of this distribution of anniversaries? It is possible, in select instances, to diagram the interaction between a temple and the time of year in which it was dedicated; the coincidence of the temple anniversaries for divine qualities with the electoral season for

156. The timing and demands of the harvest, "under the burning sun": Shaw 2013. For the seasonality of marriage in Roman Italy—peaking in the winter, bottoming out during the summer—see Shaw 1997, decisively overturning J. G. Frazer's identification of June as the preferred month. The birthing cycle in ancient Rome likewise peaked in the winter, with a secondary peak in May and August: Shaw 2001.

157. Attributes of mid-republican tufas: Jackson et al. 2005; Lancaster and Ulrich 2014, 171 on the easy susceptibility of tufa to weathering. Ancient authors recommended tuff extraction during the summer: Bernard 2018a, 142. Reliance on riverine connectivity to transport Grotto Oscura: Quaranta 2017, 42–43. Cf. the relationship of *matériel* and seasonality in aqueduct construction: Frontin. *Aq.* 2.123 with Hawkins 2016, 34–35.

158. For their slotting in and around the orientating grids of the month and the *nundinae* see Rüpke 1996, 86–87.

the major magistracies has lately invited some scrutiny.[159] However, it is not so much the temporal contingencies of any one class of dedications and their aftermath but the cumulative force unleashed by the repetitive sequencing of one anniversary after the other during the summer months that bears most directly on possible answers to this question. To demarcate the field of significations in which these temple anniversaries jostled for attention in the Roman mind, we will need first to query their resonance as *dies natales*.[160] Credited with having "birthdays," temples were perceived to have something in common with human beings and with cities qua living organisms.

Although the use of the term *dies natalis* to refer to a temple's anniversary is not first attested until the late Republic,[161] the text of Cn. Flavius's dedicatory inscription for the temple of Concordia that was cited at the beginning of this section certainly relied on the notion of a birth year from which time could be counted in the formulation of its chronographic strategy. Not a great deal of cognitive strain will have been involved in pivoting from this mental habit to an anniversary-oriented mindset, though the process by which temple anniversaries were pegged to a specific date on the calendar should not be taken for granted. It is useful to keep in mind that prior to the Julian overhaul any one date on the calendar was *not* guaranteed to be 365 days removed from its predecessor the year before or its successor the year after.[162] The repercussions of this fact for the celebration of any type of birthday or anniversary is simple but far-reaching. The date for any one anniversary had to be reckoned not by moving forward a uniform measure of time from its last instantiation but by continuous consultation of the calendrical grid's monthly divisions and salient orienting markers—the Kalends, Nones, and Ides, all of which came to be increasingly saturated with triumphal celebrations during the middle and late Republic in an obvious ploy to maximize the number of people in attendance at them.[163] By affording regular practice to those members of the

159. For an example of this interaction see Padilla Peralta 2018c on Flora's foundation date. Temple anniversaries and mid-republican consular elections: Curti 2000, 82–83.

160. Wissowa 1912, 56–57; Salzman 1990, 119; Argetsinger 1992, 175–76; Feeney 2007, 148.

161. Cic. *Att.* 4.1.4 and *Sest.* 131: the orator is tickled to have his return from exile coincide with his daughter's *natalis*, the *natalis* of the temple of Salus (a mid-republican foundation), and the *natalis* of Brundisium; cf. his contemporary Varro's epistolary references to the *natalis* of Fors Fortuna, another recipient of a mid-republican temple (*epist.* frr. 11a–b Cugusi). Gods and spectacles as reference points in Ciceronian epistolarity: Clark in progress; for Cicero's discursive strategizing around the figure of Salus, Luke 2014, 106–11 (but cf. the critique of Smith 2015, xxii).

162. Because of intercalation: see Feeney 2007, 150–56.

163. Rüpke 2012a, 307 on this last point, reemphasized in Barja de Quiroga 2018, 15.

Roman community who were learning how to wield the Flavian calendar, the expanding number of *dies natales templorum* promoted greater engagement with and social investment in the chronographic knowledge that the calendar embodied. Magistrates responsible for temple dedications and their families had to stay on top of the calibrated movement of time if they wanted the temple's dedication to retain its anniversary freshness in the eyes of the community at large. Meanwhile, members of the Roman community will have needed to know enough about the calendar to recognize the annual celebration of the temple's dedication as the annual celebration of the temple's dedication. Temple anniversaries thus served as opportunities for practicing a species of institutional and communal learning, one in which the passage of time was given new expression through the interplay between festive moment and calendrically imposed superstructure. The simple fact of anniversary repetitiveness was epistemologically meaningful, since every temple anniversary created one additional opportunity for the Roman community to experience the tension between the "reversible time" of day-to-day living and the "reversible time" of the institutional *longue durée* that came to be enshrined in monuments for cult.[164]

Furthermore, temple anniversaries were catalysts for calendrical transformation in their own right, since they modified the nature of the days on which they fell. In a sign of the authoritativeness of the F/N grid of days, the celebration of a *natalis templi* did not convert a day from F to N or vice versa,[165] but the lived experience of the day was altered by anniversary celebrations. Mary Beard has detailed how the accumulation of anniversaries and public festivals on any one date generated a concatenation of meanings—a semiotic supersaturation—that elevated especially freighted days into "conceptual pageant[s]."[166] This line of interpretation, formulated originally as a strategy for reading the multiplicity of festival meanings threading through the works of late Republican and Augustan writers such as Ovid, applies equally well to the feverishly transforming cultural climate of the fourth and third centuries. The appearance of sixty-three new *dies natales templorum* inserted sixty-three new meanings into the calendar and, in so doing, set the stage for future generations of festival-day heuristics. "Setting the stage" is no idle metaphor; the

164. I borrow these concepts from Giddens 1984, 35–36. Temples, rituals, and anniversaries as "realms of memory": Hölkeskamp 2006, 481–82, drawing on the work of Pierre Nora; cf. the contributions in Haake and Jung 2011 on Greek sanctuaries.

165. Wissowa 1912, 56: "zu jedem neuen Tempel gehört ein Festag, der nur in diesem einen Heiligtume mit einem feierlichen Opfer begangen wird, *ohne für die Allgemeinheit den rechtlichen Charakter des Tages zu bestimmen und ihn zu einem dies nefastus zu machen*" (my emphasis).

166. Beard [1987] 2003; see chapter 4 n. 11 for additional bibliography.

temples built in this period quite literally provided the seating and stages for theatrical performances that engaged with religious issues and incorporated mentions of religious festivals—proof that one did not have to be an Ovid in the time of Augustus to be immersed in a rich festival-performance metadiscourse. To paraphrase Valerius Maximus, it was above all else the "memory of cheerfulness" that was renewed with the annual cycle of temple anniversaries; the yearly repetition of dance, song, and theater engendered a "kinetic familiarity" whose socially efficacious ramifications I will consider at greater length in the next chapter.[167]

Even if it strains belief that most of Rome's citizens grasped the workings of these processes at a conscious level—if one is instead more inclined to believe that the view from these hermeneutic heights was the privilege of an aristocratic few—there are three additional aspects of the temple-birthday imaginary that merit comment. First, these temple anniversaries, each affixed to a specific temple and to the individual magistrate(s) behind the temple's vowing and dedication, helped "make real" the new patterning of political and communal life that Rome's cultic monumentalization engendered. Through their temples, magistrates entered themselves and their achievements into the annual rhythm; once "made real," these would henceforth live on in virtual counterpoint to the major festivals and *ludi* whose organization and orchestration was the prerogative of magistrates currently in office.[168] Since several major temple anniversaries and their accompanying *ludi* happened to cluster around the times of years when magistrates would depart to or return from their military or provincial assignments, it is possible that magistrates began during our period to strategize around the choice of days for *adventus* and *profectio*, and Roman audiences to respond to those choices.[169] If conspicuous expenditure on festivals—which by the beginning of the second century appears to have totaled around 465,000 denarii or 1,860,000 sesterces a year on average—was one site for strategizing and competition, the timing of this expenditure and of the logistical arrangements required to pull off a collectively satisfying orchestration of the games was another.[170]

167. Val. Max. 2.2.9 (*cuius hilaritatis memoria annuo circuitu feriarum repetitur*) with Alonso Fernández 2017, 53–54 for the case of the Lupercalia; the claim is easily generalized across the full spectrum of festival celebrations in the middle Republic.

168. "Making real": Mustakallio 2013, 72; see Rüpke 2012a on the generative tension of accumulating meanings on the one hand and the refinement of strategies for "distinction and control" on the other.

169. Meister's study (2013) of magistrate arrivals and departures does not comment on this possibility, but note Luke 2014 (with n. 161 above).

170. Taylor 2017, 157–58 for the calculations; I return to festival costs in chapter 4.

The need to cultivate and perpetuate the memory of these celebrations and their accompanying expenditures bring me to a second feature of the temple-birthday imaginary: its swelling importance to the definition and regulation of the patrician-plebeian aristocracy that rounded into form in the decades after the Licinian-Sextian Rogations. In a political system that required a decade of military service from male elites before their merits could be further tested and vetted through office holding, there were no guarantees that any one family or *gens* would enjoy sustainable political success. The disease regimes of childhood and youth combined with the odds of misfortune on the battlefield to winnow the number of elite men who made it to the opening stages of the *cursus honorum*, at which point electoral incompetence and bad luck would take their turns sorting the wheat from the chaff.[171] In this context of precarity, temples and the anniversary celebrations that sprouted to preserve the memory of their dedication amounted to deposits of symbolic capital, to be minted as social currency by future generations in their own contests for political advancement. With the caveat that correlation does not imply causation, it is instructive to observe that the payoffs to vowing a temple did not manifest solely in the vower's success in securing (for himself or a member of his family) a magistracy during which the temple could be completed and dedicated.[172] By and large members of the plebeian elite who enjoyed deep and durable connections to other regions of Italy, nearly all of the twenty-two vowers for the fourth and third centuries whose names have come down to us were remarkably successful in inscribing themselves and their families into the honor roll of Republican celebrity.[173] Until the advent of epic and prose historiography in the early decades of the second century, the burden of transmitting and magnifying the exploits of these vowers was shouldered by temple anniversaries, in particular those that by literally opening the doors to the Roman community afforded a glimpse into visual memorials of their vower's accomplishments. Rome's first histories were painted on temple walls.[174]

171. Hölkeskamp 2017, chap. 5 on the precarity of the new elite and the institutional incentives thereby generated. Statistical analysis of political succession in the last two centuries of the Republic: Hopkins and Burton in Hopkins 1983, chap. 2. Rejection at the polls: Pina Polo 2012.

172. This pattern and its institutional reverberations: Weigel 1998 and chapter 2 n. 37 above.

173. The plebeian status of most vowers, beginning with C. Junius Bubulcus (*cos.* III 311): Davies 2017a, 42–44. Well-connected elites: see, e.g., the *gens Atilia*, with its Calabrian background; Terrenato 2019, chap. 5 on the political textures of such connections.

174. Paintings of *triumphatores* at the temples of Consus and Vertumnus: Festus 228 L. s.v. "picta toga." Representations of *ferentarii* at the temple of Aesculapius: Varro *LL* 7.57. The map of Italia at the temple of Tellus: Varro *RR* 1.2.1. Contextualization: Moormann 2011, 17–27 and 47–85. Pictorial communication and historical knowledge: Adam and Rouveret 1995, 8 on

Finally, the multiplication of well-capitalized festival and anniversary celebrations spawned new incentives for travel to Rome, and these incentives grew even stronger with the introduction of commemorative anniversary *ludi* that were decked out with theatrical entertainments. Through these devices, the built structures of cult repeatedly reinforced the temporal frameworks of everyday life in mid-republican Rome. While the temple of Juno Moneta on the Arx may represent the most unambiguous instance of the era's dialectic of monumentality, temporality, and memory,[175] all of the temples dedicated during the fourth and third centuries could assert themselves as technologies for ordering time. In the manner of Janus, sacred monumentalism in mid-republican Rome looked backward as well as forward, unspooling a script for future celebrations in the form of anniversaries and *ludi*.[176] From futurity it is but a short step to perpetuity—that fever dream of statehood. This phenomenon is by no means limited to Rome, of course. That calendrical refinement and adjustment becomes a preoccupation of imperial polities throughout Eurasia during the last few centuries BCE is the clearest sign of an incipient transregional recognition of the importance of controlling time as a means of ensuring not just the viability but the longevity of the state.[177] Narrowing the focus to Italy in the era of the expansion, one might look to the epigraphic footprint of festival time's restructuration in Capua—another contender for peninsular dominance—as evidence for a growing sensitivity to the community-shaping potencies of the calendar.[178] What may well be unique about the Roman case is the binding of civic time's manipulation and orchestration to a profoundly heterarchal proliferation of temples and temple anniversaries. This pattern was above else a *republican* one; the advent of empire saw the link between temple anniversaries and the calendar severed,[179] with

---

these paintings as "une première forme d'histoire"; Holliday 2002, 1–21; Padilla Peralta 2017b and 2019.

175. Meadows and Williams 2001 for a study of this structure; Miano 2012 for the temple's role in the "mnemo-technics" of mid-republican Rome.

176. Cf. Popkin 2016, 84–86 on manubial monuments as a component of the "blueprint for future triumphs."

177. See Robinson 2016 for a groundbreaking comparative study of the unifying function of calendars in Qin China and Republican/early Imperial Rome; Kosmin 2018 for the linearization of time in the Seleucid Empire. Cf. Stern 2012, chap. 5 for the relationship between imperial disintegration and calendrical fragmentation; Dench 2018, chap. 5 for the popularization of Rome-inflected (or at the very least Rome-conscious) calendars across the Mediterranean during the Empire.

178. *Imagines* Capua 4–29 for the *iuvilas* inscriptions, with Franchi de Bellis 1981 for analysis of the texts and Zavaroni 2006 on their iconography.

179. On the spawning of new festivals and games in the Empire see, comprehensively, Salzman 1990; 2013, 492–95 for an overview.

new festivities continuing to multiply even as Roman infrastructural energies moved away from temple building and toward other monumental genres. But for those centuries during which temple construction and calendrical organization forged and maintained their synergy, the fertile commingling of space and time thereby enabled was as critical for the production of a new civic consciousness as the introduction of a Sicilian sundial to the Forum, if not more so.[180]

IV. Conclusion

"It is not hard," Andreas Bendlin has remarked, "to link the provision of religious services by temples and cults to the needs and demands of their urban and suburban base."[181] This chapter has not attempted to be systematic in documenting the entwinement of those needs and their needs with the propagation of cult. To mention only one stone left unturned, there is certainly much more to be said about the relationship between the administration of law in mid-republican Rome and the role of temples in defining and calibrating spaces for justice.[182] Nor would I contend that any of the infrastructural devices studied in this chapter represented a move toward a "thick" state. Even as the middle Republic's population expanded and its portfolio of military activities diversified, the state remained relatively "thin" in its administrative and bureaucratic capabilities.[183] Yet the magic of the "shell game" that I introduced at the beginning of the previous chapter drew its allure from the state's growing sophistication at projecting an image of the *res publica* that was greater than the sum of its parts.

Temples and their agglutinative social practices became increasingly bound to the "mnemo-scapes" and "chronotopic maps" that restructured civic life, collaborating with other civic monuments to shape the experience of urban space down to its most concrete and quotidian aspects, such as the street address.[184] At the same time, temples also became more tightly aligned with

180. For the sundial relocated from Catana to Rome in 263 see Pliny *NH* 7.60 with Feeney 2016, 124. A parasitical riff in the now-lost Plautine *Boeotia* on the sundial as a technology for regulating civic time: Gellius *NA* 3.3.3–5 with Gratwick 1979; Feeney 2007, 116–17.

181. Bendlin 2013, 476.

182. Kondratieff 2010, 99 suggestively imagines "the praetor on his tribunal . . . literally bask[ing] in the reflected glory of Rome's gods, institutions, and heroes, enjoying all the prestige that they conferred upon him and his office."

183. For the terminology of "thick" and "thin" see Tan 2017, chap. 3.

184. I borrow the concepts in quotes from Hamilakis 2014, 157–59. Temples and/as street addresses: already Plaut. *Curc.* 471 (*apud Cloacinae sacrum*) and 481 (*pone aedem Castoris*); a late antique slave collar confirms reliance on the temple of Flora as a neighborhood marker well

those public goods whose distribution secured long-term political buy-in from the Roman community. The evidence at our disposal does not enable us to determine conclusively how accessible these public goods were to the entire population, although some guided speculation on this front would not be out of line. Recent comparative work into the spatial inequities of premodern cities has laid bare the extensive disparities and differentials in elite and non-elite access to public goods.[185] To determine whether such disparities held true for mid-republican Rome and potentially fanned the flames of intraurban tension, we would need to be far better informed about patterns of residential organization in the city than we are now.[186] What can be confidently stated is that the spatial distribution of mid-republican temple construction will have privileged residents in some sections of Rome over others. Even if at first only a path-dependent outcome of the decision on the part of some Roman elites to line up their temples within view of the triumphal route, the grouping of sacred buildings not only in the vicinity of the Circus Flaminius but also the Forum Boarium and the southern side of the Circus Maximus will have most benefited those who lived in those areas.[187]

The benefits of temple construction were distributed far more equitably when it came to one specific assortment of urban practices that, enveloping much of Rome's inhabited areas, touched the life of practically every city resident during the fourth and third centuries. It was through the festival culture that sprang to life within its monumentalized landscape that Rome strengthened the social bonds of members of the urban community and enticed pilgrims to make trips to Rome for the purpose of offering dedications at city temples and shrines. The clearest signal of this enduring legacy comes centuries later: with multiple Christian polemicists "reimagining civic topography" in deliberate counterpoint to the temple-festival dyad's rootedness in pagan civic culture, the urgency of neutralizing and when possible disabling the potency of festival culture remained on the agenda of authors well into late an-

---

into the fourth century CE (*CIL* XV.7172 = *ILS* 8727). Usefully on monuments and addresses in Rome: Courrier 2014, 162–68.

185. Headlined by the work of the "Urban Organization through the Ages" research group at Arizona State University: see Dennehy et al. 2016 and (in more detail) Stanley et al. 2016.

186. Calls for the intensification of research into ancient Rome's residential fabric: Mignone 2016, chap. 5 = 2017 (Republic); Tacoma 2013 (Empire). Tensions between rival neighborhoods received ritual expression in the October Horse rite: chapter 4 n. 79. Further on intraurban violence and its significance to the life and death of neighborhood associations: cf. Purcell 1994, 673–80 (late republican Rome) and Cracco Ruggini 1980 (imperial Alexandria, Tarsus, and Lyons).

187. For visualization of this clustering see Davies 2017a, 40, figure 2.1.

tiquity.[188] By that point, of course, most mid-republican temple-festivals no longer exercised a hold on the public imagination, having been washed away by alterations to the cityscape in the centuries after their initial celebration. In the decades after the Second Punic War and by the early first century at the latest, the process of decommissioning and razing temples for new constructions was in full swing.[189] However, even if many gods and their holidays did ultimately fade into the soft twilight of oblivion, the (un)planned obsolescences of festival culture were not entirely sterile. Concern with forgetfulness as an entropic menace supercharged antiquarian intellectual projects of the late Republic and early Empire, the most prominent of which gravitated toward temples as sites for the clawing back of what had been forgotten.[190] In any case, by activating temples as places for festive gathering, the mid-republican state boosted the formation and strengthening of new circuits of human mobility that, over time, restructured individual and communal understandings of what it meant to identify as a subject of Roman rule.[191] The next two chapters of this book survey the evidence at our disposal for these developments and sketch their consequences for the history of Roman state formation.

188. For quoted phrase and general discussion see Elm 2014.

189. See Varro *ARD* fr. 45 Cardauns (*saepe censores inconsulto populo <aedes> adsolauerunt*) with Rüpke 2014b, 258. Julius Caesar's leveling of a temple: chapter 4 n. 43.

190. Varro *ARD* fr. 42 Cardauns with Ando 2015, 80–81 for the perceived urgency of the fight against *civium negligentia*. Temples and antiquarianism: Padilla Peralta 2019.

191. Cf. Kristensen's (2018) application of the "New Mobilities Paradigm" to reanimate the religious and civic textures of Greek sanctuary space.

PART II

Socialize

4

Temples, Festivals, and Common Knowledge

FROM RHYTHMS TO IDENTITIES

THE COGNITIVE AND AFFECTIVE RIPPLE EFFECTS of festivals, already a topic of vigorous discussion in classical Greek philosophy and historiography,[1] elicited commentary from Hellenistic writers across a variety of genres and discursive frames. Not otherwise charitably disposed toward organized religious observance, Epicurus is reported to have singled out festivals as the most opportune occasion for the wise man to intensify his rapport with the divine.[2] Although nowadays gaining traction in philosophically versed treatments of the role of aesthetic experience in the construction of civic identity, the socially adhesive force of festivals and public prayer—the latter commended by Epicurus for facilitating a "prosocial orientation to the laws"[3]—remain a mostly minimal addition to the literature on Hellenistic state formation. Yet communities throughout the Hellenistic world were acutely aware of the civic potency and institutional efficaciousness of public cult acts. In Polybius's lifetime, one Roman came close to theorizing this connection explicitly, in a rhetorical broadside that supplies a convenient point of departure for this chapter's line of argument.

In a surviving fragment of his speech against Gaius Gracchus's proposal of citizenship for the Latin allies in 122, the consul Gaius Fannius warned his audience of the fearful consequences in store should the legislation pass:

1. The entwinement of chorality, mimesis, and civic institutions in Plato's *Laws*: Folch 2016.

2. Philodemus *De piet.* 27–28, with Lightfoot 2002, 216–17.

3. Philodemus *De piet.* 26: τοῖς νόμοις [συμπερι]φοράς, rendered in Obbink 1996 as "social conformity to the laws."

si Latinis ciuitatem dederitis, credo, existimatis uos ita ut constitistis in contione habituros locum aut ludis et festis interfuturos. nonne illos omnia occupaturos putatis?

I think you imagine that if you give the citizenship to the allies you'll have a place in the *contio* or remain involved in the games and the festivals, just as you do now. Don't you realize they will occupy everything?[4]

Peter Wiseman cites this fragment at the beginning of his review of Frank Bernstein's *Ludi publici* in order to underline the importance of participation in the games and festivals to the construction of civic identity at Rome.[5] Fannius's positioning of the games and festivals on the same level as participation in the *contio*—and his enumeration of the three among the perks of citizenship, with other seemingly more prominent perks such as voting elided—is strong incentive for us to appreciate the cresting political importance of the *ludi* in the third and second centuries, well before games and festivals blossomed into showcases for the late republican and early Imperial elite.[6] Fannius's words, and Wiseman's engagement with them, orient this chapter's attempt to interpret the festival culture that emerged around temples and their anniversary celebrations as sites for the cultivation and dissemination of what students of collective action analyze under the rubric of "common knowledge": the distributed recognition that you know what I know, and that I know what you know.[7] My objective in the following pages is to explore how religious festivals fabricated new molds for civic self-awareness and common knowledge that were then filled in by new arrivals to the mid-republican city. By the late third century, Latins, Italians, and assorted non-Romans were making their way to Rome for *ludi*, in a migratory pattern that anticipated the post–Punic War influx of concern to Fannius. Social interaction at the games enhanced not only their knowledge of Roman institutions and their knowledge of one another but also their aggregative understanding of the extent to which others were becoming more knowledgeable about Roman institutions. This traffic in knowledge is part of Rome's mid-republican state formation story.

4. Fannius *ORF*[3] fr. 3. Cicero's praise for the speech: *Brut.* 26.99; for other ancient sources on the law and the speech see Greenidge and Clay 1986, 41. Bibliography on the Gracchan proposal and the reactions to it: Mouritsen 2006, 418 n. 2. Two complementary recent takes on the speech: Beard 2015, 236–37; Padilla Peralta 2015.

5. Wiseman 2008, 166.

6. See Cic. *Sest.* 106 with Hopkins 1983, 14–20. For a distillation of Athenian civic identity that parallels Fannius's statement in its weighting of festival culture, see Kleokritos's speech after the fall of the oligarchy: Xen. *Hell.* 2.4.20–2, stimulatingly reinterpreted in Azoulay and Ismard 2018, 50–57.

7. Definition and basic exposition: Chwe 2003. Application to classical Athens: Ober 2008.

The reconstruction of this migratory pattern's quantitative aspects will be deferred to chapter 5. This chapter's primary emphasis is on the contribution of festival culture to the promotion of a visible and exportable Roman identity, and on the role of temples in that process. My passing reference in the previous paragraph to Wiseman's critical but sympathetic dialogue with Bernstein singled out two important figures in the study of mid-republican festival culture, each wielding a different methodological rapier: in one corner, Wiseman with his meticulous if at times overzealous accent on theater and mime performed at festivals as conduits for the transmission and dissemination of history leavened with legend; at the other, Bernstein doggedly sifting through every scrap of textual evidence in an effort to piece together the origins and evolution of the public games.[8] By no means are these the only two approaches to festival culture. But even treatments that diverge substantially in focus or conclusions from those of Wiseman and Bernstein tend to share with them three basic and interlocking concerns, remarked briefly in the concluding section of the previous chapter.

The first is how best to go about reconstructing and interpreting the history of the Roman state calendar so as to situate the festivals and games of the middle Republic within their appropriate temporal rhythms. As we noted, reconstructions with this end in mind have a long scholarly history, yet interest in the process of calendar formation as dictated by and through communal engagement and consensus is a relatively recent wrinkle, one that I proposed in the last chapter to understand as inseparable from the materiality of the new temples that were springing up like mushrooms all over the mid-republican city.[9] Second is the question of how the division of time according to the grids of *feriae* and *dies fasti* and *nefasti* recast the rhythms of civic and political life. The structuring of Republican time is rich with information about the deep embeddedness of the gods in the Roman community's experience of temporality and about elite-aristocratic discourses concerned with processing that experience, as first Varro and much later Macrobius were quick to discern.[10] Last, one has to grapple with the dizzying polysemy of the festivals themselves, which made them playgrounds of interpretive possibility. Although the sometimes-contradictory significations that were ascribed to some of the major festivals in late republican and early Imperial sources were a source of great vexation to previous generations of scholarship on Roman religion—with its fixation on retrieving the "original" meaning and structure of the festivals in a hypothetically pure

8. Criticisms of Wiseman's interpretive overreach: Flower 1995 on the *fabula praetexta* (which I take up below); Purcell 1997, reviewing Wiseman 1995.

9. The "broad consensus" as prerequisite for calendrical reform: Rüpke 2012b, 107.

10. Varro *LL* 6.12 and Macr. *Sat.* 1.16.2–3 with Scheid 2003, 46–59.

Italic, non-Hellenized or otherwise nondecadent past—in recent years the field has taken on board lessons from anthropological literature on the hermeneutic lability of rituals and become more willing to embrace the notion of festivals as sites for the overproduction of cultural meaning.[11]

However, the predominantly literary slant of the scholarship has precluded a full engagement with the material signature of mid-republican Rome's festival environments. Two underappreciated aspects in particular stand out. First, the economic parameters of festival culture during the middle Republic remain in dire need of reassessment. While the drive toward conspicuous consumption in the mounting of late republican and imperial *ludi* has stimulated much conversation among both ancients and moderns, the nature and magnitude of this consumption cannot simply be retrojected to the third century. To be sure, unusual technological or logistical feats at third-century festive celebrations did earn a place in Roman cultural memory.[12] Nonetheless, the outlandish spending that elicited Cicero's chastising commentary will not have been in play for much of the middle Republic; it is only in the decades after the Second Punic War that expenditure on games escalates to the point of disruptive concern.[13] In any event, what is clear is that already in its earliest mid-republican forms festival culture created opportunities for economic transactions of various kinds. As the caretaking of temples created new job opportunities, so too did the staging of games and festivals; numerous occupational niches emerged in their wake, from the performance troupes charged with putting on commissioned productions to the *dissignatores* who after our period monitored seat assignments.[14] Yet recent studies on the economic dimensions of festivals in the Roman world have with relatively few exceptions

11. The fixation: Warde Fowler 1911; cf. Harmon 1978a and b for pristine "origins" followed by contamination and "decline." Criticism: North 1989, 602–4. The "complex of times": Beard [1987] 2003, an argument anticipated in Schilling 1964, 55; cf. Beard et al. 1998, 46–48.

12. E.g., the first time elephants were ferried across Mediterranean waters, for the triumph of L. Caecilius Metellus: Pliny *NH* 8.6.16 with Padilla Peralta 2017a, 263.

13. Cic. *De off.* 2.55 on the largess *quarum memoriam aut breuem aut nullam omnino sint relicturi*; cf. the orator's correspondence with M. Caelius Rufus over the latter's request for panthers from Cilicia (*Fam.* 2.11.2, 8.2.2); for his sharp if oversimplifying distinction between *privata luxuria* and *magnificentia publica* see *Mur.* 76–77 with Dubois-Pelerin 2016. Late republican ludic expenditure and its potential for "ruinöser Amtsobliegenheit": Bernstein 1998, 298–308. The second-century moment and the recourse to sumptuary legislation: Polyb. 31.28.6 with Chemain 2016, 127–28; see Padilla Peralta 2018a, xl n. 41 for bibliography on elite banqueting and n. xx below for distributions at sacrifices.

14. Further on seat assignments see n. 74 below. The earliest literary reference to a *dissignator* is in Plautus: *Poen.* 19–20. Epigraphic testimony for a late republican *dissignator* has raised some eyebrows: *ILLRP* 771 with Wiseman 2016, 145–46.

steered clear of the middle Republic's patchy evidence, gravitating instead toward the relative abundance of literary and epigraphic testimonies from later periods.[15]

More surprising and worrisome is the continuing lack of attention to the communicative dynamics of festival culture. At first glance, it might seem as if this topic too has earned an appropriate amount of time in the spotlight. Ancient descriptions of religious processions, such as Fabius Pictor's vivid depiction of the *ludi Romani*, have been mined for what they disclose about the performative and communicative elements of festival culture's metamorphosis of space and place, and its privileging of "distinction and control" as a primary means of social signaling.[16] Walter Burkert's classic exposition of the festival procession as "the fundamental medium of group formation" underpins much excellent recent scholarship on Greco-Roman festivals, with the agency of the gods not as detached observers but as active and engaged participants in the theatrics of procession and sacrifice eliciting particularly strong interest.[17] For Republican Rome, the literature on games and festivals as communicative consensus-building rituals has proliferated in recent years. The embodiment and replication of the Republican body politic in festival settings tapped into mechanisms for shaping and guiding civic and communal *memoria* whose general operation has been brought out quite well in recent studies.[18] But not nearly enough has been made of the specifically religious inflection and content of civic common knowledge at mid-republican festivals. This knowledge was not just about the near or distant historical past or about the aristocracy's virtuous accomplishments but about other citizens and noncitizens who happened to be participating. That Roman festivals were prime sites for the aggregation and dissemination of information—including information about cultural practices—will come as no surprise to ancient

15. On markets and fairs at festivals see De Ligt and De Neeve 1988; De Ligt 1993 on the *nundinae* or periodic markets; Frayn 1993 on *macella* and permanent markets. Comparative perspectives on preindustrial markets: Feinman and Garrity 2010.

16. *FRHist* F 15 with Rüpke 2012a, 309–12 and 316–18; the passage is preserved in Dionysius of Halicarnassus *AR* 7.72.1–15, on whose agenda here see *FRHist* III.31–33 and Barker 2017, 77–80. Further on the semantics and syntax of Republican *pompae*: Hölkeskamp 2017, chap. 7. Cf. Athenaeus 196a–203b with Cain 1995, 121 on the "museale Präsentation" of the gods in Ptolemy II Philadelphus's lavish processional exhibition in Alexandria; Xenophon of Ephesus 1.2.2–5 on the procession of Artemis at Ephesus.

17. Burkert 1985, 99. For a careful reconstruction of a historically documented procession see Rogers 1991, 80–126 on imperial Ephesus; on "civic co-operation and participation" as a central theme of Roman imperial festivals, Price 1984, chap. 5, esp. sections II–IV. The gods as active viewers: Naiden 2012b, 321–27.

18. See Flower 2009 and 2014; Hölkeskamp 2010, chap. 8 on symbolic capital.

historians of the eastern Mediterranean.[19] Nor is it all that surprising that ethnographically minded outsiders took an active interest in Roman festivals, funneling the lessons they had gleaned from autopsy or secondhand reports into their reconstructions of Roman culture.[20] To narrate how precisely the distribution of religious configured information interacted with other political and cultural mechanisms is, however, not as transparent a historiographical operation as one may think or hope, as a brief aside on scholarship about Athenian festivals will illustrate.

As with the Roman calendar, much scholarly energy was initially expended on assembling and interpreting the evidence for the Attic festival calendar, with some consideration of the political and performative features of the major celebrations.[21] Building on Felix Jacoby's insights and seeking to initiate a more explicit dialogue with historical and anthropological scholarship on the politicization of festivals in the Middle Ages and Renaissance, W. R. Connor took the step of detailing how civic festivals interacted with political developments in late archaic and classical Athens.[22] In recent years, the scholarship on civic festivals has ventured into economic issues (by taking up questions of financing) and sought to contextualize eruptions of *stasis* and civic upheaval at festivals (with the help of sociological and political scientific research into collective action). Matthew Simonton has flagged Greek festivals as prime locations not only for forms of democratic behavior and expression but also for manipulative interventions by plot-hatching insurrectionists.[23] Two of the conceptual underpinnings of his account are "interpresence" and "intervisibility," terms applied in the social-scientific literature to those contingent properties of social environments that allow participants not only to see and be seen by others but also to gauge and anticipate how others respond to a common experience. Once interpreted within this framework, explosions of *stasis* at Athenian and other Greek festivals become much more comprehensible. Thus, for example, the famous decision of the Athenian tyrannicides Harmodius and Aristogeiton to enact their deed at a festival becomes all the more intelligible in light of the degree of access, coordination,

19. The network effects of Greek and Jewish festivals: Rutherford 2017, 203–9.

20. The shock of outsiders is revealing: see Polyb. 30.22.1–12 with Champion 2018b, 38–41; on the grotesqueries of L. Anicius Gallus's *ludi* note also Gildenhard 2010, 168 and Feeney 2016, 147–49s. On the ethnographic labors of Timaeus of Tauromenium see nn. 87 and 89 below.

21. Mikalson 1975; Parke 1977; Simon 1983. The politics of Athenian festival culture, beginning with Solon: Jacoby 1944.

22. Connor 1987.

23. Simonton 2017, chap. 5. The costs and financing of Athenian festivals: Von Reden 2007, 405–6; Pritchard 2012 (repeated in 2015 and followed by Ober 2015, 500); for expenditures on the Great Dionysia note also Wilson 2008.

and (inter)visibility that were made available at festival time to the residents of the *polis*.[24]

Tacking westward from Athens, this chapter will apply the notion of intervisibility to its investigation of Roman festival culture, working toward the argument that in its mid-republican iteration this festival culture relied heavily on the physical presence of temples to communicate a very specific message about Roman identity. Some of this investigation will take the form of close readings of fragmentary literary evidence, boosted from time to time with a glance at the materiality of the monumental landscape. My main contention will be that the mid-republican promotion and regulation of intervisibility organized itself around the seemingly nonstop multiplication of temples and public festivals as a means of warding off the specter of civic insurrection—one area in which the Rome that came into being after the Licinian-Sextian Rogations differed strikingly from those classical and Hellenistic Greek poleis that were bedeviled by episodes of *stasis*—and as a means of communicating a coherent and credible message about the *res publica*'s values. The sheer amount of civic time that was colonized by public festivals and cult celebrations of all kinds, including those not explicitly linked to temple anniversaries, will have lain behind the efficient and effective circulation of this message: whereas an Athenian of the classical or Hellenistic periods could anticipate around fifty cultic celebrations a year, by the end of the third century the average Roman will have been exposed to at least double that amount.[25] To be sure, festivals did multiply across the Hellenistic East over time; what made Roman festival culture unique is how highly and repetitively concentrated it came to be in Rome itself.[26]

It should of course be stressed that Rome was no typical Greek *polis* with a typical *demos*; in terms of scale alone, Rome had already entered a league of its own by the late third century.[27] It is all the more curious, then, that one

24. The tactical and strategic affordances of Greek festivals and spectacles: Simonton 2017, 194–221.

25. The calculation for classical and Hellenistic Athens: Von Reden 2010, 166, following Rosivach 1994. Figures for festival days in the years 216–159: Taylor 1937, only counting those days available for *ludi scaenici*; for quantification of the total amount of civic time consumed by festivals see chapter 6.

26. Classical and Hellenistic Athens: Von Reden 2010, 166, following Rosivach 1994. Festival days at Rome in the years 216–159: Taylor 1937, only counting those days available for *ludi scaenici*; for a full quantification of the total amount of civic time consumed by festivals see chapter 6 below. Generally on Hellenistic festival culture: Chaniotis 2018a, chap. 15, esp. 352–53.

27. Cf. Scheidel 2010b on "the never-never land fashioned from Hellenic ideals of *demos* and *polis*." Comparison of Athenian dramatic culture and its Roman counterpart: Gildenhard 2010, 165.

has to wait until the late Republic to encounter incidents of violent civic upheaval at Roman festivals,[28] which prompts the question of what had enabled festivals to remain relatively friction-free in a city of such size for so long. Certainly part of the explanation lies in the careful management of spaces and times for political discourse within the mid-republican city. By the time of the Gracchi, if not well before, political communication between elite and the masses was primarily an affair of the *contio*, where passions ran high and simmering tensions were most likely to erupt into collective action.[29] *Ludi* and festivals seem with relatively few exceptions to have been much less fraught with danger during the middle Republic, perhaps because of the novelty appeal of their adaptation into the calendar. Since well-received games appear to have enhanced the reputation and augmented the social capital of the men responsible for organizing them,[30] praetorian and aedilician sponsors were exceedingly solicitous in introducing and fine-tuning their entertainment choices with a view to scoring points in the public eye. When festival culture and political culture do bleed into each other in the late Republic—in some cases rather literally—it is mainly because of the ingenuity of those *populares* politicians who recognized the communicative advantages of holding *contiones* during *feriae publicae*.[31] As late republican episodes would reveal time and again, the politics of festival culture extended past questions of entertainment to the means and circumstances of communal interaction and civic self-definition; the full force of Fannius's words derived equally from the sheer embodied presence of non-Roman Others at festivals and from the political sentimentality capable of being fired up by their presence. It is for this specific reason that the concept of intervisibility affords us special traction in docu-

28. Memorably in the lead-up to the Social War: the *consilium* of the disaffected allies to assassinate the Roman consuls Lucius Marcius Philippus and Sex. Julius Caesar at the Latin festival on the Alban Mount, and the murder of legates at the *ludi* in Asculum (Flor. 2.6.8–9; note also Diod. Sic. 37.12, App. *B Civ.* 1.38, and Obsequens 54). Rioting at the Compitalia of 67: Asconius 45 and 64–65C with Aldrete 2013, 434 and Flower 2017, 241–43, both citing earlier discussions.

29. The significance of the *contio*: Pina Polo 1996; Millar 1998; Morstein-Marx 2004; Hölkeskamp 2017, chap. 6. The *contio*'s religious backdrop: chapter 3 n. 57. The scale of participation in *comitia* and *contiones*: Mouritsen 2001, chap. 2; Scheidel 2006. On sites of political exchange besides the *contio*, see, e.g., Flower 2013a on *vici*, about which more below; cf. Taylor 2018, 162–64 on centurion elections as an aspect of "the political character of the Roman Republic."

30. But note the energetic volley against this position in Gruen 1992, 188–94.

31. For the most notorious episodes see now Barja de Quiroga 2018, 12–17, with n. 66 for important bibliography.

menting the inputs and outputs of mid-republican festival culture, which, although rather staid by comparison to its late-republican successor, did not lack for productive tension.

In fourth- and third-century Rome, festivals took off as prime sites for civic intervisibility because their inception and celebration was closely bound to the monumentalizing landscape, which contributed its own messaging to the consensus-building traffic in shared knowledge. The propagation of shared knowledge in festival contexts familiarized Latin and non-Latin allies with what was believed to make Rome special, facilitating their quasi-voluntary compliance with the demands of the mid-republican state in the process. Although plenty of "blood-soaked possibilities" existed for the reaffirmation of citizenship and alliance,[32] festival settings offered additional and arguably even more constructive opportunities for such affirmation, in ritual forms different from but complementary to those available through military service. The environment of festivals, games, and theater enabled community-bonding and building behaviors in part by unveiling and performing a vision of the *res publica* in which the gods were present and active; the gods were believed to be in attendance as citizens themselves—albeit uniquely powerful ones; and the rituals devoted to them had to be executed flawlessly or else repeated from scratch.[33] This concern for proper form was not merely fastidiousness for fastidiousness's sake. Through their orchestration according to a carefully monitored system of rules (that were made explicit precisely in the act of fussing over their observance), festivals and games continuously performed and reperformed the idealization of the *res publica* as a utopia of proper religious procedure. The repetitive performance of attention to ritual form over many years is what propelled festivals and games to the status of institutions; their appearance on the virtual landscape of the Roman imaginary in tandem with the monumental reproduction of temples in the urban landscape drove the coalescence of a flexible system of rules and norms that bound together the religious and political realms in the civic life of the Roman state.[34]

Behind these festival-specific rules and norms there existed real human beings, trafficking in information about one another and the wider community of which they formed part. Threading through this chapter's exposition and analysis of the relevant evidence is the desire to isolate the metamorpho-

32. Rüpke 2012b, 316.

33. Cic. *Har. Resp.* 23 with Bernstein 1998, 84–95 and North 2000, 52. The gods as citizens: Scheid 1985a, followed by Ando 2010, 60.

34. This system as a mode of *Reglementierung*: Bernstein 1998, 268–98.

sis of cultural knowledge into common knowledge as a driving factor behind the hammering of a new civic identity in the smithy of religious practice. My chief objective is to set festival culture before the reader as an attractive candidate for the engineering of what Clifford Ando has termed "the ontology of the social."[35] That festival banqueting in particular furnished opportunities for elite homosociality is as true for the Roman world as for its Greek counterpart, yet the premise and promise of social intervisibility extended to nonelites as well.[36] Reanimated every single time that animals were slaughtered and portions of their meat distributed for elite and nonelite consumption,[37] the materiality and physicality of sustained carnivalesque interaction with Rome's monumental sacred landscape contoured those habits of mind through which Romans re-cognized themselves and their community afresh, and in contradistinction to non-Roman Others.

Accordingly, the first section of this chapter examines the functions and resonances of Roman theater's staging at festivals *in conspectu dei*. The second section develops some ideas about the range and content of theater culture's communicative ambitions by analyzing fragments from the works of the Hellenistic Greek poet Callimachus and the Roman dramatists Naevius and Plautus. With these three authors, I concentrate on the transmission of cultural knowledge within settings of performance-mediated intervisibility as a powerful and lasting consequence of movements to Rome during festival time. Although the interpretations that this chapter proposes for the most part privilege sight over the other senses, the dynamics of (inter)visibility were not the only sensorial axis along which social communication unfolded during mid-republican spectacles.[38] As already mentioned, "the mnemonic force of food" in the production of the new communal sensorium that accompanied the

35. I borrow the phrase from Ando 2015, chap. 3, discussing the cognitive textures of Roman law; note also Ando 2010 on the ontology of Rome's religious institutions.

36. For the healing of the rift between Scipio Africanus and Tib. Sempronius Gracchus (father of the Gracchi) over dinner at the *epulum Iovis* see Val. Max. 4.2.3 with Mueller 2002, 72–74. The early and mid-republican background to the institution of the *epulum Iovis*: Bernstein 1998, 285–87. Banqueting at temples: chapter 3 n. 68. For overviews of the (mostly late republican and early Imperial) evidence on religious banquets, see Donahue 2003, 428–32 and Marzano 2009, 84–86; Rüpke 1995b, 277 for an attempt to compute the cost of meat as a component of the overall expenditure for *ludi* (on which see also Taylor 2017, 157–58); D'Arms 1998 and 2000, 195–97 on Caesar's precedent-shattering *epula publica*.

37. The amount of meat obtainable from the major sacrificial animals: Naiden 2012a; for the distance traveled by the smell of cooking flesh, Betts 2011, 123 n. 27; for (later) testimonies about the preferability and pricing of sacrificial meat, McDonough 2004.

38. Usefully on the visual bias of studies of movement and ritual in the city of Rome: Betts 2011.

transformation of the mid-republican state should not be overlooked.[39] Where we can monitor the operations of this sensorium more confidently, however, is in the material record of human-divine encounters at cult sites in Rome and elsewhere in central Italy. Chapter 5 will reengage some of the same questions that are explored in this chapter with the aid of a different corpus of evidence: the material record of anepigraphic and inscribed votives whose presence cues us not only to the importance of tactility in histories of mid-republican religious observance, but also to the formation of mobility corridors and networks along which information traveled—for consumption by citizens and allies alike.

I. Performative Festival Culture as Social Technology

This opening section will alight on one dimension of theatrical performance at the mid-republican *ludi* that made it unusually potent as a vehicle for the transmission of knowledge about Roman culture and specifically Rome's investment in religious practice to citizens and foreigners alike: its staging *in conspectu dei*, with temples and their cult statues supplying a para-textual and para-performative enhancement for the spectacle. Temple construction had two significant infrastructural ramifications for the institution of theater, both of which are now well studied in isolation but not sufficiently appreciated together. The first is that, until permanent theaters made their late republican debut at Rome, it was the city's temples, and space in front of and around these temples, that supplied the necessary infrastructure for the staging of theatrical performances. As a consequence, theater emerged and evolved in continuous and often intentional dialogue with the sacred structures dotting Rome's urban landscape, as numerous metatheatrical references in early Roman drama—and the social learning promoted through theatrical performance—make explicit. In the process, theater became an exceptionally fertile incubator for communal religious discourse and critique, in part because it physically manifested the wiring of Roman communal identity around cult to the gods.

At first glance, the *Agora und Theater* civic topography and institutional morphology of the classical and Hellenistic Greek city-state does not seem to apply to Republican Rome; despite numerous Roman encounters with this arrangement in the course of the *res publica*'s expansion into south Italy and

39. I borrow the quoted phrase and line of thought from Hamilakis 2014, 84–92. For the mid-third-century turn in what Hamilakis terms "gustemology" see Purcell 2003b; on Pythagoreanism and vegetarianism at Rome, Volk 2015.

Sicily,[40] the traditionalist aversion to the construction of a permanent stone theater at Rome held steadfast until Pompey's dedication of his theater in 55. Makeshift wooden structures did go up, with their construction and takedown offering the senatorial aristocracy a ritualized means of asserting control over dramatic production; a coordinated censorial attempt to erect a stone theater in the 150s ultimately came to nothing, and second-century efforts to build permanent structures were repeatedly stymied.[41] Couched in the language of *mores*, the resistance of some elites to the erection of a permanent structure was grounded in the suspicion that such structures would enjoy a second life as sites for illicit assembly.[42] In the first century, Pompey was only able to scrape away this barnacled conservatism by incorporating a temple to Venus Victrix within the *cavea* of his theater; the interarticulation of this theater to sacred ritual was further strengthened by the regular offering of sacrifices to divine qualities in the precinct.[43]

In this respect, Pompey's theater actually hewed to a different sort of convention: the centuries-old Italic paradigm of the theater-temple that has been documented archaeologically for late third- and early second-century Cagliari in Sardinia, late third- and early second-century Gabii, second-century Praeneste, late second- and early first-century Pietrabbondante, and late-second and early first-century Tibur.[44] Archaic precedents for this configuration of

40. See purely, e.g., the *Agora und Theater* complex of Hippana (mod. Montagna dei Cavalli), captured by Roman forces in 258: Vassallo 2012. Roman soldiers' exposure to Greek culture in Sicily during the First Punic War: Feeney 2016, 123.

41. Wooden theaters: Vitr. *De arch*. 5.5.7–8 with Welch 2007, 58–65 and Gruen 1992, 209; cf. Kondratieff 2010, 101–2 for the "wooden grandstands" of the Gradus Aurelii as the praetor's tribunal in post-Sullan Rome. Permanent structures: Liv. 40.51.3 on the contracting for a theater and proscenium near the temple of Apollo Medicus, with Marshall 2006, 37–38 on the theatrical associations of this neighborhood; Beare 1964, 171–72 and Bernstein 1998, 294–98 for other abortive efforts; Tan 2016 (to whose citations in n. 1 add Orosius 4.21.4) on the stone theater commissioned by the censors of 154/53.

42. For a statement to this effect see Cic. *Flac*. 15–17 with Taylor 1966, 29–33 and Frézouls 1983, 110–11. The dual-purposing of Greek theaters for *Volksammlungen*: Kolb 1981; Marconi 2012, 185–87 for evidence from late classical and Hellenistic Sicily; cf. Hansen and Fischer-Hansen 1994. On other factors behind the resistance to permanent structures see Feeney 2016, 128.

43. Beard et al. 1998, 122–23 and Davies 2017b, 491–96. Hanson 1959a, chap. 3, on the religious aspect of Pompey's theater remains essential. The Pompeian complex: Sauron 1987; Gros in *LTUR* s.v. "Theatrum Pompei"; Russell 2016, chap. 7, esp. 173–76 on the "sacred aura" of the structure. Julius Caesar's decision a decade later to demolish a temple in order to build a theater: Dubois-Pelerin 2016; see chapter 3 n. 189.

44. Hülsemann 1987, 132–37 with Abb. 37–39; Sear 2006, 44–45; Griffith 2013, 246–48; for the Hercules Victor complex at Tibur see Ceccarelli and Marroni 2011, 538–52. Hieronian Syra-

theater and temple could also be cited.[45] One lesson to derive from this history is that at Rome even change came dressed in familiar garb; if Pompey was applying himself to resolving "a specifically and uniquely Roman problem" by integrating a temple into his theater,[46] the solution that he settled on had precedents. Moreover, the association of theaters with the sacred was hardly confined to Republican Italy; the placement of theaters within sanctuary complexes is attested in the classical and Hellenistic Greek world, remained archaeologically visible in the Greek East well into the Roman Empire, and was repeatedly appropriated and customized to local specifications in the Roman provinces during the first two centuries CE.[47] Yet it is the sociocultural specificity of Italic theater-temples that will be of interest to us here, not only because their example will have informed Pompey's decision but also because they disclose how theater and temple interfaced with each other during the late third and early second centuries.

Reading the literary sources against the archaeological evidence then available, in 1959 J. A. Hanson argued that at least two sets of games and their component *scaenici* were staged directly in front of the temples of Flora and Magna Mater respectively: the *ludi Florales* and the *Megalenses*.[48] At the time of Hanson's publication, excavations on the Palatine were bringing to light the design of the temple of Magna Mater and its precinct, emboldening Hanson to speculate with some confidence that the temple's elevation on a high podium and the open space in front of the temple explained Cicero's remark that the *Megalenses* unfolded *in ipso Matris magnae conspectu*.[49] However, it was not until the Palatine excavations that Patrizio Pensabene led and Sander Goldberg's interpretation of the finds that the organization and function of the Magna Mater precinct snapped into focus.[50] At the time of its dedication in 191, the temple rose almost nine meters in the air and was approachable in

---

cuse's theater featured a stoa on its upper level that bracketed a *heroon*; Wilson 2013, 89 speculates that this design imitated sanctuary complexes at Kos and Rhodes. The second-century theaters built in Pompeii, Sarno, Capua, Cales, Teanum Sidicinum, and Lanuvium that were *not* part of temple complexes: Rawson 1991c, 471–72, citing Lauter 1976.

45. Nielsen 2007, 241–42 for the details.

46. Goldberg 1998, 12.

47. Sear 2006, 45–46 lists examples. Evocatively on theaters and urbanization in the Empire: Frézouls 1983, 112–24.

48. Hanson 1959a, chap. 1 for the reconstruction; for further exposition with a view to late republican politics see Wiseman 2009, 164–69. For the history of these two temples see now Papi in *LTUR* s.v. "Flora, aedes" and Pensabene in *LTUR* s.v. "Magna Mater, aedes."

49. Cic. *Har. resp.* 24 with Hanson 1959a, 14–15.

50. Pensabene 1979, 1985, 1988, and 1995; Goldberg 1998, 3–8. Updated topographical overview: Coarelli 2007, 135–38.

front by two sets of stairs. A fire several decades later led to the raising of the plaza and construction over the original stairs.[51] These stairs will have made excellent candidates for seating, and the paved open area immediately in front of the temple would have easily accommodated a stage. All in all, approximately 1,500 to 2,000 spectators could have been accommodated, a figure that coheres well with the evidence for actor-audience intimacy (and cheek-by-jowl seating) in Plautine comedy.[52] Goldberg went on to conclude that it was at this site and at this performative scale that the first *ludi Megalenses*, which featured an inaugural performance of Plautus's *Pseudolus*, were conducted to celebrate the temple's dedication. Future iterations of the *ludi* included four performances of Terence's plays in the 160s.

Although we cannot be certain that temples dedicated before the Magna Mater's installation also functioned as impromptu venues for the staging of theater, signs that *scaenici* and temple dedications became progressively entangled may attest to the practice's existence prior to the events of 191.[53] Not all plays were staged right in front of a temple; there is good reason to believe that Plautus's *Curculio* was staged in the Forum, for example. However, given how much public space was occupied by temples at the time of Roman drama's "birth," it would have been nearly impossible for any dramatic performance in or outside the Forum to escape having some sacred edifice as a backdrop.[54] That Hellenized Roman drama, pioneered by Livius Andronicus and Naevius and refined by Plautus and Terence, took off at the same time as the urban landscape was being populated with temples is thus significant in no small part because temple dedications supplied opportunities for dramatic performance—and because the structures provided the built environment against which drama calibrated its performance and messaging. Obviously, seeing as the emergence of a Latin dramatic literature was overdetermined,[55] I will not be suggesting that the temple construction/dramatic performance nexus is to be credited in full for its genesis and evolution. But the presence of temples in Rome's urban environment inflected and conditioned the early trajectory of that dramatic literature, with repercussions not only for that lit-

51. The fire of 111: Obsequens 39.

52. Goldberg 1998, 7–8; 13–15.

53. See chapter 3 n. 134. Cf. Nielsen 2007, 245–46 for *scaenici* at the inaugural *ludi saeculares*; 247–49 for *scaenici* in front of the temples of Apollo Medicus, Ceres-Liber-Libera, and Flora.

54. Moore 1991 on the choragus's speech in *Curculio* 462–86 and its framing by the Forum's built environment, with Marshall 2006, 40–43 for revision of Moore's reading. For dramatic performances in the Forum see now Goldberg 2018; cf. Welch 2007, 49–57 with figs. 21–28 for temporary seating structures and arrangements during the second and first centuries.

55. See chapter 1 n. 20.

erature's elite pretensions but also for its resonance and appeal to nonelites. The hesitation to decouple drama from sacred monumental structures discloses not only a determination to avoid "invalidat[ing] the strong link between performances and religious festivals" but also an awareness of this packaging's potency.[56]

Laid bare in some of the *palliata*'s most celebrated metatheatrical gestures, Roman theater's continuous and often explicit dialogue with the temples dotting Rome's urban landscape is exemplified in the types of social learning that dramatic performances promoted. The addition of festivals and their repetition through *instauratio* during and after the Second Punic War ensured regular practice in the promotion and strengthening of the associative and ideological networks that linked together sacred observance, state oversight, and theatrical entertainment.[57] At the same time, state control over dramatic production, which was supervised by aediles and praetors, communicated "public sanction for the dramatic arts and its linkage to the national religion."[58] Rome was not unlike other Hellenistic states in taking an active role in the management of theatrical entertainments, or in hitching the performance of theater to festivals.[59] However, one of the more revealing differences between Roman theater and its Greek precedents and parallels is the extremely pronounced religious content of Roman theater. Even though it is no longer plausible to hold that Hellenistic drama in the Greek East steadily divested itself of religious content,[60] the religious flavor of Roman drama is exceptional, and in the case of Plautus nearly impossible to ignore. This inflection is marked by, among other things, the many allusions to and appearances by divine figures, in some cases calibrated for obvious metatheatrical impact; the stage's sustained engagement with female-led and Bacchic cults, topics of growing political and institutional concern in the years on either side of 200; and, by the mid-second century at the latest, the mobilization of theater as a site for reli-

56. Giusti 2018, 66.

57. Roman obsession with the *instauratio* of *ludi*: Dio Cassius 12 fr. 51. *Instaurationes* and days for theater: Taylor 1937, followed by Duckworth [1952] 1994, 77 and Gruen 1992, 187; Bernstein 1998, 282–91. "Civilian morale" as the reason for *instaurationes* of *scaenici* during the Second Punic War: Konstan 1983, 23 with n. 20; cf. Leigh 2004, 3. Note Barbiero 2019, 298 on the significance of the fact that we have no evidence for the performance of *fabulae palliatae* outside of the *ludi*.

58. Gruen 1992, 197. The designation of an office in the Aventine temple of Minerva for a guild of writers and actors: Festus 446–48 L. with Jory 1970, Gruen 1990, 87–91, and Brown 2002, 226–27.

59. Jocelyn 1969, 15, distilling Tarn 1961, 113–15. For updated assessment of the Hellenistic state of affairs see the contributions to Le Guen 1997.

60. Lightfoot 2002, 216–24 for a critique of the presumption of "increasing secularisation."

gious critique.[61] The immanent sense that the Roman theater represented "a religious world" and itself pertained to the category of human-divine relations—no matter how jocular its depictions of the *dii*—would receive its most decisive confirmation in Varro's classification of theater among *res divinae.*[62] Signs of Roman drama's brewing self-conception as a genre for wrestling with questions of theology and ritual are already apparent by the end of the third century, and no later than the first few decades of the second at the absolute latest.

While a play was in itself "not a festival or ritual," early Roman drama is so thoroughly saturated with theological preoccupations as to give the lie to any reading of its religious valence or function as decorative or neutral.[63] Plautus's *Amphitruo* opens with the appearance of Mercury on stage; the god proceeds to crack a joke about Jupiter's forthcoming appearance in the comedy. For all its wrapping in coy metatheatricality, one of the more earnest preliminaries to the joke is Mercury's reiteration of the beneficence of the gods to the Roman public, characterized as a thematic fixture of Roman tragedy.[64] On one level, Mercury's remarks enact a generic differentiation between comic and tragic depictions of the gods. On another level, these generically marked depictions play off and against each other so deftly in part because of their activation through performance in the presence of those temples whose monumentality is an ever-present reminder of the gods' favor toward the Roman state, as exemplified most concretely in the *res publica*'s military exploits. It is not for nothing that Mercury's asyndetonic list consists of divinities who had not only

61. *Vicinus Apollo* in Plautus's *Bacchides* and the proximity of the play's performance to the temple of Apollo Medicus: Marshall 2006, 38–40. A possible metatheatrical temple reference in Ennius: *Tr.* frr. 94a–b Goldberg-Manuwald (*Medea*), *asta atque Athenas anticum opulentum oppidum / contempla <u>et templum Cereris ad laeuam aspice</u>*. The regular appearance of gods in Plautus: Duckworth [1952] 1994, 296–98; cf. Gellar-Goad 2013 for the situation in Terence. The religious content of Plautine comedy: Fraenkel [1922] 2007, 124–25 and 242–44 on ritual language; Toliver 1952 and Hanson 1959a for arguments over the intentions and consequences of this content; Dunsch 2009, Padilla Peralta 2017c, and Clark 2019 for updated discussions. Women and women's cult in Roman drama: Schuhmann 1977; Flower 2000 on Bacchants.

62. *ARD* fr. 4 Cardauns = *apud* Aug. *De civ.* 6.3 with Freyburger 2000, 43.

63. I am thinking of Slater 2000, 2; more congenial for my purposes is Clark 2019, 218–19.

64. Mercury's joke: *Amph.* 86–95. The reminder: *nam quid ego memorem (ut alios <u>in tragoediis</u> | uidi, Neptunum Virtutem Victoriam / Martem Bellonam commemorare quae bona / uobis fecissent) quis benefactis meus pater / deorum regnator, architectust omnibus?* (41–45). "The religious character of early Roman tragedy": Freyburger 2000. The second-century "systematization of religion" in the tragic dramas of Accius: Rüpke 2012b, chap. 4. Mercury in early Latin literature: Biggs 2019, esp. 214–15 on his Plautine appearances.

figured mightily in the war effort on land and at sea but who had also received temples during our period. While it is certainly attractive to take Mercury's designation of Jupiter as *architectus* to refer to Plautus's own labors as a leader of an acting troupe, the label also points the play's audience toward the architectural encasement of Jupiter and Rome's other gods that will have fallen within the sight lines of the stage.[65]

Evidence for the comic stage as mirror and amplifier of public religion is not restricted to Plautus; a fragment from the works of his contemporary Caecilius Statius riffs on the divergence between the auspice-taking of actors on stage and that of magistrates acting on behalf of the community.[66] But it is mostly thanks to the Plautine *palliata* that we are even in position to glimpse the complexities of the discursive process under way at the end of the third century. Even those moments when Plautine comedy's mirthful play with the gods comes off as irreverent and unserious to a modern reader had a special responsibility to discharge, by shifting attention to the Saturnalian dimension of men's relationship with the gods and the predication of that relationship on a measure of controlled chumminess—one that made some allowance for the temporary upending of norms only to reassert those norms.[67] Performed with a light touch, the moralizing sententiousness of the *palliata* worked toward the same end: the vindication of norms whose authority was believed to derive ultimately from their perceived indispensability to the good fortune of Rome and its civic body, as reified and reaffirmed by the very urban fabric within which the *palliata* were staged.[68] Seen in this light, both the appetite for Greek myth on the tragic stage and the send-ups of tragedy on the comic stage served not to displace or attenuate the semantics of the political realm,[69] but to make a political statement through the ritual act of bringing the community around

65. See Christensen 2000, 1–2 n. 5, with *TLL* s.v. "architectus" (Ausfeld) on the term as equivalent to *magister fabricarum/fabrorum*; cf. Plautus *Truc.* 3 with Richlin 2018, 386 for the "architectural" conceit of (slaves) building a city on the stage. For the possibility and payoffs of Plautine commentary on specific temple constructions note Clark 2019, 227.

66. Caecilius Statius *Plocium* fr. 14 Guardì: *insanum auspicium! <num> aliter histrionum est / atque ut magistratus publice cum auspicant?*

67. For comments to this effect see Segal 1968. Slater 2000, 65 draws a line (unnecessary in my view) between "dramaturgical necessity" and the agency of the gods.

68. Hanson 1959a, 85–88 on the Plautine principle of just deserts. For examples of sententiousness see Duckworth 1994, 298–300; cf. 300–304 on "the moral tone of Roman comedy."

69. Much ink has been spilled on Greek myth in Plautus since Fraenkel: for bibliography and assessment of the *status quaestionis*, see Barbiero 2018. On Greek mythology, Roman politics, and Latin drama see Gildenhard 2010, 160–63, whose analysis is more in line with my approach than John Scheid's contention that myth at Rome "was only a complement to the ritual, an ornament designed to charm gods and humans" (2016, 61).

an offering to the gods of the first fruits of Roman conquest: appropriated art, appropriated bodies. This was deadly serious business.

Sententiousness aligned well with the pedagogical dimension of Roman drama, and with the genre's function as a tool for promulgating and consolidating the "thought-world" that came to define Roman society in the last two centuries BCE.[70] Although the Varronian classification of theater among *res divinae* was motivated partly by the place of *ludi scaenici* in the rhythms of cultic observance at Rome, an equally powerful incentive for the classification lay in the potential of theater to teach *res divinae*. Our first sources to comment explicitly on the pedagogical function of theater are late republican in date and make no direct allusion to learning about the gods.[71] With the Christian apologists of the second century CE and after, however, the perceived connection between Roman theater and polytheistic observance, and in particular theater as a pedagogical goad for polytheistic religious practice, is stressed regularly.[72] Despite their distance in space and time from the mid-republican cultural contexts in which Roman drama first arose, the perspicacity of Christian apologists in their analysis of the pedagogical power of Roman theater is relevant to this chapter's objectives. I am not so much interested in the polemical value judgments that accompany this analysis but simply in the general conception of the theater as a site for learning about the gods. This learning drew its vigor not only from the words spoken on the stage but also from the interplay of those words with the settings of performance, as these were framed by and often directly connected to the temple constructions of the mid-republican city. The pedagogical dialectic of word, ritual, and built structure could easily be put to work to generate a fresh and elastic awareness of civic space's pluripotencies, as Plautus's *Truculentus* showcases.[73]

Theater greased the wheels for social knowledge on other fronts as well. The enactment and promotion of status and distinction is apparent from some of our earliest notices about mid-republican drama and its audiences. Although status policing at the theater only takes off in earnest after our period, the closing years of the third century witnessed the first conceptual steps in

70. Exposition of this thought-world: Kaster and Konstan 2016.

71. Bringing home education (*litteras*) from the theater: Varro *Sat. Men.* fr. 218 Cèbe. The crowd singing *quidquid didicere theatris* at the festival of Anna Perenna: Ov. *Fast.* 3.535 with Horsfall 2003, 13–14. Note Cic. *Rosc. Am.* 47 on the theater as an "image of our daily life" (*imaginem uitae cotidianae*); cf. the similar sentiment in Marcus Aurelius *Med.* 11.6.

72. Augustine is explicit about the link: Dox 2004, chap. 1; further on Christian polemic against theater see Webb 2008, chap. 8.

73. Germany 2016 for a reading of the play's manipulation of the urban landscape; Clark 2019 on the contextual resonances of its closing lines and Plautine drama's synergy with sacred urban space more generally. Further on mid-republican spatial taxonomies see chapter 3 n. 4.

this direction: the presence of slave bodies on the stage—a development we will revisit shortly—lent itself all too well to the "public semiotics" of elevation and degradation that came to figure powerfully in the dramatic culture of the later Republic and Empire.[74] But the staging of theater *in conspectu dei* also propelled the cultivation of another species of collectivizing social knowledge, by constituting not only the group of spectators at any one play but the *res publica* as a whole as the type of community whose very entertainments were hardwired to the cult of the gods. Some of the messaging will have been nourished by the design properties of mid-republican temples, which partook of a distinctively Hellenistic commitment to "fronting" the visibility of gods within cult structures; the kinesthetic and psychological imprint of staging drama *in conspectu dei* will not have been diverged appreciably from—indeed at times it would have been paired with—the aesthetics of processing to the temple to behold the god.[75] The legacy of this fusion of entertainment and cult seems also to have left its mark on the architecture and iconography of the *scaenae frons* that was eventually adopted for theater in the second and first centuries BCE: the interweaving of columniation and aedicular niches in the best-preserved *scaenarum frontes* suggests not only a desire to show off sculptural booty but also a conscious effort to mirror the architectural features of those temples that bracketed and defined the urban performance sites for Roman drama.[76] In any event, the deployment of drama in the service of what might be classed as a proto- or para-theology is unveiled in Polybius's revealing use of the verb ἐκτετραγῴδηται to characterize the Roman "performance" of piety in public and private contexts.[77] While not explicitly oriented toward theater, Polybius's choice of words can help us clarify the form that the dialogue about Rome's relationship with the gods took, in the eyes of Romans and non-Romans alike. The routine infusion of popular entertainment with

74. For quoted phrase and explication see Parker 1999, 164–66. The regularization of theater seating in 194: Gruen 1992, 202–5 and Gilula 1996; Jehne 2001, 102 on seating arrangements as *Hierarchisierungsritual*; Dench 2018, 96–98 on theater seating as "quintessentially Roman practice." Public responses to elites at late republican theater performances: Laser 1997.

75. The Hellenistic "theatricalization" of cult statues and its consequences for mid- and late republican Rome: La Rocca 2010, 104–12; on the architectural pedigree of this cultic dynamic in central Italy see the useful comments of Laird 2016, 190 on the "insistent frontality and axiality" of Etrusco-Roman temples. The gaze of the gods as an integral component of Roman urban space: Jenkyns 2013, 26–36.

76. See Klar 2006, commenting on the design properties of the *scaenae frons* as expressive of the desire of second-century Roman commanders to show off triumphal booty.

77. Polyb. 6.56.8. Walbank ad loc. chooses to read the Polybian verb through the prism of "tragic history"—not incompatible with my analysis; further on the tragic flavoring of Roman cult praxis see Jenkyns 2013, 3–4.

this dialogue and the physical embedding of these entertainments within a monumental program of public piety were in their own way public goods, as integral to the maintenance of the civic body as the infrastructural investments outlined in the first part of this book. The upshot of Rome's preoccupation with honing and disseminating public knowledge through theater is the topic of the next section.

II. Dramatic Festival Culture and the Propagation of Knowledge: Three Studies

That Roman theater-temples supplied spaces for the negotiation of "identity and alterity" was already appreciated in antiquity. Vergil, for one, capitalized on the precedent of the mid-republican theater-temple to refract Roman imperial identity through the lens of the barbarian Other.[78] But some questions about the parameters and paratexts of drama's religious spatialization demand closer examination, The premise of this section is that, by ramping up its commitment to theatrical culture in tandem with its urban monumentalization, the Roman state sharply honed its capacity to project certain messages about itself and its citizens to the greater world. I will look first at two fragmentary texts that in separate but mutually complementary ways map the circulation of Rome's messaging about itself to the Hellenistic Mediterranean. The final subsection turns to the internal messaging that the Roman state calibrated to explain to those who were uniquely and violently displaced by its military predations that their exploitation had meaning—and that those who exploited them did so in compliance with what was expected of and inculcated within them, by none other than the gods themselves.

1. *Callimachus and Rome*

One intriguing feature of the fragmentary testimonies for growing Greek awareness of Rome in the fourth and third centuries is that they bear signs of dramatic or performative mediation, the likeliest staging grounds for which would have been festivals. Timaeus of Tauromenium's report of the October Horse celebration, preserved for the purpose of withering mockery by Polybius, is perhaps the clearest example of ethnographic knowledge that drew on the sights and sounds of a Roman festival.[79] As for the theatrical flavoring of Roman culture, Duris of Samos may have been aware of the *devotio* of Decius

78. See Giusti 2019 on Verg. *Geo.* 3.1–48. For "identity and alterity" in early Roman drama see the essays in Manuwald 2000 and bibliography cited at n. 124 below.

79. *FGH* 566 F 36 (*apud* Polyb. 12.4b.1) with Baron 2012, 65–66 for the notice's place in

at Sentinum, an episode that appealed to one second-century dramatist as source material for a *fabula praetexta*; the incident may have had already received a performative workup in the first few decades after the battle.[80] Expanding on Momigliano's terse but powerful reading of these notices as suggestive of the "characteristic Roman features" that earned recognition and comment in the Hellenistic world of the third century,[81] I will engage in this subsection with the surviving scraps of a Callimachean *aition* that seems to have contained the earliest datable reference to Rome in Greek poetry: frr. 106–7 Pfeiffer of the *Aitia*. I will posit that these fragments offer insight not only into the performance context(s) through which Callimachus's Hellenistic contemporaries became acquainted with the culture and history of Italy's rising hegemon—in the generation or so before first Livius Andronicus and then Naevius began composing dramas for staging at Rome—but also in the lessons that were communicated through performance. Because these performance contexts were embedded within festivals that were structured so as to promote the acquisition and transmission of cultural knowledge, the lessons absorbed by audiences of Romans and non-Romans interacted with the full scope of these settings, including the monumental sacred backdrops that endowed Roman festivals with their manifold significations.

Meager as they are, the fragments themselves offer no direct indication that the *aition* from which they are drawn had anything to do with Rome. We owe this information instead to the corresponding summary preserved in the Milan papyrus of the *Diegeseis*, a crib to the *Aitia* that was composed sometime during the early Empire.[82]

> Φ[ησί] Πευκετίων προσκαθημένων [τ]οῖς
> τείχεσι τῆς Ῥώμης τῶν Ῥωμαίων Γά-
> ϊον ἐναλλόμενον κατακαλειν τὸν
> [ἐ]κείνων ἡγούμενον, [[σ]] τρωθῆναι δὲ εἰς
> τὸν μηρόν · μετὰ δὲ ταῦτα ἐπὶ τῷ σκάζειν
> δυσφορήσαντα παύσασθαι τῆς ἀθυμίας
> ὑπὸ τῆς μητρὸς ἐπιπληχθέντα.

Polybian polemic and Pascal 1981 for the cultural significance of the October Horse celebration.

80. *FGH* 76 F 56a–b. For Accius's play *Decius vel Aeneadae* see Flower 1995, 180, assessing Wiseman's (1994) reliance on *fabulae praetextae* as clues for "history from dramatic fiction." That Duris knew about the battle of Sentinum itself cannot be doubted; for different takes on his familiarity with the *devotiones* of the Decii Mures compare Briquel 2015 and Guittard 2015.

81. Momigliano 1975a, 16.

82. For the literary and cultural contexts of the text's composition and reception, see Cameron 1995, 123–6 and 2004, chap. III.1.

> (Callimachus) says that, while the Peucetii were conducting a siege, Gaius of the Romans leapt from the walls and killed their leader, but was wounded in the thigh. And that after these events he complained that he was limping, but that once he was upbraided by his mother he put a stop to his worrying.[83]

Since this incident is mentioned nowhere in the Roman historiographic tradition, speculation as to the historical reference points of the *Diegeseis* summary has gone in multiple directions. On the basis of the jump and subsequent limping, several scholars have identified Gaius with the legendary Horatius Cocles, while others have opted for the Spurius Carvilius known to us through Cicero.[84] That the protagonist is named Gaius does not tip the scales either way, since the *praenomen* was used in other settings to designate a generic Roman.[85] Meanwhile, the mention of an otherwise unknown siege of Rome by the Peucetii has inspired valiant efforts to connect this south Italian tribe with the Gauls of circa 390 BCE or with the Etruscans of Lars Porsenna's time.[86] Callimachus's incorporation of the Roman Gaius into his work has been sensibly linked to the rising interest of Hellenistic writers in Roman matters and specifically to the intensification of contacts between Rome and the Ptolemies, as confirmed by an exchange of embassies in 273 and by signs of Ptolemaic involvement in the western Mediterranean in the decades that followed.[87] The story has also been taken to be a Romanized calque of a Greek

83. *P.Mil.R.Univ.* (= Vogliano [1937] 1966, 66–173) Διηγήσεις Col. V 26–32. I print κατακαλειν as it appears on the papyrus but agree with Massimilla 2010, 146 that it should be corrected to κατακανεῖν *vel sim.* My translation parts ways with Vogliano on ἐναλλόμενον, which he insists "non può riferirsi al romano Gaio" because it is not in the aorist; I follow Trypanis 1958 in taking the participle to modify Gaius.

84. Comprehensively on Horatius Cocles see now Roller 2018, chap. 1. The latter figure: Cic. *De or.* 2.61.249.

85. The use of the *praenomen* Gaius to designate a "generic Roman": Plut. *QR* 30 with Forsythe 1996; Scheid 2012b, 139. For comment on Callimachus's use of "un prenomen diffusissimo come Gaio" see Vogliano ad loc.; cf. Pfeiffer *ad* fr. 107 on Gaius: "more Graeco solo praenomina introductus." The Greek habit of referring to Romans by *praenomen*: Schulze 1966, 507–9.

86. The societies and settlements of the Peucetii and their neighbors: Herring 2007. Pliny the Elder cites Callimachus as a source for the Peucetii but places them among the *gens Liburnarum* resident in Illyria (*NH* 3.139 with Pfeiffer *ad Aitia* fr. 107), they may be synonymous with the Apulian Poediculi, later a source of cavalry during the Second Punic War (Liv. 23.32.1; Val. Max.7.6.1a).

87. Historians: nn. 79–80 above. Poetry: Lycophron *Alex.* 1226–1330 and 1446–1450; on the poet's dating and on the status of these lines see variously West 1984; Hutchinson 1988, 258 with n. 70; and now Hornblower 2015 ad loc.; for the possibility that Lycophron relies on Timaeus, Humm 2016, 96–97. The awakening of Greek interest in Rome: Gruen 1984, I.317–322, following Fraser 1972, I.767–68 and II.1073–75 in assuming a Greek source and not "any direct acquain-

original,[88] though there is no prima facie reason for believing this to be the case. Most elusive of all, though, is the motivation that lay behind Callimachus's decision to incorporate this specific *aition* into his poem. In the absence of the full *aition* itself, conclusions about the poet's intentions are necessarily conjectural. It may be more productive instead to consider what Callimachus's sources for this information may have been, and which factors may have influenced the transmission of that information to the poet in Alexandria.

For Achille Vogliano, "la domanda non è oziosa" when it came to determining where the poet might have obtained the tale of Gaius: although Massimo Lenchantin had speculated that "le tradizioni verbali" could have made their way to Alexandria, the most reasonable assumption in Vogliano's view was to credit a Greek prose source that Callimachus would have consulted at the Library of Alexandria. Timaeus of Tauromenium, whose *Sicilian History* contained a Roman ethnography, was an obvious candidate.[89] But this proposal does not do much to clarify matters, seeing as it leaves unanswered the question of how the story came to the attention of the Greek source(s) responsible for transmitting it to Callimachus. My contribution here will be to hazard a provisional answer that invokes the communicative and dialogic power of Roman festivals. Lenchantin was on to something, although what I will now propose is probably not what he had in mind: that both the original performative setting for the source material behind this *aition* and its embedding within the poetic program of the *Aitia* become clearer if we read the legend of the Roman Gaius as marking the convergence of Callimachus's evident concern with festivals and their aetiological fruitfulness with Roman mid-republican festival culture.

It is generally acknowledged that Callimachus's use of narrative elegy to celebrate local and regional history is deeply rooted in an elegiac tradition of refashioning legendary and historical events for poetic performance at public festivals. The force of this tradition, reinvigorated in the poet's lifetime by Ptolemaic sponsorship of encomiastic competitions, seems to have been most pronounced in Callimachus's turn to tragedy and comedy,[90] but its traces are

tance with Roman tradition." The embassy exchange: Gruen 1984, I.62–63; Acosta-Hughes and Stephens 2012, 205–7. Ptolemaic involvement in the western Mediterranean: Wolf and Lorber 2011 for the numismatic evidence.

88. In addition to the commentaries of Vogliano and Pfeiffer, Harder 2012, II.783–86 offers an up-to-date summary of this and other lines of interpretation.

89. Vogliano [1937] 1966, 130, ruling out the possibility of a "native informant" historian; Momigliano [1959] 1977, 57. Timaeus's fragment: *FGH* 566, with Baron 2012 on his work and methods and Humm 2016 on the Roman content; other possible sources for Italic or Western Greek history are reviewed in Di Fazio 2013, 61–62.

90. Bowie 1986 on this tradition, with Barbantani 2003 on the remnants of Hellenistic

legible in the *Aitia*. One of the poem's generically most innovative features is its cross-fertilization of this strain of the elegiac tradition with an erudite curiosity about the customs and festivals of the greater Hellenistic world, with a Panhellenic sweep that is made explicit in the first of the two Gaius fragments.[91] The poem's interest in festivals spikes in Books 3 and 4, many of whose surviving fragments can be related to festivals or to ritual practices and contexts associated with festivals. The function of festivals as an organizing and content-generative principle is also on display in a work clearly influenced by and to some degree modeled on Callimachus's *Aitia*: Ovid's *Fasti*.[92] This orientation toward festivals brings me to the first proposition I want to advance regarding the Gaius episode, which is that it received aetiological exposition in Callimachus's work in part because it was linked to a Roman festival. Although other technologies for staging and disseminating the memory of the jumping Gaius may well have been available in mid-republican Rome,[93] the placement of this *aition* within the festival-dense environments of *Aitia* Books 3 and 4 is circumstantial evidence of the story's origin in and processing within festival culture. This explanation gains in persuasiveness the more we take into consideration the salience of historical dramas at Roman festivals.

Beginning with the Roman poet and playwright Cn. Naevius, who was around the age of thirty at the time of Callimachus's death according to the traditional dating of Callimachus's *floruit*, we have evidence for the performance of *fabulae praetextae* at *ludi*.[94] Wiseman has been the most forceful recent exponent of the drama-as-history theory, an idea first canvassed in nineteenth-century scholarship.[95] Substantial and well-founded objections have been raised to Wiseman's methods and conclusions, notably his insistence that the performance of historical drama can be traced to the very beginnings of the Republic. Whatever may have been the state of dramatic affairs

---

narrative elegy and Harder 2012, I.30–32 for Callimachean play with elegy. Public poetic performance in Hellenistic Alexandria: Acosta-Hughes and Stephens 2012, 86–88. Callimachus and theater: Acosta-Hughes 2012, 392–95.

91. Fr. 106 Pfeiffer: Ὧδ' ἐ[σθλοὶ?] γείνεσθε, Πανελλάδος ὧδε τελέσσαι. Harder ad loc. argues for reading the reference to the "whole of Greece" as indicative "of the perspective from which the Roman world is viewed here, i.e. as an example to be admired and followed by Greeks"; I would add that this perspective was focalized and enacted in festival settings.

92. Miller 1982 and now Wahlberg 2008 for correspondences between the two works.

93. For a highly stimulating account of these alternative strategies see Roller 2004, 10–23.

94. The titles with fragments are collected in Ribbeck; for a list see the chart at Flower 1995, 189.

95. For a full workup of the theory see Wiseman 1994, chap. 1. A review of the theory's previous iterations and development: Wiseman 1998, chap. 1 and Appendix A.

during the early Republic, there is no question that Rome's residents were becoming accustomed to historical and aetiological drama performed in public by the end of Naevius's life.[96] The likeliest venues for this drama were the festivals that emerged in connection with the introduction of new games, new cult practices, and new temples, as I argued in the previous chapter. If Naevius was not the creator of the *fabula praetexta,* he was the first to shape it into an explicitly literary form and to adapt it to the rapidly transforming cultural environment. Even before his literary intervention, however, the premier firsthand source of information on Roman customs for any Greek interested in learning about them would have been their dramatic performance in public festival settings at Rome, either as *fabulae praetextae* or as mime.[97] The tight coupling of the content and performance of mime with public religious festivals would endure well into the late Republic and early Empire, as a glance at the fragmentary corpus of Decimus Laberius confirms.[98]

The staging of the Gaius Romanus story within a festival-performative context lurks in the *Diegeseis* account's participle ἐναλλόμενον ("leaping"), which I construed earlier as modifying the hero Gaius. The identification of Gaius with Horatius Cocles was first proposed in the scholarship in part because of the immortalization of Horatius Cocles's jump in Ennius: *Horatius inclutus saltu.*[99] The Ennian *saltus* is significant as a buried clue and cue for performativity and performability. Stylized forms of jumping and dancing were routinely integrated into a range of mid-republican spectacles, from the coordinated religious dancing of the Luperci and Salii to the song-and-dance numbers of mime. Although the contribution of embodied rhythmic movement to the perpetuation of prosocial norms in ancient Rome remains in need of comprehensive study, the place of dance in the realization of this end should not be slighted, especially if comparative evidence is any indication.[100] Proverbially,

96. Flower 1995, 175 criticizes Wiseman for overlooking the aetiological aspects of the *praetexta*: one of the earliest attested compositions in the genre dramatized the summoning and arrival of the Magna Mater; another staged the origins of the *Nonae Caprotinae.*

97. For Roman mime (as distinguished from pantomime) see Wiseman 2009; Panayotakis 2009, 21–27 on the genre's origins and early development.

98. At least four of Laberius's mimes reference a religious festival in their titles: *Anna Peranna* (frs. 2–3 Panayotakis), *Compitalia* (frs. 19–21), *Parilicii* (fr. 45), *Saturnalia* (fr. 53).

99. *Ann.* 123 Skutsch. Although he leans toward identifying this Horatius as one of the triplets fighting against the Curiatii on the grounds that Festus 188–90 L. attributes the line to *Annales* II, Skutsch concedes ad loc. that "the 'famous' Horatius, especially in connection with *saltu* . . . is Cocles." The description of Cocles's leap at Dionysius of Halicarnassus *AR* 5.24.3 employs the verb καθάλλεται—a distant echo of ἐναλλόμενον.

100. Dance in Roman society: Hunt 2009, 172–73 for an overview; Torelli 1997 for material evidence of the Salian ritual's place in Roman-Etruscan relations; Wiseman 2015, chap. 3 on

the elderly mime Gaius Pomponius earned himself a place in popular tradition and gave birth to a proverb by dancing and jumping during the *ludi Apollinares* of 212 while the rest of the citizenry was called to the urban walls to defend Rome when Hannibal's forces menaced the city.[101] This story resonates not only because of its idealization of flinty Roman courage in the face of an imminent threat, but also because of its encapsulation of those interactive dynamics through which the performative moment became a historical moment (and vice versa). The semantic distinction between *saltare* as "jump" and as "dance" blurs in this story, as it does in other notices for Roman dance, for the simple reason that "jumping" and "dancing" in the realm of Roman performance were two sides of the same bodily/semiotic coin. It is the prospect of such slippage that best explains how the "Gaius"/Cocles *aition* in Callimachus may have taken shape in a performative festival setting: the saga of a man whose martial excellence came into full view as he jumped, only for him to end up lame and complain lamely has a strong whiff of the Roman stage, where multiple genres of dramatic performance sought to express *historiae* and *res gestae* through jump and dance. Here we should pause to note that, although it evolved in dialogue with other performative trends first in archaic and then in Hellenizing central Italy, Rome's distinctive fusion of dance and theater in the form of the *ludi scaenici* was explained in the annalistic tradition as a fourth-century importation from Etruria—an attribution that is revealing as an index of the middle Republic's takeover of Etruscan culture in the period of imperial expansion and as a reminder of the degree to which Roman memory and historiography equated the traffic in art to the traffic in bodies.[102]

In any event, dancing at the games and festivals in a virile manner (*uirilem in modum*) came to be viewed as appropriate for members of the senatorial elite, "even if," Seneca the Younger would write several centuries later, citing the example of a Scipio moving to the beat, "they were being watched by their

dancing at Rome prior to the emergence of Latin literature; Alonso Fernández 2015 for women and Roman dance, to be supplemented with Glinister 2011 on the Salian virgins.

101. Festus 436 L.: "Salva res <est; saltat> senex"; cf. Serv. *ad Aen.* 3.279 and 8.110 for slight variation on the wording of the proverb. The story's place in the history of Roman mime: Panayotakis 2009, 24–25. Plautine reminiscence at *Bacch.* 772 (*saluos sum, iratus est senex*): Slater 2000, 89. Cocles's lameness: Serv. *ad Aen.* 8.646 on the hero as *laesus in coxa*, referencing a tradition not mentioned in Polybius or Livy; for the exemplary semiotics of Cocles's injuries see Roller 2004, 12–15 and 2018, 38–43. *Histriones* on stage who "performed [*demonstrabant*]" *historiae* and *res gestae* by dancing: Isid. *Etym.* 18.48; but see the comments of Panayotakis 2009, 6–11.

102. Liv. 7.2.4: *sine carmine ullo, sine imitandorum carminum actu ludiones ex Etruria acciti, ad tibicinis modos saltantes, haud indecoros motus more Tusco dabant*; read with Oakley ad loc. and Feeney 2016, chap. 4. Further on Roman-Etruscan connections see Padilla Peralta 2018c; for the special case of Etruscan dance culture, Cherici 2017 and Maras 2018a.

own enemies" (*etiam si ab hostibus suis spectarentur*).[103] This fusion of dance, exemplarity, festival culture, and memory in mid-republican culture is detectable in Callimachus's fragment. Naturally, it is impossible to confirm with certainty that Callimachus himself retrieved the story of Gaius from a Roman festival; we have no evidence that Callimachus ever went to Rome in person. But the legend likely entered the Greek literary world through performance at a Roman festival at which a visiting Greek or Greeks happened to be in attendance. The third-century Hellenistic gaze toward Rome seems to have encompassed the historical reminiscence of temple foundations, the primary vector for which at the time will have been anniversary and festival celebrations.[104] Largely because of Polybius's smack-down of Timaeus as a library-bound recluse,[105] any willingness on the part of scholars to credit the Sicilian with availing himself of autopsy has been in short supply. The Polybian disparagement of his predecessor should not, however, blind us to the presence of details in the writings of Timaeus and other early Hellenistic historians that point unequivocally toward the collection and filtration of knowledge about mid-republican Rome at festival settings. Our best source for this practice is, of course, none other than Polybius himself, who cites the Horatius Cocles story in the midst of Book VI's lengthy disquisition on the relationship between Rome's performance culture and the inculcation of virtue among its citizenry.[106] Whether the germ of the Callimachean *aition* traveled with Timaeus or one of his informants—another early Hellenistic historian, or even a member of the Ptolemaic embassy that came to Rome in 273—the most important aspect of the *aition*'s intercultural trajectory is that a Roman festival provided the incentive and the venue for the projection of the Gaius narrative beyond the city. Thus contextualized, Callimachus's selection of this story for inclusion in an opus of micronarratives that were related to and on occasion culled from festival settings becomes much more intelligible. In this connection it should also be stressed that the poet's knowledge of Italian culture

103. Sen. *dial.* 9.17.5 with Alonso Fernández 2016 (see bibliography cited at p. 316 n. 3 on whether this Scipio was the first Africanus; Champion 2017, 197–201 on Africanus's seriousness about his priestly obligations as a *salius*); Macr. *Sat.* 3.14.14 with Alonso Fernández 2017, 58 for the Ap. Claudius Pulcher *cos.* 143 who prided himself on being the best dancer in the Salian *sodalitas*; cf. Glinister 2011 on the probably elite pedigree of the *Saliae*.

104. Timaeus's knowledge of the archaic foundation of temple to Fortuna/Τύχη under Servius Tullius: Miano 2012; on the proximity of Sp. Carvilius's mid-republican temple of Fortuna to this "Servian" structure and the implications for cultural memory see Liv. 10.46.14 with Miano 2018, 79–80.

105. Polyb. 12.25d.1 and 25h.1 with McGing 2010, 86–88 for discussion.

106. Polyb. 6.55 on Horatius Cocles, with Erskine 2013, 127 on one peculiarity of his version.

ranged into other aspects of ritual and cultic practice that could very well have been exhibited or memorialized at festivals.[107]

For the purposes of this chapter, the inclusion of the Gaius Romanus episode into Callimachus's *Aitia* is a tantalizing indicator of how culturally specific knowledge could be catapulted into new regional and interpretative orbits through performance at festivals. As it turns out, the Callimachean *aition* is not the only product of intercultural communication to have been enabled by mid-republican festival culture. In the next subsection, I will scrutinize a comic fragment from the corpus of Naevius whose contents shed a glimpse on the cultural fault lines that came into view and were repeatedly negotiated at Roman public festivals. These fault lines came into view to generative effect, since it was precisely in the encounter and dialogue of Romans and non-Romans in festival settings that feats of knowledge aggregation and the promotion of common knowledge became possible. As disclosed by this Naevian fragment, the multistep process of intra- and intercultural learning is closely entwined with the emergence of Roman theater as a sacralized institution in the final decades of the third century. In chapter 3, I argued for the importance of the *infrastructure* of theater; with Naevius as a lens, I move now to elucidating some of the communicative processes that were unlocked by theatrical performance, and their place in the system of cultural recognition and self-identification through which the statehood processes of the fourth and third centuries were translated into messages for broad circulation.

2. *Ritualized Painting: The Religious Life of Rome's Common Folk*

A perplexing fragment from Naevius's *Tunicularia* is preserved in the lemma for *penis* in Festus (260 L.). The first hurdle to face in interpreting the fragment is a textual problem, tackled in different ways by Ribbeck's text in *SRF*[3] and Warmington's edition of the same lines:

RIBBECK	*WARMINGTON*
Theodotum	Theodotum
<u>compeiles . . .</u> qui aras Compitalibus	<u>cum Apella comparas</u> qui Compitalibus

107. Fr. 93 Pfeiffer seems to refer to a legendary human sacrifice performed by the Etruscans following the successful siege of Lipara: see Di Fazio 2013 for analysis and interpretation. Fr. 732 Pfeiffer mentions *kadmilos* (~ Lat. *camillus*, "ritual attendant") as an Etruscan epithet of the god Hermes, a datum known also to Lycophron: see the scholia to Lyc. *Alex.* 162 with Hornblower 2015 ad loc. and Combet-Farnoux 1980, 185–217; but cf. Varro *LL* 7.34 for the claim that the word *camillus* is Greek because it appears *apud Callimachum*.

sedens in cella circumtectus tegetibus	sedens in cella circumtectus tegetibus
Lares ludentis peni pinxit bubulo.	Lares ludentes peni pinxit bubulo?[108]

The Festan lemma from which these lines are drawn is partially corrupt; the obscure *compeiles* at the beginning of the second line has exercised the imaginations of numerous nineteenth- and early twentieth-century philologists. Although I will base myself on Warmington's text and its restoration of Apelles—the Hellenistic painter of extraordinary renown in his lifetime and after—to the troubled opening of the line, this subsection's analysis will not be seriously impaired if Warmington's restoration is off the mark.[109] The lines can be translated as follows:

> Do you compare Theodotus with Apelles—
> Theodotus who, at the Compitalia, sitting in a corner
> (and fenced off with mats)
> painted the playful Lares with an ox-tail?[110]

Apelles is a well-known figure, in no small part thanks to Pliny the Elder's extensive recounting of his life and accomplishments. The identity of Theodotus, on the other hand, is far more elusive; as early as 1846, efforts were afoot to pin the tail on who he was and where he came from.[111] For the line of argument that I will pursue in a moment, the generic and performance contexts of these lines are what will most concern us. The *Tunicularia* belonged to the class of *fabulae palliatae*, the comic genre known best from the twenty-one surviving exemplars of Plautus and the six of Terence. The *palliatae* were adaptations of Greek comedy, New Comedy in particular; the process of adaptation and tinkering had the effect, at least for the plays of Plautus and Terence whose full texts we have, of "creat[ing] a fantasy world" exhibiting a "mixture

108. Naevius *com.* 99–102 Ribbeck^3 = *com. pall.* 97–100 Warmington; the latter is printed in Marmorale 1950.

109. The restoration was inspired partly by Plautine verses that mention the Hellenistic painter: *Poen.* 1271 and *Epid.* 626, with Fraenkel [1922] 2007, 12–14 for a penetrating reading of these artistic allusions as illustrative not only of the Hellenizing artistic orientation of Plautine drama but also the transmutation of slave suffering into artistic experience—about which see the next section. Proposed emendation to *compeiles qui aras*: Cèbe 1966: 60 n. 3.

110. These are the compital neighborhood Lares (see below); Warmington is incorrect to render them as "household-gods."

111. This Theodotus was probably a slave or freedman: see Solin 2003, 75–76 for late republican and early imperial attestations of the Greek name.

of features appropriate to Greek and Roman settings."[112] However, the dynamics of cultural sampling and transference that simmer beneath the surface in the extant fragments of Naevius's comedies and that vibrate throughout the Plautine and Terentine corpora are not only significant as literary artifacts. They are also notable as signs of the cultural power play that was staged in theater and festival environments, where spectacle and religion came together to animate and perpetuate a carefully manicured vision of Roman life. In support of this claim, we may adduce the religious setting and content of the contrast between the compital handiwork of Theodotus and the grand artistic program of Apelles on the other.

This passage is the earliest literary testimony for an iconographic type familiar from Delian and Pompeian domestic paintings of the second and first centuries BCE: the dancing Lares, the divinities whose compital cult would be the subject of an important and far-reaching Augustan reform.[113] Our focus will be not so much on these Lares themselves as with the festival of the Compitalia and its stylization in Naevius as an appropriate setting for the juxtaposition of the humble artistic ventures of Theodotus with those of the more celebrated Apelles. In *La caricature et la parodie dans le monde romain*, Jean-Pierre Cèbe highlighted the aggressively mocking aspects of this scene. More recently, Thomas Pekáry has situated this fragment within an unfolding ancient discourse about painters and the status of their work relative to other genres of art.[114] But another and potentially fuller range of meanings for this fragment can be activated by interrogating the scene's relation to the festival environments of mid-republican Rome and the cultural confrontations that took place within them. The perceived visual contrast between Hellenistic grandeur as embodied in the figure of the painter Apelles and Roman simplicity, even rusticity, summons to mind tropes familiar from late republican literary discourses. Yet the fact that the ostensibly "Roman" painter whose playful Lares are compared to the work of Apelles bears a Greek name speaks to the changing sociocultural realities of the middle and late third century, when a literature in Latin was partly brought into being through the activities of a Tarentine Greek and prisoner of war (Livius Andronicus); Roman drama quickly emerges as a genre thoroughly saturated with and enmeshed in the historical realities of mass enslavement.[115] Meanwhile, the focalization of

112. Manuwald 2011, 148.

113. These paintings and their ritual contexts: Hasenohr 2003 on Delos, Giacobello 2008 on Pompeii, and Flower 2017 for a full treatment. Compital cult in Augustan Rome and the *vici* reform: Lott 2004; Flower 2017, 255–347.

114. Cèbe 1966, 60–61; Pekáry 2002, 59.

115. The feedback loops of mass enslavement and Roman drama: Richlin 2014a and 2018, both to be read with Barbiero 2019; Čulík-Baird 2020 on tragedy.

these processes at the festival of the Compitalia, a celebration of Roman neighborhood cult, makes explicit the physical location and generation of cultural knowledge at the crossroads festival—a place and a ceremony that was drenched in the psychosocial tensions of people from different backgrounds and social statuses who were jostling and interacting with one another. A festival as quintessentially Roman as this "neighborhood party" gave voice to and channeled the traffic in cultural (self-)awareness and projection, with network effects whose cascading force will be taken up in chapter 5.[116]

Far from being a culturally inward-facing festival, however, the Compitalia projected outward a vision of Roman culture for consumption by non-Roman observers. At first blush, this interpretation may seem strained; after all, the festival was a celebration of neighborhood cult, not of a god such as Aesculapius whose cult's stimulation of short-term movement to Rome leaves a signature in our sources.[117] Yet there appears to be evidence that features of Roman culture on display at the Compitalia came to the attention of non-Romans, in the form of a letter from a Hellenistic adversary of Rome to the citizens of a city in Thessaly. Philip V's correspondence with the townspeople of Larisa, composed and subsequently inscribed in or around 217, is a treasure trove of information about Hellenistic practices of citizenship and community-building. The first and second letters document Philip's intervention in the resolution of a dispute among the citizens of Larisa regarding the allocation of the franchise to new citizens.[118] In the second letter, Philip famously alludes to the generosity of the Romans in their grants of citizenship, in deliberate contrast to the relative stinginess of Larisa and other Greek poleis.[119] I quote only the section of the inscription most relevant to our discussion:

> βασιλεὺς Φίλιππος Λαρισαίων τοῖς ταγοῖς καὶ τῇ πόλει χαίρειν. πυνθάνομαι τοὺς πολιτογραφηθέντας κατὰ | τὴν παρ᾽ ἐμοῦ ἐπιστολὴν καὶ τὸ ψήφισμα τὸ ὑμέτερον καὶ ἀναγραφέντας εἰς τὰς στήλας ἐκκεκολάφθαι • εἴ- | περ οὖν ἐγεγόνει τοῦτο, ἠστοχήκεισαν οἱ συνβουλεύσαντες ὑμῖν καὶ τοῦ συμφέροντος τῇ πατρίδι | καὶ τῆς ἐμῆς κρίσεως. ὅτι γὰρ πάντων κάλλιστόν ἐστιν ὡς πλείστων μετεχόντων τοῦ πολιτεύματος | την τε πόλιν ἰσχύειν καὶ τὴν χώραν μὴ ὥσπερ

116. Cf. Flower 2017, 250–53 on the "compital network" of the middle and late Republic.

117. Cf. a (likely) metatheatrical reference at Ennius *Tr.* fr. 193 Goldberg-Manuwald: *namque Aesculapi liberorum saucii opplent porticus; / non potest accidi*. For material and epigraphic signs of this movement see chapter 5.

118. *SIG*³ 543 = *IG* ix.2.517 = Austin 1981 no. 60, whose translation I follow. Chronology and political background: Habicht 2006, 67–70.

119. For the tendentiousness of the comparison see Gauthier 1974. A distant echo of the letter's juxtaposition of citizenship practices is audible in Plautus's *Menaechmi*: see Jocelyn 1984, 9–10.

> νῦν αἰσχρῶς χερσεύεσθαι, νομίζω μὲν οὐδ᾽ ὑμῶν οὐθένα ἄν ἀν- | τειπεῖν, ἔξεστι δὲ καὶ τοὺς λοιποὺς τοὺς ταῖς ὁμοίαις πολιτογραφίαις χρωμένους θεωρεῖν ὧν καὶ οἱ Ῥωμαῖ-| οί εἰσιν, οἳ καὶ τοὺς οἰκετας ὅταν ἐλευθερώσωσιν, προσδεχόμενοι εἰς τὸ πολίτευμα καὶ τῶν ἀρχαίων με- | [ταδι]δόντες, καὶ διὰ τοῦ τοιούτου τρόπου οὐ μόνον τὴν ἰδίαν πατρίδα ἐπηυξήκασιν, ἀλλὰ καὶ ἀποικίας <σ>χεδὸν | [εἰς ἑβ]δομήκοντα τόπους ἐκπεπόμφασιν.
>
> King Philip to the *tagoi* and the city of Larisa, greetings. I hear that those who were granted citizenship in accordance with the letter I sent to you and your decree, and whose names were inscribed (on the stele) have been erased. If this has happened, those who have advised you have ignored the interests of your city and my ruling. That it is much the best state of affairs for as many as possible to enjoy citizen rights, the city to be strong and the land not to lie shamefully deserted, as at present, I believe none of you would deny, and one may observe others who grant citizenship in the same way. Among these are the Romans, who when they manumit their slaves admit them to the citizen body and grant them a share in the magistracies (*archai*), and in this way have not only enlarged their country but have sent out colonies to nearly 70 places. (ll. 26–34)

For decades, commentators on this letter dismissed the underlined section as a gross distortion of Roman practice, belaboring the fact that there is no other source for Roman freedmen holding magistracies.[120] However, with the help of a passage in Livy Book 34, J. Bert Lott has interpreted Philip V's ethnographic venture as a reference to the freedmen *magistri vici*—attested epigraphically from the Augustan period onward—who were entrusted with the annual celebration of the Compitalia. While these officers were not officials of the state *sensu stricto*, "since they were charged with the celebration of a holiday of the Roman state and since they dressed like officers of the state while performing their duties it would have been easy for someone not wholly familiar with Roman society to mistake the freedman *magistri vici* for officers of the whole state rather than of their own neighborhood."[121] The question to resolve next is how Philip might have obtained this information about the Romans prior to passing it on to the citizens of Larisa. Lott speculates that Philip "must have taken every opportunity to collect secondhand information about his enemies," but we should be more precise about which opportunities were available. One plausible explanation is that this information was sourced from an itinerant Greek who attended the Compitalia and gleaned some

120. See, purely e.g., Austin 1981, 119 n. 3: "Inaccurate, if this reading is correct; only sons of freedmen were admitted to office."

121. Lott 2004, 42; 41–43 for the reading of the letter alongside the testimony of Livy.

knowledge about *magistri vici*.[122] Under this reconstruction, Philip V's letter is not an archive of general knowledge in circulation about the Romans but an attestation of an element of Roman life that came into view *only* during a specific Roman festival. The Compitalia framed a very contingent enactment of Roman social relations, and it was this enactment that attracted the attention of the observer who relayed the interesting ethnographic datum to Philip.

Religious festivals were ideal for the outward projection of information about Roman practices because they enlisted the machinery of dramatic and performative art to produce a streamlined and digestible version of Roman civic identity. Not infrequently, one of the gears of this machinery was the self-aggrandizing appeal to contrast and difference, as another fragment from the works of Naevius confirms. The fixing of Roman identity as a distinct position on the spectrum between slavery and freedom is put in the mouth of a character in the *Tarentilla* ("The little girl from Tarentum"), who exclaims that she has confirmed from the applause of the audience something that no king would dare to shatter, namely, that slavery *here*—at Rome? in the theater?—trumps freedom.[123] Dramatic performance at festivals functioned as an especially amenable locus for assessing the properties and accomplishments of the cultural Other, and for staging the differentiation of oneself and of practices at Rome from that of the Other. The question of how Hellenistic Greeks came to perceive and interpret not only Roman manumission practices but also other distinctive features of Roman social life in the mid-republican period is best answered by looking to festivals as highly fertile sites for the transmission of culturally loaded knowledge. The proliferation of images of the Other on the Roman comic stage ranged along a continuum stretching from the near-at-hand, ever-so-slightly non-Roman Latin (the *Praenestini et Lanuuini hospites* of Naevius's *Ariolus*) to the Jew (the possible protagonist of Naevius's *Apella*) and the Carthaginian (Plautus's *Poenulus*).[124] The "destabilizing potential" of

122. The suspicion that foreign embassies visiting Rome were spying: Liv. 30.23.5 with Austin and Rankov 1995, 93–94; on embassies and festivals see chapter 5 n. 38. Reconnaissance at Greek festivals is documented for other periods of Mediterranean history: Simonton 2017, 139–40.

123. *Tarentilla* fr. 1 Ribbeck^3 = *com. pall.* frs. 69–71 Warmington: *Quae ego in theatro hic meis probaui plausibus / ea non audere quemquam regem rumpere / quanto libertatem hanc hic superat seruitus*. Interpretations of this fragment: Flores 1974, 33; Barchiesi 1978, 2–8.

124. The *Ariolus*: frr. 21–24 Ribbeck^3; for the *Appella* as "the earliest reference to Jews in Latin literature" see Geiger 1984. For references to allies and "provincials" in the *palliata* see Cèbe 1960, 63–64 with n. 6; cf. the denigration of non-Roman Italians in the *togata* (Titinius fr. 103 Daviault). Representations of Carthaginians in Plautus: Palmer 1997, chap. 3; Leigh 2004, chap. 2, which Clark 2019, 219 on the ambivalent texturing of Carthaginian piety complements nicely; Giusti 2018, chap. 1 on the assimilation of Carthaginians to the barbarian Others of classical

Roman drama rested in its deployment of the "supple tool" of staging alterity; the Plautine *palliata* in particular call for close reading as an archive of migration, mobility, and intercultural contact.[125]

Instead of being purely tongue-in-cheek or derisory, the stereotypes staged in these plays also fulfilled an integrative function. The audiences for comic performance at festivals were diverse and diversifying, and no doubt much of the appeal of this trading in stereotypes lay in playing up their humorous content; but it should of course be borne in mind that the troupes who bore the burden of performance were comprised in many cases of individuals who hailed from non-Roman backgrounds and had been exposed to the imperial Republic's premier institution for forced assimilation: slavery.[126] Early Roman comedy and tragedy regularly formulated claims about the content and significance of Roman identity, claims that were simultaneously capable of instilling in the audience an enhanced awareness of Rome's distinctiveness and of reifying and perpetuating cultural divides. Thus, in the temporal and spatial symbiosis of drama and festival, knowledge about Romans and non-Romans was generated by and disseminated to Romans and non-Romans in a geopolitical environment where the stakes of staging a coherent identity could not be greater.[127]

Tapping into these circuits of knowledge to retrieve a datum of potential exemplary relevance to the citizens of Larisa, Philip V's letter plots a "mental map" for locating the Thessalian polis on the same geopolitical and cultural plane as the Roman state; their difference is made to *mean* something to the residents of this city-state.[128] This difference was constructed and enacted at festivals, as the fragments of Callimachus and Naevius in separate but complementary ways make apparent: it was religious celebration that provided a pro-

---

Greece, Achaemenid Persians. Greek stereotypes: Cèbe 1960, 64–65 on Plaut. *Curc.* 288–95; Jocelyn 1984 on anti-Greek sentiment in the *Menaechmi*.

125. For quoted phrases and discussion see Feeney 2016, 147–48 and note Gildenhard 2010, 172–79 on translation's role in the toggle between identity and alterity. Interrogations of the Plautine archive of human movement and cultural friction: Isayev 2017b, chap. 6 and 2017a.

126. Richlin 2014 and 2018. On the *thusiai* and *sunodoi* of performers circulating throughout the Hellenistic world, see Gratwick 1982, 80–81; Rawson 1991c, 475 and 487; Lightfoot 2002; Brown 2002 for the situation in Roman Italy, with Gabrielsen 2008 for general comment on the political and economic aspects of these professional organizations. Even if organized troupes such as the *technītai* of Dionysus did not regularly travel from the Greek East to the western Mediterranean until the early Empire, there was plenty of artistic talent on the (coerced) move during our period.

127. For the sociopolitical maneuverings of early Latin drama, see now Giusti 2018, 66–75.

128. I reference with quotation marks a concept that is felicitously applied in John Ma's characterization of Hellenistic peer-polity interaction: Ma 2003, 19–21.

pitious opportunity for knowledge production and transmission. The union of drama and festival, especially as it became institutionalized over the course of the second half of the third century, created opportunities for regular public communication about Roman practices. The diverse backgrounds of the audience in attendance at performances of drama ensured that this knowledge was then acquired and transmitted—with the ripples extending all the way to Macedon and Alexandria—and that metaknowledge of the kind studied by Michael Chwe and other social scientists was facilitated. But we now need to drill more deeply into the phenomenology of the metaknowledge and common knowledge on vibrant display at mid-republican festivals. As the case studies we have pursued so far offer little more than tantalizing apertures into these dynamics, it is time to proceed more aggressively into the core of the communicative praxis that redefined Roman identity on the stage during this period. My contention is that the various component elements of this praxis come together to enact one coherent message, with unwavering pitch and intensity: Rome was a theocracy; its gods oversaw and legitimated the partitioning of the world into statuses of freedom and unfreedom whose calibration and refinement it was the exclusive responsibility of the imperial Republic to arbitrate. Dramatic performance in the presence of the gods was a highly effective means of wrapping and delivering this communication to a broader audience. There is perhaps no clearer indicator of the *perceived* efficacity of drama for the execution of a communicative program that foregrounded the power and omnipotence of Rome's gods than the prominence of freedom and subjection as divinely ordained conditions among the thematic obsessions of Roman comedy.

3. *What Every Person Knows: Freedom, Slavery, and Roman Civics*

The Plautine *palliata* are crammed with references to various shades of Fortuna, reflective not only of the relevance of the goddess and/as concept to the cultural imaginary of mid-republican Rome but also of her cult's monumentalized presence in the form of temples.[129] Fortuna was an important concept to leverage in negotiating a world that had been disrupted by the seesaw violence of Roman imperialism, and in imposing order on this chaos through the designation of winners and losers. Taxonomic ordering of this sort as a world-making strategy cannot be understood without reference to the discursive possibilities that were furnished by public religious observance.[130] Through public cult at Rome, distinctions between elite and nonelite religious

129. Fortuna in Plautus: Miano 2018, 114–15.

130. Cf. Purcell 2013, 444 on the Roman *ludi* as "religion with a winner."

practitioners were reified and concretized, the officiants at the *sacra publica* and their servile or freedmen assistants each enacting for visual consumption the briefs entrusted to them.[131] The praxis of sacrifice made possible not only the repetitive assertion of social hierarchy but also the public profession of conviction in a cosmic "system of being,"[132] one that retained its potency even as Romans deployed new media for projecting a culturally distinctive brand of cosmopoiesis during the last two centuries BCE.

But the pedagogical project built into public ritual accommodated even more than these gradients of signifying distinction, as a closer examination of the messages imparted by the festival culture of the middle Republic will now attempt to demonstrate. It is risky business to attempt to derive any one set of lessons from the kaleidoscopic variety and diversity of a festival scene that experienced a warp-speed renewal during our period. The methodological hazards involved in parsing the general communicative outflows of festival culture may explain why studies of Roman festivals incline either in the direction of comprehensive coverage with minimal analysis or fine-grained attention to one or two festivals with no pretense to comprehensiveness.[133] Ingo Gildenhard has sensibly postulated a distinction between illocution and perlocution in the messaging of Latin drama,[134] though the gap between these two modes of speech-act is partially bridgeable if we join Amy Richlin in concentrating our energies on the enslaved subjects and objects of the Roman stage. With these precedents in mind, I will propose that several of the most important messages encoded into and disseminated through Roman drama in the final decades of the third and beginning of the second century converge on the relationship of religious observance to the traumas of mass enslavement—and that, in sponsoring the *ludi scaenici* at which these dramas were performed, the Roman state was effectively underwriting the costs of large-scale group therapy. While not in the same vein as the therapeutic practice of airing out marital disagreements at the shrine of Viriplaca ("Man-Pleaser"),[135] the mass therapy of *ludi* and drama capitalized on the sacred monumentaliza-

131. For useful comment on the visibility of different categories of religious practitioners in the late Republic and early Empire see Rüpke 2018a.

132. Quoted phrase and discussion: Scheid 2012a, relying on Prescendi 2007; to these add now Schultz 2016, calling for a more expansively emic orientation to Roman sacrifice.

133. Beard 1987 [2003] proposed a reading of the Parilia that could be generalized to festival culture as a whole. For evocative studies of select festivals see, e.g., Favro 1999 on the Consualia and Floralia. Comprehensiveness with a sprinkling of analysis: Scullard 1981.

134. Gildenhard 2010, 154–55.

135. Val. Max. 2.1.6, with Mueller 2002, 73 and 213 n. 23 for comment on the historicity of this *sacellum*. The placement of this notice in the work and the author's fondness for mid-republican episodes make the practice's attribution to our period likely.

tion of Rome to supercharge with religious meaning the civic self-awareness of free and slave members of the *res publica*.

In order to recover the operations of this therapy, it is important to be as clear as possible about the religious standing of the enslaved in Roman culture and about the textualization of this standing in our extant sources for mid-republican religious practice.[136] Although not much effort is required to locate evidence for slaves in the everyday rhythms of central Italy during our period, their activity in sacred contexts is harder to pin down, for the simple reason that Roman slaves—despite perhaps enjoying greater religious freedom than their counterparts in classical Greece—labored under significant constraints when it came to the exercise of independent religious agency.[137] The impression one obtains from Cato the Elder's instructions in *De agri cultura*, which at the very least formulated and projected a set of realistic expectations even if it did not directly transcribe reality,[138] is that Roman slaves were subordinated as religious actors, with the range and nature of their religious practices controlled by the demands and preferences of their masters. Such control took two forms, one of which is immediately apprehensible from Cato's text and the second of which is more clearly showcased in the Plautine *palliata*: explicit imposition and regulation on the one hand; keeping slaves far too busy to do anything except assisting (as ordered) at those religious observances that were masterminded by the elite, the public *sacra* foremost among them, on the other.

Cato orders his *uilicus*, the overseer tasked with managing the estate, not to undertake any religious rituals except those conducted at crossroads shrines or at the household hearth for the winter festival of the Compitalia in honor of the Lares (*rem diuinam nisi Conpitalibus in conpito aut in foco ne faciat*); moreover, he is admonished not to consult any fortune-teller, augur, diviner, or astrologer (*haruspicem, augurem, hariolum, Chaldaeum nequem consuluisse uelit*).[139] Meanwhile, the overseer's female colleague is ordered not to perform any religious rituals on her own or to bid another to do so on her behalf except

136. What follows is a modified version of Padilla Peralta 2017c, which should be read with Čulík-Baird 2020 on enslavement in Roman tragedy. My approach to textualization's dialogue with state cult is informed by the comments of Mackey 2018, 624–25 on MacRae 2016.

137. Slaves at work in the central Italian economy: see, e.g., *Imagines* Campania or Samnium 5, carved by a *f(a)m(e)l* Mitulus Mettius on a limestone table leg; further on slaves and freedmen in artifact production, chapter 5 n. 101. The (relative) religious freedom of Roman slaves: Patterson 1982, 68–69, following Franz Bömer (but conceding at p. 66 that Bömer's contrast between Greek and Roman slave religious life "may be a little overdrawn").

138. Contrasting perspectives on Cato's transcription of the realities of early second-century Roman agriculture: Astin 1978, 240–66; Terrenato 2012; Kay 2014, 131–88.

139. *De agri cultura* 5.2–3. Even if most overseers were free(d) (Scheidel 1990), my argument

as commanded by the master or mistress of the household (*rem diuinam ni faciat neue mandet qui pro ea faciat iniussu domini aut dominae*) and to remember that the master was the one who performed religious worship for the entire household (*scito dominum pro tota familia rem diuinam facere*). The *uilica*'s religious responsibilities are restricted to placing a garland over the hearth and praying to the *lar familiaris* on the Kalends, Ides, Nones, and any other *dies festus*.[140] For the enslaved who were neither *uilici* nor *uilicae*, Cato has very little to say. Apart from specifying that either a slave or a free person could make the offering to Mars Silvanus (*eam rem diuinam uel seruus uel liber licebit faciat*), the treatise is mostly silent about the activity of slaves in religious rituals—though it is presumed that slaves will be in attendance whenever the master officiates.[141]

Perhaps even more grippingly than Cato's treatise, Plautus's plays communicate the degree to which slaves came to be imagined as prostheses in the context of cult. Amphitryon's telling Bromia to go home and have vases prepared so that he could entreat Jupiter with sacrificial offerings in *Amphitruo*; the hiring of a slave to assist Periphanes *ad rem diuinam* in *Epidicus*; Phronesium's direction to her maid to ready some myrrh and prepare the altar fire in *Truculentus*: in these and other cases, slaves are little more than cultic *instrumenta*, running around to get things ready for the execution of their masters' religious desires.[142] Evocative of this conditioning of the slave as object and accessory of the master's ritual designs is the slave Epidicus's fear that *he* will be sacrificed as an expiation.[143] The joke's macabre assimilation of the slave's

---

is not hindered, since the privilege of overseeing the care of the *lares* of the *dominus* would still in that case be a religious experience denied to the unfree.

140. *De agri cultura* 143.1–2. For the granting of permission to (slave) nurses to make nonblood sacrifices on behalf of a child see Varro *Logistorici* fr. 9 Bolisani with Holland 2008, 101.

141. *De agri cultura* 83; further on slave involvement in the cult of Silvanus in Bömer 1981–90: I.78–87. For the master's command to a Manius—likely a generic name for the overseer—to undertake the *lustratio* see *De agri cultura* 141 with Kolendo 1994, 271–72. Slaves as the presumed audience of the officiating master: El Bouzidi 2015, 142 with table 16.

142. *Amph.* 1126–27; *Epid.* 417–18; *Truc.* 476. Cf. Way 2000 on the representation of prosthetic and masterly "extensability" in *Casina*; Reay 2005 for prostheticization as a core element of aristocratic self-fashioning in Cato.

143. *Epid.* 139–40: *men piacularem oportet fieri ob stultitiam tuam / ut meum tergum tuae stultitiae subdes succidaneum*, with Duckworth 1940 *ad loc.* and Jocelyn 2001, 288 on the *hostia succidanea*. The slave later envisions his punishment as turning his backside into a work of art: *Epid.* 626, adduced by Fraenkel [1922] 2007, 13 as an instance of Plautus's "unbridled fantasy as he elaborates brutal punishments of slaves" (cf. Richlin 2018, 92–93 on the backside as hypervisible site for the semiotics of trauma). This image makes a point about the instrumentalization of the enslaved in connection with the production of art; perhaps Plautus was aware of reports that

mottled back to a *hostia succidanea* is especially devastating, not only because it entertains the possibility that subjugated human beings might actually be offered as sacrifices to the gods—a practice not unknown to Romans of Plautus's time[144]—but also because it foregrounds, to a degree almost without parallel in our other sources for the period, the indispensable role of sacrifice in the structuring of relations between slaves and slavers. Those who were free performed that freedom in part by bossing slaves around in ritual contexts, as the behavior of *Miles Gloriosus*'s protagonist Philocomasium illustrates. Having first collaborated with the slave Palaestrio to concoct a prophetic dream and deceive another slave who had seen her making out with her lover, Philocomasium next orders Periplectomenus's slaves to place a fire on the altar so that she can offer thanks to Diana.[145] Plautine comedy's turn to sacrificial ritual as an opportunity to underline subordination falls in line with the recurring and successful patterning of animal sacrifice throughout the Greco-Roman Mediterranean to represent, model, and communicate elite social control.[146] Within this configuration, slaves were expected to be quasi-permanent altar servers, both in the private domain of the house and in public ritual contexts.[147] If Roman sacrifices were "sites through which idealized modes of religiosity could be constructed and promulgated,"[148] it makes perfect sense that this idealization molded the relationship between masters and slaves, the fundamental axis of Roman religious personhood. Unsurprisingly, one of the first acts of the manumitted slave was to offer sacrifice—as token and confirmation of a newfound (or restored) ritual capacity.[149]

---

the Athenian painter Parrhesius had tortured an Olynthian slave while painting his *Prometheus* (Sen. *Contr.* 10.5).

144. Important recent treatments of the live burials of Greeks and Gauls in the Forum Boarium include Várhelyi 2007; Schultz 2010; and Champion 2017, chap. 4. The possibility that slaves were responsible for carrying out the burials: Padilla Peralta 2018a, xxxvii.

145. *Mil.* 411–12: *inde ignem in aram, ut Ephesiae Dianae laeta laudes / gratisque agam eique ut Arabico fumificem odore amoene.* The scene's progressive escalation of bewilderment: Sharrock 2009, 107–8.

146. Animal sacrifice in the Roman Empire as articulation and projection of social hierarchy: Gordon 1990, 224–31; Rives 2012. Cf. the striking absence of sacrifice in Terence: Gellar-Goad 2013, 166–72.

147. By "altar-servers," I mean the class of sacrificial attendants known as *uictimarii*, about whom now see Lennon 2015. Slave *ministri* in public settings: Bömer 1981–90, I.9–31. Domestic settings: broadly, De Marchi [1896–1903] 1975, I.113–14 on the *sacra officia* of slaves; in connection with the family cult of the Lares, Genius, and Penates, Flower 2017, 43–49.

148. I borrow this quotation from Balberg 2017, 243, discussing the imaginative and discursive work of sacrifice in the early rabbinic corpus.

149. Not the Plautine *palliata* but the *togata* of one of his contemporaries offers the most

To the extent that slave movements required slaves to acknowledge the divinities overseeing domestic and exterior spaces, as *Miles*'s Palaestrio does by saying goodbye to the *lar familiaris* before exiting the house, a semi-independent religious subjectivity would have come into being in the act of attending to the master's ritual wishes.[150] And, not unlike altar servers in more recent times, Plautus's (and Cato's) slaves were allowed to have some extra wine on the big feast days, the Compitalia and the Saturnalia.[151] Wine was god, and the celebration of its consumption lay at the heart of another mid-republican religious festival, the Liberalia so memorably upheld as an occasion for frank speech in one of Naevius's comedies.[152] But the overgenerous dispensation of alcohol to Roman slaves also facilitated the holiday stupefaction Frederick Douglass decried two millennia later: in slave regimes ancient and modern, the temporary amnesia induced by alcohol consumption is integral to the logic of the holiday as a "scene of subjection."[153] Since on the available comparative evidence even holiday merriment and intoxication have historically functioned as mechanisms for the subjection of the structurally oppressed, we should not be gulled into thinking that the religious dimension of binge consumption at these two festivals, and the general inversion of social roles lubricated by the gift of the grape, represented purely innocent fun and games for individuals of all social statuses; for slaves, these festivals and their associated rituals were *imposed*.[154]

Even the permission that was granted to slaves to officiate at the Compitalia, far from authorizing them fully as religious actors, amounted to another

---

direct (if fragmentary) testimonium for this practice: Titinius fr. 152 Daviault with commentary ad loc.

150. *Mil.* 1339: *etiam nunc saluto te, <Lar> familiaris, prius quam eo*; see Joshel and Petersen 2014, 97–114 on slave identity and movement around and within domestic spaces.

151. *De agri cultura* 57: 3 ½ *congii* per slave = 2.76 US gallons, or about fourteen bottles of wine; see analysis of Catonian food and drink rations in Roth 2007, 26–52 for whether this allotment was intended both for the slave and for his family. As one of the few privileges Cato grants his slaves: Richlin 2014, 206. Slave roles at the Saturnalia: Bömer 1981–90, II.173–95: Accius *Annales* fr. 3 Dangel with Čulík-Baird 2020, 180–81. note Plut. *Sull.* 18.5 on the festival's exceptionalism. Saturnalian inversion in Greece: Garlan 1988, 199; cf. the festival suspension of slaver hierarchies in Achaemenid Babylon (Berossus *FGH* 680 F 2).

152. Naevius *com.* fr. 113 Ribbeck^{2}: *Libera lingua loquimur ludis Liberalibus.*

153. The African American slave's holiday: Douglass [1855] 2003, 185–87, read by Roberts 2015, 80–81 through Hartman's (1997) "scenes of subjection."

154. *Pace* Kolendo 1994, 273: "Il semble que les esclaves n'avaient pas le sentiment que ces cultes et ces pratiques religieuses leur avaient été dans une certaine mesure imposés." On the special prerogatives of slaves at the Compitalia see Dionysius of Halicarnassus *AR* 4.14.4.

carceral mechanism, in the style of those other markers of "circumscribed humanity" through which slaves were distinguished from the free.[155] It is relevant to note here that the cult of the Lares also afforded a showcase for the belief that slaves did not have their own personal *genii* or *iunones*; these guardian spirits, to which slaves were expected to pay their cultic respects, were presumed to attach only to the free members of the household.[156] However, in spite of the evidence for this ontological differentiation, the psychological toll on slaves of being minimized in the ritual and theological operations of cult has been overlooked even in otherwise astute reflections on the peculiar position of the enslaved in Roman religious settings.[157] The slave's displacement from the center of the action was likely to have engendered some strong feelings, intensifying over the course of the annual festival calendar. Save from the few other Roman festivals besides the Compitalia that had a slave focus—the celebration for Aventine Diana on the thirteenth of August, a *seruorum dies festus* on which all slaves were released from work; the festival for Juno Caprotina on the seventh of July, which commemorated the slave women who had volunteered to pose as freeborn hostages when a Latin army threatened Rome in the years after the Gallic Sack—the master's orders took precedence over a slave's wish to attend other festivals in the annual rotation.[158] In any event, how plausible is it that most slaves received regular permission to participate in cultic celebrations, in the city or in the countryside? It is not exactly

155. For the phrase see Hartman 1997, 6; on the carceral function of "humanizing" gestures toward slaves, De Wet 2015, 18–19. Cf. the comments of Chaniotis 2018 on a cult association in Hellenistic Philadelpheia that exceptionally granted slaves permission to participate in its mystic rites (*Tituli Asiae Minoris* V.3.1539).

156. For indications in the *palliata* of the slave's lack of a *genius* see Dumézil 1979, 327–36; cf. Andreau and Descat 2011, 115. Broadly on the *genius* and *iuno*: Otto in *RE* 7.1. s.v. "genius," cols. 1155–70; Schilling 1979, 415–41; Dumézil 1974, 362–69 and 1983; Schultz 2006b, 124–25; Corbeill 2015, 124–28; Bettini 2016, 68–74. Imperial epigraphic evidence for slave offerings to the *genius* of owners: Antolini and Marengo 2017.

157. So, e.g., Amiri 2016, 68, on the paradoxical figuration of the slave *uictimarius* as simultaneously necessary for the physical performance of the sacrifice and marginal to its most central moment: "Il n'est évidemment pas question ici de parler . . . de l'émotion qu'il pourrait être amené à éprouver"—but why not at least speculate about the emotions likely to have been in play? *Victimarii* "proudly" stating their profession on Imperial inscriptions: Lennon 2015, 73 and 85.

158. The *seruorum dies festus*: Plut. *QR* 100 and Festus 460.32–36 L. The festival of Juno Caprotina: Macr. *Sat.* 1.11.36–40, with other versions of the aetiology in Ov. *Ars am.* 2.257–58 and Plut. *Rom.* 29 and *Cam.* 33; discussion in Perry 2014, 21–22 and Bettini 2016, 77–79. Roman slave holidays, and holidays that recognized slaves: Bradley 1994, 18.

a surprise, then, that festival time proved most delectable when the master happened to be away.[159]

However, the Plautine dramas that record the performance of religious subjection in mid-republican Rome also bring to light slaves who insisted on their religious agency, in forms that simultaneously worked within and sought to manipulate and bend the religious strictures of enslavement. The mere fact of attending a festival may have represented an act of defiance in itself: at least some *ludi* were inaugurated by a ritual formula instructing foreigners and slaves to remove themselves from the premises—although this command should be understood more as enactive of religious difference than as an enforceable injunction against the presence of the Other.[160] There were in any event other tactics of resistance beyond the praxis of presence, beginning with the covert undermining of what we might term the master's *theology*. The limitation and regulation of the slave's capacity to offer cult acted in collaboration with the insidious psychological operations of this theology, the core premise of which is expounded by the Lorarius of Plautus's *Captiui* to his two new charges: "if the immortal gods have wished for this, for you to experience this grief, it is fitting to endure it patiently; if you do that, the work will be lighter" (*si di immortales id uoluerunt, uos hanc aerumnam exsequi / decet id pati animo aequo: si id facietis, leuior labos erit*).[161] Comparison with American slaveowners' deployment of preaching to keep slaves in line not only throws into sharp relief the function of this theology as a tactic of control but also gives the lie to the supposition that Romans were not interested in the religious ideas of their slaves; drilling the idea that the gods were responsible *and* that it was best for the slave to endure the divinely ordained misfortune of enslavement mat-

159. Toxilus in *Persae* cooks up a good time with the master out of town (*Pers.* 29): *basilice agito eleutheria* ("I'm living up the Liberty-festival like a king"), with Fraenkel [1922] 2007, 130–32 on the charge of the adverb. It is clear from, e.g., Cato *De agri cultura* 2.4 that slaves were expected to work even on feast days.

160. For the formula see Paul. Fest. 72 L. with De Cazanove 2007, 45 and Scheid 2016, 80–90. By the late Republic, the admission of slaves to a major religious festival would feature among the explosive accusations lodged against one controversial magistrate: see Cic. *Har. resp.* 21–27 on his *bête noire* P. Clodius. Note also the admission of one *ancilla* to the celebration of the Matralia—for a ritual beating: Plut. *QR* 16 with Carroll 2019, 7–8.

161. *Capt.* 195–96; on the paradoxicality of these and other similarly themed pronouncements by *lorarii* in the play see Gunderson 2015, 116–17. Cf. *Amph.* 180–81 for Sosia's internalization of religious guilt, approvingly noted by Mercury: *sum uero uerna uerbero: numero mihi in mentem fuit / dis aduenientem gratias pro meritis agere atque alloqui?* The representation of slaves as recognizing their servitude to be a divinely ordered dispensation: note, purely e.g., *Pseud.* 767 with Fraenkel [1922] 2007, 123 and Richlin 2018, 29–30 on "slave laments."

tered.[162] How might slaves respond to this discourse? By staging themselves as gods.

When *Asinaria*'s Libanus and Leonida cap their mockery of the master Argyrippus by offering to hand over the coveted twenty minas if he worships them as gods (*Asin.* 712–16)—

ARG: *datisne argentum?*
LIB: *si quidem mi statuam et aram statuis*
atque ut deo mi hic immolas bouem—nam ego tibi Salus sum.
LEO: *etiam tu, ere, istunc amoues aps te atque me ipse aggredere*
atque illa sibi quae hic iusserat mi statuis supplicasque?
ARG: *quem te autem diuom nominem?*
LEO: *Fortunam, atque Obsequentem.*

ARG: You'll give me the money?
LIB: Yup, if you set up a statue and an altar to me and sacrifice right here a cow to me as you would for a god—since I'm Health to you.
LEO: Master, are you going to move that fool away from you and approach me and set up for me what he ordered for himself—and supplicate me?
ARG: What god should I call you?
LEO: Fortune—favorable Fortune.

—the cruel joke, further sharpened by the existence of Roman cults to Salus and to Fortuna Obsequens during our period, is that the transmutation of slaves into recipients of cult was impossible. But already in its very articulation this fantasy throws a wrench into Roman calibrations of the boundary between the human and the divine, a delicate negotiation normally understood to be the prerogative of the free and mighty.[163]

162. The "prominent preaching to the slaves" in antebellum America: Randolph 1893; Raboteau [1978] 2004, 294–95 on slave responses to this preaching; cf. Parker 2001 on the work of Johannes Capitein, the former slave turned apologist for slavery. Philosophy and theology as methods for controlling slaves, from the Hellenistic and Roman world to the antebellum South: De Ste. Croix 1981, 418–25; cf. De Wet 2015 on Christian preaching to slaves.

163. Overview of this negotiation's literary instantiation in Feeney 1998, 108–14. Distinguishing this passage from more run-of-the-mill personifications of benefactors as *mea Salus* elsewhere in Plautus: Hanson 1959a, 76; cf. Clark 2019, 223–24, which is not in my view sufficiently attentive to the charge of *slaves* figuring themselves as divinities. The worship of Salus and Fortuna Obsequens in Republican Rome: Clark 2007, chap. 3. Slave deification: Segal 1968, 133–35; Gellar-Goad 2013, 164–65.

The potency of mid-republican drama's engagement with mass enslavement arose not only from its entertainment value but also from the office that it discharged of verbalizing the anguish and sorrow of mass enslavement in religious terms, and in formulating these for public consumption at festivals and against the backdrop of the monumental constructions that were built from the proceeds of the same wars through which some of those watching the plays—and some of those performing in them—had been brought to Rome as slaves. Roman comedy's cultivation of an affective domain for the contemplation and scrutiny of abstractions such as hope has been well brought out in a recent essay by Laurel Fulkerson.[164] On my reading, the experience of comedy within a religious setting prompted those who were enslaved and in attendance to reassess their relationship to not only their native religious observances but also to those practiced at Rome, and to begin the mental process of imagining themselves as competent in and deserving of a place in Roman religious praxis. This dialogue would not have been restricted solely to matters of ritual practice: Catherine Connors has argued quite compellingly for locating Fides, another divine quality that received a temple in the third century, at the beating heart of Plautine comedy's meditation on the meaning and reproduction of citizenship.[165] In light of these considerations, it is justified to take the play of slaves with divine personifications as directing the Plautine craft of "transformation and identification motifs" toward an unsettling dramatization of the religiosity of the enslaved as it (and they) received fitful and fleeting expression in Roman civic spaces.[166]

That temple construction physically and virtually loomed over Roman drama's treatment of the harrowing dilemmas of civic identity is where the monumental metamorphosis of the mid-republican city left its most indelible mark. It may not be a stretch to credit the interaction of temple-facing drama and public discourses of subjection with spurring the adoption and diffusion of a vocabulary for state violence that, while overlapping to some degree with the dominance lexicon of ancient Near Eastern kingdoms, proved unusually durable in normalizing the practice of enslavement as a defining element of Rome's imperial identity.[167] In this vein, two other dimensions of Roman religion's entanglements with slavery merit underlining here. First, if we follow

164. Fulkerson 2018.

165. Connors 2016, esp. 281–84.

166. Broadly on this craft see Fraenkel [1922] 2007, chaps. 2–3, especially pp. 51–52 on the mythological self-interpellation of characters.

167. Superbly on the formulation of this vocabulary and its literary markers: Lavan 2013, chap. 2. On Plautus's interrogation of the uncertainties and mutabilities of civic status in times of war note Konstan and Raval 2018: comic violence in Plautus gives voice to "an otherwise

Jacob Mackey in his account of the properties that characterized Roman religion and grant the existence of "intentional states" behind ritual praxis, the organization of Roman religious practice around the exploitation of slaves and the formulation of belief in the gods as a subject-object relation of total domination fed on each other. As brought to life in a tantalizing fragment of Seneca the Younger's *De superstitione*, the outfitting of the statue of Capitoline Jupiter with attendants who were tasked with catering to his every "need" was one very public instantiation of the divine representations that took shape around the cross-fertilization of Roman religion and mass enslavement: the greatest god received worship as the perfect and unattainable—but therefore desirable and within moderated bounds even imitable—paragon of masterly domination over the enslaved.[168]

Second, though I have chosen to focus primarily on those who held the status of slave as recipients of this message of religious domination, the fusion of Roman state power and Roman religious authority played out on another (complementary) axis as well. Rome's coercive alliance system evolved a language of ritual and prayer for soliciting the gods' endorsement of Roman expansion and of obedience to Rome by the Latins, especially in the aftermath of the Latin League's termination in 338 BCE.[169] Roman festival culture therefore took its cues from (and at the same time provided a performance context for) the linking of religious ritual to this species of imperial world-making.

III. Conclusion

This chapter's accent on *public* religious festivals should not be taken as illustrative of the full picture. Even as the centralization of cult picked up speed, private cults of various kinds retained their salience in the religious world of the middle Republic. It was in the sphere of private cult that some tactics of

---

repressed anxiety in the citizen audience" about "the ever-present possibility of being reduced to slavery" (48, 61).

168. Mackey 2017 on Roman religion's "intentional states"; Seneca *De superstitione* frr. 35–36 Haase = fr. 69 Vottero, to be read with Vottero 1998 ad loc. For the perfection of Jupiter's divinity as deriving from its extremeness cf. Chlup 2018 on the nature of Greek (and Roman) gods.

169. Included in one of the prayers for the Augustan *ludi saeculares* is the clause "that the Latin should always obey" (*utique Latinus semper obtemperassit*: restored to the Augustan *acta* on the basis of the Severan *acta* and now accepted in place of Mommsen's creative if rather more tame *utique semper Latinum nomen tueamini*): *CIL* VI.32323.93–94 with Taylor 1934, 108–11; Pighi ad loc.; Gruen 1984, I.282–83; Scheid 2016, 78–79. On the (mandated?) religious travel of Latins to Rome see chapter 5 n. 34.

resistance to the impositions of an elite-orchestrated religious praxis could take shape and flourish.[170] Nonetheless, I have been primarily concerned with public festival culture in the previous pages because it was there that opportunities for social intervisibility and the production of common knowledge proliferated. This common knowledge orbited around the idea that at Rome, everyone had a place and a responsibility in the sight of the gods—whether to officiate or serve, whether to dance or observe. Common knowledge and the cultivation of a religious brand went hand in hand. Rome's capacity to translate its monumentalizing fixation on cult into an exportable reputation did not stop with the discourse of *Fides*/Pistis that makes its first appearance on the coin issue of a third-century ally.[171]

The lasting significance of temples in the construction and promulgation of common civic knowledge snaps into focus by the late Republic and early Empire, when antiquarian interest in sifting through their real and hyperreal archives spikes and Imperial interest in flexing the system to new ends comes into view.[172] Hitched to the epistemic revolution whose force would reverberate across the centuries, antiquarian research kept an eye on Rome's festival culture, as the works of Varro and his successors make clear. For evidence of the later commingling and conflation of construction practice with the projection of statehood, one could do worse than cite Augustus's boast of having renovated eighty-two temples in one consulship.[173] Arguably an even louder signal of the sociocognitive cross-fertilization of temples, festival culture, and antiquarianism comes through in Valerius Maximus's curation of a list of gods in Book 1 of his *Facta et dicta memorabilia,* headlined by the brother-divinities whose early republican temple was repaired and rededicated with accompanying games by the future emperor, Tiberius, in 6 CE.[174]

In the long run, one important phenomenological and discursive outcome of the fusion of temples and festivals was the emergence of "religion" as a category of cultural and historical analysis in its own right, its birth midwifed by the application of intellectual energy to processing and reactivating the performance culture whose birth is traceable to the middle Republic. One

170. On the blurring of boundaries between "public" and "private" religious ceremonial see the comments of Russell 2016, 102–5 on Festus 284 L.

171. The silver stater of Lokri Epizephyrii minted c. 270, with a head of Zeus on the obverse and Pistis (*Fides*) crowning a seated Roma on the reverse: *SNG* 3.531, with Hölkeskamp 2000 for contextualization; Crawford 1974, II.724–25 for personified Roma on coins.

172. On this practice see Padilla Peralta 2019.

173. *RG* 20: *duo et octoginta templa deum in urbe consul sextum ex decreto senatus refeci, nullo praetermisso quod eo tempore refici debebat.*

174. Val. Max. 1.8.1 with Rüpke 2015, 106–7; for Tiberius's investment in the Dioscuri and their temple see Champlin 2011.

symptom of this process is that public spectacles of varying stripes became to a degree almost synonymous with the presence and experience of the divine.[175] But another and in the long run even more definitive outcome was Rome's emergence as a center of pilgrimage. In order for the messages examined in this chapter to attain general circulation, residents of the city had to be in a position to participate in their reception and interpretation—ideally in the company of out-of-towners, whether citizen or non-Roman, who were themselves digesting the contents of those messages. The next chapter proposes pilgrimage as an explanation for how these interactions occurred, and human mobility for religious purposes as simultaneously a consequence of and a catalyst for mid-republican state formation.

175. Ciceronian evidence for this equation: Clark in progress; cf. Clark 2018, 104 on religion and public oratory as equally capable of "connect[ing] immediacy with some level of 'transcendence,' albeit in rather different ways."

5

Pilgrimage to Mid-Republican Rome

FROM DEDICATIONS TO NETWORKS

AMONG THE MORE INTRIGUING CONSEQUENCES of Rome's multicentury investment in the monumentalization of its sacred urban landscape is the gentle fade into insignificance of cultic centers elsewhere in Latium within a century and a half after our period.[1] Despite the mentions in late republican authors of religiously motivated travel to extraurban sites that were hallowed by tradition and legend—Cicero's allusion to the *vestigia* of Castor and Pollux at Lake Regillus is especially notable—there is no question that the city of Rome itself had by that point become dominant in religious affairs, as it had in other matters.[2] While this development could be read simply as another epiphenomenon of the funneling of central Italy's population toward the city of Rome in the closing decades of the Republic,[3] we should be wary of positing a direct causal relationship between this large-scale migration and the hollowing out of Latium's sacred landscapes. Complicating matters, it is hard to find other Hellenistic parallels for the centralization of cult within an imperial core region, although the interaction between synoecism and the increasingly urbanized morphology of public religious observance in the world of Alexander the Great's successors presents some attractive possibilities for comparison.[4]

1. Rous 2009 for the archaeological trends; Bouma and van 't Lindenhout 1996 for cult and settlement in Latium in the archaic and early republican periods. Cf. n. 27 below on Rome's assertion of control over the major regional cults; Dillon 2015 for the contrast with Rome's handling of Greek sanctuaries. Comprehensive overviews of Latium's sanctuaries: Ceccarelli and Marroni 2011.

2. Cic. *ND* 3.11—but Cotta's reference to the hoofprints is sneering. On epiphanies of the Dioscuri see now Platt 2018.

3. On which see Strabo 5.2.9 and 5.3.1–2 with Morley 1996, 178–79.

4. Synoecism and civic cult in the Greek East: Boehm 2018, chap. 3. On the need for a more concerted investigation of this dynamic in the Roman world see Ando 2017.

The monumentalization of Rome's cultic landscape in the preceding centuries, in conjunction with the emergence of a curatorial and preservationist sensibility in the management of public cult, drove the city's ascendance to religious dominance. It was not only that new structures were going up, but also that older structures transitioned into objects of care and veneration.[5] Between the monumental sedimentation of the city on one end and its calendrical accumulation of festivals on the other, mid-republican Rome evolved a palimpsestic urban texture whose success at propagating the "virtual presence" of both living divinities and of the Romans alive and deceased who had worshipped them enhanced its appeal as a destination for pilgrimage.[6] Although Rome's enticement of out-of-town visitors was not confined solely to its growing importance as a center for cult, the infrastructural choices made by multiple generations of mid-republican elites attest a determination on their part to make the city's sacred profile impossible for new arrivals to miss—perhaps nowhere more conspicuously than in the area of the Porta Capena, where the extramural temple of Mars was outfitted with a paved path from its podium to the city gate by action of the curule aediles for 295.[7]

While the sociocultural dynamics of human mobility up and down Italy come to the fore in the literary record for the late third and early second centuries (as we saw in chapter 4), centripetal and centrifugal movement of the voluntary and forced varieties had been a fact of peninsular life well before then. Studies of *longue durée* patterns of migration in mid-republican Rome and Italy are receiving a new boost from fields such as bioarchaeology, though the limited availability of skeletons sufficiently well preserved for scientific analysis and securely datable to our period imposes some restrictions on that front.[8] Exploiting more traditional veins of evidence, Laurens Tacoma's *Moving Romans* and Elena Isayev's *Migration, Mobility, and Place in Ancient Italy* have recently brought a new and more exacting focus to bear on the study of mobility in Roman history. Both studies are meticulous in their

5. Evidence for this phenomenon in the vicinity of the future Palatine sanctuary of Apollo: Zink 2015, 369.

6. Introduction and application of the terminology of "palimpsest" and "virtual presence" to the study of Hellenistic sanctuaries: Petsalis-Diomidis 2017.

7. Liv. 10.23.12 with Laurence 1999, 18–19 on the relationship of this temple to the first stage of the Via Appia and Oakley ad loc. for comment on the cost of the paving. For the identification of this temple and others in the area with archaeological remains see now Dubbini 2016, 343–46.

8. See, e.g., Killgrove 2013, 50–55 for the results of isotope analysis of Republican-era skeletons from Castellacio Europarco and 55–57 for the osteobiography of an individual who likely immigrated to Rome from the vicinity of Naples in the fourth or third century.

representation of the "pluriformity" of migration, as differentiated not only according to agency—voluntary, state-organized, forced—but also according to category: elite, administrative, educational, intellectual, artistic, seasonal/temporary labor, economic destitution, traders, slaves, soldiers.[9]

These last two categories are exceptionally important. During the fourth and third centuries, at least two institutions were steering people to Rome on a short-term basis, even if the demographic scale of that movement defies precise reckoning. The first was the annual cycle of elections; the second was the *dilectus*. Whatever one makes of the increasing gap between the numbers of enfranchised Romans in central Italy and the infrastructural capacity to accommodate their exercise of the franchise, or of the obviously anachronistic flavor of Polybius's description of the procedure for the *dilectus*,[10] by the end of the third century the city's population was swelling and contracting with each intake and discharge of out-of-town visitors. Another contributor to the city's periodic inflation and deflation was closely tied to the demands and outcomes of militarization: the *res publica's* orchestration of forced displacements, with battlefield captives of elite and nonelite backgrounds being warehoused in the city and its environs, for delivery either to ransom or to enslavement.[11]

At the same time as, and in tandem with, these institutional movers of men, the *ludi* and entertainments that we examined in chapter 4 were drawing people into the city. This chapter's primary intervention will consist of the argument that pilgrimage to participate in cult at Rome was yet another lever by which the mid-republican *res publica* bootstrapped itself into statehood. The burnishing of Rome's credentials as a destination for pilgrimage followed closely on the heels of the cresting popularity of a specific brand of religious observance in mid-republican central Italy, the healing cults that "formed a religious infrastructure that transcended political boundaries" and whose assimilation into the Roman matrix of statehood were the focus of chapter 3.[12] Although the interaction between premodern state formation and intercultural pilgrimage has surfaced on the radar of scholars working in other periods and regions, few studies of the middle Republic grant much space or recogni-

9. See Tacoma 2016, chap. 2 for a typology accompanied by a sketch of geographic catchments and construction of interval-estimate quantification for each of the individual categories.

10. Polyb. 6.19–21 with Walbank ad loc. and Brunt 1971, 625–34.

11. Jewell 2019 is sharp on the mid- and late republican landscapes of forced displacement. On captivity and ransoming see chapter 3 n. 42; for the conspicuousness of enslavement in Roman festival culture, pp. 165–75.

12. Quotation: Rüpke 2014c, 219.

tion to this cultural process. However, mid-republican Rome was not unlike other imperial cities in its reliance on monumentality to elicit and sustain waves of pilgrimage.[13] One of this chapter's primary goals is to identify where in the material record these waves can be detected and their impact gauged. One of its secondary aims is to model religiously motivated mobility as conducing to what Charles Tilly in his late-career work defined as a "trust network": that "ever-present form of commitment-maintaining connection" that binds two parties to each other in a situation of fraught encounter and risk.[14] I will suggest that the reproduction of these networks in and through cultic practices at Rome supplied yet another jolt to the mid-republican state formation project.

This chapter is organized into four main sections. In the first, I argue for the applicability of the concept of pilgrimage to the sacred mobilities of mid-republican Italy, and I introduce some of the epigraphic and literary evidence that can be marshaled to clarify its workings. The second section concentrates on the anepigraphic anatomical votives whose recovery and interpretation have moved to the center of Roman republican religious studies in recent years; the emphasis here will be on deriving conclusions about the scale of pilgrimage to Rome from quantitative analysis of the material record. To reanimate and flesh out further the existence of a pilgrimage network centered on Rome, the third section turns to the inscribed *pocola* ceramics, and their role within a souvenir economy that emerged in connection with the practice of pilgrimage. Finally, in the fourth section, I revisit the second section's quantitative findings to build a network model of pilgrimage's outcomes and thereby show how the material record can be manipulated to yield a series of representations of those social interactions that took place between city dwellers and out-of-towners when the latter came to make dedications at Rome's temples. The conclusion pulls these strands together, arguing for their relevance to our understanding of the political-religious economy of the mid-republican state and in the process clearing the way for the book's final chapter.

A supercharged version of this chapter's argument would posit a deliberate and highly coordinated campaign spanning the better part of two centuries, by which the city of Rome centered itself in the religious imaginations of those Italian communities that came under the Republic's sway. Fortunately, the actual positions staked out below do not require ascribing calculation or intent to a monolithically conceived Roman state. What I hope to demonstrate instead is that investments in temple construction and festival culture

13. For pilgrimage and state formation see, e.g., McCarriston 2017 on the ancient Near East; on monumentalized "imperial cities" as hubs for pilgrimage, Gutiérrez et al. 2015, 537–38.

14. Tilly 2010, 271.

created opportunities for nonresident central Italians to participate in cult at Rome, as sacred monumentalization began to exert its charismatic pull. Whether by conscious design or through the cumulative force of more than two centuries of contingent and serendipitous decisions, the city's capacity to entice visitors into spending time at its sanctuaries supplied a cultic boost to the centralizing motor of Roman statehood.[15]

I. Pilgrimage in Mid-Republican Italy: Prolegomena

I begin with some remarks on the conceptual and heuristic utility of pilgrimage and its relevance to the history of sacred movement in the Greco-Roman Mediterranean in general and mid-republican Italy in particular.

A practice of long-standing interest to historians of medieval and modern Christianity and Islam, pilgrimage has in recent years received more attention from historians working on other religious traditions. The rising interest in pilgrimage among scholars of Greco-Roman antiquity has prompted complaints that notions of pilgrimage modeled on Christianity and Islam are being uncritically retrofitted onto the ancient Mediterranean.[16] Criticisms of pilgrimage's application to the pagan Greco-Roman world have not been without their own lapses into uninterrogated assumption. It has been contended that for a trip to a sanctuary to count as pilgrimage the *primary* motivation had to have been religious, and that such a religious motivation had to be freely embraced, or that sacred movement has to exhibit some impressive measure of scale, either in chronological terms (by spanning multiple centuries) or in the volume of human traffic (to be reckoned in the four or five digits) or in geographic extent (the more distance traveled the better) to be classed as pilgrimage. On each of these fronts, however, studies of pilgrimage in Christian and non-Christian settings have advanced a more nuanced vision.

Pilgrims' reasons for travel were multiple and sometimes muddled, and in some cases originated in social or institutional pressures that verged on coercion; pilgrimage could be temporally restricted, waxing and waning with the fates of specific shrines; it could be limited in demographic scope, manifesting

15. See chapter 1 n. 7 on centrality and statehood; cf. Collins-Kreiner 2010, 448–50 on theories of pilgrimage as a center-seeking (and, I would add, center-making) activity.

16. Pilgrimage and human mobility in the ancient Mediterranean: Horden and Purcell 2000, 445–49. Specific studies: Dillon 1997; the essays in Frankfurter 1998; the essays in Elsner and Rutherford 2005; Kiernan 2012. Attention to and management of Mediterranean "heritage sites," many of which continued to receive pilgrims in late antiquity: Moralee 2018, 64–66. Terminological and conceptual debates over the use of the term *pilgrimage*: Graf 2002 and Scullion 2005; Kristensen 2012, 67–69; Eade and Albera 2017, 6–9. Pilgrimage studies bibliography: Eade and Mesaritou 2018.

not (only) in the teeming humanity that converged on major regional sanctuaries but also in the steady but slender trickle to an isolated remote shrine; and it could be local as well as global, since for every well-heeled pilgrim who covered extensive distances there were others who by choice or from lack of resources chose a day trip instead.[17] In the spirit of this work, my own application of the concept of pilgrimage is intended to highlight the small-scale but nonetheless time- and resource-consuming movement of individuals for the explicit purpose of visiting Rome's sanctuaries and participating in the *ludi*. Even individuals who traveled to Rome primarily for nonreligious reasons (military, economic, political) but made a point of stopping by the city's shrines can also be accommodated under the rubric of pilgrimage; the motives of pilgrims in other historical periods were regularly overdetermined, and sometimes "not strictly spiritual."[18]

That members of Rome's elite performed pilgrimages to extraurban and extrapeninsular destinations is well documented. The fourth and third centuries witnessed the dispatching of embassies staffed by Roman aristocrats to secure and relocate new gods for worship at Rome, resulting in the importations of cults of Aesculapius and Magna Mater from the Greek world.[19] These movements foreshadowed the increasing prominence of sanctuary visits in the "tours of duty" of Roman commanders and administrators during the second century.[20] Yet these embassies were only the tip of the iceberg. The frequenting of Italian sanctuaries outside of Rome by travelers during major festivals is indisputable. Some of those travelers were Roman; others came from farther afield. One Hellenistic literary source specifies the festival of Hera at Lacinium as one "to which all the Italians came"; a contemporaneous Greek text singles out two cult sites on the Tyrrhenian coastline—the Kirkaion approximately sixty miles south of Rome, and a monument to Elpenor in its vicinity—as orientation markers on a navigational guide, indicating that at the very least some Greeks traveling to the peninsula were keeping an eye out for these cult sites.[21] There is also evidence of pilgrimage to Lake Avernus in Campania, which at some point during our period—if not be-

17. In laying out these counters, I have relied mainly on the exposition of pilgrimage in Bartlett 2013, esp. 421–25; Oldfield 2014, esp. 226 and 264; McCarriston 2017, 12–13.

18. Bartlett 2013, 421 for quotation and discussion.

19. See chapter 3 for discussion of Aesculapius.

20. On these tours and their material traces compare Lo Monaco 2016 and Padilla Peralta 2018b, 252–53; cf. Kowalzig 2005 on *theōria* in the Greek Mediterranean.

21. Hera's festival: Ps.-Arist. *De mir. aus.* 96: εἰς ἣν συμπορεύονται πάντες Ἰταλιῶται; on Hannibal's visit and dedication, Polyb. 3.33.18 and Liv. 28.46.16. The Kirkaion: Ps.-Scylax *Periplous* 8; cf. Theophrastus *HP* 5.8.3 and Strabo 5.3.6 (the latter with Roller ad loc. for the botany of the region, implicated in the rise of a Hellenistic market in healing medicine).

fore—became home to a cult of the dead and perhaps even an oracle.[22] The fame of healing springs in Latium and Etruria traveled far and wide; though we cannot be certain of significant pilgrimage to these springs during our period, it is not unreasonable to assume that they were steadily accruing celebrity status in the two centuries before their first mentions in late republican and Imperial literary sources.[23] In Latium itself, the dedication of a blue necklace of Phoenician-Carthaginian manufacture at an extraurban republican sanctuary of Ardea at some point in the second half of the fourth or early third century may attest the presence of a culturally Punic pilgrim in the area. The literary record of treaties between Rome and Carthage makes it clear that Carthaginians were not strangers to the coast of Latium; the archaeological record confirms Punic visitors at sanctuaries in central Italy already in the archaic period.[24]

No later than the final decades of the third century, the movements of elite and nonelite Romans to locations in central Italy for the purpose of participating in cult and making offerings can be tracked in the material record. Although this movement, as documented in the dedicatory inscriptions commissioned or set up by these travelers, is not usually classed as pilgrimage, there is no reason why it should not be. The standard line is that the movement of Rome's elites was dictated at least in part by Rome's burgeoning interest in asserting its authority over major sanctuary centers in central Italy,[25] but such an explanation does not on its face preclude our reconceptualizing this movement as pilgrimage. At the extraurban sanctuary of Diana in Nemi, the site of a temple whose first construction phase is datable to the late fourth or

22. Lake Avernus: Hornblower 2018, 110–11 on Lyc. *Alex.* 694–711, with bibliography on Hannibal's stopover in the area; cf. Panayotakis 2009, 277–78 for Decimus Laberius's eponymous mime and Cicero's derisive allusion (*Tusc. Disp.* 1.37) to rituals performed there.

23. E.g., the *fontes Clusinae*: see Hor. *Epist.* 1.15 with Donahue 2014. The Ponte di Nona sanctuary and spring: Potter and Wells 1985; cf. Turfa 2006b, 73 on water at Italian sanctuaries.

24. Necklace deposited at the sanctuary at Banditella: Ceccarelli and Marroni 2011, 40; note p. 80 for the recovery of another necklace of the same style in a mid-republican deposit at Nemi. The treaties, and in particular the first with its reference to Ardea: Polyb. 3.22–7 with Serrati 2006. The Pyrgi tablets and Punic presence in Italic sanctuaries: Cornell 1995, 212–14 on the archaic period; Fentress 2013, 161–65 on Punic-Etruscan contacts and Punic visits to central Italian cult sites; Moser 2019b on activity at Latium's port sanctuaries. The circulation of fourth- and early third-century Carthaginian currencies in Rome and central Italy: Frey-Kupper 1995 and Susanna 2016. Punic merchants were active elsewhere in the peninsula: *Imagines* Buxentum 3 (dating to the third or second century) may name one; see commentary and bibliography ad loc.

25. For comment on this process see Scheid 2006, 79–80. Cf. Belfiori 2018 on the effects of Roman colonization on sanctuary centers in north-central Italy.

Table 5.1. Roman Magistrate Dedications, Nemi

CIL I² no.	Text	Other references
41	*Diana* | *M. Livio(s) M.f.* | *praitor dedit.*	*ILLRP* 76 = Ceccarelli and Marroni 2011, 70
610	*C. Aurilius C.f.* | *praitor* | *iterum didit* | *isdim consl* | *probavit.*	*ILLRP* 75
N/A	*Dian*[*ai*] | *C. Atini*[*us C(ai)* (?) *f(ilius)*] | *pr.* [*don(um) dat*].	Coarelli 2012, 277–278[1]

1. On the first praetor see Brennan 2001, 655; Degrassi *ILLRP* ad loc. for the second; Coarelli 2012 for the third. Roughly contemporaneous with these three dedications: the inscribed offering of a C. Manlius who traveled from Ariminum to make an offering *pro poplo Arimenesi* in his capacity as consul of a Roman colony (*CIL* I².40 with Bertrand 2015, 181–82); he may have been the grandfather of L. Manlius Acidinus, *pr. urb.* 210, and great-grandfather of L. Manlius Acidinus Fulvianus, *cos.* 179.

early third century,[26] several Roman magistrates made dedications (table 5.1): the praetor Marcus Livius, son of Marcus, possibly the consul of 219 whose *cognomen* was Salinator; the praetor Gaius Aurelius, son of Gaius, praetor in 202 and 201 en route to a consulship in 200; and the praetor Gaius Atinius, son of Gaius, who held office sometime in the first two decades of the second century. Roman magistrates also traveled to Lavinium for cultic reasons, although when they began doing so is unclear. By the late Republic, it had become customary for Roman consuls to journey there and offer sacrifice immediately after assuming and just prior to stepping down from office.[27] Revealingly, Lavinium appears to have been outfitted, either during our period or not long thereafter, with a pilgrimage-site fixture in the form of a dutifully tended relic: the city's priests preserved in brine the body of the sow whose prodigious birthing of thirty white pigs Aeneas had been advised to interpret as a sign of his arrival at his final destination.[28]

26. The *lucus* was frequented perhaps as early as the middle Bronze Age: Ceccarelli and Marroni 2011, 71–72. The temple's construction: Ghini and Diosono 2012.

27. Consuls: Varro *LL* 5.144 and Macrob. *Sat.* 3.4.11. *Imperatores* en route to *provinciae*: Servius *ad Aen.* 3.12 with Ando 2008, 119. The presence of Roman magistrates at this and other federal sanctuaries: Scheid 2006, esp. 79–80; Hölkeskamp 2011 on the theatricality of consular ritual performance. The consular circuit Capitol-Alban Mount-Lavinium: Grandazzi 2010.

28. Varro *RR* 2.4.18 for the pig's preservation; for the prodigy, Verg. *Aen.* 3.390–393; for an alternative version of the story, Cassius Hemina *FRHist* F14 with commentary *ad loc.* and Stucchi 2018. By Timaeus's lifetime, Lavinium claimed to possess relics from the Trojan War: *FGH* 566 F 59 (*apud* Dionysius of Halicarnassus *AR* 1.67.4), punctuated with the comment that the historian had learned about these relics "from the inhabitants"; further on Timaeus see chapter

As for other cities prominent in magistrate tours of sacred duty, we may note Praeneste, where Q. Lutatius Cerco, *cos.* 241, traveled to consult the *sortes* at the sanctuary of Fortuna Primigenia in an effort to undermine or sidestep senatorial authority prior to commencing his term as consul.[29] As visits by Roman magistrates morphed into spectacles of ritualized power, communities that did not make the proper accommodations for their arrivals began to feel the heat, as a disrespected visiting magistrate's surly response to a perceived slight would later make menacingly obvious.[30]

But pilgrimage to Italian sanctuaries was by no means the exclusive prerogative of Roman magistrates. At Nemi, the epigraphic record preserves third- and early second-century dedications from visitors in nonofficial capacities, from a humble nurse who dedicated an inscribed bronze spear tip and bronze breast to a Poublilia Turpilia who had a statue erected on behalf of her son (table 5.2). In the case of these dedicators, it is important to bear in mind a point recently stressed by Wiebke Friese in a study of women's sacred travel in Greece: "female agency outside the domestic environment was, if not ubiquitous, at least commonly accepted."[31] Similarly embedded in patterns of religiously motivated movement are the inscribed dedications at the grove of Feronia near Capena in Etruria, frequented in connection with an annual fair that attracted people from all over the peninsula. Although it was primarily through high-end offerings that the sanctuary amassed its renowned wealth—which was targeted for looting by Hannibal in 211—nonelite dedications are mostly what survive for us to examine, several of which are clearly the work of women.[32] A small, damaged statue base records the offering of a Plaria, freedwoman of Titus; another base that of three freedmen Genucilii; and a third that of a freedman Porcius. Much like the sanctuary at Nemi, Feronia's grove was an extraurban site to which most prospective worshippers will have had to travel, with journeys taking anywhere from a few hours to a few days.

---

4. Relics in the Hellenistic Greek world: see, e.g., Pliny *NH* 7.20 with Beagon ad loc. on King Pyrrhus's right toe.

29. Val. Max. 1.3.2 with Dillon 2015, 123–26; Miano 2018, 27 on the sanctuary's appeal to out-of-town worshippers. Further on this curious incident: Padilla Peralta 2018c, 293–94.

30. See Liv. 42.17 with Miano 2018, 30–31.

31. Statement and discussion: Friese 2017, 55–56; cf. Holland 2008, 101 on limits to the religious agency of slave women (and chapter 4 above).

32. The fair at the grove: Dionysius of Halicarnassus *AR* 3.32.1. The looting episode: Liv. 26.11; cf. Sil. *Pun.* 13.83–90. The wealth of the sanctuary: Granino Cecere 2009, updating Bodei Giglioni 1977 on temple repositories of wealth in Roman Italy. Accumulation of wealth at Mediterranean sanctuaries in other regions and periods: cf. (e.g.) Chankowski 2011 on the Hellenistic East; SanPietro 2014, chap. 4 on late antique Christian churches.

Table 5.2. Select Dedications, Nemi and the Lucus Feroniae

CIL I² no.	Text	Other references
42	*Poublilia Turpilia Cn. uxor | hoce seignum pro Cn. filiod | Dianai donum dedit.*	*ILLRP* 82 = Ceccarelli and Marroni 2011, 71
45	*Diana mereto | noutrix Paperia.*	*ILLRP* 81 = Ceccarelli and Marroni 2011,70[1]
2867	*[.]esco[.]al || vod A[- - -] | Plaria T.l. || dedet libes || Fero(niae) dono||m mereto.*	*ILLRP* 93a; Bloch 1952; Bloch and Foti 1953; Di Fazio 2013, 123 no. 3
2869a	*M. T. V. Genucilio Sen. l. | Feroneai dedit.*	*Nuove scoperte e acquisizioni* 1975 no. 40; Di Fazio 2013, 123 no. 6[2]
2869c	*[- - -]rcius L(uciae?) l. | [Fer]oneae | [- - -?]M[- - -?]*	Di Fazio 2013, 123 no. 1

1. This inscription on a bronze spear point was reported to have been found together with a bronze breast; note Holland 2008, 98–100 for the possibility that the breast was not intended as part of *noutrix Paperia*'s dedication. For another exemplar of the bronze-breast votive offering see De Cazanove 2016, 289, fig. 9.
2. Cf. Torelli 2014, 423–24, dating the freedmen Genucilii to the second century.

While we cannot know whether any of these dedicators came from Rome, at a minimum these artifacts attest the existence of religiously motivated mobility in mid-republican Italy.

That these extraurban locations were in the business of receiving pilgrims would therefore appear to be uncontroversial. These sites were not, however, alone in this regard: the city of Rome was also receiving pilgrims in the fourth and third centuries. By the second century, this movement to and from Rome during festival time is obvious,[33] but its prominence in the post-Hannibalic cultural dispensation owed much to state-overseen initiatives in the fourth and third centuries, one of which is detailed in Livy. In 344, reports of multiple prodigies ultimately resulted in the dispatching of instructions to supplicate not only to Rome's citizen tribes but also to the *finitimi populi*, a curious designation for what were likely communities at the remotest points of the *ager Romanus*. Bernhard Linke has persuasively interpreted this notice to mean that these *populi* were required to participate in *supplicationes* at Rome, presumably through ambassadors.[34] Initiatives like the one recorded for 344 established a precedent for what occurred over a century later during the

33. See, e.g., the ill fortune of the *eques* and his daughter on their return to Apulia in 114 after the *ludi Romani*: Obsequens 37 with Erdkamp 2008, 421 and Isayev 2017a, 30. Embassies: n. 38 below.

34. Liv. 7.28.6–8 with Linke 2013, 81. One precedent for this may have been the travel of Latins

Second Punic War: the requirement that people come from out of town to supplicate in moments of acute crisis, as is apparent from the directions that were circulated to the urban population and to those residing in the countryside at the height of the Hannibalic menace.[35] With Livy's books for most of the third century now lost to us, it is impossible to track in detail how public supplications gained prominence over the course of the fourth and third centuries as a mechanism for religiously motivated travel to Rome, or how the catchment area specified for those commanded to participate expanded and shrunk according to the particulars of any one expiation and the dynamics of Roman expansion. What is beyond a doubt, however, is that those communities (or at the very least their representatives) that traveled to Rome for the purpose of supplication were engaging in pilgrimage. While different in its initial impetus from the pilgrimage of the magistrates who ventured to Nemi and Lavinium or the individuals who visited Nemi and the *lucus Feroniae*, it was pilgrimage all the same. By reading the notices from Livy alongside the epigraphic evidence for visits to extraurban sanctuaries, we can cautiously postulate the existence of a dyadic structure for pilgrimage in the mid-republican peninsula: centripetal movement toward Rome followed by centrifugal movement away from it. Both types of movement will have been facilitated by Rome's escalating investments in road networks during our period.[36]

By the second century, there is unambiguous literary testimony for individuals traveling to Rome for the purpose of checking out the sacred sights. Not infrequently, they traveled long distances. Prominent figures from the Greek world who were seeking audiences with the Roman Senate led the way; the visit of Prusias II of Bithynia to tour "the temples of the gods and the city" (*templa deum urbemque*—an arresting hendiadys) was among the most memorable and high-profile of these episodes.[37] Embassies from communities

---

to Rome to offer crowns at the Capitoline Temple of Jupiter: see Liv. 2.22.6 (495) and 3.57.7 (448). Usefully on *supplicatio* in Republican Rome: Février 2009, 173–91.

35. E.g., Liv. 22.10.8: *supplicatumque iere cum coniugibus ac liberis non urbana multitudo tantum sed agrestium etiam.*

36. Cf. the distribution of reported *prodigia* along Roman roads: Rosenberger 2005. The road-enabled mobility of sacred embassies is not irreconcileable with the argument of Terrenato 2019, 230–36 that Rome's road network grew out of the transportation needs of *domi nobiles*—though I am skeptical that this was the primary factor behind the massive outlay in funds for their construction. I revisit the road network's importance to mid-republican religious history below.

37. Liv. 45.44.4–6, with Jenkyns 2013, 228 on Prusias's inclusion of the gods among "the three classes of the population"; Miano 2018, 31 on his tour of central Italic sanctuaries. Polyb. 30.18's scathingly tendentious characterization of this trip: chapter 3 n. 88.

that were already allied to or seeking to broker new terms of alliance made the journey as well, and on at least four separate occasions they requested and obtained permission from the Senate to make votive offerings at the Capitoline temple of Jupiter.[38] Although adapted to a new geopolitical dispensation after Rome's victory in the Second Punic War, these dynamics were already in motion during the third century, when signs of a rising human traffic to Rome's shrines and temples first appear in the material record. The main evidence comes in the form of a class of artifact whose popularization throughout central Italy in the fourth and third centuries has been taken to herald a sea change in religious sensibility. These are the anatomical votives whose quantification and analysis will enlist our energies next.

II. Anatomical Votives and Italy's Pilgrimage Networks

My argument in this section is that one of the most effective ways to reconstruct mid-republican pilgrimage is by quantifying the number of anatomical votives that were deposited at sanctuaries in the city of Rome during the fourth and third centuries. In turning to the analysis of these votives, I follow the lead of recent work on central Italian material culture that has teased out the subtleties and possibilities of this unique archive.[39] As a preliminary to my exposition of the argument, some comment on the history of these votives and of their study is in order.[40]

Characterized for the most part by dedications of ceramics or small objects wrought from precious metal, the votive trends of archaic central Italy steadily gave way in the course of the fourth and early third centuries to a new religious order in which offerings made out of terracotta predominated—expressive of the so-called Etrusco-Latial-Campanian (ELC) regime.[41] Of the approximately two hundred Italian sanctuary locations that have been excavated to date, about 130 have yielded anepigraphic anatomicals: uninscribed terracotta, and less frequently metal, artifacts shaped as body parts

38. The embassies: Liv. 28.39.18 (Saguntum, 205 BCE); 36.35.12 (legates of King Philip V, 191); 43.6.6 (Alabanda and Lampsacus, 170); 44.14.3 (Pamphylia, 169). Timing of embassy visits: note Gibson 2012, 264–65 on embassies and festivals in the Hellenistic world. The granting of a similar privilege to the *collegium* of *scribae* and *histriones* at the Aventine temple of Minerva (chapter 4 n. 58): Jory 1970, 229–30.

39. Moser 2019 is exemplary in this regard.

40. In referring to the material record of dedications below, I will use the terms "votive" and "ex-voto" more or less interchangeably; although efforts are now afoot to devise a more stringently differentiated lexicon for votive offerings, adoption of, for example, the taxonomic strictures of Zeggio 2016 would not significantly alter this chapter's conclusions.

41. The transition: Gentili 2005, 367–69.

that were mass-produced in considerable quantities (figure 5.1).[42] At least some of this mass production will have been the responsibility of workshops that were under the supervision of the very sanctuaries in whose vicinity the items came to rest; the most outstanding illustration of this coupling is to be found at the sanctuary to the goddess Angitia in the Luco dei Marsi, where excavations have uncovered a kiln—presumably for the firing of votives—underneath the terrace.[43] In any case, the number of surviving inscribed terracotta dedications is meager by comparison to the abundance of anepigraphic anatomical ones; other types of terracotta votives that were produced by Italic communities during the fourth and third centuries likewise do not compare in terms of scale.[44]

Following the pioneering publications of 1975 and 1981 that first synthesized all the then-available evidence for the geographical distribution of the anatomical ex-votos, it was long held that the ELC regime corresponded more or less perfectly with the spread of Romanization. Resistance to this line of interpretation subsequently stiffened among scholars who were calling into question Romanization's relation to the history of religious transformation in Italy.[45] One of the most perceptive concerns voiced was that the rubric of Romanization shoehorned religion into the category of epiphenomenal signals of the conquest, denying religious action and motivation any measure of

42. Although the scale of the votive finds left a deep impression on scholars at the turn of the twentieth century—see, e.g., De Marchi [1896–1903] 1975, I.296–97, and Lanciani at n. 51 below—it took decades for their significance to be fully digested: see North 1989, 580 for alertness to their importance. Exposition of the ELC: Fenelli 1975a and 1975b (ninety-six sites surveyed); Comella 1981 (161 sites surveyed); De Cazanove 1991; Turfa 2004 and Dicus 2012, chap. 4 for updated figures. The ELC and Etruscan culture before and during the Roman conquest: Haack 2017; further on votive deposits in Etruria note also Jannot 2005, 139–42. Mass production under the control of sanctuaries: Bodei Giglioni 1977; Edlund 1983; Morel 1989–1990, 512–14. Postdepositional recyling of metal is partly accountable for the underrepresentation of bronze votives in the material record, although more are now coming to light: see Galinsky 2018 on "Sabellian" bronze figurines of Hercules.

43. Mass production under the control of sanctuaries: Bodei Giglioni 1977; Edlund 1983; Morel 1989–90, 512–14. The sanctuary of Angitia: Cairoli 2001, with additional bibliography in Estienne and De Cazanove 2009, 9; for more on this divinity see the Appendix.

44. Nonnis 2016, 352–57 for discussion and 359–63 for a dossier of inscribed dedications; for other types of terracotta votives note (e.g.) Söderlind 2002 on Etruscan terra-cotta heads and Battiloro 2018, 88–96 on Lucanian figurines. Coroplastic trends further afield: Lancel 1995, 339–50 on Carthaginian terracottas.

45. See De Cazanove 2000 for a précis of the earlier position. Robust challenges to the use of Romanization for interpreting the ELC: Glinister 2006a; cf. Griffith 2013, 239. For summary and evaluation of other critical treatments note Stek 2015; Scopacasa 2015b, 1–5.

FIGURE 5.1. Votive uterus, third–second century BCE. Princeton University Art Museum. Museum Purchase, Classical Purchase Fund. (Photo credit: Princeton University Art Museum)

independent agency in their own right.[46] In response, Olivier de Cazanove has insisted repeatedly on the need to contextualize the anatomicals as products of a third-century imperializing moment, defined by Rome's adoption of the cult of Aesculapius and by the propulsive dissemination of Roman cultic practices through colonization.[47] Typological study of the anatomicals, notably of the uterine specimens that can be differentiated into at least four different genera, lends some support to De Cazanove's general argument. Although certainty will be elusive so long as a comprehensive investigation of anatomical typologies along the lines of J.-P. Morel's classification of Campanian ceramics remains a pipe dream, it seems reasonable to conclude with De Caza-

46. Terrenato 2013, 43–48 for a sophisticated expression of this stance, and 53–60 for an alternative.

47. De Cazanove 2015 and 2016; cf. Glinister 2015 on colonies as vehicles for "religious dynamism."

nove that the distribution of the anatomical *ex-votos* is reflective, if not of top-down Romanization, then at the very least of the agency of those Roman and Latin colonists who were busy forging a new culture in the era of the first Great Migration.[48] However, for those areas of the peninsula that directly abutted or interacted with colonial foundations, the decision to adopt the anatomical votive habit interacted with preexisting cultural preferences that "seem to have been long-standing"; it would therefore be misguided to slight the agency of those communities who manipulated and adopted the ELC to their own specific ends and needs.[49]

In any event, other approaches to the study of the anatomicals that do not index it solely or primarily to the operations of Roman military and economic power have proven equally if not more productive, especially as archaeological finds force a reconsideration of the votives' geographic scatter.[50] Responding to the call to move beyond Romanization or its critique as an interpretive paradigm, investigations into the ritual lives of women and nonelites, the practice and valuation of reproductive and popular medicine, and the distribution and representation of ideas about personhood and disability have all received a boost from scholars willing to work with the anatomicals.[51] Attention to tactility as a component of the ritual sensorium of the anatomical votives has also increased in recent years, as the full spectrum of manual work involved in the management and upkeep of sanctuary spaces comes into clearer view.[52] Then there is the matter of the socioeconomic background of the votive dedicators. First floated by a generation of archaeologists who had been trained to read patterns of material culture in Roman Italy through a *marxisant* lens, the

48. De Cazanove 2015, 52 on distinguishing between the "impatto di Roma" and the "impatto dei coloni, romani e latini," in the votive record; cf. Torelli 1999, chap. 2, Stek 2016, 295–98, and Belfiori 2018 on the relationship between "Roman" colonization and religious Romanization. With the phrase "Great Migration," I nod both to Scheidel 2004b, 10–12 on the four colonization programs of the Republic and early Empire and to the twentieth-century "Great Migration" of African Americans in the United States.

49. Scopacasa 2015b, 18 for quotation and 14–22 for the details; further on cultural adaptation and appropriation note also Hughes 2017b, chap. 3. For the spread of the anatomical votive habit to Gallo-Roman communities after our period see De Cazanove 2009.

50. Note, e.g., Scopacasa 2016, 51–52 on excavations in the central Apennines and Adriatic Italy.

51. A call to escape the reductive hermeneutic constraints of Romanization: Termeer 2016. Ritual lives and agencies of women: Schultz 2006b; Glinister 2006b. Reproductive knowledge and popular medicine: Flemming 2016 and 2017. Personhood: Graham 2017. Disability: Graham 2016; Adams 2016.

52. On the latter note, e.g., the handling and disposal of architectural terracottas, "sacred rubbish": Glinister 2000.

possibility that some or even most of the anatomicals represent the religious agency of the lower classes should not be dismissed out of hand,[53] although the presumption that mass-produced votives straightforwardly mirror the socioeconomic background of their dedicators does not have much to commend it. Oddly, however, no global quantitative synthesis of the anatomical habit has been attempted, even though many of the publications of these votives in the *Corpus delle stipi votive* series do tabulate site finds.[54]

With the caveat that the etic classification of these votives as "anatomical" only imperfectly captures their varied significations,[55] the purpose of this section will be to move the conversation about these items onto the quantitative plane in order to gain a firmer handle on the habit's wax and wane in Rome, and thereby determine whether the activity of out-of-town travelers to Rome can be glimpsed behind the habit's imprint on the material record of the city. The votive record opens the door to the prospect of envisioning temporary migration flows in numerical terms.[56] Although depressingly in line with other historical episodes in the archaeology of nonprecious artifacts, the discovery of these anatomical votives in modern Rome is noteworthy in part because the scale of the first finds prompted some efforts to think quantitatively.

In the course of dredging and construction work to redirect and wall up the Tiber's flow during the 1880s, heaps of votives were unearthed in the general vicinity of the Tiber Island. Under the terms of an agreement reached between the Ministero della Pubblica Istruzione and the Ministero dei Lavori Pubblici at the time, materials recovered by the Ufficio Tecnico Speciale Per La Sistemazione del Tevere—the body directly responsible for oversight of the construction and dredging—was transferred to the archaeological authorities. The product of this collaboration was a compilation of numbered lists of the finds and their find-spots, the so-called *Verbali di consegna di oggetti provenienti dal Tevere*.[57] Unfortunately, however, many items were then sucked into the black hole of the antiquities market or were destroyed before they could be

53. Comments to this effect in Guarducci 1971, 275; *RMR* 1977; Pensabene et al. 1980; and Torelli 1995. The possibility that these votives reflect the agency of an unostentatious "middle class": Turfa 2006b, 72; cf. the warnings of Glinister 2006b, 96–97 against taking the votives as "lower class" offerings.

54. The publications do not always make the sorting and tabulation of different categories of votives and votive deposits possible: see Ammerman's 1991 criticisms of Iacobone 1988 and Ginge's 1993 comments on several of the other volumes.

55. For illustration of this point see Termeer 2016, 120.

56. Cf. Isayev 2017b, 19 on her reasons for *not* "creat[ing] a numerical model of migration flows."

57. The source for catalogues raisonnés such as the entry in *RMR* and Pensabene et al. 1980,

cataloged and stored away, with the result that only a limited number are now preserved in the storerooms of the Museo Nazionale. The 352 terracotta ex-votos that are documented as having been found on the right bank of the river in the vicinity of the modern Ponte dei Quattro Capi represent a fraction of the original finds in the area.[58] In 1893, the archaeologist Rodolfo Lanciani claimed that the votive specimens had to be counted not by the thousands but by the millions.[59] Even if one is inclined to dismiss Lanciani's words as exaggeration, the 16,000 items enumerated in the *Verbali* speak loudly about the magnitude of Rome's votive praxis during and after our period. I will return to this point momentarily.

The area around the Tiber has not been the only source of votive finds in Rome. In the decades since the river's dredging, deposits with contents that are datable to the fourth and third centuries have come to light in other parts of the city.[60] But the Tiber region has certainly been the most bountiful of the city's sectors in terms of the volume of votives recovered, and the main reason usually cited in explanation of the concentration of votives seems obvious enough: most if not the overwhelming majority of these votives were dedicated to the healing god Aesculapius, whose temple on the Tiber Island we examined in chapter 3. That most of the recovered votives were found upstream and lining the Tiber banks, as opposed to on the island itself, does not fatally undermine this explanation.[61] For one, the habit of clearing out votives at highly frequented temples is well known from other Greco-Roman sanctuary contexts. The sanctuary of Aesculapius accumulated enough wealth in the form of dedications for two late republican junior magistrates to tap into it as funding for the building of another structure;[62] dedications that could not be monetized or commodified would have been relocated to make space for new offerings. Other proposed explanations of these votives and their find-spots—

---

the *Verbali* provide a bare description of the item and find-spot but do not give detailed descriptions of find-context.

58. For this number see Carafa and Pacchiarotti in Carandini 2017, I.552, with citations.

59. Lanciani 1893, 62; cf. Lanciani 1897, 26–28 for an overview of the types of finds recovered from the riverbed. It is to be hoped that the resumption of archaeological excavation on the Tiber Island by the University of Florida will unearth not only more inscriptions (on which see already Bruce and Wagman 2012) but anatomicals as well.

60. See, e.g., Gatti Lo Guzzo 1978 and Martini 1990 on the deposits near the temple of Minerva Medica; Zeggio 1996 on the deposit at the Meta Sudans; Gentili 2005, 370–71 for overview of urban and peri-urban finds.

61. Cf. Glinister 2006a, 22.

62. *CIL* I^2.800 = *ILS* 3836 = *ILLRP* 39: [- - - -], *A.L*[- - - -]*s L.f. Flaccus* | *aid(iles) d(e) stipe Aesculapi* | *faciundum locauere,* | *eidem pr(aetores) probauere.* Bibliography on this inscription: Estienne and De Cazanove 2009, 27 n. 112.

that these votives were dedications to the divine personification of the Tiber, or that the Tiber was converted over time into one large *favissa* for use by all of the temples close to the banks, or that these represent the dedicatory caches of merchants whose stalls may have lined the left bank of the river—run into logical or evidentiary problems of various kinds and will not be considered here.[63] Even if, in light of potentially distorting taphonomic factors, one remains skeptical that the recovered votives were dedicated to Aesculapius, the volume of anatomicals tells us something about the scale of personalized engagement with cults at Rome during our period; whether worshippers were dedicating votives to Aesculapius or to Minerva Medica or other temples close to the Tiber, what matters most for my reconstruction is that these mid-republican foundations were on the receiving end of considerable foot traffic.

Despite the lack of rigorously detailed archaeological context for the riverine votives, there is plenty that one can do with the evidence at hand once quantitative analysis is brought to bear. For starters, we can build a relatively simple yet powerful model for the number of votives dedicated in mid-republican Rome, taking the aforementioned number of 16,000 items in the *Verbali* as a convenient point of departure. This figure is intended as nothing more than a speculative foundation, and the edifice that surges from it as a highly stylized (and necessarily simplified) approximation of one possible historical reality. A brief glance at quantitative trends in the deposition of votives throughout the peninsula outside of Rome will give us an idea of how to proceed with the first stages of model building. Tabulating and graphing the aggregate total of anatomical ex-votos recovered from five sites and published in the *Corpus delle stipi votive* yields some interesting results (color plate 3).[64] To hurdle past the depositional, postdepositional, and recovery processes that have rendered it difficult to assign most terracotta votives anything more precise than a general dating based on typology,[65] I created and plotted three

63. The *favissa* and merchant theories: Lanciani 1893 and Besnier 1902. The dedications-to-Tiber theory: Le Gall 1953, dismissed by Guarducci 1971, 269 n. 8. Assessment and criticism of these theories: *RMR* 1977, 140; Pensabene et al. 1980, 50–51. Use of the term *favissa* in modern archaeological reports: Zeggio 2016.

64. $N = 855$ for each trend line. The data were culled from Comella 1986; D'Ercole 1990; Comella 2001; Guidobaldi 2002; Bartolini and Benedettini 2011. The five sites: Falerii and Veii, both in Etruria; Punta della Vipera, an extraurban sanctuary near Caere; Belvedere a Lucera, near the town in Samnite/Daunian country that was colonized after the Second Samnite War; and Rapino, a settlement in the Abruzzo that was occupied by the Marrucini.

65. Griffith 2013, 239 for a concise review of the dating issues. For an ingenious attempt to establish a chronological distribution for Etruscan terracotta votive heads see Söderlind 2002, 348–50 with figure 166.

datasets for the votive corpora of these sites: one in which all artifacts were biased early (BE) and assigned a date corresponding to the earliest possible year within their typology-based chronological range; another in which all artifacts were biased to the middle (BM) and assigned a date corresponding to the halfway point of their chronological range; and a third in which all artifacts were biased late (BL) and assigned a date corresponding to the last year possible within their chronological range. Two of the three trend lines situate the peak of votive dedications in the third century, either in the first quarter (BE) or third (BM). In view of the cultic developments unfolding at Rome during these two periods, the timing is appealingly suggestive.

With a small peak before the major one, the BE line registers the possibility that dedications at Etruscan sites were on the rise some decades before the early third-century explosion. The one trend line that does strain credulity is BL: its peak in the second half of the second century combined with a long tail well into the second half of the first seems implausible on independent grounds.[66] Its inclusion here only serves to reinforce visually the likelihood that BE and BM are more accurate representations of what may have historically transpired. If the anatomical votive habit did persist in attenuated form after the end of the second or first few decades of the first century, it did so not in terracotta but in precious metal.[67]

With these broad trends as the backdrop, the next issue in need of resolution is how to leverage the 16,000 items listed in the *Verbali* in order to arrive at a global estimate of the number of anatomical ex-votos—the one class of votive whose association with the efflorescence of the ELC habit from the late fourth to the late second centuries is secure—that were dedicated at Rome during our period. Two steps are required to generate this estimate, which (it should be emphasized) will not pretend to accuracy except in the most general order-of-magnitude terms. The first is to establish the percentage of the items in the *Verbali* that are identifiable as anatomical ex-votos. Instead of slogging through the catalog to determine a precise figure, I have made use of a convenient shortcut. In the deposits of five Italian sanctuary sites whose publication catalogs I chose more or less at random, the average proportion of anatomical ex-votos to all other votives comes out to 36.5 percent.[68] Since

66. Religious activity at sanctuary sites throughout Italy undergoes a significant shift around 100 BCE: chapter 1 n. 57. The decline of votive terracotta production "in the whole of Central Italy" during the first century: Söderlind 2002, 355–58.

67. See, e.g., the second-century CE silver spleen dedicated at the temple of Aesculapius by an imperial freedman: *IGUR* I.105 with Estienne and De Cazanove 2009, 18–19.

68. The five sites whose *Corpus delle stipi votive* publications were consulted: Rapino (29.2 percent of votives were anatomicals), Veii (14.1 percent), Belvedere a Lucera (38.7 percent), Cumae (53.4 percent), and Punta della Vipera (47.2 percent).

anatomical ex-votos are almost certainly overrepresented in most deposits that survived to be excavated (coins will have been stolen in antiquity or looted from sites before and during excavation, while other metal objects will have been repurposed and organics will have disintegrated),[69] we should adjust this percentage downward and assume that, in the case of mid-republican Rome, no more than 30 percent of the votives dedicated during the fourth and third centuries at Rome were anatomical ex-votos. Multiplying 16,000 by 30 percent yields a baseline figure of 4,800 anatomical votives. In light of the loss or destruction of anatomical votives over time, this figure cannot account for more than a fraction of the original number of anatomical dedications in mid-republican Rome. Therefore, the second step to take is to settle on the percentage of the original global total that is represented by the 4,800. For simplicity's sake, I limit myself to three arithmetically straightforward possibilities: that the figure represents 10 percent, 5 percent, or 1 percent of the original amount of anatomical votives that were dedicated. Taking my cue from the trend lines for the ELC discussed above, I have broken up the hypothetical original quantities across fifty-year intervals from 325 to 125 BCE such that their distribution corresponds very roughly to a statistical normal distribution. The result is a simple demonstration of what the rate of dedications of anatomicals in the vicinity of Rome's Tiber Island may have looked like during the fourth and third centuries (table 5.3). Of course, the material record of dedicated anatomical ex-votos would be even under the most felicitous circumstances only a partial reflection of the total number of individuals who traveled to a shrine, and not only because of postdepositional processes. As Diogenes of Sinope once memorably quipped in response to a friend gawking at the heaps of dedications on Hellenistic Samothrace, disappointed—or unsuccessful—pilgrims did not leave behind votives.[70]

The true leap of faith comes at the next stage in the design of the model. First, in order to exploit these figures as proxies for mobility, we will need to convert numbers of dedications into human beings. The dilemma to iron out here is whether there was a one-to-one correspondence between any single ex-voto and a human dedicator. Tilting against this idea is the likelihood that reasonably well-off individuals would have been able to afford and dedicate more than one anatomical terra-cotta; inclining in favor is the likelihood that the relatively well-off opted for more impressive dedications of statuary or metal objects in lieu of or as complement to an anatomical terracotta offering.

69. The overrepresentation of terracotta relative to metal and organic offerings (such as fabrics and wood panels) at excavated republican sanctuaries: Estienne and De Cazanove 2009, 8–9.

70. Diog. Laert. 6.59 credits the line to Diogenes of Sinope but adds that some attributed it to Diagoras the Atheist; Cic. *ND* 3.37.89 attributes the one-liner to Diagoras.

Table 5.3. Anatomical Ex-Votos Dedicated in the Tiber Island Region

	Under the 10% rule		5% rule		1% rule	
Years	No. of dedications	Yearly avg.	ND	YA	ND	YA
325–275	4,800	96	9,600	192	48,000	960
275–225	19,200	384	38,400	768	192,000	3,840
225–175	19,200	384	38,400	768	192,000	3,840
175–125	4,800	96	9,600	192	48,000	960
Totals	48,000		96,000		480,000	

Without yielding fully to the position that these ex-votos were mostly dedications made by the socioeconomically middling or distressed, I will accept the latter argument and its implications: those who had more resources at their disposal were much more likely to set up another votive that was not an anatomical terracotta. On the assumption that this premise is generally correct, I will take each ex-voto as representing the one-time dedicatory act of a single individual.

Finally, in order to harness the votive record and quantitatively focused insights gleaned from it as testimonies to human mobility, we will need to establish some probabilistic parameters for the proposition that some of those whose activity has been conjured by these numbers were coming to Rome to make their dedications. Undeniably, many of those making these dedications will have been residents of the city at the time of the dedication. How might one go about informed speculation as to the number of dedicators who were not? One advantageous tool at the disposal of the probabilistically minded is Bayes' theorem. A staple of inferential statistics, this theorem is regularly employed to calibrate and recalibrate a set of probabilities against observed data and is for this reason beginning to gain traction among archaeologists.[71] The theorem enables the calibration of an anticipated outcome (a *prior* probability) according to new facts, as these come in.[72] The theorem calculates a *posterior* probability through the formula $xy / [xy + z(1\text{-}x)]$, where x is the *prior* probability; y is the *probability conditional on the hypothesis being true*; and z is the *probability conditional on the hypothesis being false.*

71. For a recent application of Bayesian statistics to the study of the Roman economy, see Rubio-Campillo et al. 2017; for an application of the theorem to the interface between religious practice and economic transactionality, Padilla Peralta 2020.

72. Formal textbook exposition of theorem: the last two chapters of Wonnacott and Wonnacott 1990. Popularizing, with real-world applications for polling: Silver 2012, chap. 8.

For this subsection, I wish to evaluate the following hypothesis: "of the individuals making votive offerings in mid-republican Rome, some came from out of town to make their dedications." Stacking the deck against the hypothesis, I will grant it only a 1 percent probability of being true and set this as my prior. To update this prior, I will now introduce some additional information from Rome's material record, in the form of inscribed votive bases that have also been recovered from the Tiber and that appear to be of mid-republican date.[73] These bases preserve the names of their dedicators and the gods to whom they were dedicated, who range from Aesculapius and Hercules to the more obscure Numisius Martius. Intriguingly, several of the individuals responsible for these dedications sport names that might betoken non-Roman origins (table 5.4). At the very least, each of these dedicators can be linked prosopographically to gentilician networks that extended beyond Rome to other regions of central Italy.[74] Mid-republican Albanii are attested in Etruria and at Firmum Picenum on the Adriatic, and a semilegendary member of the *gens* was credited in the annalistic tradition with guiding a *flamen* and the Vestals to Etruscan Caere at the time of the Gallic Sack.[75] Bruttius is an ethnonym; the connections of the *gens* to Bruttium and Lucania are attested well into the Empire.[76] Populicii (a variant spelling of Publicii) are active in central Italy, with two members of the *gens* involved in the vowing and dedication of a temple to Flora at Rome following the suppression of an insurrection

73. All but one were recovered during the Tiber's dredging and realignment in the 1880s. I restrict myself to this body of inscriptions because the other republican-era epigraphic votives published in *CIL* are either too fragmentary to merit discussion, not securely datable to the third/early second century, or not securely traceable to a find-context in Rome. For disagreement over the dating of *CIL* I^2.31, which is carved in travertine, compare Frank 1924, 32 n. 14 (dating to c. 125 on the grounds that travertine entered regular use at Rome in the second half of the second century); Panciera 1995, 323–24 (mid-third-century date for travertine's adoption); Jackson and Kosso 2013 (late second-century date); Ferraro in the *EDR* entry for the inscription (opting to rely on paleography for a third-century dating). Note now Bernard 2018a, 224–26 with table 7.2 for the lag between the date of Rome's acquisition of quarry zones and the first confirmed appearance of stone from those zones in monumental construction at Rome.

74. Usefully on onomastics, epigraphy, and mobility in archaic and mid-republican central Italy: Bourdin 2012, 575–85.

75. *CIE* 2603 bis = *TLE* 740 = *ET* OA 3.9: *tite : alpnas : turce : aiseras : θuflθicla : trutvecie* (on a fourth-century statue base; for *alpna(s)* = *Albinius/Albanius* see Schulze 1966, 118–19); *CIL* I^2.383 = IX.5351 = *ILS* 6132 = *ILLRP* 593 = Ernout no. 79 for a M. Albanius among Firmum Picenum's quaestors. The legendary Albanius: Liv. 5.40.9 with Ogilvie *ad loc.*; Luce 1990, 131–32 with n. 25 on *CIL* VI.1272 = *InscrIt* 13.3.11.

76. Arnheim 1972, 139–41; Settipani 2000, 340–41; Scalfari 2009, 128–29.

Table 5.4. Mid-Republican Inscribed Votives from the Tiber Area

CIL I² no.	Text	Other references
26	*Aiscolapio dono(m) | L. Albanius K(aesonis) f(ilius) dedit.*	*CIL* VI.30842 = *ILS* 3833 = *ILLRP* 36 + *Imag.* 21 = Ernout no. 20 = *RMR* 145 no. 180 = Renberg no. 1
27	*C. Bruttius | Aescolapi[o] | dono(m) dedit | meritod*	*ILS* 3835 = *ILLRP* 38 = Renberg no. 7
28	*Aescolapio | donom dat | lubens merito | M(arcus) Populicio M(arci) f(ilius)*	*ILS* 3834 = *ILLRP* 35 + *Imag.* 22A = *RMR* 145-46 no. 181 = Renberg no. 2
30	*M. C. Pomp(i)lio(s) No(vi?) f(ilii) | ded(e)ron(t) | Hercole*	*CIL* VI.30898 = *ILS* 3422 = *ILLRP* 123 + *Imag.* 63 = Ernout no. 21
31	*M(arcus) (?) Bicoleio(s) V(ibi) l(ibertus) Honore | donom dedet mereto*	*CIL* VI.3692 = *ILS* 3794 = *ILLRP* 157 + *Imag.* 77 = Ernout no. 25
32	*[- - -]onius Q(uinti) f(ilius) | Numisio Martio | donom dedit | meretod*	*ILS* 3148 = *ILLRP* 247 + *Imag.* 109
33	*[Nu]misio Mar[tio] | M(arcus) Terebonio(s) C(ai) l(ibertus) | donum dat liben(s) | meritod*	*ILS* 3147 = *ILLRP* 248 + *Imag.* 110

at Falerii Veteres.[77] Republican-era Pompilii appear in Etruria and Campania.[78] The freedman Bicoleius is linked by the Oscanizing ending of his *gentilicium* to the non-Latin-speaking center and south of the peninsula.[79] Lastly, the T(e)rebonii, here seen making a dedication to a poorly known Sabellic divinity, surface at Praeneste and also in Etruria.[80]

77. Schulze 1966, 216 for the *gentilicium* and its variant spellings (Poblicius, Poplicius). The aedile Publicii Malleoli: Padilla Peralta 2018c.

78. Schulze 1966, 183. For the Oscanizing *praenomen* Novius cf. the Novius Plautius of the Ficoroni *cista*: *CIL* I².562 with Terrenato 2014 and 2019, chap. 5.

79. BICOL[- - - -] on a fragmentary text from Brundisium: *CIL* IX.214. Cf. *Hinoleius* (*CIL* I².399 = X.4632 = Ernout no. 89 with Nonnis 2016); *Canoleius* (*CIL* I².406 = X.8054 = Ernout no. 90); *Bacculeius* (*NSc* 1921: 461 = *CIL* IV supp. 3: 9256; *CIL* X.8055.67 = *Imagines* Pompei 86).

80. This epiklesis of Mars is attested in this exact form only in a dedication from the *ager Capenas* by the Oscan-sounding Marcus Popius son of Statius, but cf. Ferrante 2008, 19–22 for variant spellings of the theonym. T(e)rebonii at Praeneste: *CIL* XIV.3272. Etruria and elsewhere: Schulze 1966, 246 and 375; Kaimio 1975, 122–24 on alternation of *o* and *u* in Latin transliteration of Etruscan names (*trepu̱* > *T(e)rebo̱nius*); Crawford et al. 2011, 1620 for attestations

FIGURE 5.2. Two inscribed votives from the Tiber area. Su concessione del Ministero per i beni e le attività culturali e per il Turismo—Museo Nazionale Romano. (Photo credit: Author)

Although these connections are not in themselves incontrovertible evidence that the dedicators traveled to Rome from elsewhere, they at least gesture toward that possibility.

With these inscriptions and the prosopography of their dedicators in mind, we can now revisit Bayes' theorem. For any one of these inscribed dedications, let us assume that its probability of being put up by a noncity dweller is 50 percent (y) if the hypothesis with which I began is true, but only 5 percent (z) if the hypothesis is false. Plugging these values into Bayes' theorem results in a posterior probability of 9 percent for the proposition's truthfulness. We can perform a simple Bayesian experiment by running this new posterior probability through the Theorem twice, holding constant the y and z values (table 5.5). Each run-through would correspond to the addition of a new piece of evidence—for example, another inscription of the type examined in the previous paragraph. The virtue of structuring the testing of the hypothesis as a Bayesian experiment is that we can see how quickly the statistical plausibility of the hypothesis would spike were new evidence to materialize.

Once again, I emphasize that it is not certain beyond a reasonable doubt that any one of the inscribed votives was in fact dedicated by a person not resident in Rome. However, if any of them stands an even decent chance of having been dedicated by an out-of-towner, the general hypothesis makes a small but meaningful gain in plausibility—and if two or three of the dedications make

---

of names beginning with *treb-* in Italic epigraphy. Liv. 10.40.7 places a (T.?) Trebonius among the cavalry commanders at the battle of Aquilonia in 293; see Oakley ad loc.

Table 5.5. Three Bayesian Iterations for Out-of-towners Dedicating at Rome

	SIMULATION 1	SIMULATION 2	SIMULATION 3
x = prior	1%	9.1%	49.7%
y = prob cond, true	50%	50%	50%
z = prob cond, false	5%	5%	5%
Posterior prob	9.1%	**49.7%**	**90.8%**

the cut, the hypothesis rises to the level of near-certainty. Lending still greater plausibility to this scenario are finds of Hellenistic Greek and Carthaginian coinage on the banks of the Tiber; in the case of those exemplars that can with confidence be dated to the fourth and third centuries, the most parsimonious explanation is that they traveled to Rome in the hands of out-of-town visitors. A connection between the coins and the votive deposits in the neighborhood of the Tiber Island has been proposed, although such a reading will necessarily remain speculative given the lack of detailed documentation for the find-context of the coins.[81]

As it turns out, yet another category of artifact offers strong circumstantial evidence for sacred mobility as a catalyst for these dedications at Rome. The significance of these artifacts, however, lies in the fact that they register the movement of individuals away from Rome *after* having visited the city. This category consists of inscribed *pocola*, ceramics that furnish such unique insight into the rhythms of mid-republican pilgrimage as to warrant a standalone treatment.

III. Pottery and Pilgrims: The Religious Life of Souvenirs

Despite its capacity to speak to the complexity and texture of religious life in third-century Italy, pottery has not occupied a central place in histories of Roman republican religion.[82] Nor do religious meanings enjoy particularly high visibility among those contextualizing and interpretive strategies that specialists in Roman ceramics employ.[83] Part of the challenge lies in the fact that, even in the case of ceramics whose religious or sacred import seems undeniable, it can be difficult to delineate their ritual and cultic functions with anything resembling precision. To single out only one beguiling ex-

81. Discussion and catalog of these coins: Frey-Kupper 1995, with figure 1 (p. 36) for their chronological distribution and p. 38 for the possible connection to votive offerings.

82. Beard et al. 1998, I.41 figure 1.7 for an example of how the *pocola* have been handled.

83. Greene 1992, 16–23 omits religion in a review of the approaches brought to bear on the study of Roman pottery; likewise Roth 2007 in a social history of mid-republican ceramics.

ample, third-century Black Gloss finewares marked "H" (*Herculi?*), "HV" (*Herculi Victori?*), and "HVI" (*Herculi Victori Invicto?*) seem to have circulated in Rome and throughout several of the mid-republican colonial foundations but we are lacking the sort of contextual information that could help us connect the dots.[84] Much the same could be said for the so-called *Heraklesschalen*, or even those Genucilia plates whose capacity to fire the imagination is in inverse proportion to what is actually known about them.[85] However, there is one category of ceramics in production during the third century for which we are in a position to reconstruct both sacred meanings and histories of use and mobility. These are Black Gloss ceramics that are inscribed with an epigraphic formula: the name of a deity in the genitive followed by the noun *pocolom*.[86] This section will track the journeys of these *pocola*, many of which were produced in or around Rome, beyond the city. Although resembling the Gnathian potteries of central and southern Hellenistic Italy in form, fabric, and style of decoration,[87] the *pocola* have a distinctive story. Their spatial trajectories offer the clearest material evidence we will encounter in this chapter of a pilgrimage network for which the city of Rome was a central node.

Having proved itself more than capable of stirring a tempest in a teapot,[88] the study of Black Gloss wares is not without controversies. The interpretation of the *pocola* is no exception. On the basis of late republican and early imperial literary references, some scholars have likened them to the Greek γραμματικὰ ἐκπώματα, vases inscribed with the names of gods in the genitive

84. *RMR* 1977: 49 no. 2 for overview. The discovery of the Roman exemplars: Pietrangeli 1941, 144–46. Additional discussions of these wares: Franchi de Bellis 1995, 385–87; Nonnis in Cifarelli et al. 2002–3, 289–90; Nonnis 2010, 125–26; on the finds at colonial Alba Fucens see Stek 2018, 159-60; cf. Ciaghi 1993 on ceramic production in Roman colonies. "H" ceramics at the Villa of the Auditorium: D'Alessio and Di Giuseppe 2005, 12–14. Hercules cult in Samnite Italy: Scopacasa 2015a, 199–200 on the Black Gloss from Campochiaro inscribed [**herek**]**lui aiserniui**; on Hercules in pre-Roman central Italy see now Galinsky 2018.

85. On the former, see Scott Ryberg 1940, 123–25; *RMR* 1977, 49 no. 1; Smith 2013, 31; note Olcese 1998, 142–44 for the attribution of the *Heraklesschalen* and the "H" ceramics to workshops in or around Rome. The Genucilia plates: Del Chiaro 1957; Torelli 2014.

86. I will refer to the wares with the archaic form *pocola* (sing. *pocolom*), not *pocula* (sing. *poculum*); I limit myself to those ceramics with the inscribed formula and set aside uninscribed wares similar to the *pocola* in decoration or form (such as the elephant plates: Pedroni 2001, 119). I do not use the term as a proxy for "dedication" (see, e.g., Turfa 2006a, 67 n. 17 for the Veientine dish inscribed *C<e>ere L. Tolonio(s) dedet* [*ILLRP* 64 = *Imag.* 32 = *CIL* I.2^4.2908]).

87. Green 2001 provides an overview of Gnathian and other Italic painted potteries.

88. See the criticisms offered by Roth 2007, 40–64 to Morel's 1981 comprehensive synthesis; the response of Morel 2009, and Roth 2013a.

and employed for toasting and libations at banquets.[89] Besides their use in homosocial symposiastic settings, these wares might have first made an appearance at the Greek-style *lectisternia* that the Roman Senate commissioned in moments of serious social turbulence.[90] Although any one of these may be a viable explanation for the original or primary use of the *pocola*, none accounts for the geographic scatter of their depositional distribution. In any case, J. Theodore Peña has shown that patterns of reclamation and reuse structure the life spans of Roman pottery,[91] an observation as relevant to the study of fine wares as it is for coarse wares. Extending this claim, I will attempt to line up the circulatory reuse of the *pocola* beyond their place of manufacture and first use with the artifactual and human movements that have been discussed earlier in this chapter. Thus reframed, the *pocola* open a window onto the experiential variety of pilgrimage in the third century and to the role of the Roman state in incentivizing the spread of knowledge about opportunities for cultic worship on offer in the city. For this reason alone, they matter a great deal not only to the history of religion in mid-republican Italy,[92] but to the history of mid-republican Roman state formation as well.

A. *The* Pocola*: Overview, Characteristics, and Spread*

In his 1947 study of Etruscan vases, Sir John Beazley was the first to posit that a majority of the *pocola* should be attributed to the same hand or the same shop, which he termed the Volcani Painter/Group on the basis of one of the inscriptions. Two decades after the publication of Beazley's work, J.-P. Morel undertook an examination of the potteries produced by the so-called Atelier des petites estampilles, in the course of which he demonstrated that in form and in decorative technique the *pocola* conformed to the atelier's production pattern.[93] In the same essay, Morel also offered a set of mutually reinforcing arguments for why the atelier was likely to have been based in Rome or its immediate vicinity. This localization of the atelier's operations, contested in

89. For *pocola* as *sacrata instrumenta* see Sall. *Hist.* fr. 298 Maurenbrecher = II fr. 73 Ramsay; *loci* for libation use are gathered under *TLL* s.v. "poculum" (Schrickx). Examples of γραμματικὰ ἐκπώματα: *SEG* 45.780 and 55.705. The comparison: Jessen 1975, 34–35; Peruzzi 1998, 23–40; for additional references see Nonnis in Cifarelli et al. 2002–3, 293 ns. 161–62. Religious banqueting at Rome: chapter 4 n. 36.

90. Analogous to the use of the *choes* at the Anthesteria, on which see Van Hoorn 1951 and Ham 1999. The *lectisternium* theory: Simon 1982, 186, endorsed in Ambrosini 2014, 358–59.

91. Peña 2007.

92. Comments to this effect: Smith 2013, 29–30 and Miano 2015, 263–65.

93. Morel 1969.

FIGURE 5.3. The *pocolom* of Aesculapius. (*CIL* 1^2.440 = *RMR* no. 13 = Appendix no. 2). Antikensammlung Berlin. (Photo credit: WikiMedia Commons)

recent scholarship but integral to any positioning of the *pocola* within an emergent pilgrimage network, will be taken up for scrutiny in a moment.

The appendix to this book offers an annotated catalog of the thirty-one extant *pocola*. In lieu of a full-spectrum study of their design affordances,[94] I concentrate in this subsection on providing a synoptic account of their historical features, proceeding from general comment on their material aspects and find-locations (where these are known or knowable) to scrutiny of the deities that are referenced in the inscriptions themselves—many of which were painted on the finished ceramic surface. The overwhelming majority of *pocola* are bowls designed for use as libations (*paterae*: figure 5.3 is one exemplar), measuring anywhere from 13 to 15 cm in diameter; *oenochoai* and cups account for the remainder.

The inscriptions of twenty-four *pocola* are sufficiently well preserved to enable identification of the deity in the genitive. In the vast majority of cases, the divinities mentioned are ones whose cult was alive and well in mid-republican Rome, from Aesculapius and Bellona and a trinity of divine qualities (Concordia, Fortuna, Salus) to those fixtures of state cult who either received new

94. For an introductory application of design theory to Roman material culture see Swift 2017. The "banausic identity" of mid-republican ceramics: Richlin 2018, 13 with n. 21, to whose bibliography add Bernard 2018a, 188–91.

temple structures or gained a renovated monumental face during the fourth and third centuries (Ceres, Juno, Minerva, Saturn, Vesta, Vulcan). Even some of the obscure deities mentioned in the *pocola*, such as Laverna and possibly Aequitas and Cura, may have had a mid-republican urban presence. Inscribing the names of divine qualities on the ceramics will have been one means of rendering tangible and giving physical form to an abstraction.[95] The single most noteworthy aspect of the *pocola* for our purposes, however, is that only one of them has been recovered from Rome itself; at least thirteen are traceable to Etruscan find-contexts (funerary in the better-documented cases), while others seem to have been scattered throughout Latium and Umbria; and a few have been recovered in Rimini. These last exemplars were probably produced in or around the colony at Ariminum and have been regularly cited in connection with those processes of Romanization that occupied our attention earlier.[96] The ones that will hold our concentration in what follows, however, are those that appear to have been produced in and disseminated from the city of Rome itself.

Both in the previous paragraph and in the catalog, I make a point of underscoring the relationship of the inscribed theonyms to developments in mid-republican cult at Rome. But this decision may strike the reader as question-begging, all the more so if most of the *pocola* can be securely traced to depositional contexts well outside of the city. Rather than reflexively associating these ceramics with cults as they were practiced within Rome, why should we not instead situate the *pocola* within a central Italian religious *koine* spanning Latium and Etruria?[97] And why privilege public worship as the primary context for these artifacts when they might have originated in and have been employed for private religious observance? To arrive at answers to these questions, I will first review J.-P. Morel's ascription of many of the *pocola* to a production site in or in the immediate vicinity of Rome and recapitulate subsequent refinements to the atelier model that underpinned Morel's theories. Next, I will comment on the suggestive relationship of the *pocola*'s find-spots to mid-republican Rome's road infrastructure.

Several considerations guided Morel's assignment of *pocola* manufacture to what he branded the Atelier des petites estampilles, a workshop whose pottery featured a varied but relatively standardized array of stamps with designs in relief. These designs ran the spectrum from letters and palmette-and-rosette

95. Cf. Spannagel 2000 on the *Vergegenwärtigung* of abstractions in Republican culture. Abstractions mentioned in the *pocola*: Miano 2015, 263–65.

96. See Minak 2006a and Stek 2009, 138–45, with n. 45 above on Romanization and its discontents; n. 84 for ceramics and colonization.

97. Note in this regard Miano 2015, 266–67 on Capua.

patterns to representations of helmeted divinities such as Minerva and Hercules that bear unmistakable affinities with numismatic iconographies.[98] As a whole, the atelier's productions are also distinguished by the color of the glaze and the texture of the surface, the form of many of the wares, and the broad uniformity in decorative technique and preferred motifs.[99] Since these design properties and decorative iconographies characterize many of the *pocola*, Morel argued for attributing them to the activity of one atelier, which he proposed to locate in Rome or on its outskirts. Although the inscribed *pocola* supplied important indirect evidence for location in the form of the aforementioned theonyms, these were not sufficient reason for locating the atelier in the city or its immediate vicinity, nor was the remarkable similarity between some of the figural motifs on the stamps and those on Rome's *aes grave* issues in the generation before and after Pyrrhus enough for an authoritative determination.[100] At best, these gestured to connections between the atelier's productions and the city of Rome but did not amount to definitive proof of the atelier's installation in Rome itself. The ceramics' deployment of the dolphin-rider motif, for instance, could with equal sense be construed to justify the placement of the atelier in Tarentum, where the dolphin rider had enjoyed a long numismatic vogue.[101] The truly dispositive facts, in Morel's view, were the primary circulation of this atelier's production within central Italy and the finds of uninscribed Black Gloss pottery in the atelier's style within Rome itself.[102] That fineware whose iconographic and material properties bespoke a

98. Morel's iconographic argument was anticipated in Scott Ryberg 1940, 137. Catalog and discussion of the stamps: Morel 1969, 71–81 with figs. 5 and 6; for similar stamps see *CIL* I^2.2882.

99. "Les dimensions . . . remarquablement constantes": Morel 1969, 63–65 with the table on p. 64; 90–94 for motifs. For the Hellenizing aspects of the Erotes motif—dismissed by Beazley 1947, 11—see Schmidt 1990. Painting technique: Torelli 2006, 89 on Roman visual parallels to the "compendiary" style of the *pocola*. Further on these motifs and the dating of early Roman coinage: Starr 1980, 33–34 and 44–45.

100. Scott Ryberg 1940, 126–28; Morel 1969, 107–8 with figs. 28 and 29. The motifs are helmeted Minerva, Pegasus, an open left or right hand, a dolphin, and a shell.

101. Morel 1969, 108–9 with figure 30, taking this motif as a sign that the workshop "subit une influence tarentine" with the arrival of (enslaved?) Tarentine potters in the train of Rome's defeat of Tarentum in 272. Endorsement of this line: Nonnis in Cifarelli et al. 2002–3, 284; Ambrosini 2014, 347. Migrant-artist rhythms in third-century Italy: Richlin 2018, 12–14; cf. Crawford et al. 2011, 4 with *Imagines* Teanum Sidicinum 25 for the itinerant Messapian potter Plator; cf. Fentress 2013, 177 on second-century evidence.

102. Thus Morel 1969, 113–14. Uninscribed wares found on the Tiber banks and in the area of the Esquiline necropolis: Bernardini 1986, no. 299; Scott Ryberg 1940, 136. Atelier products in Gabii: Pérez Ballester 2003, 222–23. Beyond central Italy: e.g., Bechtold 2007, 65, and 2018, 39–40 on finds in western Sicily.

shared origin that was mostly traceable to Roman or Latial find-contexts was what confirmed for Morel the hypothesis that the atelier was based in or immediately outside of Rome, an idea that received a further boost from the evidence for ceramic workshops (*figlinae*) located on the periphery of the city's core.[103]

Since the publication of Morel's essay, the atelier model at its core has been refined and queried.[104] Specifically with respect to the Atelier des petites estampilles, fabric and typological differences among its various productions have prompted several scholars to posit the emergence of competitor or imitator workshops. The application of X-ray fluorescence testing to Black Gloss ceramics has generated results consistent with the existence of workshops elsewhere in Latium.[105] Renewed attention to and reevaluation of the movement of Black Gloss in central Italy inspired E. A. Stanco to propose in place of one central or primary atelier a "Gruppo dei Piccoli Stampigli" whose output could be differentiated into five phases of production, with the production of the *pocola*—at least some of which Stanco is willing to credit to a workshop in Rome—falling in GPS's third phase.[106] Although Stanco's synthesis and explication of the material are compelling, the existence of multiple workshops does not vitiate Morel's fundamental claim that a large workshop or set of workshops operated in Rome and its environs, nor does it rule out the possibility that workshops based in or near Rome were contributing at higher levels to the volume of Black Gloss traffic than other workshops scattered across central Italy, seeing as the status of the mid-republican city as a production center for ceramics and as an "intermediary for the movement of artisans and the circulation of molds" is apparent from other evidence.[107] Elsewhere

103. Scott Ryberg 1940, 120 for *figlinae* on or near Oppius and Esquiline hills and Morel 1987 on the topography of *artisanat* in republican Rome; Ferrandes 2017 for an up-to-date synthesis of the available evidence for the location of workshops within the city and on its periphery.

104. Critiques of the traditional workshop model: Kristensen and Poulsen 2012. Elaboration and testing of eight different theories for workshop production in mid-republican central Italy: Söderlind 2002, chap. 6, esp. pp. 311–14 on traveling workshops. Epigraphic documentation of ateliers: *Imagines* Teanum Sidicinum 26–30 for the commercial enterprises of the Berii.

105. XRF findings: Olcese 1998; 2003 for application of the method to coarse-wares. Forti 1970 located the atelier in Vulci; for a skeptical riposte see Nonnis in Cifarelli et al. 2002–3. Catalog and discussion of regional production centers identified on the basis of kiln remnants: Di Giuseppe 2012, 33–83.

106. Stanco 2004 and 2009, with expansion of the model in Ferrandes 2008. A plea to ditch the Morelian vision of the Atelier des petites estampilles as "an exclusively Roman production": Roth 2013b, 98–99.

107. Papini 2015, 103. For a synthetic account of this process with explicit attention to eco-

FIGURE 5.4. The distribution of *pocola* in central Italy. (Drawing: Author)

in peninsular Italy, at least some Black Gloss production appears to have been directly affiliated with sanctuaries.[108] It is not a stretch to link the theonyms on the *pocola* to the sanctuaries that may have overseen their production; the most obvious location for several of these sanctuaries will have been Rome.[109]

Proceeding, then, from the assumption that the workshop or workshops responsible for the production of most of the *pocola* operated in Rome or its suburbs, the interlinked questions of how these wares traveled to their final destinations and how such travel inflected the meanings that were attached to them loom large. The alignment of *pocola* find-spots with Rome's expanding

nomic and commercial particulars see Panella 2010. Cf. Bertrand 2015, 160 for skepticism that the Ariminum *pocola* hailed from a local atelier.

108. Exposition of the evidence in Di Giuseppe 2012, 82–84. Cf. n. 43 above.

109. The embedding of ceramic production within sanctuary precincts: Ferrandes 2017.

road grid is an important fact to keep in mind (figure 5.4).[110] If indeed the *pocola* are indices of a sacred economy whose lines of communication and exchange spoked outward from Rome—in synergy with the developing road network—they deserve to be grouped together with the explosion in anatomical terracottas throughout central Italy, the appearance of votive dedications within Rome, and the temple building that created the structures at which these dedications were deposited. The depositional record of *pocola* lines up well with the possibility that individuals were traveling to and from sanctuaries in Rome, leaving a votive dedication at their destination and taking an artifact with them back home. Once this prospect is entertained more seriously, pilgrimage gains in credibility as a compelling explanation for how these phenomena defined and fueled one another.

B. Worshippers in Motion

Some forty years ago, Filippo Coarelli and Jean-Paul Morel expanded on an interpretation of the *pocola* first proposed by Giancarlo Susini. In their write-up for *Roma medio repubblicana*, the two scholars cited find-context as the primary reason for taking the ceramics not as votive dedications but as "oggetti-ricordo," purchased by an individual after a visit to one of Rome's sanctuaries.[111] Mary Beard, John North, and Simon Price subsequently accepted this idea in their own brief exposition of the *pocola*: "to judge from their find-spots, they were not dedications (which would have been found in the particular temple of the deity), but may have functioned as temple souvenirs (taken away from the temple, and so found widely dispersed)."[112] The deposition of several of the *pocola* in tombs coheres with this theory. At least initially, as Erika Simon has proposed, some of the *pocola* may have been produced or intended for use at Roman *lectisternia* and supplications, in which out-of-towners would have participated, but in their journey to tombs the *pocola* would have been infused with a new set of meanings through the paired operation of movement and memory. If, as speculated for the contemporaneous Genucilia plates,[113] the overpainted labels on the *pocola* evoked an asso-

110. Cf. the interarticulation of pilgrimage patterns and road networks in medieval Europe: Cohen 1980.

111. *RMR*: 57, developing the suggestion of Susini 1970, 165–66; the proposal is reiterated in Coarelli 2011, 232. Whether this reading can be applied to the Ariminum *pocola* is unclear: see the remarks of Bertrand 2015, 160.

112. Beard et al. 1998, 1.41 figure 1.7; echoed in Smith 2013, 30. One possible example of a ceramic dedication at a city sanctuary is a small dish inscribed SEMP[--]OS FICOLOS FEKED MED that was unearthed in the excavations at Curiae Veteres; see Ferrandes 2017, 33–34.

113. See Torelli 2014, 418.

ciation with specific rituals, the wares were not only generic souvenirs but also souvenirs of involvement in a particular religious act—the memory of which some participants were happy to take with them to their graves. This complex of ritual and memory as mediated by a traveling artifact is very much in line with the example of other historically documented pilgrimage systems.

Also characteristic of other pilgrimage systems, including those that emerged during the High Roman Empire and remained vibrant well into late antiquity, is the diagnostic pattern of travelers leaving an offering at a sanctuary and taking a souvenir with them for the road.[114] Mass-produced, cheap pottery is on a par with the types of objects—low in financial value but rich in commemorative meaning—that were acquired and taken home by pilgrims in many religious traditions, from scrolls to "singing toilet-paper roll holders" to "Martin Luther's socks."[115] In Roman late antiquity, at least one mass-production technology was hitched to the making of souvenirs: glass manufacture, responsible for the souvenir flasks of Puteoli and Baiae.[116] If some Roman sanctuaries oversaw Black Gloss workshops, it would not be unreasonable to assume that the production or repurposing of ceramics as souvenirs was directly controlled by the sanctuaries themselves.[117] The presence of Black Gloss wares in extraurban sanctuaries under Roman control lends additional plausibility to the mid-republican coupling of these ceramics with religious cult and practice.[118] Finally, the fit between the journeys of the *pocola* and the branching of Rome's road system mirrors the importance of roads to the development and geographic patterning of pilgrimage traditions in other times and places.[119]

Here two potential criticisms deserve to be aired. First, one could object that the relatively small number of extant *pocola* do not seem congruent with the operations of a pilgrimage network. To respond to such an objection and

114. The Empire's souvenir economy: Koeppel and Künzl 2002; for comment on the omission of *pocola* from this work see Nonnis in Cifarelli et al. 2002–3, 293 n. 160. Note also Hughes 2017a on "non-purpose-made" votives that were dedicated as "souvenirs of the self" in ritual contexts.

115. See the discussion in Reader 2014, chap. 6. Souvenirs "of little intrinsic value" in late medieval and early Renaissance pilgrimage in western Europe: Stopford 1994, 68; cf. Bartlett 2013, 442 on pilgrim badges as "cheap consumer items."

116. For these souvenirs see Popkin 2018.

117. Note in this connection the evidence for the re-sale of dedicated offerings at Italian sanctuaries: *CIL* I^2.756 (the *lex aedis Furfensis*) with García Morcillo 2013, 244. Cf. Moser 2019b, 69–70 on the production and sale of "crafted objects" at Satricum's acropolis sanctuary.

118. Purely e.g., an exemplar of Morel 2783g unearthed in a foundation deposit at the temple of Sol Indiges in Lavinium: Jaia and Molinari 2012, 375 with n. 20.

119. See Kiernan 2012, 83 for roads and pilgrimage in the Roman West.

to correct against the scale-specific prejudices that sometimes impede the identification of religiously motivated mobility as pilgrimage, it may be helpful to compare the volume of souvenirs circulating in other pilgrimage economies to the output of the *pocola*. Consider the case of the well-studied late antique and early medieval European *ampullae* (containers for storing holy water or anointing oil), six hundred exemplars of which have been found.[120] The production of these *ampullae* lasted about four centuries. If this production was distributed evenly across 400 years, with about 150 datable to each century, the roughly thirty *pocola* seem like a measly quantity by comparison until we recall that thirty wares produced in a twenty- to twenty-five-year period translate to between 100 and 150 over a full century. A second and arguably more powerful objection is that the *pocola* were not custom made for pilgrims in the manner of medieval European pilgrim badges. But this objection falls away in the face of the evidence from other pilgrimage traditions for the reuse of artifacts that had been originally commissioned for other purposes as souvenirs. One such instance of reuse involving ceramics has been proposed for the interpretation of Spanish pottery found in medieval England.[121] It is quite probable that additional instances of this phenomenon have escaped the attention of ancient and medieval historians and archaeologists simply because of the tendency to advance nonsacralizing readings of quotidian artifacts such as pottery.

Pilgrimage souvenirs derive much of their power from their capacity to function both "as advertising and marketing tools" and as "key formative elements in pilgrimage cults and their popularity."[122] These functions are evident in the *pocola*, texts-qua-artifacts capable of summoning to mind the experience and memory of the trip to Rome's sanctuaries. Articulated to the reminiscence of travel is the talismanic power of the divinity's name, foregrounded as the key to reading the text that has been painted on the surface of the vase by the fact of being placed first.[123] At the same time, as multiple scholars have noted, the naming of the divinity fulfills a marketing imperative: the circulation of information about which gods were being worshipped at Rome. How would the resident of Vulci know that Aesculapius had a new temple in Rome? Possibly by word of mouth; possibly by handling one of the gleaming *paterae* making their way up into Etruria. The theonyms painted on their shiny sur-

120. Quantification of the *ampullae*: Lambert and Pedemonte Demeglio 1994, figures 1–5.

121. These Spanish ceramics were initially believed to reflect small-scale luxury trade but have since been reinterpreted as pilgrim souvenirs: Stopford 1994, 63–64.

122. Reader 2014, 160.

123. Cf. Byzantine *eulogiai* for an analogous use of the genitive on a souvenir: Foskolou 2012, esp. 60–61.

faces converted the *pocola* into voiced media for communication, platforms for spreading the word as to which divinities could be sought and entreated in Rome. Cumulatively, all of these features endowed the *pocolom* with an added value distinct from its original context of use, one most transparently reflected in the choice of several individuals to have *pocola* deposited in their tombs.[124]

I opened this section by positing that the *pocola* ought to be interpreted in relation to the inscribed and uninscribed votives whose wax and wane were described in the previous sections. Embedded within the same votive economy, the *pocola* will have been a testament to what was experienced and communicated through the process of pilgrimage. As a class of artifacts, the *pocola* had life histories of their own, but their full resonance is appreciable only through juxtaposition with the other markers for religious mobility to Rome in the material record. On my reading, the *pocola*'s status as souvenirs will have been integral to the operation of a multidimensional sacred economy of pilgrimage. Much like other pilgrimage systems, this mid-republican regime linked different categories of artifacts to each other in networks of complementarity, with votives being offered up and left behind while *pocola* were acquired for the journey home. To internalize fully the historical reality of this process will require us to ditch skepticism about mid-republican Rome's viability as a religious center.[125] The odds are rather more strongly in favor of the city's slow but assured metamorphosis into a place that came "to embody a valued ideal."[126] Although this historical transition may be difficult to piece together from the literary sources that are normally privileged in the writing of Roman republican religious history, it can be reimagined through a synthesizing approach to the material record.

What, if anything, does the rise of pilgrimage during this period have to offer the student of state formation? It is to the task of developing some answers to this question that I proceed next. It has been argued in other state formation contexts that the advent of pilgrimage as a "costly signal" is a sure sign of increasing sophistication in the structuring of social cooperation around ritual practice.[127] Both the scale of this political economy of religion and the interpersonal mechanisms that boosted it are the subject of the next section.

124. Cf. Aravantinos [2000] 2009 on the inscribed vases in a Hellenistic tomb in Thebes.

125. Of the sort paraded in, e.g., Cancik 2008. For imperial Rome as a destination for pilgrimage see Apul. *Met.* 11.26 (and cf. *Flor.* 1.1–2).

126. I quote the definition of pilgrimage offered by Morinis 1992, 4.

127. Thus Kantner and Vaughn 2012, in a study of the prestate cultures of Chaco Canyon in the US Southwest and Cahuachi in Peru.

IV. Mid-Republican Pilgrimage as Network Activity

Roman religion's efficacy in bootstrapping the *res publica* into statehood capitalized on the reach and power of public ritual to drive institutionalized integration, the formation of a civic consciousness, and the elicitation of quasi-voluntary compliance. In chapter 4, I underlined those processes of communication and knowledge transfer that found expression in mid-republican Rome's festival environments. I argued on the basis of literary evidence that such knowledge transfer moved down, along, and across cultural gradients as people from diverse backgrounds mingled in the city's performative and communicative spaces. But I cautioned that, given the limitations of the textual evidence at our disposal, it is difficult to recover more than a skeletal version of this dynamic; that we needed to entertain more seriously the questions of when and to what ends people were coming to Rome; and that in pursuit of answers the material record had to be our major port of call. Precisely to this end, the previous sections of this chapter have sought to establish the main patterns of religiously mediated mobility by interpretation of a select group of artifacts through a quantitative and statistical lens. Circling back to the findings of section II, the next few pages will develop and analyze models for the catchment areas of those coming to Rome on pilgrimage trips and for their interactions once in Rome with resident Romans, with a view to specifying the magnitude of the pilgrimage phenomenon and the implications of that magnitude for our understanding of mid-republican religion's state-shaping capabilities. Therefore, the overarching objective of this section is to explain (at a necessarily abstract level) how sacred mobility, as an urbanized network phenomenon, interacted with the twin drives for "reproduction" and "control" that fueled Roman state formation during the fourth and third centuries.[128]

Although military service provided one setting for the integrative interaction of city dwellers with other central Italians,[129] visits to the city of Rome provided another. As one of the peninsula's *domi nobiles*, you might head to the city to broker a political bargain for your home community or a marriage alliance by which you or your family could amass social capital for a run at the *cursus honorum*; as a merchant, to hawk your wares; as a *iunior* on the military rolls, to report for the *dilectus* and *sacramentum*. Even if your primary intention

128. For "reproduction" and "control" as characteristics of state centralization through network formation note, e.g., Padgett and Ansell 1993, 1259–60 on Renaissance Florence. On urbanization and "small-world" network effects note Smith 2003.

129. Jehne 2006 for the army as integration zone, to which now add Taylor 2018 on the army's inculcation of political culture.

was not to offer cult at Rome, the sheer number of opportunities in the form of temples and festivals made enough of an impression to guide you to a sanctuary. What kinds of relationships might you strike up in the immediate context of this sanctuary visit? How many resident and nonresident Romans might you cross paths with, if only fleetingly?

I have already speculated on the basis of the material record that non-Romans (a term that will in what follows encompass both non-Roman citizens and Roman citizens not normally resident in Rome) were coming into the mid-republican city to dedicate votives. But we still have no concrete sense of where most visitors to Rome came from, how long on average each visit was, how many person-to-person encounters each visitor had in the course of a visit to Rome, or which forms of networking ensued from their encounters with city dwellers. In the first subsection below, I will set out some basic "rules" for the interactions of Romans and non-Romans in sacred settings at Rome, including the catchment areas for these non-Romans and the duration of their trips to and stays at Rome. In the second, I will design and execute a social-network visualization of these interactions and undertake an analysis of the model's implications for the study of interpersonal interaction. To conclude, I will explain how this two-tiered approach clarifies and consolidates arguments introduced earlier in this chapter and preceding chapters.

A. Geographies, Proportions, Durations

The question of how many human interactions any one traveler could have managed during their trip to Rome is approachable only through the most indirect of means given our lack of direct evidence. In order to sketch the outlines of an answer, another set of models will have to be conjured into being. If only as exposition of the a priori commitments that will dictate the form of these models, a brief comment on the current state of affairs in research on the network analysis of human social interaction is warranted.

Recent anthropological and neuroscientific investigations into the maximum capacity of individual human networks provide a useful, if unavoidably oversimplifying, frame of reference. In 1992, the British anthropologist Robin Dunbar famously posited 150 people as the upper bound for any one human being's network of close friends. In the two decades since, this figure, colloquially termed "Dunbar's Number," has come in for criticism and adjustment; several anthropologists have contended on the basis of field studies that a more realistic number for the upper bound of any one individual's close (friend) ties might be in the vicinity of 300.[130] The average figure for a human

130. Dunbar 1992, popularized by (e.g.) Gladwell 2000. Dunbar derived the number by running a regression equation on figures for neocortex size and group size among various species

being's maximum number of acquaintances is probably higher: already in 1961, Michael Gurevitch found in a dissertation study of individual acquaintance networks (differentiated according to the socioeconomic status of the study's subjects) that these networks could range in size from 240 to 500 acquaintances contacted during a 100-day interval.[131] The sometimes staggering "Friend" agglomerations of some Facebook profiles might be taken not so much as proof of the obsolescence of Dunbar's Number but as a testament to Gurevitch's insight into the capaciousness of acquaintance networks.

Gurevitch's delimited research interval of 100 days notwithstanding, the research literature has mostly danced around the questions of how best to characterize the temporal flux of friend and acquaintance networks and how to progress from a descriptive/static model of friend networks at any one instant to a more dynamic model of how these networks expand or contract over time.[132] Dunbar's Number is a global maximum network figure for any one human being, not a discrete or segmentable number that can be broken up by period of life or demarcated temporal unit into, say, the 50 friends you make in high school, the 50 you make in college, or the 50 you make after college *vel sim.*—let alone even narrower slivers of annual or monthly life. While techniques for modeling social interactions within networks across time have been developed in a number of scientific fields, these techniques tend to require either very refined mathematical approaches or troves of data.[133] Lacking both, I will content myself in what follows with building a rough model that can clear a path to engaging the findings of research into network size while also shedding light on the issues most pertinent to this book.

The data I tap over the next few pages were generated in table 5.3's reconstruction of the numbers of anatomical ex-votos deposited at Rome from the late fourth to late second centuries BCE, whose orders of magnitude I reconstructed under several different hypothetical scenarios. Having first proposed

---

of primates; for reassessment of this study and strong skepticism regarding its conclusions see De Ruiter et al. 2011. Confirmation for Dunbar's model through analysis of user activity on Twitter: Gonçalves et al. 2011. On 290 (or 230) and not 150 as the upper bound for any one person's strong social ties: Bernard and Shelley 1987 and McCarty et al. 2000; cf. Wellman 2012.

131. Gurevitch 1961, chap. 3, finding that socioeconomic status was correlated to acquaintance network size, with lower-SES individuals having on average smaller networks than their higher-SES counterparts.

132. Burt 2000 drew attention to the rarity of longitudinal network studies. Bibliography of studies committed to rectifying this deficit: Lewis et al. 2008, 332.

133. Even "simple" models tend to be anything but: see Starnini et al. 2013 for an example.

that each votive dedication be understood to represent the act of *one* individual who did not make a subsequent anatomical ex-voto dedication, I suggested that we interpret these numbers as proxies for the number of persons who made anatomical dedications at Rome. The annual numbers in themselves do not overwhelm even at the 1 percent hypothesis; it is over time that the dedicatory acts pile up. These acts will take on a new bundle of responsibilities in this subsection as secondary proxies for interactions between residents of the mid-republican city and out-of-town visitors. As a means of carving up the mass of potential dedicators at Rome's sanctuaries—Roman as well as non-Roman—into heuristically useful components, consider the following three basic scenarios:

Under *scenario 1*, two-thirds of all votive dedicators reside in Rome, with the remaining one-third consisting of non-Roman visitors;
Under *scenario 2*, half of all votive dedicators reside in Rome, and half are non-Roman visitors;
Under *scenario 3*, one-third of dedicators reside in Rome, and the remaining two-thirds are non-Roman visitors.

Multiplying these scenarios across the hypothetical conditions from table 5.3, we can derive a chronological distribution for Roman and non-Roman dedicators at city sanctuaries from the late fourth to late second centuries (table 5.6). Relative to the six-figure population of Rome over the fourth to second centuries—which rose from approximately 125,000 in the fourth to somewhere in the vicinity of half a million by the beginning of the first—the numbers are small.[134] But in any one year even a trifling number of non-Roman visitors could be seen by and interact with a sizable number of Romans, with momentous and lasting effects as the volume of contacts steadily increased over time. Although this short-term migration will have been at least an order of magnitude lower than the volume of travelers to Rome in later periods,[135] its importance to the social dynamics of the mid-republican city should not be taken lightly.

In order to measure the scope of this effect, it would be very useful to know how many Roman residents interacted with those non-Romans who were coming into the city to make dedications. With no concrete quantitative testimonies from the historiographical tradition to guide us, a set of secondary assumptions will have to suffice as parameters for the approximations. While these secondary assumptions can be modified in any number of ways—the

134. On Rome's demography in this period see chapter 2 nn. 82–86.

135. Quantification of migration patterns to Rome in the early Principate: Tacoma 2016, 61–72.

Table 5.6. Individual Roman and Non-Roman Dedicators per Year, 325–125 BCE[1]

Interval	Totals	Scenario 1	Scenario 2	Scenario 3
	10% hypothesis			
325–275	96	64—32	48—48	32—64
275–225	384	256—128	192—192	128—256
225–175	384	256—128	192—192	128—256
175–125	96	64—32	48—48	32—64
	5%			
325–275	192	128—64	96—96	64—128
275–225	768	512—256	384—384	256—512
225–175	768	512—256	384—384	256—512
175–125	192	128—64	96—96	64—128
	1%			
325–275	960	640—220	480—480	220—640
275–225	3,840	2,560—1,340	1,920—1,920	1,340—2,560
225–175	3,840	2,560—1,340	1,920—1,920	1,340—2,560
175–125	960	640—220	480—480	220—640

1. In the scenario columns, the numbers on the left side of the em-dash (long dash) represent the "Roman" individuals; those on the right side are the out-of-towners.

conclusion of this section will entertain some possible tweaks—for present purposes I have formulated them with several restrictions in mind.

First, recall from the summary of Gurevitch's research into human acquaintance networks that his subjects—depending on their socioeconomic background—contacted anywhere from an average of 240 to an average of 500 persons over a 100-day period. These contacts were for the most part *not* of new, hitherto-unknown individuals. Since many of them were not face-to-face contacts but rather through the phone or correspondence, the amplifying effects of modern technology should be borne in mind when bending Gurevitch's figures to the purposes of this section. I will therefore assume that it is best to begin at the low end of Gurevitch's range: 240. Turning our eyes to mid-republican Rome, we have no reason for presuming that each non-Roman's trip to Rome averaged 100 days in length—a possibility that would be unlikely in light of some of the seasonal constraints addressed in chapters 2 and 3. Let us assume instead that each traveler spends an average of 5 days in Rome. Dividing 240 by 20 (100 / 20 = 5 days) gives 12 contacts per day, which I will round down to 10. Finally, we need to consider the likely statistical composition of this group of 10. In the interests of computational simplicity, I will specify two linked parameters for this interaction: (a) each group *n* of visitors to Rome contacts exactly the same and only the same 10 Romans during its time in Rome; (b) each non-Roman individual in this group *n* contacts 10

Romans, with no two (or more) non-Romans contacting the same Roman, during their time in Rome.[136]

Feeding these inputs into the previous table's matrix of possibilities moves us closer in the direction of a three-dimensional re-creation of mid-republican Rome's social interactions (color plate 4). As emphasized in connection with other models in this book, what matters most about these figures is their orders of magnitude. Even under the rather optimistic 10 percent hypothesis for the survival of votives, the volume of interactions in any given year between Romans and non-Romans who traveled to the city to dedicate will not have been inconsiderable. During the period 275–225 BCE, the same years when Roman temple construction hit its peak, the volume of contacts hit four digits. If the bulk or even just a portion of these dedications represented the activity of out-of-towners who had traveled to Rome to work on the construction of its temples, the relationship between sacred travel to Rome and temple construction in Rome would be even tighter—although it is not necessary to insist on that connection. As for the long-term arc of these interactions, two points merit special emphasis. Were we to extrapolate fifty-year aggregates from the table, the absolute minimum number of interactions would be 500, but the low figure under assumption (b) as stipulated in the previous paragraph would be 320 x 50 = 16,000, while the high figure would be 25,600 x 50 = 1,280,000.

At two very different orders of magnitude, each of these numbers evokes the networking power that could be generated through the accumulation of contacts over time. Under the 1 percent hypothesis, annual contact figures range into the five digits. Although it may initially seem unreasonable to suppose that in the years 275–225 and 225–175 up to a quarter of the resident Roman population interacted with non-Romans who came into town to dedicate, the sheer repetition of opportunities for such interactions as detailed in the previous chapters lends some support to this scenario. Nonetheless, and in the interests of caution, it would be sensible to take the numbers obtained through the 1 percent hypothesis as the absolute maxima for the sum of social interactions realized through non-Roman encounters with Romans.

The virtue of this model is that it takes the votive evidence of section II as a launching pad for the formulation of a transparent and flexible quantitative representation of interpersonal contacts. By developing an interpretation and periodization of votives and the human agency behind them (the 10-5-1 per-

136. The probability of group *n* of visitors meeting the exact same ten people from a population of 150,000–200,000 is lower than the probability of each individual in group *n* meeting ten people chosen at random (even with the condition of no overlap) from a population of 150,000–200,000.

cent hypotheses, broken down into four time periods each), we proceeded from a minimum tally for the number of human interactions to a quantification of a numerical range for these interactions, corresponding roughly to what the composition of the non-Roman groups venturing to Rome might have looked like. Naturally, as with any quantitative model seeking to capture a slice of social life, these findings are very crude. Even as a blunt tool, however, this model provides a new perspective on the scale and volume of the connectivity that came into being as a consequence of sacred mobility toward Rome in fourth- and third-century Italy.

Suppose now that we wished to ground the interactions of color plate 5 in the mobility of those non-Romans who traveled from multiple parts of the peninsula to Rome, by differentiating them according to their region of origin. The basic premise for this next model will be that the likelihood of traveling to the city to make a dedication decreased the farther away from Rome the prospective dedicator resided. Relics of the votive economy do seem to decrease as a function of distance away from the core Etrusco-Latial-Campanian axis,[137] although this may be a by-product of the spatial distribution of modern archaeological excavations. To incorporate this geographical variation into the model, let us suppose that 50 percent of non-Roman dedicators lived within a day or two of Rome; that another 25 percent were traveling from areas three to four days away from the city; that 12.5 percent were traveling from locations five or six days away; and that the remaining 12.5 percent are traveling from locations a week or more away, with a negligible number of these coming from outside the peninsula. We will also assume that they were traveling cheaply. While the numbers of non-Romans set forth above are such that we might unobjectionably assume them to have been (mostly) well-off elites, it is reasonable to suppose that they were not burning to get to the city as quickly as humanly possible. Because travel is a function of cost as well as of distance, upgrading to the claim that non-Romans traveled as quickly as possible would necessarily imply that they incurred substantially more expense to do so; if true, such a willingness to incur expense would say much about the emergent appeal of Rome as a religious center, but for now I will limit myself to the proposition that those traveling to Rome sought to get there as cheaply as possible. With the help of ORBIS, the Stanford Geospatial Network Model of the Roman World, we can quite easily and quickly relate financial expense to the duration of travel in reconstructing movement across Roman landscapes.[138]

137. See, e.g., maps of the artifact scatter, beginning with Comella 1981, 760–61 figures 1 and 2. But this decrease is not uniform.

138. ORBIS was launched in 2012: orbis.stanford.edu. For the methodology adopted in its design see the website introduction.

For present purposes, however, I will be using ORBIS as a tool for layering the percentage distribution proposed earlier in this paragraph onto the Italian peninsula. I have generated time-to-Rome calculations for twenty-one different sites in order to delineate catchment areas for different groups of prospective pilgrims as a function of distance from Rome (plate 5).[139] This static cartographic representation is a highly schematized approximation of what was necessarily a fluid process. The region fenced off in yellow—within a day or two at the most of cheap travel to Rome, and where I will assume the 50 percent of non-Roman dedicators originated—extends from southern Etruria *trans Tiberim* into Sabine country and then south into Latium. Hedged by red is the second catchment area—within three to four days' travel range to Rome, and accounting for another 25 percent of non-Roman dedicators—encompassing central Etruria, the Sabine highlands, and the remainder of Latium. Marked in blue is the region whose boundary points were five to six days' cheap travel away from Rome; this sliver, responsible for about 12.5 percent of non-Roman dedicators, takes in northern Etruria, the edge of Picenum, the territories of the Marsi and the Paeligni, and northern and central Campania. Beyond the blue are the regions of peninsular Italy that could be accessed by a week or more of cheap and slow travel; these (along with areas beyond peninsular Italy) will have accounted for the remaining 12.5 percent of non-Roman dedicators.

This visualization should not be taken as authoritative. It is perfectly plausible that such a cartographic gridding, by indexing the probability of a traveler's origins in any one part of Italy strictly to distance, downplays that special connection between Rome and its colonies whose involvement in peninsula-wide religious and political innovation remains a subject of intense debate. For colonists who hailed originally from Rome or its immediate environs, the prospect of a trip to the *Hauptstadt* may have held substantially more appeal than for members of allied city-states or tribes. On the whole, however, distance to travel will have been one of the major structuring forces—and potential deterrents—for the mobility of pilgrims. What remains now is to scrutinize the nature of those interpersonal connections that religiously motivated travel to Rome nurtured between non-Romans and

139. The search parameters: cheapest travel possible and travel during the summer months. The sites: Tibur, Reate, Cosa, Volsinii, Spoletium, Alba Fucens, Casinum, Populonium, Arretium, Ariminum, Asculum, Corfinium, Beneventum, Capua, Neapolis, Venusia, Sipontum, Tarentum, Hipponion/Vibo Valentia, Regium, and Irna/Salernum. Although ORBIS derives terrestrial travel values that are based on the road network as it existed by the Empire, significant stretches of the peninsular *viae* had been largely completed by the beginning of the second century BCE: see chapter 2 n. 96.

Romans. In illustration of this, I will pivot to a social network scheme that fuses this subsection's conjectured components into one coherent system for further analysis.

B. *The Interpersonal Regime: A Middle Republic of Networks*

Although the religiously motivated mobility under study in this chapter will have given rise to the emergence of "strong tie" trust networks, information about Rome's cultic offerings will have traveled on the back of "weak ties" as well—of the kind whose form and function the sociologist Mark Granovetter memorably described in a classic article.[140] To be sure, the connective power of strong ties is more easily recoverable from the religious archives of Hellenistic literature, which dramatizes several alluring examples of strong-tie dynamics at work in cultic contexts. One of Herodas's *Mimes* imagines two women arriving at an Asklepieion to make their offerings, with one switching between devotional speech-acts and the insistent verbal denigration of her slave attendant; the conversation between the two free women about the artwork exhibited at the sanctuary has much in common with the dialogue (by turns lighthearted, reverential, and abrasive) of the women in Theocritus's Fifteenth *Idyll*.[141] Even if Theocritus's poem "constructs a parody of women's perspectives of a religious festival,"[142] one takeaway relevant to our purposes is the attachment of knowledge transfer—personal, religious, civic—to a festival setting. Pegged to personal or private encounters with the divine (and conditioned always by distinctions of status and practices of domination), this knowledge entered social circulation not only through the disclosure of confidences to friends, but also through chance divulgence to an acquaintance or social inferior, or even an overheard conversation.[143] The likelihood of such exchanges in the religious landscapes of mid-republican Rome invites the application of social network analysis (SNA) as a means of shoring up some of this chapter's arguments about sacred mobility, the traffic in common knowledge, and community formation.

140. Granovetter 1973; cf. Tilly 2005, 12–17 on the properties of trust networks and Padgett and Ansell 1993, 1274–75 n. 28 for an inductive distinction between strong and weak ties in their study of Medicean Florence's networks. Refinements to the strong/weak tie model: Knappett 2011, 126–27.

141. Herodas *Mim.* 4 with Headlam and Knox ad loc. for the code switching; Barbantani 2017, 382–89 for general remarks on mime.

142. Lambert 2001 on the *Idyll* as a send-up of "women's superficial religiosity," responding to (among others) Skinner 2001; cf. Philippides 2018 for Plautine reworking of this motif in the *Poenulus*.

143. Cf. Small 2017 on the significance of meaningful personal disclosures to nonintimates.

SNA has emerged in recent decades as one of the more promising methods for ordering, conceptualizing, and interpreting human and nonhuman interactions. However, despite its growing prominence among digital humanists and archaeologists, applications of SNA in the domain of ancient history remain few in number.[144] It will be the contention of this subsection that SNA can open up some heuristically rewarding avenues for gauging the extent and variety of those interpersonal connections that were enabled in a mid-republican Rome fast evolving into a site for pilgrimage. Taking to heart Ian Rutherford's provocative characterization of pilgrimage networks in the Greco-Roman Mediterranean as predicated on weak ties,[145] I will build and analyze a network model for the temporary person-to-person bonds that were formed between out-of-town arrivals and the city's residents as a consequence of pilgrimage. Again, as with the other models developed in this chapter, I do not aspire to unassailable comprehensiveness or accuracy, only to a method of structuring and representing social relations that enables their cumulative impact to be grasped and their significance to be better appreciated. Claudia Moser has encouraged us to study the "relational network" manifested and enacted through certain types of votive deposits at Rome;[146] I hope to visualize the potential scope and variety of that relational network as it came into being during the peak festival periods of the middle Republic. In settling on a model to represent this network, one question to ponder is whether the picture of multiethnic interaction and interpersonal knowledge in contexts of religiously mediated mobility shifts according to whether we center the agency of the Gaius Romanus who resided in the city or the out-of-town traveler who came to dedicate a votive. In the language of network theory, how much does it matter if we privilege the resident or the visitor as a primary node for social traffic?

This network model will rely on the data that were generated for plate 4. Instead of producing network graphs for every single one of the possibilities represented in the graph, I will confine myself to the study of one scenario: row 1 of condition #2 of the 5 percent hypothesis. This row enumerates the interactions between non-Romans and Romans that took place annually in

144. Basic introductions: Easley and Kleinberg 2010; Koput 2010. Proof of concept: Alexander and Danowski 1990; Cline 2012. Systematic application: Ruffini 2008. "Soft" and "small world" versions: Malkin et al. 2009 and Malkin 2011; cf. criticisms in Ruffini 2012. SNA and classical Athens: Sobak 2015. SNA and maritime religious connectivity: Kowalzig 2018. SNA and Roman religion: Collar 2007 and 2013; Price 2012, 10–11. SNA centrality measures and settlement formation in early Iron Age central Italy: Fulminate 2012.

145. Rutherford 2017, 201, condensing a proposal first canvassed in Rutherford 2007.

146. Moser 2019a, chap. 2, examining deposits of *arulae* at Largo Argentina sanctuaries.

the period 325–275 BCE within the following parameters: that archaeologically documented votives represent 5 percent of the original total and that 50 percent of those responsible for making the dedications were non-Roman. The annual total number of Roman and non-Roman dedicators postulated under this scenario was 192. In accordance with the percentage distribution of dedicators that was outlined at the end of the previous subsection, I will now assign half of the ninety-six non-Roman dedicators a geographic origin in the area enclosed by the yellow line of plate 5; of the remaining forty-eight, twenty-four will be assigned to the area between the yellow and red lines, twelve to the area between the red and blue lines, and twelve to the territory beyond the blue. Having completed this assignment, we can now map a list of nodes and ties that credits each non-Roman visitor with ten nonoverlapping contacts among the urban population during the period of his or her visit to Rome.[147]

The list of nodes and ties is easily converted into a visualization of the connections formed between non-Roman dedicators and city dwellers in the course of any one year during the period 325–275 BCE (color plate 6).[148] What may seem at first glance like little more than a colorful mass of dots is a proxy for the social universe of the city of Rome in this era. The visualization is an important first step in resurrecting that universe, but not the last. Our next task will be to take a closer look at some of the interpersonal processes that conspired to shape the distribution of various types of knowledge in this network—personal, interpersonal, and civic.

It is through a clearer understanding of these processes that we might, finally, be in position to fulfill chapter 4's call to foreground intervisibility as one of the phenomena by which the Roman state reconstituted and consolidated itself during the middle Republic. Even if the representation of religiously mediated person-to-person interactions as a tangle of nodes and ties is not the most direct prod to clear-minded concentration, I want to underline a secondary feature of the graph that, while not immediately discernible from the resolution of plate 6, has a more easily apprehensible meaning for the study of sacred mobility and its social effects. As a close-up shot of one of the nodes demonstrates (color plate 7), the nodes cluster into self-contained groups, one obvious outcome of my specifications: I set each non-Roman to interact with ten nonoverlapping Romans. This compartmentalization into noninteractive bubbles would have held true even under the network theory of triadic clo-

147. For this constraint, see n. 136 above. The source-target inventory of nodes and ties was prepared as a .CSV file, available for download at scholar.princeton.edu/dpadilla/Materials.

148. This visualization was generated by entering the contents of the .CSV file into the network-graph tool Gephi.

sure, according to which any system of nodes A-B-C in which A and B and A and C are linked by ties will develop a tie between B and C.[149]

Nonetheless, on the assumption that triadic closure occurred during the annual time span of interactions captured by this model, some Romans probably developed closer ties to each other as a result (plate 7). These ties were made possible because some of those non-Romans who came into town mediated the formation of bonds among city dwellers. In other words, because out-of-towners came to the city for the purpose of dedicating votives, residents who might otherwise not have interacted with each other did.

If we were to tweak the network such that a Roman (hereafter designated R1) interacted with a minimum of one non-Roman visitor from each peninsular region (designated Y, Re, B, and O, with reference to the color designations of plate 6), each Roman would establish four ties: to a Y, a Re, a B, and an O. The result would be a very well-connected R1, with at least 44 connections emanating from this Roman in two steps—a powerful node in the network (color plate 8). Under this scenario, then, the formation of a bond between one Roman and four non-Romans translates into connections with up to forty additional Romans.

According to the principle of triadic closure, both these non-Romans and those Romans with whom they interacted will forge ties with one another, for a final tally of no fewer than 88 new social connections. Other modifications to the model are relatively easy to implement and offer equally nourishing food for thought. I offer one example of a tweak to the attributes of a non-Roman node. Suppose that one non-Roman Y1 has, among the 10 connections forged on a visit to the city, seven Romans and three non-Romans (Re1, B1, and O1). Under this new set of assumptions, the seven ties to Romans and three to non-Romans, which yield a total of 10 ties at distance, will have generated 10 ties through each of the non-Roman nodes at distance two, for a cumulative total of 40 ties.

Then, through triadic closure, the 10 nodes at distance one will have sprouted ties with one another, and each bundle of 10 at distance two as well, with the result that the sum total of ties will have doubled to 80 (color plate 9). The difference between this figure and the one calculated through the recalibration of a Roman node at the start of the paragraph is not terribly meaningful; we could have, for example, raised the number of non-Roman nodes that were contacted by Y1 to ensure a higher aggregate tally of ties. But the difference does bring into view two final issues for discussion: First, who was better positioned to be the routing point for multiethnic interaction and

149. Triadic closure was first proposed by Georg Simmel; Easley and Kleinberg 2010, chap. 3 offer an explanation with illustrations.

interpersonal knowledge, the Roman insider or the visiting outsider? Second, what bearing does an answer to this question have on the state-formation processes of interest to this book?

Any decisive answers on either front would have to account for the dynamics of elite networking and mobility freshly reexamined by Kathryn Lomas and Nicola Terrenato, among others.[150] A network model of the kind introduced in this subsection makes it easier not only to discern the ripple effects of interpersonal contact at Rome but also to see how these effects shift depending on the weight and frequency of social interactions that are assigned to insider or outsider respectively. Potentially as a means of entering into even more rewarding dialogue with recent scholarship on elite networking, one could modify my network model to incorporate a class-specific component, or introduce a probabilistic element for varying the number of social interactions according to the length of a visitor's length of stay in Rome. Or one might ditch the human beings altogether and focus entirely on the epigraphic and anegraphic artifacts of the ELC and the network relations that can be posited for them.[151] Whichever option for future refinement proves most attractive, the objective of this subsection's exercise was to showcase SNA as a spark for the imagination and to demonstrate how the movement of non-Romans to Rome spurred improvements in social connectivity among those already residing in the city.

This last point is crucial for understanding how pilgrimage flows to mid-republican Rome interacted productively with the social practices that were documented earlier in this book as holding the Roman state together. Working from the material laid out earlier in this chapter, this subsection's application of network theory sought to elucidate the scope of pilgrims' social power. I had suggested through my readings of the dedicatory record that a relatively small number of religiously motivated travelers could have wielded a communicative potency disproportionate to their actual numbers. However, the utility of network theory does not lie solely in its reiteration on an abstract level of the power of small numbers, or the implications of this power for the religious and cultural trajectory of the middle Republic. This subsection's model also helps furnish a structural explanation for what is arguably the most convincing circumstantial corroboration for social networking at Rome in the final decades of the third century: the surge in immigration to the city from Latin settlements in the years after the Second Punic War. Although the movement of tens of thousands of Latins to Rome (and the eventual expulsion of

150. Lomas 2012; Terrenato 2014.

151. For an archaeological network approach, centered on objects, that wears its debts to Latour and Deleuze proudly see Knappett 2011, chaps. 7–9.

12,000 from the city) was motivated and mediated by a host of factors—exercise of the *ius migrandi* and recourse to *hospitium* prominent among them[152]—the settlement of these individuals in the city would have depended at least in part on the strength of those preexisting friend and kinship networks through which immigrants could secure both lodging and opportunities for employment.

This networking was not limited to those elites for whom the technology of the *tessera hospitalis* had greased the wheels of mobility since the archaic period.[153] Mid-republican Rome saw the appearance of migrant neighborhoods that were associated not only with a distinct ethnic profile but also with the worship of those divinities that had ascended to prominence in the public and monumental life of the third-century cityscape.[154] With comparative histories of migration offering ample evidence of nonelites striking up and sustaining systems of migrant aid through the mediation of religious observances (such as pilgrimage), it would not be entirely unreasonable to speculate that, among those out-of-towners whose first journey to Rome was marked by a trip to a shrine, a not-insubstantial number settled down in the city later on—perhaps with the help of those people they had encountered on that initial visit, and even in the vicinity of the shrine that they had first visited.

V. Conclusion

The exercises pursued in each of this chapter's sections are, in the first instance, a means of exploiting material culture to re-create those "knowledge and information exchange networks" that we examined from the different angle of Roman comedy in chapter 4.[155] But the more ambitious project is to harmonize the appearance and function of these networks with the state-formation thesis at the heart of this book. Critiquing and refining political theorist Margaret Levi's conception of trust, Charles Tilly proposed in its

152. The events of 187 and 177 BCE: Liv. 39.3.4–6, 41.8.6–12, 41.9.9–12 and 42.10.3; Isayev 2017b, 39–42 for discussion. The *ius migrandi* in the second century: Broadhead 2001. *Hospitium privatum* and *publicum*: Bourdin 2012, 569–74.

153. See, e.g., the inscribed ivory lion from the Sant'Omobono sanctuary (Holloway 1995, 71 with figure 5.6) and the inscribed ivory boar from a Carthaginian cemetery (Isayev 2017b, 101–3); Bourdin 2012, 521–27 and 542–51 on gentilician mobility and interethnic relations.

154. A statue of Vertumnus rose in the Vicus Tuscus (Varro *LL* 5.46; for his mid-republican temple see chapter 3 n. 174); a statue of Mercury may have graced the Vicus Sobrius (Festus 382 L.; Andrews and Flower 2015, 53–54 on the relationship of a travertine monument restored by Augustus to this statue). The latter neighborhood's association with a cult of Mercury attested otherwise only in Carthaginian North Africa: Palmer 1997, chap. 6; Biggs 2017, 357.

155. Isayev 2017b, 212–13 on the *palliata*.

stead a transactional account of trust that moved away from systemic or dispositional approaches to emphasize the interactive and repetitive procedures by which trust between social actors was strengthened and perpetuated. Fundamental to his analysis was the distinction between trust networks and public politics per se, the latter encroaching on or interfacing with trust networks through coercion, capital, or "commitment" (in the form of a relational ideology), and between trust networks and other coordinating social structures, such as authoritative organizations and collaborative institutions.[156]

Determined by a historically contingent constellation of institutions and amplified through multiple discursive practices, the emergence of the city of Rome as a religious center conduced to the trust-building envisaged by Tilly.[157] There are longer-term repercussions to this process that call for study in their own right, such as the subsequent redefinition and reconceptualization of the city of Rome as a paradigm for reduplication in municipal charters.[158] What this chapter has sought to do is identify and track the trust-generative efficacies of religiously motivated movement to the city during the fourth and third centuries. By creating opportunities for face-to-face contact in sacred settings, this movement promoted the formation and consolidation of trust networks centered on Rome. This centering of Rome, and in particular the Capitoline, in the political and religious operations of Roman domination was not fated to last forever, Horace's powerfully evocative tableau in *Odes* 3.30 notwithstanding; already by the early Principate, signs of the "decentralization of Rome's symbolic topography" were in evidence. In several important respects, however, this centering benefited from a new lease on life under the Empire, as emperors reinvigorated the practice of sacred monumental dedications to their preferred divinities.[159] But the practice originated in a mid-republican system that paired dedicatory acts with pilgrimage and face-to-face connectivity, in the service of a new cultural protocol for fostering social cohesion as the state expanded in size and population.

In positing pilgrimage as a force for social connectivity, I am committing to the proposition that during our period the religious status of Rome shifted in the minds of prospective visitors: the city was no longer religiously periph-

156. Tilly 2005, chaps. 1–2.

157. Carlà 2017 investigates this process.

158. On the cognitive tensions that ensue from this development, see Festus 146 L. s.v. "municipalia sacra" with Ando 2008, 114–35.

159. Moralee 2018, 43–44 for the quoted phrase in the preceding sentence and for an overview of the process. The *longue durée* of sacred monumental construction at Rome: figure 2.3 above.

eral to their lives, but central.[160] This transition comes into clearest focus when contextualized against the broader meshworks of social and political relations that characterized the mid-republican res publica. The next and final chapter will weld together the varied components of religious practice under examination in this book into a unified structure. Before turning the page on this chapter's arguments, however, we should bear in mind that the emergence of Rome as a religious center for interpersonal networking was not some unalloyed good for all parties in central Italy. The progressive abandonment of sanctuaries elsewhere in Latium during the final two centuries BCE is one symptom of a much more sweeping erosion of locally situated cultic knowledges, precipitated at least in part by Rome's religious self-amplification. In a pattern increasingly characteristic of the imperializing Mediterranean, city-centric forms of religious life came to eclipse their rural and village counterparts, setting the stage not only for new political economies of religion but also for those processes of epistemicide that rode their coattails. The road from local religious independence—as exemplified by those archaic Italian peoples who partook of meat at the festival on the Alban Mount, or by those communities that joined Egerius Baebius of Tusculum to offer a dedication at Aricia—to religious subordination ran through mid-republican Rome.[161]

160. Cf. Cohen 1992, who differentiates the tourist who travels from center to periphery from the pilgrim who journeys from periphery to center.

161. The decrease in foot traffic to Latium's sanctuaries: n. 1 above. Mediterranean political economies of religion that privilege urban over nonurban communities: Ando 2017. Epistemicide and the Roman expansion: Padilla Peralta in progress a. The fifty-three *populi* who shared the meat at the Alban Mount: Pliny *NH* 3.68–70 (with Palmer 1970, 10–11 for some problems with the notice). Egerius Baebius and the dedicating communities at Aricia: Cato *FRHist* F 36.

6

Conclusion

RELIGION AND THE ENDURING STATE

THE PROCESSES THAT HAVE BEEN CHARTED in this book all came to the forefront during the Second Punic War, when the Roman state exploited practically every means at its disposal to stabilize and when necessary repair the relationship of its human community to the gods. As an early imperial writer later insisted, "the most effective hardening agent is necessity."[1] It was in the pressurizer of those Hannibalic years that the mid-republican state was rigorously tested for durability, and its major institutions—religious observance foremost among them—subjected to intense and exacting scrutiny. Supplying fuel and momentum to those religious changes that had been phased in during the First Punic War and its aftermath, the numerous crises in the state's management of the *sacra* that surface during the final two decades of the third century would clear the way for a substantially different religious landscape after 200 BCE—which is one of the reasons why my story ends where it does.[2] The purpose of this conclusion is to offer a two-part assessment of this book's major findings, first through an examination of one of the institutional religious procedures that arose from the repetitive patterning of those collective commitments that we surveyed in the earlier chapters, and second through the formulation of one final model that attempts to visualize the cumulative force of religious practice on the design and experience of civic time. I begin with the institutional procedure: prodigy expiation.

1. Val. Max. 2.7.10: *efficacissimum duramentum est necessitas.*

2. See the introduction on periodization; cf. Arnhold and Rüpke 2017, 415–16 on the religious ferment of the final decades of the third century.

I. Prodigy Expiation and State Coordination

Much of the recent work on the Roman state's coordination of responses to reported prodigies has underlined how the system enabled major political organs—and in particular the Roman Senate—to assert expertise and control at moments of pervasive social anxiety, and to assure citizens and allies alike that Rome would go to any lengths to enlist and retain the support of the gods.[3] Prodigies, most often in the form of disruptions to the Roman sense of the natural order—atmospheric and climatic phenomena such as lightning and hail, or perceived aberrations from the biological status quo such as mules birthing or babies talking—were understood to convey information about the community's standing before the gods, and their expiations were seen as integral to securing the *pax deorum*.[4] Whenever a prodigy was reported, the Roman Senate would decide whether to accept or reject the report. If the *prodigium* was accepted, the Senate proceeded to solicit the advice of the priestly colleges, who would rely on their repositories of institutional expertise—from the *commentarii* of the *pontifices* to the Sibylline Books in the case of the *decemviri* and the so-called *Etrusca disciplina* of the *haruspices*—to propose expiatory *remedia*. These were then carried out as the Senate decreed.[5]

The reconstruction of this system's workings is heavily reliant on Livy, whose third decade furnishes twenty-one notices of announced and expiated prodigies for a total of approximately 160 individual *prodigia* and *portenta*.[6] Concerned as it is with summarizing elite deliberations and resolutions regarding the *prodigia*, Livy's narrative does not offer much direct insight into whether the actions of magistrates, Senate, and priestly *collegia* had more than a temporary calming influence on the population at large. In engaging the content and tenor of Livy's presentation of prodigies, modern scholarship has lapsed repeatedly into broad-brush characterizations of popular "morale" or "fear" as manipulated and assuaged by the political savvy of a presumably more rational aristocracy. As Craige Champion has cogently argued, an elite-

3. Already North 1989, 596 for this functionalist reading; Rosenberger 1998 for a comprehensive study in a similar vein.

4. For the meaning and significance of this slippery term compare Santangelo 2011 and Satterfield 2015.

5. Only one rejection is attested, well after our period: the Senate's determination in 169 that certain prodigies were not relevant to public matters (Liv. 43.13).

6. Catalog with citations and summaries: MacBain 1982, Appendix A. The sources for prodigy lists that were consulted by historians such as Livy: Rawson [1971] 1991b and n. 21 below.

instrumentalist approach of this sort will not do; there is no legitimate reason for assuming that the Roman aristocratic elite was not itself gripped by fear and anxiety in receiving prodigy reports and while working out how best to address them.[7] The objective of this section is to outline how the prodigy-expiation system paired coordinated large-scale activity at Rome by boosting the ritual commitments that brought Romans and non-Romans alike to Rome. Three points should be noted at the outset.

First, the announcement and expiation of prodigies created a space for collaborative activity by enabling a range of actors (elite and nonelite, urban and rural, Roman and allied) to participate in the maintenance of the *res publica*.[8] Constituencies of various kinds and from multiple areas voiced concerns regarding their sensory-religious world to the Senate; this body, whose corporate identity I examined in chapter 3, then took action; and over time the repeated application of the process served to validate the status and sense of belonging appropriate to each constituency. Similarly fundamental to the perceived success of this process was the alignment of repetition with innovation, as the compulsion to resort to traditional expiatory practices such as *lectisternia* entered into a homeostatic relationship with the appeal of the new. The monumentalized sacred infrastructure of the mid-republican city and of its allied peers contributed to this alignment: temple spaces and precincts were routinely the sites where *prodigia* manifested and where their expiation took place. The infrastructural investment detailed in chapters 2 and 3 of this book therefore yielded a double dividend, supplying structures that were used by humans to communicate with the gods and by gods to communicate with humans.

Second, the prodigy system structured movement to Rome, within Rome, and from Rome, by routinizing human and nonhuman physical activity in ways that underwrote the formation of a more integrated cooperative ecology. The formation of this ecology began with the traffic in prodigy news, the operations of rumor that brought notices of alarming developments in Rome or among the allies to the Senate. These notices traveled in space—from the site of the reported occurrence to members of the Senate—and through many mouths. While this oral transmission increased the chance of distortion, it also facilitated the dissemination of the ritualized verbal mimicry through which members of the community received instruction and practice in a common language of the sacred. Moreover, the expiatory rituals enacted to reassert and promote collective solidarity standardized not only speech but also

7. Champion 2017—although prodigies do not receive much attention in his work.

8. Orlin 2010, 127.

physical movements and sight lines, through activities such as supplications, festivals, and processions. In chapter 5, I referenced one historical example of communities traveling to Rome for supplication; the Senate could also determine that it was appropriate for priestly elites to travel beyond the city in expiatory pilgrimage, as a means of affirming Rome's religious ties to other communities.

Third, the prodigy system was a historically contingent outcome of Roman state formation.[9] The majority of the prodigy notices preserved in the annalistic tradition date to the second half of the third century: Julius Obsequens begins his *Liber prodigiorum*, which draws on Livy, with a prodigy notice for 249 BCE; the number and frequency of notices in Livy and other sources drops off considerably after the period of the Second Punic War. The explanations proposed for this temporal clustering range from appeals to the mysterious whims of the annalists, to speculation about changes to recording practice involving the shadowy *Annales maximi*, to insistence on Livy's primarily literary intentions in wielding the prodigy notices as a stylizing tool for his Hannibalic War narrative.[10] These all have some merit but are partial explanations at best. As far as this book is concerned, the abundance of prodigy notices during this particular period is a powerful signal of a shift in Roman state formation. The prodigy-expiation system around which these reports congregate marks the successful crystallization of those mid-republican structures of religious expression that we studied in previous chapters: not only the material investment in cult that yielded temples capable of serving as sites for the performance of the prodigious, but also the formation of an increasingly specialized and differentiated elite that strove to collaborate with nonelites in order to implement the techniques and rituals through which Rome's social cohesion was maintained.

The temple-and-*ludi* complex remained alive and well during the Second Punic War; both temples and games continued to be vowed, often in response to *prodigia* or other portents.[11] But for the remainder of this section I will

9. Cf. Bloch 1963, 77 for the call to study the prodigy system from "le point de vue évolutif"; discussion of this issue in Engels 2005, 151–54.

10. The wax and wane of prodigy reporting and expiation: Rosenberger 1998, 205–33. Statistics on Livy's references to religious phenomena as compared to other ancient historians: Newbold 1982. *Prodigia* as narrative devices: Levene 1993 on the third decade, and especially 65–66 on 27.37; Levene 2010, 37–38. Livy's religiosity: Walsh 1961, 61–64; Levene 1993, 16–34; Liebeschuetz [1967] 2009.

11. Temples: Liv. 22.9.9 and 10.10 on the vowing of temples to Venus Erycina and Mens; 29.10.4–8 on the solicitation of the Magna Mater. Games: Liv. 25.12 on the celebration of the *ludi Apollinares* following the discovery of the *carmina Marciana*.

concentrate on a prodigy notice that conveys a sense of the experiential feel of the prodigy system and its success at bringing people together. The year is 218, and Hannibal had already arrived in Italy. I quote the notice in full below so as to give a flavor both of the nature of the *prodigia* reported and of the responses devised to remedy them; the details of particular relevance to this section's argumentative brief are underlined.[12]

> *Romae aut circa urbem multa ea hieme prodigia facta aut, quod euenire solet motis semel in religionem animis, multa nuntiata et temere credita sunt, in quis ingenuum infantem semenstrem in foro holitorio triumphum clamasse, et <in> foro boario bouem in tertiam contignationem sua sponte escendisse atque inde tumultu habitatorum territum sese deiecisse, et nauium speciem de caelo adfulsisse, et aedem Spei, quae est in foro holitorio, fulmine ictam, et Lanuui hastam se commouisse et coruum in aedem Iunonis deuolasse atque in ipso puluinari consedisse, et in agro Amiternino multis locis hominum specie procul candida ueste uisos nec cum ullo congressos,*[13] *et in Piceno lapidibus pluuisse, et Caere sortes extenuatas, et in Gallia lupum uigili gladium ex uagina raptum abstulisse. Ob cetera prodigia libros adire decemuiri iussi; quod autem lapidibus pluuisset in Piceno, nouendiale sacrum edictum; et subinde aliis procurandis prope tota ciuitas operata fuit. Iam primum omnium urbs lustrata est hostiaeque maiores quibus editum est dis caesae, et donum ex auri pondo quadraginta Lanuuium Iunoni portatum est et signum aeneum matronae Iunoni in Auentino dedicauerunt, et lectisternium Caere, ubi sortes attenuatae erant, imperatum, et supplicatio Fortunae in Algido; Romae quoque et lectisternium Iuuentati et supplicatio ad aedem Herculis nominatim, deinde uniuerso populo circa omnia puluinaria indicta, et Genio maiores hostiae caesae quinque, et C. Atilius Serranus praetor uota suspicere issus, si in decem annos res publica eodem stetisset statu. Haec procurata uotaque ex libris Sibyllinis magna ex parte leuauerant religione animos.*

> At Rome or in the vicinity of the city many prodigies occurred that winter or, as tends to occur on occasion when minds are moved to religious fear, many were announced and rashly believed. Among them: that a freeborn six-month-old had shouted "Triumph" in the Forum Holitorium, and that in the Forum Boarium a cow of its own will ascended to the third level (of a building) and then, terrified by the tumult of the residents, threw itself

12. Liv. 21.62. Case studies of this notice that inform my reading: Rosenberger 1998, 176–79; Engels 2005, 158–60.

13. The grammar of this clause is confusing, and emendation of *specie* and *uisos* to *species* and *uisas* has been proposed; cf. Weissenborn and Müller *ad loc.* who gloss the clause with the remark that "im Griechischen würde ὄντας hinzutreten."

> down, and that an apparition of ships had gleamed in the sky, and that the temple of Spes in the Forum Holitorium was struck by lightning, and that at Lanuvium a spear moved itself and a crow flew down into the temple of Juno and sat on Juno's couch, and that in the territory of Amiternum at multiple locations individuals in the guise of men dressed in white were seen from afar—but did not encounter anyone—and that in Picenum it rained stones, and that at Caere the *sortes* shrunk in size, and that in Gaul a wolf snatched and carried off a sentry's sword from its scabbard. On account of the other prodigies the *decemviri* were ordered to consult the Sibylline Books; but because it had rained stones in Picenum, a sacred nine-day period was pronounced; and immediately the attention of almost the entire citizen body was given to the expiation of the other prodigies. For first of all, the city was purified and mature victims that were stipulated for the gods were killed, and a gift of forty pounds of gold was brought to Juno of Lanuvium and the matrons dedicated a bronze statue to Juno on the Aventine, and at Caere—where the *sortes* had shrunk in size—a *lectisternium* was ordered, and a supplication to Fortuna at Algidum; and at Rome both a *lectisternium* to Iuventas and a supplication at the temple of Hercules[14] were undertaken by name,[15] and then by the entire community around all the couches of the gods; and five mature victims were sacrified to Genius, and C. Atilius Serranus the praetor was ordered to undertake vows if in ten years the *res publica* remained in the same state. These expiations and vows from the Sibylline Books relieved minds from religious fear, for the most part.

Much has been written about the tone, diction, syntax, and arrangement of this and other prodigy reports; about the fusion of these elements to create a historiographic emplotment of the prodigy system, and the relation of that emplotment to the historicity of the reports; and about the likelihood that annalistic transmission had manipulated and deformed the contents of this and other notices even before Livy got his hands on them. For our purposes, I will assume that this notice preserves the substantive truth of how the prodigy reporting and procuration of 218 functioned. My narrow focus in what follows will be on the administrative and institutional dimensions of the process, especially in the urban context of Rome itself. The clauses and phrases underlined reflect moments in the prodigy-expiation complex where a *prodigium* happened in a public space and/or where the expiation ordered was carried out in front of and actively involved the general public.

14. We do not know which temple of Hercules is meant here.

15. *Nominatim* has defied clear interpretation; see Rosenberger 1998, 178 for the rueful comment that "Das Procedere hierbei ist unklar."

How many people are likely to have actually heard a baby shouting "Triumph" in the Forum Holitorium? I pose this question in the belief that the social significance of this *prodigium* was amplified by its occurrence in a highly frequented space in the city; the same amplification, this time flagged through explicit mention of the crowd of local residents that terrified a wayward cow into jumping off a building, occurred with the prodigy reported from the Forum Boarium. That prodigious events were imagined and reported as spectacles visible to a plurality of Romans cuts two ways. It is tempting to read the reports as indices of "collective hallucination" or "effervescence," both phenomena with a rich literature in the field of sociology and group psychology from the time of Émile Durkheim. Although the collective hallucination model has some purchase here, the preoccupation with public manifestation is best appreciated from an institutional and participatory standpoint. The prodigy system was predicated on the understanding that many people might have seen the reported event; the perception of the *prodigium* as highly visible and therefore much bruited, whether at Rome or elsewhere in Roman Italy, will have factored into the Senate's determination to respond to it with a high-visibility expiation that could travel along the mouths of gods and men. Spaces of high social visibility were not only sites of human-human interaction; the sites specified in the report were spaces crowded with gods, and in the case of the Forum Holitorium and Forum Boarium temples to the gods. The (rumored) baby's shout of "Triumph" in the Forum Boarium thus became the catalyst for a type of common knowledge, both for those human beings who believed themselves to have heard the shout and to know others who had heard it, and for the numinous beings whose cults delineated the Forum's spatial extent and who themselves knew not only about the shout but also about those humans who had heard it. Failing to act on common knowledge of this sort came with potentially dire personal consequences.[16]

This line of analysis differs in one important respect from Bruce MacBain's appealing interpretation of the *prodigia* as implicated in Roman state efforts to establish and maintain religious communication with its colonists and allies.[17] Through such communication, MacBain's theory goes, those members of the coalition outside the city of Rome had their religious fears recognized and resolved by the Senate; the scale of this communication is manifest in the more than one hundred towns and territories—many of which were not on *ager Romanus*—that are named in Livy's prodigy re-

16. Cf. the fate of the plebeian who was visited by Jupiter in a dream after a slave was beaten at the *ludi Maximi*: Macr. *Sat.* 1.11.3–5 with Padilla Peralta 2018a, xxvii–xxix.

17. MacBain 1982, 34–42.

cords.[18] What I am suggesting is that an inchoate awareness of the operations of common knowledge was structured into the apparatus. On one front, this awareness acted to build up trust, in that the encouragement to confide any disquieting or upsetting phenomenon was a necessary precondition of the system's smooth operation. At the same time, however, the involvement of the public and of public spaces in the reporting and expiation of prodigies was also hitched to the "strategic manufactur[ing of] fear" whose contribution to the Roman war efforts of the post–Second Punic War period has been investigated by James Quillin. In his "fear propaganda game," Quillin modeled the efficacy of fear as a means of motivating the Roman citizen body to recommit to military activity.[19] Fear alone, though, was not enough; *directed* fear, fear with referents in view and clear consequences in mind, was what proved most decisive in the long run. For such fear to be managed successfully, there had to be a mechanism that perpetuated fear and at the same time reinforced a sense of strategic resolution and purpose. The monumental buildup of the Roman city, and the training of the citizen body through regularized cultic observance to attend ever-vigilantly to those spaces in which the gods were worshipped,[20] created conditions for the (re)production of fear and for the ritual release from that fear, following which military activity could be resumed with the guarantee of the gods' backing and endorsement.

The single clearest indicator of the importance of the prodigy system to the management of the Roman war effort is the calendrical timing of the expiations. To judge from the arrangement of the notices in Livy, every single episode of prodigy expiation was immediately followed by preparations for military activity.[21] Moreover, the presentation of these preparations for military activity as described by Livy explicitly connects the resolution of expiation with the turn to military matters, since the former had to be carried out prior

18. The geographical distribution of prodigy reports has excited much debate among scholars of Roman religion: for the major lines of interpretation see Rawson [1971] 1991b; for the connection between prodigy reporting and the road network, Rosenberger 2005.

19. Quillin 2004 for a game-theoretic approach to the stoking of *metus hostilis*.

20. Usefully on the genuine fear felt before the gods: Lacam 2010, 141–42.

21. Even accounting for Livy's literary molding of the narrative (bibliography at n. 6 above), the order probably reflects historical realities: Satterfield 2012. The mean interval between second-century prodigy notices in Julius Obsequens is 1.8 years; at the very least, reports were accepted and expiations carried out biannually. If the original source for annalistic prodigy lists was the pontifical *tabula dealbata* (on which see *Annales Pontificum* fr. 2 = Cato *Origines* 4.1 Chassignet; for the possible mediation of its contents through the published *Annales Maximi*, Frier 1979), an annual patterning for the reports would gain in plausibility. Annualized lists in Roman state records: Riggsby 2019, chap. 1.

to the latter's initiation.[22] This sequencing falls in line with the standard assortment of rituals performed by higher magistrates annually as they readied to depart to their provinces; the offering of sacrifices, the stipulation of vows, and the taking of auspices were all strategies for managing the transition from *domi* to *militiae*, and for ensuring that the gods were consulted and properly acknowledged prior to the initiation of the campaign season.[23] The practice of articulating the expiation of prodigies to the resumption of military operations was one extension of this sacro-institutional logic. The great fear lurking in these reports of extraordinary and supernatural phenomena—that the gods whose monumental cultic presence was so richly realized in the city were displeased or dissatisfied—was first acknowledged in public and then assuaged through the enactment of public rituals in which all residents of the city participated and saw one another participate, not least of all the gods themselves. Common knowledge reigned supreme. To be sure, mid-republican Rome was not unique among its Mediterranean peers in rushing to implement novel ritual remedies prior to embarking on or resuming military activity. Following a rash of epidemics and a string of battlefield defeats during its seesaw conflicts with Syracuse, Carthage introduced the worship of Demeter and Kore and appointed the most preeminent men of the state to the a newly created priesthood for her cult.[24] But it was the frequency with which the Roman state commissioned and oversaw these public rituals that may have distanced it from its Mediterranean competition—although caution is in order here given the gaps in our evidence for the religious life of Rome's rivals.

Two final implications of this setup, as it imprinted itself in the minds of Romans and of their allies, merit recognition here. The first is that temples were validated as constitutive features of Roman civic life with every prodigy report of an incident in their precincts or vicinity that was accepted by the Senate, and with every expiatory procedure that was orchestrated before them. The second is that even signs of divine displeasure in the urban spaces overseen by Rome's temples acted to entrench the city's status as a religious center, since many of the expiations undertaken in this period entailed the assertion of control either of these spaces or of sanctuary spaces outside of the city through prescribed ritual movements—pilgrimage.

22. One example will suffice: in 208, praetors were permitted to head to their assigned provinces, but the consuls were kept at Rome after failing to obtain *litatio*: Liv. 27.23.1.

23. Comprehensively on these rituals: Rüpke 1990. Vows: chapter 2 n. 10; Lacam 2010, 57–60 on the extraordinary vows of the Second Punic War.

24. Diodorus 14.77.4–5, with Melliti 2010, 92–93 for the claim that this cult to the thesmophoric goddesses was intended in the first instance to satisfy "les intérêts immédiats d'une aristocratie maritime."

II. Rhythm and Quantity: The Magnitude of the Consensus

This one notice of prodigies and their expiation offers a mere snapshot of what was a far more fluid, interactive, and above all else psychosomatically engrossing social practice, threading through Roman culture year after year for many decades. To evaluate how this social practice interacted with the full range of institutional behaviors that contributed to holding the Roman state together, especially in times of crisis, I will now propose and comment on one final model. As will have been apparent from chapter 2's quantification of temple construction demands in relation to military service, it is hard to escape the conclusion that military service was by an order or more of magnitude the single most influential driver of integration during the middle Republic.[25] The claim should be hedged with the observation that many aspects of military service, from the regular rituals of the *sacramentum* and auspice-taking to the more infrequent rituals of *devotio* and *evocatio*, were highly sacralized, but given how many troops the Roman state pressed into campaigning, and the lengthening of their service commitments during the final decades of the third century, it might seem rather curious that this book has been harping on religion and not the army as a primary catalyst for state formation. Furthermore, in light of the spirited and at times fractious debates over the political power of the *populus* in mid- and late republican Rome that have consumed much of the scholarship in recent years, the reader might wonder what this book has to offer those more interested in the constitutional machinery of state formation.

In homage to the adoption of quantitative approaches to the study of political access and participation in mid- and late republican Rome,[26] this book's parting shot will take the form of a model that represents the apportionment of Roman civic time across political, religious, and military commitments during our period. The model will tabulate the person-hours expended on military service in the years 225–200 BCE and compare them to the equivalent cumulative expenditures in the domains of political activity and religious observance. Since this model will of necessity be reliant on judicious speculation, I will be as explicit as possible about its orientating assumptions for those readers who might wish to falsify it.

a. First, I disaggregated religious activity into four components: annual festivals, expiatory activities, temple construction, and pilgrimage. For temple construction I relied on the figures for $n = 500$ and $n = 2{,}000$ generated in

25. Scheidel 2006, 224–26; cf. Taylor 2018 on centurion elections and the practice of politics.

26. See, e.g., the calculations in Mouritsen 2001, chap. 2.

chapter 2 for the period 225–200: 2,700,000 for the former; 10,800,000 for the latter. For the remaining three, I proceeded as follows:

The category of annual festivals was divided into (1) temple anniversaries and (2) major state festivals. Chapter 3 calculated that 63 new *dies natales templorum* were incorporated into the calendar during the fourth and third centuries. For a "low" condition for participation, I assumed that on average 500 people participated in the celebration of each of these anniversaries, at an average of 4 hours per person; for a "high" condition for participation, I raised the number to 1,000 but kept the same per-person average number of hours. To obtain the number of major state festivals, I counted all capitalized celebrations in the Republican *fasti* (the Agonalia, the Carmentalia, etc.) as well as *conceptivae* by the number of days marked off for each in the calendar; the total is 49. For these major festival days with their associated *ludi* and processions, I again set low and high conditions: for the former, an average of 2,000 people participating for 4 hours each; for the latter, an average of 10,000 participating for 4 hours each. I then multiplied the annual low and high results ([63 × 500 × 4] + [49 × 2,000 × 4] for the first; [63 × 1,000 × 4] + [49 × 10,000 × 4] for the second) by 25 to arrive at tallies for the period 225–200. The result is 12,950,000 person-hours at the low end, and 55,300,000 at the high end. I chose not to account for the rising incidence of ludic *instaurationes* at the tail end of the Second Punic War; correcting for this would not affect the result's order of magnitude.

Next, I sifted through all the expiatory notices preserved in Livy for the years 218–200 and converted each ritual into a person-hour figure.[27] To give a sense of what this procedure entailed, let us return briefly to the notice for 218 examined in the first section of this chapter. The *decemviri* consulted the Sibylline Books: here we have a body of ten men whom I will assume spent two hours consulting the Books and reporting their findings to the Senate. A *novendiale sacrum* was announced: for nine days of *feriae*, I speculated that each day around 5,000 people participated in daily religious observance, averaging 3 hours per person. A *lustratio urbis* was carried out: I assumed that a group of approximately 50 people—senior magistrates, members of the priestly colleges, and attendants—was involved in undertaking the *lustratio* and averaged about 4 hours per person; the remaining inhabitants of the city and its environs (200,000) saw the *lustratio* taking place or engaged with it, averaging 2 hours per person. A 40-pound gift was dedicated at the temple of Juno in Lanuvium: I assumed that 50 people devoted 1 hour to offer the dedication.

27. The notices, with their corresponding years: Liv. 21.62 (218); 22.1.8–20 and 22.9–10 (217); 22.57.2–6 (216); 24.10.6–13 (214); 25.7.7–9 and 25.12 (212); 26.23.4–6 (211); 27.4.11–15 (210); 27.11.1–6 (209); 27.23.4 (208); 27.37.4–15 (207); 28.11.1–7 (206); 29.14.2–5 (204); 30.2.9–13 (203); 30.38.8–10 (202); 31.12.5–10 (200).

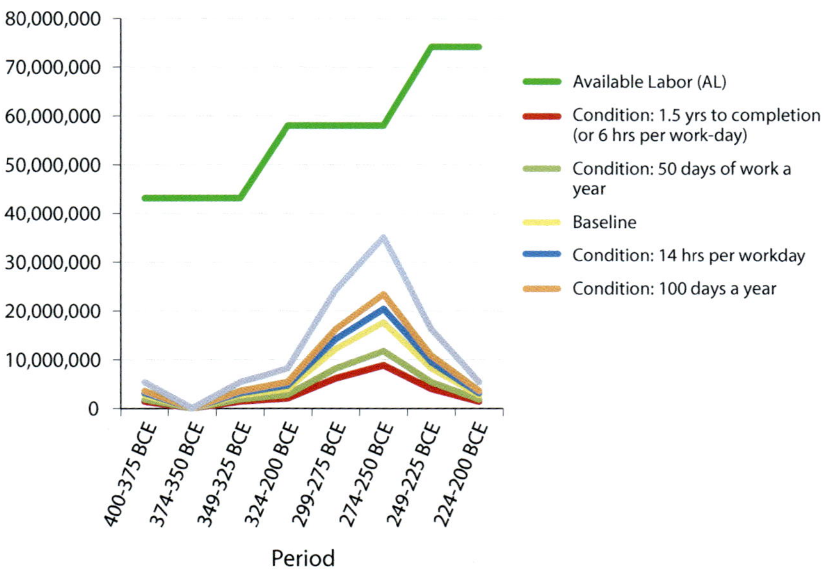

Plate 1. Alterations to the model, holding n = 500.

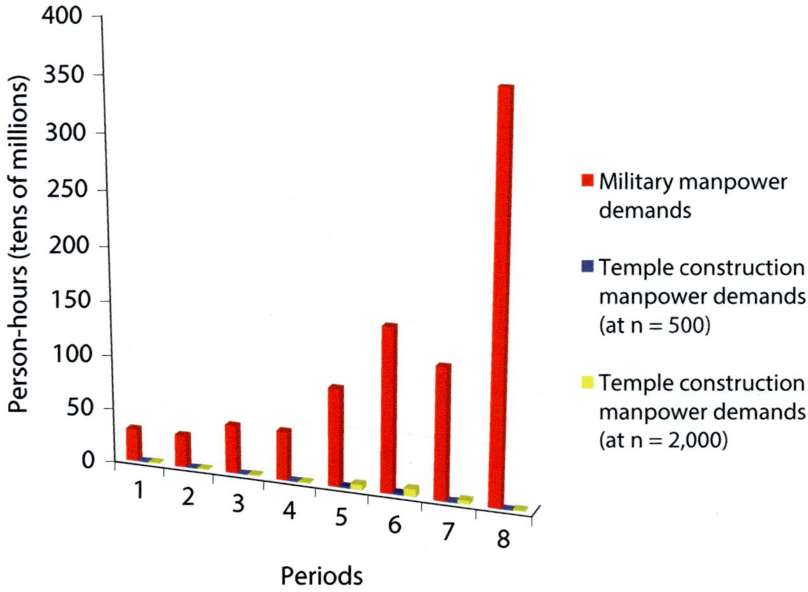

Plate 2. Military campaigning vs. temple construction: manpower demands, 400–200 BCE.

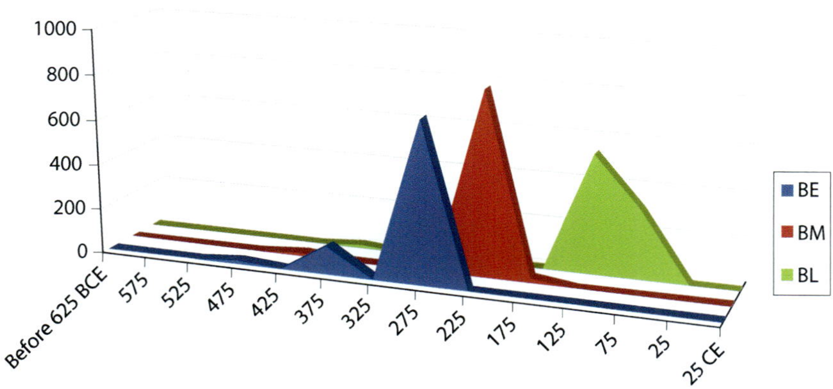

Plate 3. Chronological distribution of anatomical ex-votos: five Italian sanctuaries.

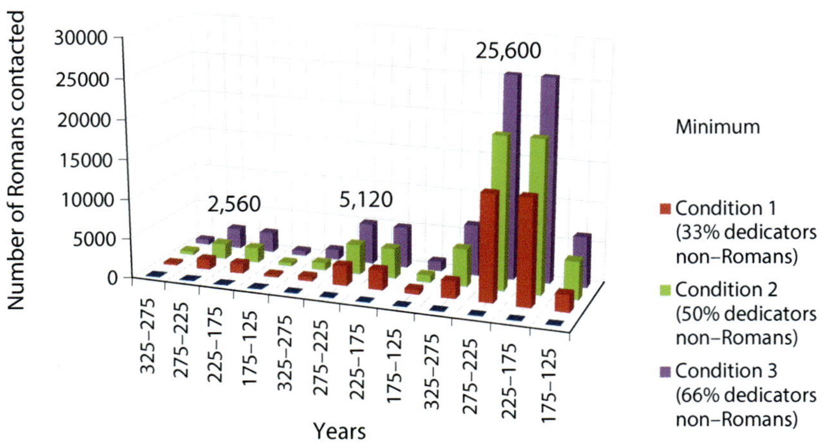

Plate 4. Conjectured number of annual interactions between non-Roman dedicators and city residents, 325–125 BCE.

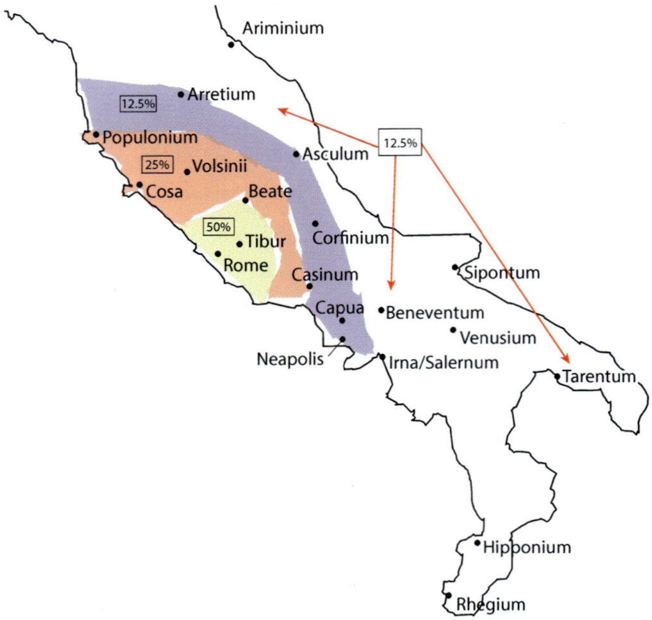

Plate 5. Sacred mobility in mid-republican Italy: the home regions of prospective pilgrims to Rome. (Drawing by the author)

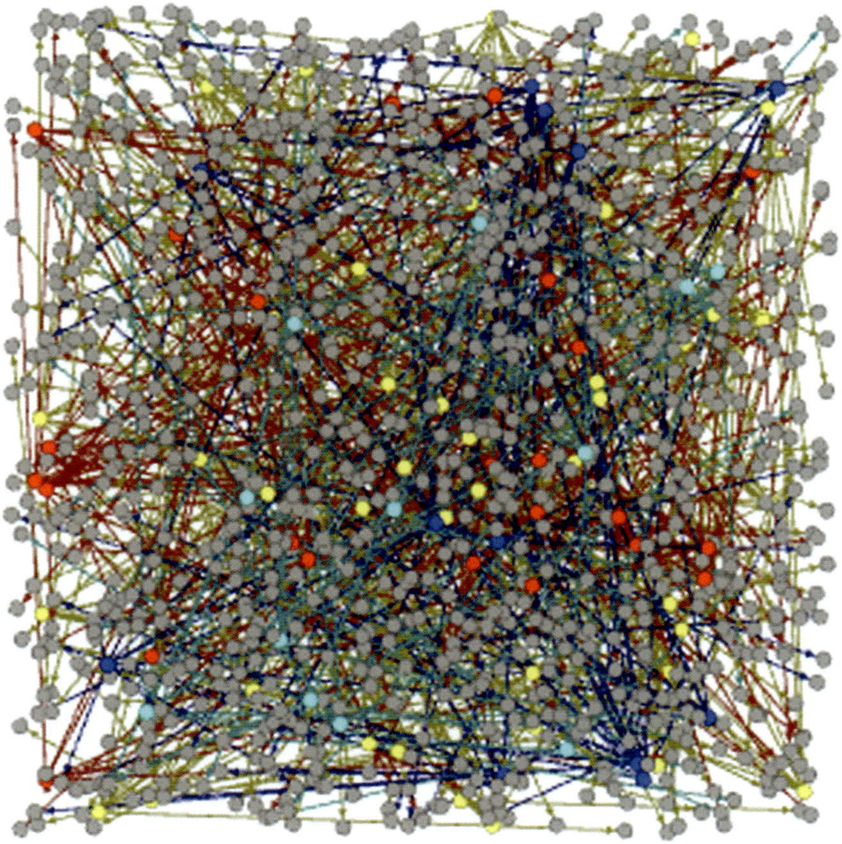

Plate 6. Annual interactions between residents of Rome and out-of-town pilgrims, 325–275 BCE. Color coding of nodes: Yellow (Y) = Individual hailing from catchment area bounded in yellow (as per Plate 5); Red (Re) = catchment area between red and yellow lines; Dark Blue (B) = catchment area between red and blue lines; Sky Blue (O) = outside the catchment areas; Gray = Gaius Romanus, resident of the city.

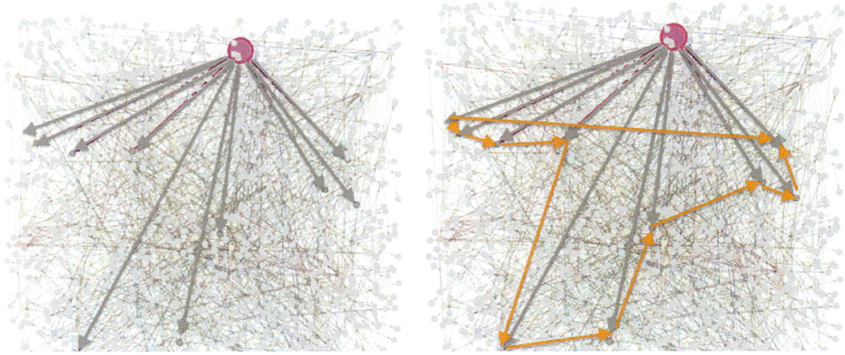

Plate 7. Close-up of non-Roman node Y1 in network universe. (Left) = no triadic closure; (right) = with triadic closure, marked in orange. Here and following, I supply only one set of triadic closures for each pair of "spokes on the wheel." Although more triadic closures could be counted and represented, introducing them would (1) make my graphs unreadable and (2) not materially enhance my main argument.

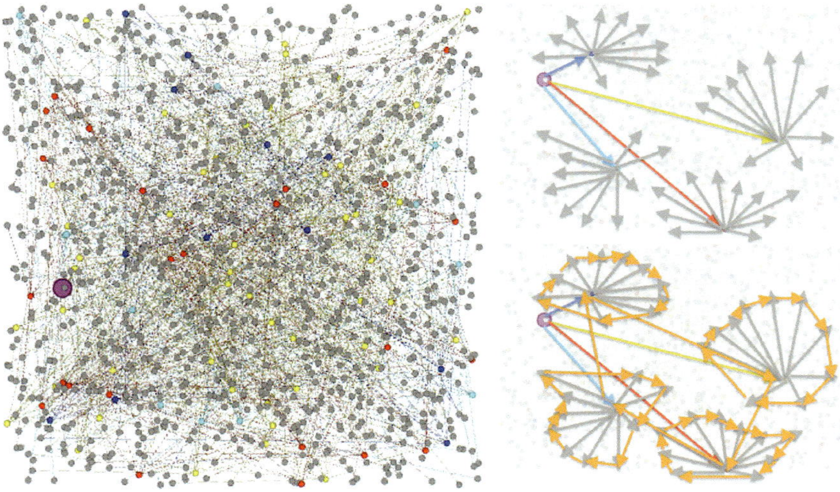

Plate 8. A Roman (R1) forges ties with four non-Romans (Y1-Re1-B1-O1). (Left) = node in network universe (purple, left margin); (right, top) = close-up; (right, bottom) = close-up with triadic closure (marked in orange).

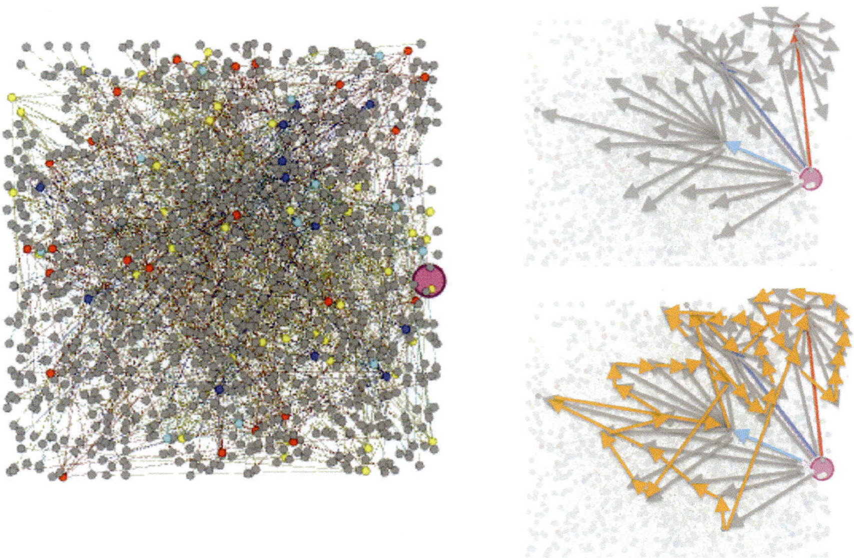

Plate 9. A Y1 forges ties with seven Rs and Re1-B1-O1. (Left) = node in network universe (purple, right margin); (right, top) = close-up; (right, bottom) = close-up with triadic closure.

The *matronae* dedicated a statue to Aventine Juno: here I envisioned 500 elite women devoting 1 hour to their dedication.

For the *lectisternium* at Caere, I imagined 5,000 local residents expending 3 hours on average in traveling within, around, and back from the area where the *lectisternium* was being held; for the *supplicatio* at Algidum, 10,000, again at 3 hours on average; for the *supplicatio* and *lectisternium* at Rome, 10,000 at 3 hours on average; and for the *universus populus* approaching all the *pulvinaria*, 50,000 at 6 hours on average. I proceeded in much the same fashion and following the same guiding assumptions for all of Livy's notices, summing up the time allotments for the rituals that are specified in each annual notice (or two) to arrive at a total for each year. I then added up the totals, divided this sum by the number of years for which we have reported notices (fifteen) to obtain an annual average,[28] and multiplied that average by 25 to obtain an aggregate reconstructed total for the period 225–200: 8,237,834 person-hours, rounded down to 8 million.

Finally, to account for pilgrimage, I extrapolated from the numbers in chapter 5. For the low condition, I took Scenario 1 of the 10 percent hypothesis for years 225–175, according to which 128 out-of-towners came to dedicate at Rome annually; I assumed that they averaged one full day traveling to Rome and one full day traveling back to their city or region of origin. For the high condition, I took Scenario 3 of the 1 percent hypothesis for years 225–175, according to which 2,560 out-of-towners came annually, and made the same assumption about average length of travel to and from Rome. (To avoid double-counting, I will not account for the time spent by these pilgrims *in* Rome, having already generated the figures for the person-hour commitments to festival celebration.) The low condition yields a total of 153,600 person-hours (128 × 48 hours × 25) for the period 225–200; the high condition yields 3,072,000 (2,560 × 48 × 25).

To sum up: on the low end (expiatory rituals + festivals [low] + temple construction [low] + pilgrimage [low]), approximately 24 million person-hours were expended in the years 225 to 200; on the high end (expiatory rituals + festivals [high] + temple construction [high] + pilgrimage [high]), approximately 77 million.

b. For political activity in the period 225–200, I went through a typical year's political cycle and tried to pin some numbers on the cycle's time commitments, taking my cue from Henrik Mouritsen's figures for the physical capacity of mid- and late republican political venues.[29]

28. Livy has no prodigy notices for 215, 213, or 201, and we are missing the books that would have recorded notices prior to 218.

29. Mouritsen 2001.

I began with the obscure *comitia curiata*, which met either in the Comitium or the Capitol. The responsibilities of this assembly were twofold: (1) the conferral of *imperium* to senior magistrates and (2) approving adoptions. We are completely in the dark about how the *curiae* were organized and populated. Although by the late Republic participation was down to one token lictor for each of the thirty *curiae*, I assumed purely for the sake of this exercise that participation during the middle Republic was substantially higher and stipulated one of two conditions: a low of 1,000 and a high of 3,600, at the high end of what the Comitium could reasonably accommodate. Next, I assumed that the *comitia curiata* convened six times in the course of a calendar year, once for the conferring of *imperium* on newly elected magistrates and another five for adoptions; finally, I assumed that on average each participant spent an hour at each of these meetings. Running the low and high conditions through these assumptions gives a low total of 6,000 person-hours per year and a high of 21,600.

I then turned to the activities of the *comitia centuriata*, which met in the Campus Martius. The centuriate assembly was responsible for the election of consuls, praetors, and censors; the declaration of war and peace and the ratification of treaties; and the passage of legislation. For each of these procedures, voting had to be initiated and concluded within the same day. We do not know how long it took to vote during any one of these, but there is good reason to think it was not long. Given the peculiarities of the centuriate assembly's configuration, a majority could be reached without a sizable number of the centuries coming up to vote; drawn-out elections appear to have been rare.[30] For the number of participants, I stipulated a low of 5,000 and a high of 15,000, and I have also assumed that on average each voter spent 2 hours in the process of casting his vote. Consular and praetorian elections took place once a year, and censorial elections once every four years. For meetings to approve declarations of war and peace and the ratification of treaties, I counted 6 for the period 225–200.[31] For other legislation, I arbitrarily settled on the number of 5 meetings per year during our period and lengthened the average duration of legislative sessions—so as to have Gaius Romanus spending 4, not 2, hours at each proceeding—to account for preliminary *contiones*.

Third to be tabulated were the activities of the *concilium plebis* and the *comitia tributa*, which for our period probably met in the Forum. These bodies

30. An unusually long consular election in 45 lasted a little under four hours (five Roman hours): Cic. *Fam.* 7.30 with Mouritsen 2001, 30–31.

31. The initiation and conclusion of hostilities with the Gauls of northern Italy counts as 2; the declaration of war and the ratification of peace with Carthage counts as 2; and the initiation and conclusion of the First Macedonian War counts as 2.

were responsible for the election of tribunes and aediles, the approval of special commissions, and (again) the passage of legislation. The number of participants I set at a low of 3,500 and a high of 10,000. As with consular, praetorian, and censorial elections held in the centuriate assembly, I assumed that tribunal and aedilician elections required on average about 2 hours from Gaius Romanus; I made the same assumptions about time required for legislation and the number of times legislation was voted on as above; for the approval of special commissions, I settled on 10 for the period 225–200.[32]

Last to be calculated were the time investments of the Roman Senate. The mid-republican Senate was smaller than its late republican counterpart, as implied by the quorum figure mentioned in the *SC de Bacchanalibus*. I have assumed—generously—that there were on average 200 senators in attendance at each session; that these senators averaged 5 hours per session; and that the Senate met 20 times a year for the discussion of political and military matters, the awarding of contracts, the receiving of embassies, and the resolution of *prodigia* and other matters brought to its attention by the priestly colleges. Adding up figures for all these different political bodies in order to arrive at a total for time expended on political activity in the last quarter of the third century yields 6,190,000 person-hours at the low end and 18,100,000 at the high end.

These figures are now ripe for visualization, and the resulting logarithmic graph provides a rather intriguing perspective on how religious activity and participation stack up relative to other sectors of Roman civic life (figure 6.1). That the military retains its place of prominence is no surprise, but arguably the more important takeaway is that only under high conditions of participation does the amount of aggregate human time spent on political participation reach the same scale as the amount of time expended on religious activities. Although the figures on this graph do not pretend to be authoritative, this quantification of the mid-republican distribution of civic time could with some adjustments be reformulated as an estimate of human labor expenditure in the middle Republic. In that respect, the model exemplifies how one might go about generating the sorts of "systematic data" through which the history of premodern political economies can more effectively be analyzed.[33]

For present purposes, however, the model's main selling point is that it crystallizes the temporal demands of religion in relation to those of politics. On this representation, the mid-republican state looks less like classical Athens and more like classical Sparta, perhaps the only other Mediterranean pol-

32. Four are listed in *MRR*; I chose ten to account for any missing from Livy's text, and for those that were appointed in the period before Livy's text resumes.

33. The significance of collecting and analyzing such data: Hoffman 2017, 1566.

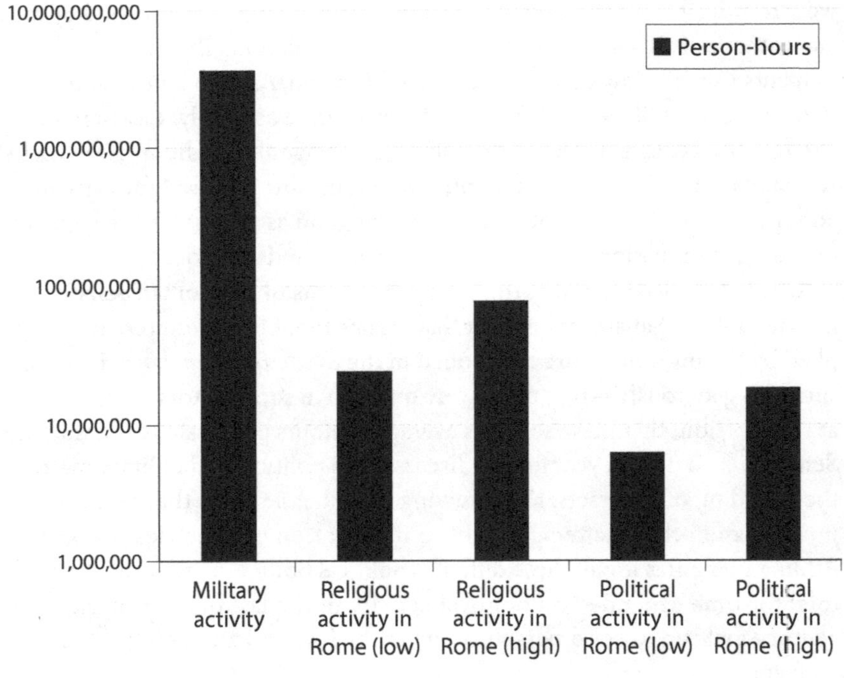

FIGURE 6.1. The distribution of civic time in mid-republican Rome, 225–200 BCE.

ity for which it can confidently be asserted that religious ritual consumed far more civic time than the practice of politics.[34] Whether an incipient awareness of this similarity gave a nudge to mid- and late republican interest in credentializing Rome as genealogically and culturally indebted to Sparta awaits further study.[35] In any case, the model's disentanglement of the political from the religious actually understates the time commitment to religious praxis in the Roman political realm. As stressed in the analysis of the Senate in chapter 3, political units frequently met in or in the immediate vicinity of temples. Moreover, all assembly meetings opened with religious rituals and could be terminated by religious infelicities. Even if we set these facts aside, the graph is a convenient illustration of two key dimensions of the middle Republic's timescapes that bear directly on our understanding of Roman state formation during the fourth and third centuries and that will therefore serve as the closing notes of this book.

34. For an overview of Spartan religion see M. Flower 2017.

35. A connection mediated by the Sabines: see, e.g., Cato the Elder *FRHist* F 50 with commentary *ad loc.* on the historian's handling of the "strong and the weak version of the Spartan tradition." On the cultural valence of monetization in both classical Sparta and mid-republican Rome note Humm 2005, 327 with n. 182.

III. Envoi

The first is that religious practice must be mentioned in the same breath as political engagement in any study of what held the *res publica* together. It is in cult and its associated commitments that "the core of the consensus" of long-standing interest to Karl-Joachim Hölkeskamp and other students of Republican political culture undoubtedly resided. As the summary sketch of the commitments that I listed in explaining the model's setup makes clear, there were many more opportunities to participate in religious practice than there were opportunities to engage in electoral or bureaucratic activity. Whereas, under the Empire, "the ritual life of the Roman citizen" became increasingly crowded with the protocols of state administration (foremost among them the census),[36] during the fourth and third centuries BCE this life consisted in the main of religious acts. Furthermore, opportunities for religious engagement exhibited considerable variation not only in scale—from the relatively small numbers participating directly in the construction of temples to the far larger numbers for processions and *supplicationes*—but in the status of participants: in sharp contrast to the political cycle, many religious activities were open to noncitizens. Although elite management of some of these religious activities often literally took center stage, this book has also lingered over slave and freedmen involvement in the operations of cult and tracked the operations of a votive economy that over the course of two centuries involved both elites and nonelites. Time spent together was what made the development and reinforcement of trust through face-to-face interaction, small- and large-group collective action, and the cultivation of common knowledge possible.

The second proposition is about method, and about quantitative methods in particular. Systematic quantification is a great boon to those seeking to study the interrelation of religious observance and state formation, and in particular those who are seeking to build bridges between otherwise isolated or (artificially) partitioned bodies of evidence. In generating figure 6.1, I attempted to model this habit one final time by mobilizing some quantitative techniques to facilitate comparison. The methodological sensibility that informs the design of figure 6.1's model and that streaks through this book draws strength from the belief that the interaction between religious practice and state formation should be understood as a system amenable to quantification—one whose component parts, participant volumes, and cumulative time investments can be reconstructed and disarticulated for closer scrutiny.

Without a fine-tuned comprehension of the scales and rhythms of Rome's religious world, it becomes all too easy to recapitulate the standard line that the story of the middle Republic's state-formation trajectory is fundamentally

36. Ando 2000, 351–62.

about politics and conquest. I hope to have confirmed by now the deep social penetration of the middle Republic's "government by ritual"[37] and the premium it placed on the public intervisibility of members of the Roman community and of the divinities who were believed to lend (and on occasion withhold) their critical support. This book has insisted on the value and enduring rewards of the Republic's promotion of a cultural space, defined above all by the channeling of resources to monumentality and the restructuring of civic time, through which religious experience became an indispensable foundation for the consolidation and regeneration of the Roman state. The building block for Roman Republican statehood was not, on my reconstruction, the political constitution idealized by Polybius, nor was the infrastructural reflex of that statehood limited to roads and aqueducts, those signature enterprises of Roman imperial engineering. Rather, what so defined that statehood as to become a candidate for repackaging and export as a coherent assemblage under the late Republic and Empire were temples, theaters, and festivals. These were eventually joined by a new religious form that for all its seeming incongruity with Republican culture nonetheless was incubated and nourished alongside it: ruler cult.[38] But the bundling of ruler cult together with the trinity of theaters, temples, and festivals takes us well beyond our period. It will suffice to end here with the observation that, through its diversion of so much time and labor to religious praxis and through that diversion's gravitationally charismatic pull, the Roman middle Republic morphed into a type of state better known to anthropologists than to ancient historians. It was a Geertzian theater state, locking down the continuing support of its various constituencies across the generations not only by waging warfare and by systematizing rent extraction but also by enticing members of the community into a seemingly endless and all-consuming cycle of ritual.[39]

37. Hölkeskamp 2011, 165–66, drawing on the terminology and concepts of the Renaissance historian Edward Muir.

38. The communicative rituals of ruler cult: Price 1984; Ando 2000, 385–98.

39. Geertz 1980 for the concept; Holt 2009 for refinement. Cf. Azoulay and Ismard 2018 for the thought-provoking characterization of classical Athens as a "choral" state.

APPENDIX

The *Pocola Deorum*: An Annotated CATALOG

1. *CIL* 1^2.439 = *RMR* no. 24. This is a Black Gloss *patera* that measures 13.7 cm in diameter and is decorated with a branch painted over the gloss in white and yellow. Found in the environs of Vulci, it is now held at the British Museum in London. The text reads: AECETIAI POCOLOM. The identity of the divinity AECETIAI is disputed: Aequitas/Aequitia and Angitia have been proposed; a hypothesized eponymous goddess of the central Italian Aequi was first suggested by A. Ernout but later dismissed by Degrassi-Krummrey.[1]

2. *CIL* 1^2.440 = *RMR* no. 13. This is a Black Gloss *patera* that measures 15 cm in diameter and is decorated with a painted Eros. Probably from Clusium or its *suburbium*, it is currently in the possession of the Antikensammlung of the Staatliche Museen in Berlin. The inscription reads: AISCLAPI POCO[[CO]] LOM. This is not the only orthographic peculiarity among the *pocola*: see nos. 3 and 7 below.[2] Aesculapius's receipt of a temple and cult in mid-republican Rome are discussed in chapter 3.

1. Ernout no. 99 with discussion ad loc. for the connection to the *signum Aequitatis* from Praeneste (*CIL* XIV.2860); cf. Massa-Pairault 1992, 133 on this *pocolom*'s relevance to the interpretation of a Praenestine *cista* in the Morgan Library collection. The Oscan dedication to *Angitia Dia* of uncertain origin, currently in the Collection Froehner of the Cabinet des Médailles: *Imagines* Bovianum/Saepinum 1. A dedication to Angitia found in the vicinity of her *lucus*: *ILLRP* 7 = *AE* 1991.567 with Scheid 2006, 84. Angitia as an alternative name for Angerona and the secret name of Rome: Tommasi 2014, 195–200. The rostering of Angitia alongside other Italic "fertility goddesses" such as Feronia and Mater Matuta: Poccetti 2005, 96–96; but cf. Carroll 2019 for deconstruction of this category.

2. One word (*poco[[co]]lom*) exhibits anaptyxis while the other (*Aisclapi*) does not. Wachter 1987, 467–68 explains that the "Lokalform von Epidaurus" accompanying the god on his installation at Rome around 290 would have experienced anaptyctic expansion after our

3. *CIL* 1^2.441 = *RMR* no. 21. This is a Black Gloss *patera* of unreported measurements that is decorated with a female head, ivy leaves, and berries. The head's hair is not arranged neatly; some early commentators interpreted the disorderly locks as snakes, but this reading did not find favor with Beazley. Of unknown provenience, the *pocolom* is currently held in the Louvre's Campana Collection. In light of Giampietro Campana's collecting habits, it is not unreasonable to assume that the ware was originally recovered from a site in central Italy. The inscription reads: BELOLAI POCOLOM. BELOLAI is a variant spelling of *Bel(l)onai*, the divinity to which Ap. Claudius Caecus vowed and dedicated a temple; this structure is discussed in chapter 3. It is not clear whether the female head represents Bellona herself.

4. *CIL* 1^2.442 = *RMR* no. 25. This is a Black Gloss *patera* whose diameter measurements have not been reported. Found at Orte together with *CIL* 1^2.2871 and ten Etruscan-language texts in a tomb, the *pocolom* is held at the Museo Nazionale Etrusco di Villa Giulia. The inscription reads: COERA POCOLO(M). Degrassi in *ILLRP* dismissed readings of the first word as *Coira, Coera(e),* or *Cofra*; A. Ernout took *Coera* as an archaic genitive (= *Coeras,* with omission of –s paralleled in other *pocola*) of *Cura*. While no cult to Cura is attested in the ancient sources, such a cult's existence would be in keeping with the worship of abstract qualities in mid-republican Rome and the attestation of other abstract deities among the *pocola* themselves, as discussed in chapters 2 and 5.

5. *CIL* 1^2.2883 = *RMR* no. 31. This is a small *oenochoe,* 9.5 cm tall and 6.7 in diameter, with striated belly and painted white lettering. Its precise find-spot is unknown, although its subsequent acquisition by the Pansa Collection makes an origin in the vicinity of ancient Teate likely. The *pocolom* is currently in the possession of the Museo Archeologico Nazionale in Chieti. Its inscription reads: CUCORDIA POCOLO(M).[3] Presumably the decorator wanted to paint CONCORDIA, though the spelling might also reflect pronunciation habits at the time of the *oenochoe*'s production.[4] As with no. 4 above, the divinity's name is in the genitive but with –s omitted. A shrine to Concordia at Rome was dedicated by Cn. Flavius, the *scriba*-turned-aedile, in the last dec-

period; cf. *CIL* I^2.3107a for the inscription AISCLAP[IO] on the remains of an altar—likely of third- or second-century date—recovered during the 1978–79 excavations at Fregellae.

3. Note Wachter 1987, 465 n. 1044 on *RMR*'s incorrect printing of the text as *Cucordie pocolom*.

4. Wachter 1987, 467: "Offenbar hat der Schreiber genauso geschrieben, wie er es hörte: das kurze *o* vor Nasal noch dunkler als sonst . . . und den Nasal als in der Schrift nicht festhaltbare Nasalierung."

ade of the fourth century. Chapter 2 briefly discusses the controversy surrounding its dedication.[5]

6. *CIL* 1^2.443 = *RMR* no. 26. This is a small and fragmentary *oenochoe* that is 7 cm tall and is missing the mouth and almost all of the handle. Of uncertain origin—a final deposition in Otranto (Hydrantum) has been speculated—the *pocolom* is now in the possession of the Cabinet des Médailles. The inscription reads: FORTUNAI POCOLO(M), with the divinity's name given as a standard first-declension archaic genitive. While worship of Fortuna reaches back far in Rome's past and is attested in central Italy outside of Rome, innovations to her Roman cult—possibly influenced by Hellenistic cults of *Tyche*—gained momentum over the course of the fourth and third centuries. The cultural resonance of her worship is assessed in chapter 4.[6]

7. *CIL* 1^2.444 = *RMR* no. 15. This is a Black Gloss *patera* that measures 15 cm in diameter; its center is decorated with the figure of an Eros riding a dog. Found in the vicinity of ancient Vulci at Cellere—where it was recovered from a tomb—the dish was subsequently acquired by a museum in Gotha before disappearing during the course of World War II.[7] The inscription reads: IUNO[[NE]]NES POCOLOM, another dittography (cf. nos. 2 and 3 above). In addition to her worship as a member of the Capitoline triad, Juno received cult at Rome under new and sharply differentiated guises during the fourth and third centuries.[8]

8. *CIL* 1^2.445 = *RMR* no. 19. This is a Black Gloss *patera* that measures 13.2 cm in diameter and is decorated with a flute-playing Eros. Originally from Vulci, it is now at the Museo Gregoriano Etrusco in Vatican City. The inscription reads: KERI POCOLOM. The divine name could be construed as Ceres, though this genitive form of her name is otherwise unattested; another, more

5. Chapter 2 n. 24. The structure: Ferroni in *LTUR* 1.316–17 s.v. "Concordia, aedes"; Bernard 2018a, 245.

6. The Roman cult of Fortuna from the archaic period through the end of the Republic: Champeaux 1982–87; Miano 2018, esp. 64–67 on this *pocolom*. The connections between the mid-republican cult of Pudicitia Plebeia (Coarelli in *LTUR* 4.168–69 s.vv. "Pudicitia Patricia, sacellum, ara, templum" and "Pudicitia Plebeia, sacellum") and Fortuna Muliebris: Clark 2007, 39–49.

7. The funerary find-context: Scott Ryberg 1940, 136 with n. 113.

8. See Andreussi in *LTUR* 3.125–26 and 5.269 s.v. "Iuno Regina, aedes"; Gianelli in *LTUR* 3.122–23 s.v. "Iuno Lucina, aedes"; Gianelli in *LTUR* 3.123–25 and 5.269 s.v. "Iuno Moneta, aedes"; and Coarelli in *LTUR* 3.128–29 s.v. "Iuno Sospita." Juno in archaic and mid-republican Italy: Palmer 1974, 3–56. Roman *matronae* and the cult of Juno Regina during the Second Punic War: Hänninen 1999; Schultz 2006b, 33–38. Juno Moneta and the Republican coin mint: Meadows and Williams 2001. Juno Sospita and the management of relations with the Italian allies: Schultz 2006a, especially 209–10.

exotic possibility is the Cerus mentioned in the *Carmen Saliare*.[9] Placed on a monumental footing in the early Republic with the installation of a temple on the Aventine and woven into the fabric of festival life with the introduction and regularization of the *ludi Ceriales* sometime in the third century, the worship of Ceres enjoyed a high degree of public visibility during the middle Republic.[10]

9. *CIL* 1^2.446 = *RMR* n. 20. This is a Black Gloss *patera* that measures 13.8 cm in diameter and depicts an Eros holding a tray. Originally from Orte, it is now at the Museo Gregoriano Etrusco in Vatican City. The inscription reads: LAVERNAI POCOLOM. As best can be gleaned from the scant literary evidence, the goddess Laverna was an underworld divinity who received cult not at a temple but at an altar near the eponymous Porta Lavernalis, which was probably located on a stretch of the Servian Wall that ran on the Aventine.[11]

10. *CIL* 1^2.447 = *RMR* no. 29. This striated *oenochoe* is 10 cm tall and is decorated with garland and twig. Found in Tarquinii, it is now in the possession of the Museo Archeologico Nazionale Tarquiniense. The inscription reads: MENERVAI POCOLOM. In addition to receiving cult on the Capitoline, Minerva was worshipped on the Esquiline under the *epiklesis* of Minerva Medica; there, she received many republican-era dedications, as reflected by a sizable votive deposit unearthed on the Esquiline.[12]

11. *CIL* 1^2.448 = *RMR* no. 23. This fragmentary Black Gloss *patera* measures 9 x 7 cm. Found on the Esquiline, it is now held at the Antiquarium Comunale in Rome. The fragment only contains two letters: ME; plausible restorations are ME[NERVAI POCOLOM] or ME[RCURI POCOLOM].[13]

12. *CIL* 1^2.449 = *RMR* no. 30. This is a small *oenochoe* whose measurements have not been reported and whose glaze appears to have been distributed

9. Citing Festus 109 L. and Varro *LL* 7.26, Degrassi *ILLRP ad* 68 gives only the second reading. But the engraver may not have been a native Latin speaker: see Wachter 1987, 467. On the Aventine structure see Coarelli in *LTUR* 1.260–61 s.v. "Ceres, Liber, Libera, aedes"; this entry comes in for robust criticism in Mignone 2016, Appendix 1.

10. The *ludi Ceriales*: Bernstein 1998, 163–71. Public prominence: the testimony of Plautine drama, e.g., Ceres's inclusion in mock oaths (*Bacch.* 892). Usefully on Republican Ceres: Spaeth 1996, 81–102.

11. Laverna as the patron goddess of thieves: Plaut. *Corn.* fr. 4; Nonius 134.35, citing Lucilius fr. 549 Marx; recapitulation of what little else we know of this divinity in Wissowa 1912, 236. Location of the Porta Lavernalis: Varro *LL* 5.34 with Mignone 2016, 99 n. 98.

12. See chapter 5 n. 60 for publications of this deposit; Carlucci in *LTUR* 3.255–256 for the cult structure.

13. Combet-Farnoux 1980 remains the major treatment of Mercury's cult under the Republic, although Turcan's 1982 withering review exposed many of the book's shortcomings; see now Biggs 2019 and the other essays in Miller and Clay 2019.

somewhat unevenly. Its original find-spot is unknown, but it is now at the Louvre's Campana Collection in Paris, in the company of no. 3 above. The inscription reads: SAETURNI POCOLOM. After Saturn received a temple at Rome in the first century of the Republic, his festival of havoc came to assume a prominent position in the ritual life of the city.[14]

13. *CIL* 1^2.450 = *RMR* no. 16. This is a Black Gloss *patera* that measures 13.8 cm in diameter and is decorated with the figure of a flute-playing Eros. Found in Orte, it is now at the Museo Gregoriano Etrusco in Vatican City. The inscription reads: SALUTES POCOLOM. The abstract deity *Salus* received a temple during the middle Republic but was probably being worshipped before our period. *Prodigia* involving the temple occur sometime in the years 275–269, and again in 206.[15]

14. *CIL* 1^2.451 = *RMR* n. 28. This striated Black Gloss *oenochoe*, 7 cm tall, is decorated with a garland on the neck that is painted in white and yellow and a twig on the handle that is painted in red. Found in Tarquinii, it is now in the possession of the Museo Archeologico Nazionale Tarquiniense, in the company of no. 10. The inscription reads: VENERES POCOLOM. During the third century, Venus accumulated new temples at Rome and emerged as a central figure in the genealogically premised narratives of Rome's origins and cosmic mission.[16]

15. *CIL* 1^2.2495.[17] This is a fragmentary Black Gloss jug, of which only the rim is preserved. Found in Caere, its modern location was reported by Degrassi-Krummrey as the Museo Nazionale Etrusco di Villa Giulia in Rome; but Cifarelli et al. 2002–3 place a question mark under the entry for location in their catalog. The inscription reads: VENERE[S POCOLOM?].

16. *CIL* 1^2.452 = *RMR* no. 27. This is a striated Black Gloss *oenochoe* that is missing its rim and much of the handle. Found in Lanuvium, it is now at the British Museum in London. The inscription reads: VESTAI POCOLO(M). The cult of Vesta, whose flame famously symbolized the preservation and

14. For his temple see Coarelli in *LTUR* 4.234–36 s.v. "Saturnus, aedes." The god appears in the earliest lines of Latin literature, earning multiple mentions in Livius Andronicus's *Odusia*: *pater noster, Saturni filie* (fr. 2 Blänsdorf); *sancta puer Saturni filia regina* (fr. 13).

15. Previous worship: Clark 2007, 35. The *prodigia* notices: Orosius 4.4.1 for the first; Liv. 28.11.1–7 for the second. The temple: Coarelli in *LTUR* s.v. 4.229–230 "Salus, aedes."

16. Papi in *LTUR* 5.118 s.v. "Venus Obsequens, aedes ad Circum Maximum;" Coarelli in *LTUR* 5.114 s.v. "Venus Erycina, aedes in Capitolio." Venus in Rome's new third-century narratives: Feeney 1991, 109–12; Orlin 2010, 73–76 examines the political and diplomatic dimensions.

17. Not published in *RMR*, it is described as a *vasculum* in *ILLRP* 274 and as a "bracchetta" in Nonnis in Cifarelli et al. 2002–3, Appendix II.

flourishing of Rome, grew in prestige during the middle Republic, as the complex of quasi-legendary stories about her priestesses that take shape in the fourth and third centuries and the archaeological evidence for the rebuilding and (probable) expansion of her shrine confirm.[18]

17. *CIL* 1^2.453 = *RMR* no. 14. This is a Black Gloss *patera* that measures about 15 cm in diameter and is decorated with the figure of an Eros. Found in Vulci, it is now at the Antikensammlung of the Staatliche Museen in Berlin, in the company of no. 2. The inscription reads: VOLCANI POCOLOM. Vulcan was worshipped at Rome not only in the *area Vulcani* adjacent to the Comitium but also at a temple in the Campus Martius that was dedicated not long after the disastrous fire of 241, the repercussions of which are explored in chapter 3.

18. *CIL* 1^2.2884 = *RMR* no. 32. This is a fragment of a Black Gloss *oenochoe* that will have been around 8 cm tall; its belly is striated, and the handle is double-ribboned. A dove painted in white and a garland painted in yellow on the neck round out the decorative scheme. Found in a votive deposit at Carsioli (Carseoli), it is now at the Museo Archeologico Nazionale of Chieti. The inscription reads: VESTAI POCOLOM.

19. *CIL* 1^2.2884a.[19] This is a Black Gloss *patera* of which two fragments survive and whose diameter has been estimated at 16 cm; it is decorated with an ivy crown. Reported to have been found in a tomb at Caere, it came into possession of a private owner residing in Bern in 1972. The incompletely preserved inscription reads: [- - -?]CRI POCOLOM. Restoration of the first word is highly uncertain. In her publication of the text, Bettina Jessen proposed *[Lu]cri* and took the text to refer to the obscure *dei Lucrii* mentioned in Arnobius.[20] Mindful of the orthographic peculiarities of the *pocola* inscriptions as a whole, Degrassi-Krummrey elected not to exclude alternative restorations such as C<E>RI (cf. *Keri* in no. 8) or even [ME- or [MIR]C<V>RI.

20. *CIL* 1^2.2884b = *RMR* p. 370. This is a fragment of a Black Gloss *patera* with an estimated base diameter of 5 cm. Its decoration consists of a now-faded image of an elephant that was traced in red line between two yellow lines, and lettering in white. Found at Norchia sul colle S. Pietro in 1973, together with other pottery of the fourth and third centuries, it is now at the Museo Nazionale Etrusco di Villa Giulia. The inscription reads: [- - -] ES POCOLO(M). Restoration of the first word is uncertain; possibilities include [VENER]- or [IUNON]-.

18. On Vesta's shrine see Scott in *LTUR* 5.125–28 s.v. "Vesta, aedes" and Bernard 2018a, 213. The cult of Vesta at Lanuvium: Pailler 1997, 517–23; his claim that this *pocolom* was "fabriquée sans doute en Campanie" is not substantiated.

19. This item was not published in *RMR*.

20. Jessen 1975, citing Arnob. *Adv. gen.* 4.9.

21. *CIL* 1^2.2885 = *RMR*: 370.[21] This is a fragment of a Black Gloss *patera* decorated with yellow lettering; its measurements have not been reported. Unearthed in Ariminum, it is now at the Museo della Città of Rimini. The inscription reads: [- - -?]IIRVS POCLOM. Restoration of the first word is uncertain. Since the double I is used in central Italic inscriptions from this period to designate "E," [VEN]ERUS and [CER]ERUS—third-declension genitives in *–us* that are attested in second-century epigraphy[22]—have been proposed.

22. *CIL* 1^2.2886 = *RMR*: 370. This is a fragment of a Black Gloss *patera* decorated with yellow lettering; its measurements have not been reported. It was also found in Ariminum and is currently in the possession of the Museo della Città of Rimini. The inscription reads: [- - -?]AI POCOL[OM]. The archaic genitive in *–ai* calls to mind the BELOLAI of no. 3, the MENERVAI of nos. 10 and 11, or the VESTAI of nos. 16, 18, and 25; either restoration is plausible.

23. *CIL* 1^2.2887. This is a fragment of a Black Gloss *patera* that is decorated with yellow lettering; its measurements have not been reported. It was also found in Ariminum and is currently in the possession of the Museo della Città of Rimini. The inscription reads: [- - -?] POC[OLOM] or POC[LOM].

24. *CIL* 1^2.2887a.[23] This is a fragment of a Black Gloss *patera* that is decorated with white lettering; its measurements have not been reported. Found at Cosa in the course of the 1948/49 excavations conducted by the American Academy in Rome, its current whereabouts are unknown.[24] The inscription reads: [- - -?] POCO[LOM].

21. This and the next two artifacts are dated to the period after the foundation of a Roman colony at Ariminium in 268. For follow-up discussions see Franchi de Bellis 1993, nn. 1–3; 1995, 373; Minak 2006a; and Bertrand 2015, 158–61. Excluded from this catalog's sampling of ceramics from the colony are two Black Gloss fragments that name Apollo in the dative (for which see Franchi de Bellis 1993, 45 nn. 4–5 and 56–57); several Black Gloss fragments sporting the abbreviations "H" or "HC" ("Hercules" and/or "Hercules Custos": Franchi de Bellis 1993, nn. 6a–f and chapter 5 n. 84); a Black Gloss fragment inscribed [DA]EIRAI (an epithet of Persephone declined in the dative: Braccesi 2006); and various Black Gloss ceramics that appear to reference a *uicus* or *pagus* (*CIL* I^2.2897a, 2897b, 2898, 2899a, 2899b, and 2899; Stek 2009, 138–45).

22. The magistrate dedications from Capua: *CIL* I^2.675 = Ernout no. 94 (*Heisce magistreis Venerus Ioviae murum | aedificandum coiraverunt* etc.) and *CIL* I^2.677 = Ernout no. 96 (*Heisce magistreis Cererus murum | et pluteum* etc.); cf. the form Venerus on an inscribed *thesaurus* from Aragnia (IllRP 721) and the form *Kastorus* in the second-century *SC de Tiburtibus* (*CIL* I^2.586 = 14.3584 = Ernout no. 127). Other examples: Franchi de Bellis 1993, 48–49.

23. This and all subsequent items in the catalog were not published in *RMR*.

24. The excavation also turned up other, uninscribed Black Gloss wares at Cosa that were published in Taylor 1957 and reevaluated in Scott 2008.

25. Simon 1982, 186 no. 118.[25] This is a fragmentary Black Gloss jug whose measurements are not reported. Its provenience is not known; it was formerly at the Kurashiki Ninagawa Museum but is now held at the Kake Museum, in Okayama, Japan. The inscription reads: VESTAI POCOLO(M).

26. Manconi and De Angelis 1987, 25–27 with figure 30. This is a fragmentary Black Gloss *patera* decorated with plant motifs; its measurements have not been reported. Found in the *ager Nursinus* in the course of excavations at Ancarano, it is now held at the Museo Archeologico Nazionale of Perugia. The inscription reads: [VOL]CANI POCOLOM.

27. Cordella and Criniti 1996, 36. This is a fragmentary Black Gloss *patera* decorated with plant motifs; its measurements have not been reported. Also found in the *ager Nursinus*, its present location is unknown. The inscription reads: [ME]RCVRI POCOLOM.

28. Ambrosini in Cifarelli et al. 2002–3 = *AE* 2005, 304b. This Black Gloss vase survives in two fragments, each decorated with dark-red lettering. Unearthed at Signia in the course of the 1985–89 excavations conducted on the acropolis, it is now the property of the Museo Archeologico Comunale of Segni. The inscription reads: [- - - -?]NI PO[COLOM] on one fragment of the inside of the vase; [- - - -?] VELI AV[- - - -?] on another fragment of the outside. This is the only surviving *pocolom* to contain two different texts.[26] Proposed restorations of the theonym include [VOLCA]NI, [SAETUR]NI, and [NEPTU]NI.[27] Neptune—worshipped in Rome from the archaic period onward—shares with Vulcan and Saturn the distinction of receiving a mid-republican temple, in his case near the Circus Flaminius; its place in the infrastructural complex of the Campus Martius is examined in chapter 3.

29. Minak 2006b. This is a fragment of the rim of a Black Gloss cup, with off-white lettering; the fragment is 4.3 cm tall, and the diameter of the bowl has been estimated to be 18 cm. Recovered in Ariminum during the 1978 season of the San Francesco excavations, it is now held at the Museo della Città of Rimini. The inscription reads: [- - - -?]POLLO or (more likely) POCLO.

30. Ambrosini 2014. This is a Black Gloss *patera* approximately 15 cm in diameter, photographs of which surfaced in the papers of Giuseppe Fabbri (the "Carte Fabbri") now held by the Biblioteca Comunale di Vetralla "Alessandro Pistella." Although there is no mention of a find-context in the papers, Ambrosini has suggested that because of the state of preservation apparent in the photographs the *pocolom* was likely retrieved from a burial chamber—probably one in the San Giuliano necropolis. The current whereabouts of the

25. This and all subsequent items in this appendix were not published in *CIL*.

26. The second text may be the name of the owner in the genitive (*Velius Aulus*?).

27. Thus Ambrosini in Cifarelli et al. 2002–3.

cup are unknown, but it is believed to be in a private collection. The inscription reads: [V]OLUPTATES PỌCỌLỌM. Associated with (and/or known as) Volupia—who was worshipped at a *sacellum* in the vicinity of the Porta Romanula—Voluptas was one of the abstract divinities worshipped in mid-republican Rome.[28]

31. Princeton University Art Museum y1989-58. This unpublished Black Gloss *patera,* which survives in two fragments that have been reattached, measures 6.36 cm from the center to the rim, for a reconstructed diameter of 12.7 cm. It is decorated with a rooster in profile, rendered with tawny and white plumage. One logical iconographic comparison is with the cocks that appear on Roman *aes signatum (RRC 12/1).*[29] The *patera* entered a private collection before being donated to the Princeton University Art Museum in 1989; nothing about the provenance is known. Its inscription reads: [---?] AI POCOLOM. As noted for no. 22, the archaic genitive in -ai could be restored either as BELOLAI (no. 3), MENERVAI (nos. 10–11), or as VESTAI (nos. 16, 18, 25). The existence of coin issues from the First Punic War, whose iconography pairs helmeted Minerva with cocks, tips the scales in favor of MENERVAI.[30]

28. See Aronen in *LTUR* 5.213 s.v. "Volupia, sacellum," updated in Ambrosini 2014, 348–54.

29. These are normally interpreted as pecking chickens, possibly of the sort used for auspice-taking; but Liv Yarrow has made a compelling case for identifying them as fighting cocks: http://livyarrow.org/2014/03/03/258-out-of-410-days-fighting-cocks-and-sacred-chickens/.

30. For the iconography's appearance on coin issues of Rome's colonies and allies, see Crawford 1985, 47–48. Publication and analysis of this *pocolom*: Padilla Peralta in progress b.

REFERENCES

Aberson, M. 1994. *Temples votifs et butin de guerre dans la Rome républicaine*. Rome.

———. 2010. "Dire le voeu sur le champ de bataille." *MEFRA* 122, no. 2: 493–501.

Abrams, E. M. 1987. "Economic Specialization and Construction Personnel in Classic Period Copan, Honduras." *American Antiquity* 52, no. 3: 485–99.

Abrams, P. 1988. "Notes on the Difficulty of Studying the State." *Journal of Historical Sociology* 1, no. 1: 58–89.

Acosta-Hughes, B. 2012. " 'Nor When a Man Goes to Dionysus' Holy Contests' (Theocr. 17.112): Outlines of Theatrical Performance in Theocritus." In *Theater Outside Athens: Drama in Greek Sicily and South Italy*, edited by K. Bosher, 391–408. Cambridge.

Acosta-Hughes, B., and S. Stephens. 2012. *Callimachus in Context: From Plato to the Augustan Poets*. Cambridge.

Acton, P. 2014. *Poiesis: Manufacturing in Classical Athens*. Oxford.

Adam, A.-M., and A. Rouveret. 1995. "Cavaleries et aristocraties cavalières en Italie entre la fin du VIe siècle et le premiers tiers du IIIe siècle av. notre ère." *MEFRA* 107, no. 1: 7–12.

Adams, E. 2017. "Fragmentation and the Body's Boundaries: Reassessing the Body in Parts." In *Bodies of Evidence: Ancient Anatomical Votives Past, Present and Future*, edited by J. Draycott and E.-J. Graham, 193–213. London.

Aldrete, G. S. 2006. *Floods of the Tiber in Ancient Rome*. Baltimore.

———. 2013. "Riots." In *The Cambridge Companion to Ancient Rome*, edited by P. Erdkamp, 425–40. Cambridge.

Alexander, M. C., and J. A. Danowski. 1990. "Analysis of an Ancient Network: Personal Communication and the Study of Social Structure in a Past Society." *Social Networks* 12, no. 4: 313–35.

Alonso Fernández, Z. 2015. "*Docta saltatrix*: Body Knowledge, Culture, and Corporeal Discourse in Female Roman Dance." *Phoenix* 69, no. 3–4: 304–33.

———. 2016. "Choreography of Lupercalia: Corporeality in Roman Public Religion." *GRMS* 4: 311–32.

———. 2017. "Re-thinking Lupercalia: From Corporeality to Corporation." *GRMS* 5: 43–62.

Ambrosini, L. 2014. "Le divinità dei *pocola deorum*: Un nuovo *pocolom* di *Voluptas* del *Volcani Group*." *RPAA* 85: 337–63.

Amiri, B. 2016. "La religion des esclaves: Entre visibilité et invisibilité." In *Religion sous contrôle: Pratiques et expériences religieuses de la marge?*, edited by B. Amiri, 65–76. Besançon.

Ammerman, R. M. 1991. "Votive terracottas from Taranto (6th–2nd c. B.C.)." *JRA* 4: 195–99.

Ampolo, C. 1990. "Aspetti dello sviluppo economico agl'inizi della repubblica romana." In *Staat und Staatlichkeit in der frühen römischen Republik. Akten eines Symposiums 12.–15. Juli 1998. Freie Universität Berlin*, edited by W. Eder, 482–93. Stuttgart.

Anderson, G. 2018. "Was There Any Such Thing as a Nonmodern State?" In *State Formations: Global Histories and Cultures of Statehood*, edited by J. L. Brooke, J. C. Strauss, and G. Anderson, 58–79. Cambridge.

Ando, C. 2000. *Imperial Ideology and Provincial Loyalty in the Roman Empire*. Berkeley.

———. 2008. *The Matter of the Gods: Religion and the Roman Empire*. Berkeley.

———. 2010. "The Ontology of Religious Institutions." *History of Religions* 50, no. 1: 54–79.

———. 2015. *Roman Social Imaginaries: Language and Thought in Contexts of Empire*. Toronto.

———. 2017. "City, Village, Sacrifice: The Political Economy of Religion in the Early Roman Empire." In *Mass and Elite in the Greek and Roman Worlds: From Sparta to Late Antiquity*, edited by R. Evans, 118–36. London.

Ando, C., and S. Richardson, eds. 2017. *Ancient States and Infrastructural Power: Europe, Asia, and America*. Philadelphia.

Andreani, C., M. P. Del Moro, and M. De Nuccio. 2005. "Contesti e materiali votivi dell' 'area sacra' di Largo Argentina." In *Depositi votivi e culti dell'Italia antica dall'età arcaica a quella tardo-repubblicana*, edited by A. Comella and S. Mele, 111–25. Bari.

Andreau, J., and R. Descat. 2011. *The Slave in Greece and Rome*. Translated by M. Leopold. Madison.

Andrews, M., and S. Bernard. 2017. "Urban Development at Rome's Porta Esquilina and Church of San Vito over the *longue durée*." *JRA* 30: 244–65.

Andrews, M., and H. I. Flower. 2015. "Mercury on the Esquiline: A Reconsideration of a Local Shrine Restored by Augustus." *AJA* 119, no. 1: 47–67.

Antolini, S., and S. M. Marengo. 2017. "Dediche servili al *genius* dei padroni." In *Esclaves et maîtres dans le monde romain: expressions épigraphiques de leurs relations*, edited by M. Dondin-Payre and N. Tran. doi:10.4000/books.efr.3207.

Aravantinos, V. [2000] 2009. "Θήβα." *Archaiologiko Deltio* 55, B1: 377–94.

Argetsinger, K. 1992. "Birthday Rituals: Friends and Patrons in Roman Poetry and Cult." *CA* 11, no. 2: 175–93.

Arizza, M., and D. Rossi. 2018. "Tuff Quarrying in the Territory of Veii: A 'Status' Activity of the Landowning Aristocracy of the Archaic Period, from Construction to Craft." *Scienze dell'Antichità* 24, no. 1: 101–9.

Armstrong, J. 2016. *War and Society in Early Rome: From Warlords to Generals*. Cambridge.

Arnheim, M.T.W. 1972. *The Senatorial Aristocracy in the Later Roman Empire*. Oxford.

Arnhold, M., and J. Rüpke. 2017. "Appropriating and Shaping Religious Practices in the Roman Republic." In *Politische Kultur und soziale Struktur der römischen Republik. Bilanzen und Perspektiven*, edited by M. Haake and A.-C. Harders, 413–28. Stuttgart.

Arnold, D. 1999. *Temples of the Last Pharaohs*. New York.

Astin, A. E. 1978. *Cato the Censor*. Oxford.

Attema, P.A.J. 2018. "Urban and Rural Landscapes of the Pontine Region (Central Italy) in the Late Republican Period, Economic Growth between Colonial Heritage and Elite Impetus." *BABESCH* 93: 143–64.

Auliard, C. 2002. "Les esclaves dans les butins républicains des premiers siècles de la conquête." In *Routes et marchés d'esclaves (26e colloque du GIREA: Besançon, 27–29 septembre 2001)*, edited by M. Garrido-Hory, 51–64. Paris.

Aust, E. 1889. *De aedibus sacris populi Romani inde a primis liberae rei publicae temporibus usque ad Augusti imperatoris aetatem Romae conditis*. Marburg.

Austin, M. M., ed. and trans. 1981. *The Hellenistic World from Alexander to the Roman Conquest: A Selection of Ancient Sources in Translation*. Cambridge.

Austin, N.J.E., and N. B. Rankov. 1995. *Exploratio: Military and Political Intelligence in the Roman World from the Second Punic War to the Battle of Adrianople*. London.

Azoulay, V., and P. Ismard. 2018. "The City in Chorus: For a Choral History of Athenian Society." In *Ancient Greek History and Contemporary Social Science*, edited by M. Canevaro, A. Erskine, B. Gray, and J. Ober, 47–67. Edinburgh.

Badian, E. 1958. *Foreign* Clientelae *(264–70 BC)*. Oxford.

Baker, P. 2013. *The Archaeology of Medicine in the Greco-Roman World*. Cambridge.

Balberg, M. 2017. *Blood for Thought: The Reinvention of Sacrifice in Early Rabbinic Literature*. Oakland.

Barbantani, S. 2003. "Callimachus and the Contemporary Historical 'Epic.'" *Hermathena* 173–74: 29–47.

———. 2017. "Lyric for the Rulers, Lyric for the People: The Transformation of Some Lyric Subgenres in Hellenistic Poetry." *Trends in Classics* 9, no. 2: 339–99.

Barbiero, E. A. 2018. "Myth, Letters, and the Poetics of Ancestry in Plautus' *Bacchides*." *Ramus* 47, no. 1: 1–25.

———. 2019. Untitled Review: A. Richlin, *Slave Theater in the Roman Republic: Plautus and Popular Comedy*. *CPh* 114, no. 2: 296–300.

Barchiesi, A. 2008. "*Senatus consultum de Lycaone*: Concili degli dèi e immaginazione politica nelle *Metamorfosi* di Ovidio." *Materiali e discussioni per l'analisi dei testi classici* 61, no. 2: 117–45.

Barchiesi, M. 1978. *La* Tarentilla *revisitata: Studi su Nevio comico*. Pisa.

Barja de Quiroga, P. L. 2018. "The *Quinquatrus* of June, Marsyas and *Libertas* in the Late Roman Republic." *CQ* 68, no. 1: 143–59.

Barker, A. 2017. "Dionysius of Halicarnassus on Rome's Greek Musical Heritage." *GRMS* 5: 63–81.

Baron, C. A. 2012. *Timaeus of Tauromenium and Hellenistic Historiography*. Cambridge.

Barro, R. J. 2004. "Spirit of Capitalism: Religion and Economic Development." *Harvard International Review* 25: 64–67.

Barro, R. J., and R. M. McCleary. 2003. "Religion and Economic Growth." NBER Working Paper no. 9682 = "Religion and Economic Growth across Countries." *American Sociological Review* 68: 760–81.

Bartlett, R. 2013. *Why Can the Dead Do Such Great Things? Saints and Worshippers from the Martyrs to the Reformation*. Princeton.

Bartolini, G., and M. Gilda Benedettini. 2011. *Veio: Il deposito votivo di comunità (Scavi 1889–2005)*. Corpus delle stipi votive in Italia XXI, Regio VII-3. Rome.

Battiloro, I. 2018. *The Archaeology of Lucanian Cult Places: Fourth Century BC to the Early Imperial Age*. London.

Battiloro, I., and M. Osanna. 2011. "Le aree di culto lucane: Topografia e articolazione degli spazi." In Brateís Datas: *Pratiche rituali, votivi e strumenti del culto dai santuari della Lucania antica*, edited by I. Battiloro and M. Osanna, 15–37. Potenza.

———. 2015. "Continuity and Change in Lucanian Cult Places between the Third and First Centuries BC: New Insights into the 'Romanization' Issue." In *The Impact of Rome on Cult Places and Religious Practices in Ancient Italy*, edited by T. D. Stek and G.-J. Burgers, 169–98. London.

Beagon, M. 2005. *The Elder Pliny on the Human Animal. Natural History* Book 7. Translated with introduction and historical commentary. Oxford.

Beard, M. 1980. "The Sexual Status of Vestal Virgins." *JRS* 70: 12–27.

———. 1987. "A Complex of Times: No More Sheep on Romulus' Birthday." *PCPS* 33: 1–15. = 2003. In *Roman Religion*, edited by C. Ando, 273–88. Edinburgh.

———. 1990. "Priesthood in the Roman Republic." In *Pagan Priests: Religion and Power in the Ancient World*, edited by M. Beard and J. North, 19–48. Ithaca.

———. 1998. "Documenting Roman Religion." In *La mémoire perdue: Recherches sur l'administration romaine*, 75–101. Rome.

———. 2007. *Roman Triumph*. Cambridge, MA.

———. 2015. *SPQR: A History of Ancient Rome*. New York.

Beard, M., J. North, and S. Price. 1998. *Roman Religions*. 2 vols. Cambridge.

Beare, W. 1968. *The Roman Stage: A Short History of Latin Drama in the Time of the Republic.*[3] London.

Beazley, J. D. 1947. *Etruscan Vase-Painting*. Oxford.

Bechtold, B. 2007. "Alcune osservazioni sui rapporti commerciali fra Cartagine, la Sicilia occidentale e la Campania (IV–metà del II sec. a.C.): Nuovi dati basati sulla distribuzione di ceramiche campane e nordafricane/cartaginesi." *BABESCH* 82: 51–76.

———. 2018. "Rapporti commerciali fra la Sicilia occidentale e l'Italia centro-tirrenica fra IV–III sec. a.C.: I dati della cultura materiale." *HEROM: Journal on Hellenistic and Roman Material Culture* 7, no. 1–2: 25–61.

Beck, H. 2005. *Karriere und Hierarchie. Die römische Aristokratie und die Anfänge des* cursus honorum *in der mittleren Republik*. Stuttgart.

Becker, M. 2017. Suntoque aediles curatores urbis: *Die Entwicklung der stadtrömischen Aedilität in republikanischer Zeit*. Stuttgart.

Beerden, K. 2018. "Trees and Streets: Current Directions in the Study of Roman Religions." *Mnemosyne* 71: 881–91.

Belfiori, F. 2018. "Il ruolo dei luoghi di culto e l'espansione di Roma in Italia centrale." *Athenaeum* 106, no. 1: 94–110.

Beloch, K. J. 1926. *Römische Geschichte bis zum Beginn der punischen Kriege*. Berlin.

Bendlin, A. 1997. Untitled Review: R. B. Ulrich, *The Roman Orator and the Sacred Stage*. *JRS* 87: 282–83.

———. 2000. "Looking beyond the Civic Compromise: Religious Pluralism in Late Republican Rome." In *Religion in Archaic and Republican Rome and Italy: Evidence and Experience*, edited by E. Bispham and C. Smith, 115–35. Edinburgh.

———. 2001. "Rituals or Beliefs? 'Religion' and the Religious Life of Rome." *SCI* 20: 191–208.

———. 2006. "Nicht der Eine, nicht die Vielen: Zur Pragmatik religiösen Verhaltens in einer polytheistischen Gesellschaft am Beispiel Roms." In *Götterbilder—Gottesbilder—Weltbilder. Polytheismus und Monotheismus in der Welt der Antike*. Bd. II: *Griechenland und Rom, Judentum, Christentum und Islam*, edited by R. Kratz and H. Spieckermann, 279–311. Tübingen.

———. 2013. "The Urban Sacred Landscape." In *The Cambridge Companion to Ancient Rome*, edited by P. Erdkamp, 461–77. Cambridge.

Bernard, H. R., and G. A. Shelley. 1987. "How Much of a Network Does the GSS and RSW Dredge Up?" *Social Networks* 9: 49–61.

Bernard, S. 2016. "Debt, Land, and Labor in the Early Republican Economy." *Phoenix* 70, no. 3–4: 317–38.

———. 2017. "*Aedificare, res damnosissima*. Building and Historiography in Livy, Books 5–6." In Omnium annalium monumenta: *Historical Writing and Historical Evidence in Republican Rome*, edited by K. Sandberg and C. Smith, 404–21. Leiden.

———. 2018a. *Building Mid-Republican Rome: Labor, Architecture, and the Urban Economy*. Oxford.

———. 2018b. "Kings and States in Archaic Central Italy." *JRA* 31: 573–80.

———. 2018c. "The Social History of Early Roman Coinage." *JRS* 108: 1–26.

Bernardini, P. 1986. *Museo Nazionale Romano: Le ceramiche*. Vol. 1: *La ceramica a vernice nera dal Tevere*. Rome.

Bernstein, F. 1998. Ludi publici. *Untersuchungen zur Entstehung und Entwicklung der öffentlichen Spiele im republikanischen Rom*. Stuttgart.

Bertrand, A. 2015. *La religion publique des colonies dans l'Italie républicaine et impériale (Italie médio-adriatique, IIIe s. av. n.è.–IIe. s. de n.è.)*. Rome.

Besnier, M. 1902. *L'Île Tibérine dans l'antiquité*. Paris.

Bettini, M. 2016. "Per una 'biologie sauvage' dei Romani: Prime proposte." *EuGeStA* 6: 66–85.

Betts, E. 2011. "Towards a Multisensory Experience of Movement in the City of Rome." In *Rome, Ostia, Pompeii: Movement and Space*, edited by R. Laurence and D. J. Newsome, 118–32. Oxford.

Beyerlein, K., and J. R. Hipp. 2005. "Social Capital, Too Much of a Good Thing? American Religious Traditions and Community Crime." *Social Forces* 84, no. 2: 995–1013.

Biddau, F. 2005. "I templi di Forte Fortuna: Un nuovo contributo all'identificazione da Terenzio Scauro." *RFIC* 133, no. 4: 443–51.

Bierbrier, M. 1982. *The Tomb-Builders of the Pharaohs*. London.

Biggs, T. 2017a. "*Primus Romanorum*: Origin Stories, Fictions of Primacy, and the First Punic War." *CPh* 112, no. 3: 350–67.

———. 2017b. "A Second First Punic War: (Re)spoliation of Republican Naval Monuments in the Urban and Poetic Landscapes of Augustan Rome." In *Rome, Empire of Plunder: The Dynamics of Cultural Appropriation*, edited by M. P. Loar, C. S. MacDonald, and D. Padilla Peralta, 47–68. Cambridge.

———. 2019. "Did Mercury Build the Ship of Aeneas?" In *Tracking Hermes/Pursuing Mercury*, edited by J. F. Miller and J. Strauss Clay, 209–24. Oxford.

Bispham, E. 2007. *From Asculum to Actium: The Municipalization of Italy from the Social War to Augustus*. Oxford.

Blanton, R. 2016. "The Variety of Ritual Experience in Premodern States." In *Ritual and Archaic States*, edited by J.M.A. Murphy, 23–49. Gainesville.

Blanton, R., and L. Fargher. 2008. *Collective Action in the Formation of Pre-Modern States*. New York.

Bleicken, J. 1963. "*Coniuratio*. Die Schwurszene auf den Münzen und Gemmen der römischen Republik." *JNG* 13: 51–70.

Bloch, R. 1963. *Les prodiges dans l'antiquité classique (Grèce, Étrurie et Rome)*. Paris.

Blösel, W. 2003. "Die *memoria* der *gentes* als Rückgrat der kollektiven Erinnerung im republikanischen Rom." In *Formen römischer Geschischsschreibung von den Anfängen bis Livius. Gattungen—Autoren—Kontexte*, edited by U. Eigler, U. Gotter, N. Luraghi, and U. Walter, 53–72. Darmstadt.

Bodei Giglioni, G. 1977. "*Pecunia fanatica*: L'incidenza economica dei templi laziali." *Rivista storica italiana* 89: 59–76.

Boehm, R. 2018. *City and Empire in the Age of the Successors: Urbanization and Social Response in the Making of the Hellenistic Kingdoms*. Berkeley.

Bömer, F. 1981–1990. *Untersuchungen über die Religion der Sklaven in Griechenland und Rom*.[2] 2 vols. Wiesbaden.

Bond, S. E. 2015. "Curial Communiqué: Memory, Propaganda, and the Roman Senate House." In *Aspects of Ancient Institutions and Geography: Studies in Honor of Richard J. A. Talbert*, edited by L. L. Brice and D. Slootjes, 84–102. Leiden.

Bonnefond-Coudry, M. 1979. "Le Sénat républicaine dans l'*atrium Libertatis*?" *MEFRA* 91: 601–22.

———. 1989. *Le Sénat de la république romaine de la guerre d'Hannibal à Auguste: Pratiques délibératives et prise de décision*. Rome.

Bouma, J. W., and E. van 't Lindenhout. 1996. "Light in Dark Age Latium: Evidence from Settlements and Cult Places." In *Debating Dark Ages. Caeculus. Papers on Mediterranean Archaeology and Greek and Roman Studies*, edited by M. Maaskant-Kleibrink and M. Vink, 3: 91–102.

Bourdin, S. 2012. *Les peuples de l'Italie préromaine: Identités, territoires et relations inter-ethniques en Italie centrale et septentrionale (VIIIe–Ier s. av. J.-C.)*. Rome.

Bowie, E. L. 1986. "Early Greek Elegy, Symposium, and Public Festival." *JHS* 106: 13–35.

Bowman, A. 2017. "The State and the Economy: Fiscality and Taxation." In *Trade, Commerce, and the State in the Roman World*, edited by A. Wilson and A. Bowman, 27–52. Oxford.

Braccesi, L. 2006. "In margine ai *pocola*: Una nuova testimonianza, 2." In *Ariminum: Storia e archeologia*, 47–50. Rome.

Bradley, G., E. Isayev, and C. Riva. eds. 2007. *Ancient Italy: Regions without Boundaries*. Exeter.

Bradley, K. 1994. *Slavery and Society at Rome*. Cambridge.

Brañas-Garza, P., M. Rossi, and D. Zaclicever. 2009. "Individual's Religiosity Enhances Trust: Latin American Evidence for the Puzzle." *Journal of Money, Credit, and Banking* 41, no. 2–3: 555–66.

Bravo, B., and M. Griffin. 1988. "Un frammento del libro XI di Tito Livio?" *Athenaeum* 66: 447–521.

Brelich, A. 1961. "Un libro dannoso: La '*Römische Religionsgeschichte*' di K. Latte." *Studi et materiali di storia delle religioni* 32, no. 2: 311–54.

Bremer, F. P., ed. 1896. Iurisprudentiae antehadrianae quae supersunt. Pars prior: Liberae rei publicae iuris consulti. Leipzig.

Brennan, T. C. 2000. *The Praetorship in the Roman Republic*. 2 vols. Oxford.

Briquel, D. 2002. *Le Forum brûle (18–19 mars 210 av. J.-C.): Un épisode méconnu de la deuxième guerre punique*. Paris.

———. 2015. "Un événement capital de l'histoire de Rome, la bataille de Sentinum: Le témoignage de Douris et ses limites." In *De Samos à Rome: Personnalité et influence de Douris*, edited by V. Naas and M. Simon, 291–301. Nanterre.

Broadhead, W. 2001. "Rome's Migration Policy and the So-Called *Ius Migrandi*." *Cahiers du Centre Gustave Glotz* 12: 69–89.

Brown, P. G. McC. 2002. "Actors and Actor-Managers at Rome in the Time of Plautus and Terence." In *Greek and Roman Actors: Aspects of an Ancient Profession*, edited by P. Easterling and E. Hall, 225–37. Cambridge.

Bruce, W. N., and R. S. Wagman. 2012. "*Frustula tiberina*: Epigraphical Fragments from the Tiber Island and Environs." *Epigraphica* 74, no. 1–2: 374–78.

Brunt, P. A. 1971. *Italian Manpower, 225 BC–AD 14*. Oxford.

Bruun, C. 2000. *The Roman Middle Republic: Politics, Religion, and Historiography, c. 400–133 BC*. Rome.

———. 2003. "*Medius Fidius . . . tantam pecuniam Nicomedenses perdiderint!* Roman Water Supply, Public Administration, and Private Contractors." In *Tâches publiques et enteprise privée dans le monde romain*, edited by J.-J. Aubert, 305–25. Geneva.

———. 2007. "*Aqueductium* e *statio aquarum*: La sede della *cura aquarum* di Roma." In Res Bene Gestae: *Ricerche di storia urbana su Roma antica in onore di Eva Margarita Steinby*, edited by A. Leone, D. Palombi, and S. Walker, 1–14. Rome.

Budesheim, J. 2006. "Versammlungen des republikanischen Senates in den *templa* Roms." *Hephaistos* 24: 73–78.

Bulbulia, J., M. Frean, and P. Reddish. 2013. "Ecological Signalling." In *A New Science of Religion*, edited by G. W. Dawes and J. Maclaurin, 100–110. New York.

Burford, A. 1969. *The Greek Temple Builders at Epidauros: A Social and Economic Study of Building in the Asklepian Sanctuary during the Fourth and Early Third Centuries BC*. Toronto.

Burkert, W. 1985. *Greek Religion*. Translated by J. Raffan. Cambridge, MA.

Burnett, A. M. 1989. "The Beginnings of Roman Coinage." *AIIN* 33: 33–64.

Burt, R. S. 2000. "Decay Functions." *Social Networks* 22: 1–28.

Cain, H.-U. 1995. "Hellenistiche Kultbilder. Religiöse Präsenz und museale Präsentation der Götter im Heiligtum und beim Fest." In *Stadtbild und Bürgerbild im Hellenismus*, edited by M. Wörrl and P. Zanker, 114–30. Munich.

Cairoli, R. 2001. "L'area sacra di Anxa-Angitia." In *Il tesoro del Lago: L'archeologia del Fucino e la Collezione Torlonia*, edited by A. Campanelli, 258–61 and 271–79. Pescara.

Cairoli Giuliani, F. 1982. "Architettura e tecnica edilizia." In *Roma repubblicana fra il 509 e il 270 a.C.*, edited by I. Dondero and P. Pensabene, 29–36. Rome.

Cameron, A. 1995. *Callimachus and His Critics*. Princeton.

Cancik, H. 2008. "Auswärtige Teilnehmer an stadtrömischen Festen." In *Festrituale in der römischen Kaiserzeit*, edited by J. Rüpke, 5–18. Tübingen.

Capogrossi Colognesi, L. 2014. *Law and Power in the Making of the Roman Commonwealth.* Translated by L. Kopp. Cambridge.

Carandini, A., ed. 2017. *The Atlas of Ancient Rome.* Translated by A. Campbell Halavais. Princeton.

Carini, A. 2016. "I grandi santuari dell'Italia tra il II e il I secolo a.C." In *Orte der Forschung, Orte des Glaubens: Neue Perspektiven für Heiligtümer in Italien von der Archaik bis zur Späten Republik. Akten der internationalen Tagung in Darmstadt am 19. und 20. Juli 2013,* edited by M. Bolder-Boos and D. Maschek, 165–71. Bonn.

Carlà, F. 2017. "*Caput mundi*: Rome as Center in Roman Representation and Construction of Space." *Ancient Society* 49: 119–57.

Carrelli, C. W. 2004. "Measures of Power: The Energetics of Royal Construction at Early Classic Copan." In *Understanding Early Classic Copan,* edited by E. E. Bell, M. A. Canuto, and R. J. Sharer, 113–27. Philadelphia.

Carroll, M. 2019. "Mater Matuta: 'Fertility Cults' and the Integration of Women in Religious Life in Italy in the Fourth to First Centuries BC." *PBSR* 87: 1–45.

Castagnoli, F. 1984. "Il tempio romano: Questioni di terminologia e di tipologia." *PBSR* 52: 3–20.

Caygill, H. 2011. "Historiography and Political Theology: Momigliano and the End of History." In *The Western Time of Ancient History: Historiographical Encounters with the Greek and Roman Pasts,* edited by A. Lianeri, 99–116. Cambridge.

Cèbe, J.-P. 1966. *La caricature et la parodie dans le monde romain antique: Des origines à Juvénal.* Paris.

Ceccarelli, L., and E. Marroni. 2011. *Repertorio dei santuari del Lazio.* Rome.

Champeaux, J. 1982–87. *Fortuna: Recherches sur le culte de la Fortune à Rome et dans le monde romain des origines à la mort de César.* 2 vols. Rome.

Champion, C. B. 2017. *The Peace of the Gods: Elite Religious Practices in the Middle Roman Republic.* Princeton.

———. 2018a. "Extralimitación imperial: Impedimentos estructurales y culturales para el Imperio en la Roma de la República media." In *Estudios interdisciplinarios de historia: Antigua V,* edited by C. Ames, M. Sagristani, A. Moreno, and Á. M. Moreno Leoni, 284–94. Cordova.

———. 2018b. "Polybian Barbarology, Flute-Playing in Arcadia, and Fisticuffs at Rome." In *Polybius and His Legacy,* edited by N. Miltsios and M. Tamiolaki, 35–42. Berlin.

Champlin, E. 2011. "Tiberius and the Heavenly Twins." *JRS* 101: 73–99.

Chaniotis, A. 2018a. *Age of Conquests: The Greek World from Alexander to Hadrian.* Cambridge, MA.

———. 2018b. "Epigraphic Evidence." In *The Oxford Handbook of Greek and Roman Slaveries,* edited by S. Hodkinson, M. Kleijwegt, and K. Vlassopoulos. doi: 10.1093/oxfordhb/9780199575251.013.3.

Chankowski, V. 2011. "Divine Financiers: Cults as Consumers and Generators of Value." In *The Economies of Hellenistic Societies, Third to First Centuries BC,* edited by Z. H. Archibald, J. K. Davies, and V. Gabrielsen, 142–65. Oxford.

Chassignet, M. 2017. "Caesar and Roman Historiography Prior to the *Commentarii.*" In *The*

Cambridge Companion to the Writings of Julius Caesar, edited by L. Grillo and C. K. Krebs, 249–62. Cambridge.

Chaves, M., and D. E. Cann. 1992. "Regulation, Pluralism, and Religious Market Structure." *Rationality and Society* (July): 292–90.

Chemain, J.-Fr. 2016. *L'économie romaine en Italie à l'époque républicaine*. Paris.

Cherici, A. 2017. "Dance." In *Etruscology*. Edited by A. Naso, 233–44. Boston.

Chevallier, R. 1997. *Les voies romaines*. Paris.

Chlup, R. 2018. "On the Nature of the Gods: Methodological Suggestions for the Study of Greek Divinities." *History of Religions* 58, no. 2: 101–27.

Christenson, D. M., ed. 2000. *Plautus*: Amphitruo. Cambridge.

Chwe, M. 2003. *Rational Ritual: Culture, Coordination, and Common Knowledge*. Princeton.

Ciaghi, S. 1993. *Le terrecotte figurate da Cales del Museo Nazionale di Napoli: Sacro—stile—committenza*. Rome.

Cifarelli, F. M., L. Ambrosini, and D. Nonnis. 2002–3. "Nuovi dati su Segni medio-repubblicana: A proposito di un nuovo *pocolom* dall'Acropoli." *RPAA* 75: 245–325.

Cirucci, G. 2013. "The Roman Conquest of Sicily and Its Consequences." In *Sicily: Art and Invention between Greece and Rome*, edited by C. L. Lyons, M. Bennett, and C. Marconi, 134–43. Los Angeles.

Clark, A. 2007. *Divine Qualities: Cult and Community in Republican Rome*. Oxford.

———. 2018. "Gods, Change, and Civic Space in Late Republican Oratory." In *Institutions and Ideology in Republican Rome*, edited by H. van der Blom, C. Gray, and C. Steel, 88–104. Cambridge.

———. 2019. "Gods and Roman Comedy." In *The Cambridge Companion to Roman Comedy*, edited by M. Dinter, 217–28. Cambridge.

———. In progress. "Ciceronian Correspondences? Gods as Elements of Social Communication (*Att.* 1.13, 1.16 and 1.18)." www.academia.edu/4805230/Ciceronian_Correspondences_Gods_as_elements_of_social_communication_Att._1.13_1.16_1.18_. Last accessed October 5, 2018.

Clemente, G. 2018. "When the Senators Became 'The Best.'" In *Institutions and Ideology in Republican Rome*, edited by H. van der Blom, C. Gray, and C. Steel, 203–21. Cambridge.

Cline, D. H. 2012. "Six Degrees of Alexander: Social Network Analysis as a Tool for Ancient History." *AHB* 26, no. 1–2: 59–70.

———. 2018. "Entanglement, Materiality, and the Social Organization of Construction Workers in Classical Athens." In *Ancient Greek History and Contemporary Social Science*, edited by M. Canevaro, A. Erskine, B. Gray, and J. Ober, 512–28. Edinburgh.

Coale, A. J., and P. Demeny. 1983. *Regional Model Life Tables and Stable Populations*.[2] New York.

Coarelli, F. 1968. "Il tempio di Bellona." *BullCom* 80: 37–72.

———. 1983. "I santuari del Lazio e della Campania tra i Gracchi e le guerre civili." In *Les "Borgeoisies" municipales italiennes aux IIe et Ier siècles av. J.-C. Centre Jean Bérard, Institut français de Naples, 7–10 décembre 1981*, 217–40.

———. 1985. *Il foro romano* (II). *Periodo repubblicano e augusteo*. Rome.

———. 1987. *I santuari dei Lazio in età repubblicana*. Rome.

———. 1997. *Il Campo Marzio: Dalle origini alla fine della repubblica*. Rome.

Coarelli, F. 2007. *Rome and Environs: An Archaeological Guide*. Translated by J. J. Clauss and D. P. Harmon. Berkeley.

———. 2010. "*Substructio et tabularium*." *PBSR* 78: 107–32.

———. 2011. *Le origini di Roma: La cultura artistica dalle origini al III secolo a.C.* Rome.

———. 2012. "Un'iscrizione dal tempio di Diana a Nemi e i *Bacchanalia*." In *Lazio e Sabina 8, Atti del Convegno: Ottavo incontro di studi sul Lazio e la Sabina*, edited by G. Ghini and Z. Mari, 277–78. Rome.

———. 2017. "Le origini dei santuari laziali. Satricum, Lanuvium, *Lucus Aricinus*. In *Quand naissent les dieux. Fondation des sanctuaires antiques: Motivations, agents, lieux*, edited by S. Agusta-Boularot, S. Huber, and W. Van Andringa, 173–81. Rome.

Coffee, N. 2016. *Gift and Gain: How Money Transformed Ancient Rome*. Oxford.

Cohen, E. 1980. "Roads and Pilgrimage: A Study in Economic Interaction." *Studi Medievali* 13, no. 21: 322–41.

———. 1992. "Pilgrimage and Tourism: Convergence and Divergence." In *Sacred Journeys: The Anthropology of Pilgrimage*, edited by A. Morinis, 47–61. Westport.

Collar, A. 2007. "Network Theory and Religious Innovation." *MHR* 22, no. 1: 149–62.

———. 2013. *Religious Networks in the Roman Empire: The Spread of New Ideas*. Cambridge.

Collar, A., and T. M. Kristensen, eds. 2020. *Going, Gathering, and Giving: Economies of Sacred Travel in the Ancient Mediterranean*. Leiden.

Collins-Kreiner, N. 2010. "Researching Pilgrimage: Continuity and Transformations." *Annals of Tourism Research* 37, no. 2: 440–56.

Colonna, G. 1984. "Un 'trofeo' di Novio Fannio, comandante sannita." In *Studi di antichità in onore di Guglielmo Maetzke*, vol. 2, pp. 229–41. Rome.

Colonna, G., ed. 1985. *Santuari d'Etruria*. Milan.

Combet-Farnoux, B. 1980. *Mercure romain: Le culte public de Mercure et la fonction mercantile à Rome de la république archaïque à l'époque augustéenne*. Rome.

Comella, A. 1981. "Tipologia e diffusione dei complessi votivi in Italia in epoca medio e tardo-repubblicana." *MEFRA* 93, no. 2: 717–803.

———. 1986. *I materiali votivi di Falerii*. Corpus delle stipi votive in Italia I, Regio VII–1. Rome.

———. 2001. *Il santuario di Punta della Vipera. Santa Marinella, Comune di Civitavecchia*. I: *I materiali votivi*. Corpus delle stipi votive in Italia XIII, Regio VII–6. Rome.

Connor, W. R. 1987. "Tribes, Festivals, and Processions: Civic Ceremonial and Political Manipulation in Archaic Greece." *JHS* 107: 40–50.

Connors, C. 2016. "Nothing to Do with *Fides*? Female Networks and the Reproduction of Citizenship in Plautus' *Casina*." In *Roman Drama and Its Contexts*, edited by S. Frangoulidis, S. J. Harrison, and G. Manuwald, 275–88. Berlin.

Corbeill, A. 2015. *Sexing the World: Grammatical Gender and Biological Sex in Ancient Rome*. Princeton.

Cordella, R., and N. Criniti. 1996. "Regio IV, Sabina et Samnium. Nursia—Ager Nursinus." In *Supplementa Italica (nuova serie)*, vol. 13, edited by M. Guarducci and S. Panciera, 11–189. Rome.

Cornell, T. J. 1995. *The Beginnings of Rome: Italy and Rome from the Bronze Age to the Punic Wars (c. 1000–264 BC)*. London.

———. 2000a. "The City of Rome in the Middle Republic (c. 400–100 BC)." In *Ancient Rome: The Archaeology of the Eternal City*, edited by J. Coulston and H. Dodge, 42–60. Oxford.

———. 2000b. "The City-States in Latium." In *A Comparative Study of Thirty City-State Cultures*, edited by M. H. Hansen, 209–28. Copenhagen.

———. 2000c. "The *Lex Ovinia* and the Emancipation of the Senate." In *The Roman Middle Republic: Politics, Religion, and Historiography*, edited by C. Bruun, 69–90. Rome.

———. 2004. "Deconstructing the Samnite Wars: An Essay in Historiography." In *Samnium: Settlement and Change; The Proceedings of the Third E. Togo Salmon Conference on Roman Studies*, edited by H. Jones, 115–31. Providence.

Coudry, M. 2009. "Partage et gestion du butin dans la Rome républicaine: Procédures et enjeux." In *Praeda: Butin de guerre et sociétee dans la Rome républicaine / Kriegsbeute und Gesellschaft im republikanischen Rom*, edited by M. Coudry and M. Humm, 21–79. Stuttgart.

Courrier, C. 2014. *La plèbe de Rome et sa culture (fin du IIe siècle av. J.-C.–fin du Ier siècle ap. J.-C.)*. Rome.

Cracco Ruggini, L. 1980. "Nuclei immigrati e forze indigene in tre grandi centri commerciali dell'impero." In *The Seaborne Commerce of Ancient Rome*, edited by J. H. D'Arms and E. C. Kopf, 55–76. Rome.

Crawford, M. H. 1974. *Roman Republican Coinage*. 2 vols. London.

———. 1985. *Coinage and Money under the Roman Republic: Italy and the Mediterranean Economy*. Berkeley.

———. 1989. "*Aut sacrom aut poublicom*." In *New Perspectives in the Roman Law of Property*, edited by P. Birks, 93–98. Oxford.

Crawford, M. H., and F. Coarelli. 1977. "Public Building in Rome between the Second Punic War and Sulla." *PBSR* 45: 1–23.

Crawford, M. H., W. M. Broadhead, J.P.T. Clackson, F. Santangelo, S. Thompson, and M. Watmough, eds. 2011. *Imagines Italicae: A Corpus of Italic Inscriptions*. 3 vols. London.

Crise et transformation des sociétés archaïques de l'Italie antique au Ve siècle av. J.-C. 1990. Rome.

Čulík-Baird, H. 2020. "Staging Roman slavery in the second century BCE." *Ramus* 48, no. 2: 174–97.

Curti, E. 2000. "From Concordia to the Quirinal: Notes on Religion and Politics in Mid-Republican/Hellenistic Rome." In *Religion in Archaic and Republican Rome and Italy: Evidence and Experience*, edited by E. Bispham and C. Smith, 77–91. Edinburgh.

———. 2001. "Toynbee's Legacy: Discussing Aspects of the Romanization of Italy." In *Italy and the West: Comparative Issues in Romanization*, edited by S. Keay and N. Terrenato, 17–26. Oxford.

Curti, E., E. Dench, and J. R. Patterson. 1996. "The Archaeology of Central and Southern Roman Italy: Recent Trends and Approaches." *JRS* 86: 170–89.

Daguet-Gagey, A. 1997. *Les* opera publica *à Rome (180–305 ap. J.-C.)*. Paris.

D'Alessio, M. T. and H. Di Giuseppe. 2005. "La villa dell'Auditorium a Roma tra sacro e profane." In *Roman Villas around the* Urbs*: Interaction with Landscape and Environment, Proceedings of a Conference Held at the Swedish Institute in Rome, September 17–18, 2004*, edited by B. Santillo Frizell and A. Klynne, 1–20. Rome.

D'Arms, J. H. 1998. "Between Public and Private: The *epulum publicum* and Caesar's *horti trans Tiberim*." In *Horti Romani: Atti del Convegno Internazionale, Roma 4–6 Maggio 1995*, edited by M. Cima and E. La Rocca, 33–44. Rome.

D'Arms, J. H. 2000. "P. Lucilius Gamala's Feasts for the Ostians and Their Roman Models." *JRA* 13, no. 1: 192–200.

David, J.-M. 1996a. *The Roman Conquest of Italy*. Translated by A. Nevill. Oxford. Orig. pub. 1994. *La romanisation de l'Italie*. Paris.

———. 1996b. Untitled Review: R. B. Ulrich, *The Roman Orator and the Sacred Stage: The Roman* templum rostratum. *L'Antiquité Classique* 65: 505–7.

Davies, J. K. 2001. "Rebuilding a Temple: The Economic Effects of Piety." In *Economies beyond Agriculture in the Classical World*, edited by D. J. Mattingly and J. Salmon, 209–29. London.

———. 2018. "State Formation in Early Iron Age Greece: The Operative Forces." In *Defining Citizenship in Archaic Greece*, edited by A. Duplouy and R. W. Brock, 51–78. Oxford.

Davies, J. P. 2004. *Rome's Religious History: Livy, Tacitus, and Ammianus on Their Gods*. Cambridge.

Davies, P.J.E. 2014. "Rome and Her Neighbors: Greek Building Practices in Republican Rome." In *A Companion to Roman Architecture*, edited by R. B. Ulrich and C. K. Quenemoen, 27–44. Chichester.

———. 2017a. *Architecture and Politics in Republican Rome*. Cambridge.

———. 2017b. "Constructing, Deconstructing and Reconstructing Civic Memory in Late Republican Rome." In Omnium annalium monumenta: *Historical Writing and Historical Evidence in Republican Rome*, edited by K. Sandberg and C. Smith, 477–511. Leiden.

———. 2017c. "A Republican Dilemma: City or State? Or, The Concrete Revolution Revisited." *PBSR* 85: 71–107.

De Angelis, F. 2016. *Archaic and Classical Greek Sicily: A Social and Economic History*. Oxford.

De Callataÿ, F. 2014. "Long-Term Quantification in Ancient History: A Historical Perspective." In *Quantifying the Greco-Roman Economy and Beyond*, edited by F. de Callataÿ, 13–27. Bari.

De Cazanove, O. 1991. "*Ex-voto* de l'Italie républicaine: Sur quelques aspects de leur mise au rebut." In *Les sanctuaires celtiques et leurs rapports avec le monde méditerranéen*, edited by J.-L. Brunaux, 203–14. Paris.

———. 2000. "Some Thoughts on the 'Religious Romanisation' of Italy before the Social War." In *Religion in Archaic and Republican Rome and Italy: Evidence and Experience*, edited by E. Bispham and C. Smith, 71–76. Edinburgh.

———. 2001. "Itinéraires et étapes de l'avancée romaine entre Samnium, Daunie, Lucanie et Étrurie." In *Le censeur et les Samnites: Sur Tite-Live, Livre IX*, edited by D. Briquel and J.-P. Thuiller, 147–93. Paris.

———. 2005. "Les colonies latines et les frontières régionales de l'Italie." *Mélanges de la Casa de Velázquez* 35, no. 2: 107–24.

———. 2007. "Pre-Roman Italy, before and under the Romans." In *A Companion to Roman Religion*, edited by J. Rüpke, 43–57. Malden.

———. 2009. "Oggetti muti? Le iscrizioni degli ex voto anatomici nel mondo romano." In *Dediche sacre nel mondo greco-romano: Religious Dedications in the Greco-Roman World*, 355–71. Rome.

———. 2011. "Quadro concettuale, quadro materiale delle pratiche religiose lucane: Per una revisione dei dati." In *Brateís Datas: Pratiche rituali, votivi e strumenti del culto dai santuari della Lucania antica*, edited by I. Battiloro and M. Osanna, 295–310. Potenza.

———. 2015. "Per la datazione degli ex voto anatomici d'Italia." In *The Impact of Rome on Cult Places and Religious Practices in Ancient Italy*, edited by T. D. Stek and G.-J. Burgers, 29–66. London.

———. 2016. "Offerte della e dall'Italia centrale: Teste e uteri di terracotta come spie delle dinamiche di diffusione." In *E pluribus unum? L'Italie, de la diversité préromaine à l'unité augustéenne*. Vol. 2: *L'Italie centrale e la creazione di una koiné culturale? I percorsi della "romanizzazione,"* edited by M. Aberson, M. C. Biella, M. Di Fazio, P. Sánchez, and M. Wullschleger, 273–89. Bern.

Degrassi, A., ed. 1963. *Inscriptiones Italiae XIII: Fasti et elogia*. Vol. 2: *Fasti anni Numani et Iuliani*. Rome.

De Haas, T. C. 2011. *Fields, Farms, and Colonists: Intensive Field Survey and Early Roman Colonization in the Pontine Region, Central Italy*. Groningen.

DeLaine, J. 1997. *The Baths of Caracalla: A Study in the Design, Construction, and Economics of Large-Scale Building Projects in Imperial Rome*. Portsmouth.

———. 2001. "Bricks and Mortar: Exploring the Economics of Building Techniques at Rome and Ostia." In *Economies beyond Agriculture in the Classical World*, edited by D. J. Mattingly and J. Salmon, 230–68. New York.

———. 2002. "The Temple of Hadrian at Cyzicus and Roman Attitudes to Exceptional Construction." *PBSR* 70: 205–30.

Del Buono, G. 2009. "Il tempio di Portuno: Una nuova periodizzazione per le fasi medio-repubblicane." *BullCom* 110: 9–30.

Del Chiaro, M. 1957. *The* Genucilia *Group: A Class of Etruscan Red-Figured Plates*. Berkeley.

De Ligt, L. 1993. *Fairs and Markets in the Roman Empire: Economic and Social Aspects of Periodic Trade in a Pre-Industrial Society*. Amsterdam.

De Ligt, L., and P. W. de Neeve. 1988. *Ancient Periodic Markets: Festivals and Fairs*. Pavia.

De Marchi, A. [1896–1903] 1975. *Il culto privato di Roma antica*. 2 vols. New York.

Dench, E. 1995. *From Barbarians to New Men: Greek, Roman, and Modern Perceptions of Peoples of the Central Apennines*. Oxford.

———. 2003. "Beyond Greeks and Barbarians: Italy and Sicily in the Hellenistic Age." In *A Companion to the Hellenistic World*, edited by A. Erskine, 294–310. Malden.

———. 2018. *Empire and Political Cultures in the Roman World*. Cambridge.

Dennehy, T. J., B. W. Stanley, and M. E. Smith. 2016. "Social Inequality and Access to Services in Premodern Societies." *Archeological Papers of the American Anthropological Association* 27: 143–60.

De Nuccio, M. 2011. "La decorazione architettonica del tempio di Bellona." *BullCom* 112: 191–226.

De Polignac, F. 1984. *La naissance de la cité grecque: Cultes, espace et société VIII*[e]*–VII*[e] *siècles avant J.-C.* Paris.

D'Ercole, M. C. 1990. *La stipe votiva del Belvedere a Lucera*. Corpus delle stipi votive in Italia III, Region II–2. Rome.

De Ruiter, J., G. Weston, and S. M. Lyon. 2012. "Dunbar's Number: Group Size and Brain Physiology in Humans Reexamined." *American Anthropologist* 113, no. 4: 557–68.

Deschamps, L. 1983. "Varron, les lymphes et les nymphes." In *Hommages à Robert Schilling*, edited by H. Zehnacker and G. Hentz, 67–83. Paris.

De Ste. Croix, G.E.M. 1981. *The Class Struggle in the Ancient Greek World from the Archaic Age to the Arab Conquests.* Ithaca.

De Wet, C. L. 2015. *Preaching Bondage: John Chrysostom and the Discourse of Slavery in Early Christianity*. Oakland.

Dicus, K. D'Arcy. 2012. "Actors and Agents in Ritual Behavior: The Sanctuary at Grasceta dei Cavallari as a Case-Study of the E-L-C Votive Tradition in Republican Italy." PhD diss., University of Michigan.

Di Fazio, M. 2012. "I luoghi di culto di Feronia: Ubicazioni e funzioni." In *Il* Fanum Voltumnae *e I santuari comunitari dell'Italia antica*, edited by G. M. della Fina, 379–408. Rome.

———. 2013. "Callimachus and the Etruscans: Human Sacrifice between Myth, History, and Historiography." *Histos* 7: 48–69.

Di Giuseppe, H. 2012. *Black-Gloss Ware in Italy: Production Management and Local Histories.* Oxford.

Dillon, J. N. 2015. "Trojan Religion: Foreign Sanctuaries and the Limits of Roman Religious Exclusivity." In *The Impact of Rome on Cult Places and Religious Practices in Ancient Italy*, edited by T. D. Stek and G.-J. Burgers, 113–44. London.

Dillon, M. 1997. *Pilgrims and Pilgrimage in Ancient Greece*. London.

DiLuzio, M. J. 2016. *A Place at the Altar: Priestesses in Republican Rome*. Princeton.

Domingo Gygax, M. 2016. *Benefaction and Rewards in the Ancient Greek City: The Origins of Euergetism*. Cambridge.

Donahue, J. F. 2003. "Toward a Typology of Roman Public Feasting." *AJP* 124, no. 3: 423–41.

———. 2014. "The Healing Springs of Latium and Etruria." In *Aspects of Ancient Institutions and Geography: Studies in Honor of Richard J. A. Talbert*, edited by L. L. Brice and D. Slootjes, 314–32. Leiden.

Dondin-Payre, M. 1987. "Topographie et propagande gentilice: Le *compitum Acilium* et l'origine des *Acilii Glabriones*." In *L'urbs, espace urbain et histoire (1er siècle av. J.-C.–IIIe siècle ap. J.-C.)*, 87–109. Rome.

Döring, K. 1978. "Antike Theorien über die staatspolitische Notwendigkeit der Götterfurcht." *Antike und Abendland* 24: 43–56.

Douglass, F. [1855] 2003. *My Bondage and My Freedom*. New York.

Dox, D. 2004. *The Idea of the Theater in Latin Christian Thought: Augustine to the Fourteenth Century*. Ann Arbor.

Draycott, J. 2016. "Literary and Documentary Evidence for Lay Medical Practice in the Roman Republic and Empire." In Homo patiens: *Approaches to the Patient in the Ancient World*, edited by G. Petridou and C. Thumiger, 432–50. Leiden.

———. 2017. "When Lived Ancient Religion and Lived Ancient Medicine Meet: The Household Gods, the Household Shrine and Regimen." *RRE* 3, no. 2: 164–80.

———. 2019. *Roman Domestic Medical Practice in Central Italy: From the Middle Republic to the Early Empire*. London.

Driediger-Murphy, L. G. 2014. "M. Valerius Messala to Teos (*Syll.*³ 601) and the Theology of Rome's War with Antiochus III." *ZPE* 189: 115–20.

———. 2019. *Roman Republican Augury: Freedom and Control*. Oxford.

Dubbini, R. 2016. "A New Republican Temple on the *via Appia*, at the Borders of Rome's Urban Space." *JRA* 29: 327–47.

Dubois-Pelerin, E. 2016. "Luxe privé/faste public: Le thème de l'*aedificatio* du IIe siècle av. J.-C. au début de l'Empire." *MEFRA* 128, no. 1. doi: 10.4000/mefra.3227.

Dubourdieu, A., and J. Scheid. 2000. "Lieux de culte, lieux sacrés: Les usages de la langue; L'Italie romaine." In *Lieux sacrés, lieux de culte, sanctuaires: Approches terminologiques, méthodologiques, historiques et monographiques*, edited by A. Vauchez, 59–80. Rome.

Duckworth, G. E., ed. 1940. T. Macci Plauti Epidicus. Princeton.

———. [1952] 1994. *The Nature of Roman Comedy: A Study in Popular Entertainment.*[2] Norman.

Dumézil, G. 1974. *La religion romaine archaïque, avec un appendice sur la religion des Étrusques.* Paris.

———. 1979. *Mariages indo-européens*. Paris.

———. 1983. "Encore *Genius*." In *Hommages à Robert Schilling*, edited by H. Zehnacker and G. Hentz, 85–92. Paris.

Dunbar, R.I.M. 1992. "Neocortex Size as a Constraint on Group Size in Primates." *Journal of Human Evolution* 20: 469–93.

Duncan-Jones, R. 1990. *Structure and Scale in the Roman Economy*. Cambridge.

———. 1997. "Numerical Distortion in Roman Writers." In *Économie antique: Prix et formation des prix dans les économies antiques*, edited by J. Andreau et al., 147–59. Saint-Bertrand-de-Comminges.

Dunsch, B. 2009. "Religion in der römischen Komödie: Einige programmatische Überlegungen." In *Römische Religion im historischen Wandel: Diskursentwicklung von Plautus bis Ovid*, edited by A. Bendlin and J. Rüpke, 17–56. Stuttgart.

Dutsch, D. 2014. "The Beginnings: Philosophy in Roman Literature before 155 B.C." In *The Philosophizing Muse: The Influence of Greek Philosophy on Roman Poetry*, edited by M. Garani and D. Konstan, 1–25. Cambridge.

Eade, J., and D. Albera. 2017. "Pilgrimage Studies in Global Perspective." In *New Pathways in Pilgrimage Studies: Global Perspectives*, edited by D. Albera and J. Eade, 1–17. London.

Easley, D., and J. Kleinberg. 2010. *Networks, Crowds, and Markets: Reasoning about a Highly Connected World*. New York.

Eckstein, A. M. 2000. "Brigands, Emperors, and Anarchy." *International History Review* 22: 862–79.

———. 2006. *Mediterranean Anarchy, Interstate War, and the Rise of Rome*. Berkeley.

Edelstein, E. J., and L. Edelstein. 1998. *Asclepius: A Collection and Interpretation of the Testimonies.*[2] 2 vols. Baltimore.

Eder, W., ed. 1990. *Staat und Staatlichkeit in der frühen römischen Republik. Akten eines Symposiums 12.–15. Juli 1998. Freie Universität Berlin*. Stuttgart.

Edlund, I.E.M. 1983. "Sacred and Secular: Evidence of Rural Shrines and Industry among Greeks and Etruscans." In *Crossroads of the Mediterranean: Papers Delivered at the International Conference Held at Brown University, 1981*, edited by T. Hackens et al., 283–87. Louvain-la-Neuve.

Edlund-Berry, I. 2006. "Healing, Health, and Well-Being: Archaeological Evidence for Issues of Health Concerns in Ancient Italy." *ARG* 8: 81–88.

Ehmig, U. 2016. "Bauten als Gegenwert göttlicher Hilfe im Zeugnis lateinischer Votivinschriften." *MH* 73: 56–77.

Eich, A., and P. Eich. 2005. "War and State-Building in Roman Republican Times." *SCI* 24: 1–33.

El Bouzidi, S. 2015. *La familia rustica catonienne: Structure, contrôle et exploitation*. Munich.

Ellis, S.J.R. 2018. *The Roman Retail Revolution: The Socio-economic World of the* Taberna. Oxford.

Elm, S. 2014. "Church—Festival—Temple: Reimagining Civic Topography in Late Antiquity." In *The City in the Classical and Post-Classical World: Changing Contexts of Power and Identity*, edited by C. Rapp and H. A. Drake, 167–82. Cambridge.

Elsner, J., and I. Rutherford, eds. 2005. *Pilgrimage in Graeco-Roman and Early Christian Antiquity: Seeing the Gods*. Oxford.

Elvira Barba, M. A. 1982. "Terracotas votivas." In *El santuario de Juno en Gabii*, edited by M. Almagro-Garbea, 263–300. Rome.

Engels, D. 2005. "*Eo anno multa prodigia facta sunt*. Das Jahr 218 als Wendepunkt des römischen Vorzeichenwesens." In *Mantik: Profile prognostischen Wissens in Wissenschaft und Kultur*, edited by W. Hogrebe, 151–66. Würzburg.

Erdkamp, P. 2008. "Mobility and Migration in Italy in the Second Century BC." In *People, Land, and Politics: Demographic Developments and the Transformation of Roman Italy, 300 BC–AD 14*, edited by L. De Ligt and S. Northwood, 417–49. Leiden.

Ernout, A. 1957. *Recueil de textes latins archaïques.*[2] Paris.

Erskine, A. 2013. "Making Sense of the Romans: Polybius and the Greek Perspective." In *Le point de vue de l'autre: Relations culturelles et diplomatie* (*DHA* Supplément 9), edited by A. Gonzalez and M. T. Schettino, 115–29. Besançon.

Estienne, S. 2017. "Fonder un sanctuaire romaine: Droit et pratiques." In *Quand naissent les dieux: Fondation des sanctuaires antiques; Motivations, Agents, Lieux*, edited by S. Agusta-Boularot, S. Huber, and W. Van Andringa, 247–57. Rome.

Estienne, S., and O. de Cazanove. 2009. "Offrandes et amendes dans les sanctuaires du monde romain à l'époque républicaine." *ARG* 11: 5–56.

Evans, N. 2010. *Civic Rites: Democracy and Religion in Ancient Athens*. Berkeley.

Favro, D. 1999. "The City Is a Living Thing: The Performative Role of an Urban Site in Ancient Rome, the Vallis Murcia." In *The Art of Ancient Spectacle*, edited by B. Bergmann and C. Kondoleon, 205–19. New Haven.

Fears, J. R. 1981. "The Theology of Victory at Rome: Approaches and Problems." *ANRW* II.17.2: 736–826.

Feeney, D. 1991. *The Gods in Epic: Poets and Critics of the Classical Tradition*. Oxford.

———. 1998. *Literature and Religion at Rome: Cultures, Contexts, and Beliefs*. Cambridge.

———. 2005. "The Beginnings of a Literature in Latin." *JRS* 95: 226–40.

———. 2007. *Caesar's Calendar: Ancient Time and the Beginnings of History*. Berkeley.

———. 2016. *Beyond Greek: The Beginnings of Latin Literature*. Cambridge, MA.

Feinman, G. M. 2016. "Variation and Change in Archaic States: Ritual as a Mechanism of Sociopolitical Integration." In *Ritual and Archaic States*, edited by J.M.A. Murphy, 1–22. Gainesville.

Feinman, G. M., and C. P. Garrity. 2010. "Preindustrial Markets and Marketing: Archaeological Perspectives." *Annual Reviews in Anthropology* 39: 167–91.

Fenelli, M. 1975a. "Contributo per lo studio del votivo anatomico: I votivi anatomici di Lavinio." *Archeologia Classica* 27: 206–52.

———. 1975b. "Votivi anatomici (D)." In *Lavinium II: Le Tredici Are*, edited by F. Castagnoli et al., 253–55. Rome.

Fentress, E. 2013. "Strangers in the City: Élite Communication in the Hellenistic Central Mediterranean." In *The Hellenistic West: Rethinking the Ancient Mediterranean*, edited by J.R.W. Prag and J. Crawley Quinn, 157–78. Cambridge.

Ferrandes, A. F. 2008. "Produzioni ceramiche a Roma tra IV e III secolo a.C." *Rei Cretariae Romanae Acta* 40: 363–72.

———. 2017. "Gli artigiani e Roma tra alta e media età repubblicana." *Scienze dell'antichità* 23, no. 2: 21–53.

Ferrante, C. 2008. "Una brocca di bronzo con dedica a NVMISIVS MARTIVS dalla necropoli delle Saliere a Capena." *Cahiers du Centre Gustave Glotz* 19: 7–25.

Février, C. 2009. Supplicare deis: *La supplication expiatoire à Rome*. Turnhout.

Finke, R., and L. R. Iannaccone. 1993. "Supply-Side Explanations for Religious Change." *Annals of the American Academy of Political and Social Sciences* (May): 27–39.

Fischer-Bovet, C. 2014. *Army and Society in Ptolemaic Egypt*. Cambridge.

Flaig, E. 2003. *Ritualisierte Politik. Zeichen, Gesten und Herrschaft im alten Rome*. Göttingen.

Fleck, R. K., and F. A. Hanssen. 2018. "What Can Data Drawn from the Hansen-Nielsen *Inventory* Tell Us about Political Transitions in Ancient Greece?" In *Ancient Greek History and Contemporary Social Science*, edited by M. Canevaro, A. Erskine, B. Gray, and J. Ober, 213–38. Edinburgh.

Flemming, R. 2016. "Anatomical Votives: Popular Medicine in Republican Italy?" In *Popular Medicine in Graeco-Roman Antiquity: Explorations*, edited by W. V. Harris, 105–25. Leiden.

———. 2017. "Wombs for the Gods." In *Bodies of Evidence: Ancient Anatomical Votives Past, Present, and Future*, edited by J. Draycott and E.-J. Graham, 112–30. London.

Flores, E. 1974. *Letteratura latina e ideologia del III–II a.C: Disegno storico-sociologico da Appio Claudio Cieco a Pacuvio*. Naples.

———, ed. 2011. Cn. Naeui Bellum Poenicum. *Introduzione, edizione critica e versione italiana*. Napoli.

Flower, H. I. 1995. "*Fabulae praetextae* in Context: When Were Plays on Contemporary Subjects Performed in Republican Rome?" *CQ* 45, no. 1: 170–90.

———. 1996. *Ancestor Masks and Aristocratic Power in Roman Culture*. Oxford.

———. 1998. "The Significance of an Inscribed Breastplate Captured at Falerii in 241 BC." *JRA* 11: 224–32.

———. 2000. "*Fabula de Bacchanalibus*: The Bacchanalian Cult of the Second Century BC and Roman Drama." In *Identität und Alterität in der frührömischen Tragödie*, edited by G. Manuwald, ed., 23–35. Würzburg.

———. 2009. "Alternatives to Written History in Republican Rome." In *The Cambridge Companion to the Roman Republic*, edited by A. Feldherr, 322–43. Cambridge.

———. 2010. *Roman Republics*. Princeton.

———. 2013a. "Beyond the *contio*: Political Communication in the Tribunate of Tiberius Gracchus." In *Community and Communication: Oratory and Politics in Republican Rome*, edited by C. Steel and H. van der Blom, 85–100. Oxford.

———. 2013b. "Consensus and Community in Republican Rome." Todd Lecture, University of Sydney.

Flower, H. I. [2004] 2014. "Spectacle and Political Culture in the Roman Republic." In *The Cambridge Companion to the Roman Republic*², edited by H. I. Flower, 377–98. Cambridge.

———. 2017. *The Dancing Lares and the Serpent in the Garden: Religion at the Roman Street Corner*. Princeton.

Flower, M. 2017. "Spartan Religion." In *The Blackwell Companion to Ancient Sparta*, edited by A. Powell, 425–51. Malden.

Folch, M. 2016. *The City and the Stage: Performance, Genre, and Gender in Plato's* Laws. Oxford.

Forsythe, G. 1996. "*Ubi tu Gaius, ego Gaia*: New Light on an Old Roman Legal Saw." *Historia* 45, no. 2: 240–41.

———. 2005. *A Critical History of Early Rome: From Prehistory to the First Punic War*. Berkeley.

———. 2012. *Time in Roman Religion: One Thousand Years of Religious History*. London.

Forti, L. 1970. "Una officina di vasi tarantini a Vulci." *Rendiconti Napoli* 45: 233–65.

Foskolou, V. 2012. "Blessing for Sale? On the Production and Distribution of Pilgrim Mementoes in Byzantium." *BZ* 105, no. 1: 53–84.

Fracchia, H. 2015. "Cult Places in the Ancient Landscape of Roccagloriosa (Western Lucania), Third to First Centuries BC: Aspects of Change and Continuity." In *The Impact of Rome on Cult Places and Religious Practices in Ancient Italy*, edited by T. D. Stek and G.-J. Burgers, 97–112. London.

Fraenkel, E. [1922] 2007. *Plautine Elements in Plautus*. Translated by T. Drevikovsky and F. Muecke. Oxford.

Franchi de Bellis, A. 1981. *Le iovile capuane*. Florence.

———. 1993 "Il latino nell'*ager Gallicus*: I *pocula* riminesi." In *Caratteri e diffusione del latino in età arcaica*, edited by E. Campanile, 35–63. Pisa.

———. 1995. "I *pocola* riminesi." In *Pro poplo Arimenese: Atti del Convegno Internazionale, Rimini antica, Una respublica fra terra e mare*, edited by A. Calbi and G. Susini, 367–91. Faenza.

Frank, T. 1924. *Roman Buildings of the Republic: An Attempt to Date Them from Their Materials*. Rome.

———. [1933] 1975. *An Economic Survey of Ancient Rome*. Vol. 1: *Rome and Italy of the Republic*. New York.

Frankfurter, D., ed. 1998. *Pilgrimage and Holy Space in Late Antique Egypt*. Leiden.

Fraser, P. M. 1972. *Ptolemaic Alexandria*. 3 vols. Oxford.

Frayn, J. M. 1993. *Markets and Fairs in Roman Italy: Their Social and Economic Importance from the Second Century BC to the Third Century AD*. Oxford.

Freyburger, G. 1977. "La supplication d'action de grâces dans la religion romaine archaïque." *Latomus* 36: 283–315.

———. 1988. "Supplication grecque et supplication romaine." *Latomus* 47, no. 3: 501–25.

———. 2000. "Der religiöse Charakter der frührömischen Tragödie." In *Identität und Alterität in der frührömischen Tragödie*, edited by G. Manuwald, 37–48. Würzburg.

Frey-Kupper, S. 1995. "Monete dal Tevere: I rinvenimenti 'greci'" *Bollettino di Numismatica* 25: 33–73.

Frézouls, E. 1983. "Le théâtre romain et la culture urbaine." In *La città antica come fatto di cultura: Atti del Convegno di Como e Bellagio, 16–19 Giugno 1979*, 105–30. Como.

Frier, B. W. 1979. Libri annales pontificum maximorum: *The Origins of the Annalistic Tradition.* Ann Arbor.

Friese, W. 2017. "Of Piety, Gender, and Ritual Space: An Archaeological Approach to Women's Sacred Travel in Greece." In *Excavating Pilgrimage: Archaeological Approaches to Sacred Travel and Movement in the Ancient World,* edited by T. M. Kristensen and W. Friese, 47–66. London.

Fukuyama, F. 2011. *The Origins of Political Order: From Prehuman Times to the French Revolution.* New York.

Fulkerson, L. 2018. "*Deos speravi* (*Miles* 1209): Hope and the Gods in Roman Comedy." In *Hope in Ancient Literature, History, and Art: Ancient Emotions* 1, edited by G. Kazantzidis and D. Spatharas, 153–69. Berlin.

Fulminante, F. 2012. "Social Network Analysis and the Emergence of Central Places: A Case Study from Central Italy (Latium Vetus)." *BABESCH* 87: 1–27.

Gabrielli, C. 2003. "Lucius Postumius Megellus at Gabii: A New Fragment of Livy." *CQ* 53: 247–59.

Gabrielsen, V. 2007. "Brotherhoods of Faith and Provident Planning: The Non-Public Associations of the Greek World." *MHR* 22, no. 2: 183–210.

Galinsky, K. 2018. "The Popularity of Hercules in Pre-Roman Central Italy." In *At the Crossroads of Greco-Roman History, Culture, and Religion: Papers in Memory of Carin M. C. Green,* edited by S. W. Bell and L. Holland, 191–202. Oxford.

García Morcillo, M. 2013. "Trade and Sacred Places: Fairs, Markets, and Exchange in Ancient Italic Sanctuaries." In *Religiöse Vielfalt und soziale Integration: Die Bedeutung der Religion für die kulturelle Identität und politische Stabilität im republikanischen Italien,* edited by M. Jehne, B. Linke, and J. Rüpke, 236–74. Heidelberg.

Gargola, D. J. 2017. *The Shape of the Roman Order: The Republic and Its Spaces.* Chapel Hill.

Garlan, Y. 1988. *Slavery in Ancient Greece.* Translated by J. Lloyd. Ithaca.

Garland, R. 1992. *Introducing New Gods: The Politics of Athenian Religion.* London.

Gatti Lo Guzzo, L. 1978. *Il deposito votivo dall'Esquilino detto di Minerva Medica.* Florence.

Gauthier, P. 1974. "'Générosité' romaine et 'avarice' grecque: Sur l'octroi du droit de cité." In *Mélanges d'histoire ancienne offerts à William Seston,* 207–16. Paris.

Geertz, C. 1980. *Negara: The Theater State in Nineteenth-Century Bali.* Princeton.

Geiger, J. 1984. "The Earliest Reference to Jews in Latin Literature." *JSJ* 15: 145–47.

Gellar-Goad, T.H.M. 2013. "Religious Ritual and Family Dynamics in Terence." In *A Companion to Terence,* edited by A. Augoustakis and A. Traill, 156–74. Chichester.

Gentili, M. D. 2005. "Riflessioni sul fenomeno storico dei depositi votivi di tipo etrusco-laziale-campano." In *Depositi votivi e culti dell'Italia antica dall'età arcaica a quella tardo-repubblicana,* edited by A. Comella and S. Mele, 367–78. Bari.

Germany, R. 2016. "Civic Reassignment of Space in the *Truculuntus.*" In *Roman Drama and Its Contexts,* edited by S. Frangoulidis, S. J. Harrison, and G. Manuwald, 263–74. Berlin.

Ghini, G., and F. Diosono. "Il Tempio di Diana a Nemi: Una rilettura alla luce dei recenti scavi." In *Lazio e Sabina 8: Atti del Convegno; Ottavo incontro di studi sul Lazio e la Sabina,* edited by G. Ghini and Z. Mari, 269–76.

Giacobello, F. 2008. *Larari pompeiani: Iconografia e culto dei Lari in ambito domestico.* Milan.

Giangiulio, M. 1986. "Appunti di storia dei culti." In *Neapolis: Atti del venticinquesimo convegno di studi sulla Magna Grecia*, 101–54. Taranto.

Gibson, B. 2012. "Festivals and Games in Polybius." In *Imperialism, Cultural Politics, and Polybius*, edited by C. Smith and L. M. Yarrow, 263–77. Oxford.

Giddens, A. 1984. *The Constitution of Society: Outline of the Theory of Structuration*. Cambridge.

Gildenhard, I. 2003. "The 'Annalist' before the Annalists: Ennius and His *Annales*." In *Formen römischer Geschichtsschreibung von den Anfängen bis Livius. Gattungen—Autoren—Kontexte*, edited by U. Eigler, U. Gotter, N. Luraghi, and U. Walter, 92–114. Stuttgart.

———. 2007. "Virgil vs. Ennius—or: The Undoing of the Annalist." In Ennius perennis: *The* Annals *and Beyond*, edited by W. Fitzgerald and E. Gowers, 73–102. Cambridge.

———. 2010. "Buskins and SPQR: Roman Receptions of Greek Tragedy." In *Beyond the Fifth Century: Interactions with Greek Tragedy from the Fourth Century BCE to the Middle Ages*, edited by I. Gildenhard and M. Revermann, 153–86. Berlin.

Gilula, D. 1996. "The Allocation of Seats to Senators in 194 BCE." In *Classical Studies in Honor of David Sohlberg*, edited by R. Katzoff, 234–44. Ramat-Gan.

Ginge, B. 1993. "Votive Deposits in Italy: New Perspectives on Old Finds." *JRA* 6: 285–88.

Giusti, E. 2018. *Carthage in Virgil's* Aeneid: *Staging the Enemy under Augustus*. Cambridge.

———. 2019. "Bunte Barbaren Setting Up the Stage: Re-inventing the Barbarian on the *Georgics*' Theatre-Temple (*G.* 3.1–48)." In *Virgil's* Georgics: *Reflections and New Perspectives*, edited by B. Xinyue and N. Freer. 105–14. London.

Gladwell, M. 2000. *The Tipping Point: How Little Things Make a Big Difference*. Boston.

Glinister, F. 2000. "Sacred Rubbish." In *Religion in Archaic and Republican Rome and Italy: Evidence and Experience*, edited by E. Bispham and C. Smith, 54–70. Edinburgh.

———. 2006a. "Reconsidering 'Religious Romanization.'" In *Religion in Republican Italy*, edited by C. Schultz and P. Harvey Jr., 10–33. Cambridge.

———. 2006b. "Women, Colonization, and Cult in Hellenistic Central Italy." *ARG* 8: 89–104.

———. 2011. "'Bring on the Dancing Girls': Some Thoughts on the Salian Priesthood." In *Priests and State in the Roman World*, edited by J. H. Richardson and F. Santangelo, 107–36. Stuttgart.

———. 2015. "Colonies and Religious Dynamism in Mid-Republican Italy." In *The Impact of Rome on Cult Places and Religious Practices in Ancient Italy*, edited by T. D. Stek and G.-J. Burgers, 145–56. London.

Goldberg, S. M. 1998. "Plautus on the Palatine." *JRS* 88: 1–20.

———. 2018. "Theater without Theaters: Seeing Plays the Roman Way." *TAPA* 148, no. 1: 139–72.

Goldstone, J. A., and J. F. Haldon. 2009. "Ancient States, Empires, and Exploitation." In *The Dynamics of Ancient Empires: State Power from Assyria to Byzantium*, edited by I. Morris and W. Scheidel, 3–29. Oxford.

Gonçalves, B., N. Perra, and A. Vespignani. 2011. "Modeling Users' Activity on Twitter Networks: Validation of Dunbar's Number." *PloS ONE* 6, no. 8: e22656. doi: 10.1371/journal.pone.0022656.

Goodchild, H. 2013. "GIS Models of Roman Agricultural Production." In *The Roman Agricultural Economy: Organization, Investment, and Production*, edited by A. Bowman and A. Wilson, 55–84. Oxford.

Gordon, R. 1990. "The Veil of Power: Emperors, Sacrificers, and Benefactors." In *Pagan Priests: Religion and Power in the Ancient World*, edited by M. Beard and J. North, 201–31. Ithaca.

Graf, F. 2002. Untitled Review: M. Dillon, *Pilgrims and Pilgrimage in Ancient Greece. History of Religions* 42, no. 2: 193–96.

Graham, E.-J. 2016. "Mobility Impairment in the Sanctuaries of Early Roman Italy." In *Disability in Antiquity*, edited by C. Laes, 248–66. London.

———. 2017. "Partible Humans and Permeable Gods: Anatomical Votives and Personhood in the Sanctuaries of Central Italy." In *Bodies of Evidence: Ancient Anatomical Votives Past, Present, and Future*, edited by J. Draycott and E.-J. Graham, 45–62. London.

Grandazzi, A. 2010. "Lavinium, Alba Longa, Roma: À quoi sert un paysage religieux?" *Revue de l'histoire des religions* 4: 573–90.

Granino Cecere, M. G. 2009. "*Pecunia sacra* e proprietà fondiaria nei santuari dell'Italia centrale: Il contributo dell'epigrafia." *ARG* 11: 37–62.

Gratwick, A. S. 1979. "Sundials, Parasites, and Girls from Boeotia." *CQ* 29, no. 2: 308–23.

———. 1982. "Drama." In *The Cambridge History of Classical Literature*. Vol. 2: *Latin Literature*, edited by E. J. Kenney, 77–137. Cambridge.

Greco, E. 1986. "L'impianto urbano di Neapolis Greca: Aspetti e problemi." In *Neapolis: Atti del venticinquesimo convegno di studi sulla Magna Grecia*, 187–219. Taranto.

Green, J. R. 1976. "An Addition to the Volcani Group." *AJA* 80, no. 2: 188–89.

———. 2001. "Gnathia and Other Overpainted Wares of Italy and Sicily: A Survey." In *Céramiques hellénistiques et romaines* 3, edited by P. Lévêque, J.-P. Morel, and E. Geny, 57–103. Besançon.

Greene, K. 1992. *Roman Pottery*. Berkeley.

Greenidge, A.H.J., and A. M. Clay. 1986. *Sources for Roman History, 133–70 B.C.* 2nd ed. Rev. by E. W. Gray. Oxford.

Gregori, G. L., and D. Nonnis. 2013. "Il contributo dell'epigrafia allo studio delle cinte murarie dell'Italia repubblicana." *Scienze dell'antichità* 19, no. 2–3: 491–524.

Griffith, A. B. 2013. "Reconstructing Religious Ritual in Italy." In *A Companion to the Archaeology of the Roman Republic*, edited by J. D. Evans, 235–49. Malden.

Gruen, E. S. 1984. *The Hellenistic World and the Coming of Rome*. 2 vols. Berkeley.

———. 1990. *Studies in Greek Culture and Roman Policy*. Leiden.

———. 1992. *Culture and National Identity in Republican Rome*. Ithaca.

Guarducci, M. 1971. "L'Isola Tiberina e la sua tradizione ospitaliera." *Rendiconti Lincei* 8, no. 26: 267–81.

Guidobaldi, M. P. 1999. "La *Via Caecilia*: Riflessioni sulla cronologia e sul percorso di una *via publica romana*." In *La Salaria in età antica*, edited by E. Catani and G. Paci, 277–90. Rome.

———. 2002. *I materiali votivi della Grotta del Colle di Rapino*. Corpus delle stipi votive in Italia XV, Regio IV–1. Rome.

Guittard, C. 2015. "Douris et la tradition de la *devotio* des *Decii*." In *De Samos à Rome: Personnalité et influence de Douris*, edited by V. Naas and M. Simon, 329–39. Nanterre.

Gunderson, E. 2015. *Laughing Awry: Plautus and Tragicomedy*. Oxford.

Gurevitch, M. 1961. "The Social Structure of Acquaintanceship Networks." PhD diss., Massachusetts Institute of Technology.

Gutiérrez, G., N. Terrenato, and A. Otto. 2015. "Imperial Cities." In *Early Cities in Comparative Perspective. The Cambridge World History* 3, edited by N. Yoffee, 532–45. Cambridge.

Haake, M., and M. Jung, eds. 2011. *Griechische Heiligtümer als Erinnerungsorte: Von der Archaik bis in den Hellenismus. Erträge einer internationalen Tagung in Münster, 20.–21. Januar 2006*. Stuttgart.

Haack, M.-L. 2017. "Ritual and Cults, 450–250 BCE." In *Etruscology*, edited by A. Naso, 1117–28. Leiden.

Habicht, C. 2006. *The Hellenistic Monarchies: Selected Papers*. Ann Arbor.

Ham, G. 1999. "The *choes* and Anthesteria Reconsidered: Male Maturation Rites and the Peloponnesian Wars." In *Rites of Passage in Ancient Greece: Literature, Religion, Society*, edited by M. W. Padilla, 201–18. Lewisburg.

Hamilakis, Y. 2014. *Archaeology and the Senses: Human Experience, Memory, and Affect*. Cambridge.

Hands, A. R. 1968. *Charities and Social Aid in Greece and Rome*. Ithaca.

Hänninen, M.-L. 1999. "Juno Regina and the Roman Matrons." In *Female Networks and the Public Sphere in Roman Society*, edited by P. Setälä and L. Savunen, 39–52. Rome.

Hansen, M. H., and T. Fischer-Hansen. 1994. "Monumental Political Architecture in Archaic and Classical Greek *poleis*: Evidence and Historical Significance." In *From Political Architecture to Stephanus Byzantius: Sources for the Ancient Greek Polis*, edited by D. Whitehead, 23–90. Stuttgart.

Hansen, M. H., and T. H. Nielsen, eds. 2004. *An Inventory of Archaic and Classical* poleis: *An Investigation Conducted by the Copenhagen Polis Centre for the Danish National Research Foundation*. Oxford.

Hanson, J. A. 1959a. "Plautus as a Source Book for Roman Religion." *TAPA* 90: 48–101.

———. 1959b. *Roman Theater-Temples*. Princeton.

Hanson, J. W. 2016. *An Urban Geography of the Roman World, 100 BC to AD 300*. Oxford.

Harder, A., ed. and trans. 2012. *Callimachus*: Aetia. *Introduction, Text, Translation, and Commentary*. 2 vols. Oxford.

Hardie, A. 2016. "The Camenae in Cult, History, and Song." *CA* 35, no. 1: 45–85.

Harmon, D. P. 1978a. "The Family Festivals of Rome." *ANRW* 2.16.2: 1592–1603.

———. 1978b. "The Public Festivals of Rome." *ANRW* 2.16.2: 1440–68.

Harris, W. V. 1979. *War and Imperialism in Republican Rome, 327–70 BC*. Oxford.

———. 2013. "Defining and Detecting Mediterranean Deforestation, 800 BCE to 700 CE." In *The Ancient Mediterranean Environment between Science and History*, edited by W. V. Harris, 173–94. Leiden.

———. 2016. *Roman Power: A Thousand Years of Empire*. Cambridge.

Hartman, S. V. 1997. *Scenes of Subjection: Terror, Slavery, and Self-Making in Nineteenth-Century America*. New York.

Hartnett, J. 2017. *The Roman Street: Urban Life and Society in Pompeii, Herculaneum, and Rome*. New York.

Harvey, P., Jr., and P. H. Baldi. 2002. "*Populus*: A Reevaluation." In *Proceedings of the Thirteenth*

Annual UCLA Indo-European Conference, edited by K. Jones-Bley et al., 145–64. Washington, DC.

Hasenohr, C. 2003. "Les Compitalia à Délos." *BCH* 127, no. 1: 167–249.

Hawkins, C. 2016. *Roman Artisans and the Urban Economy*. Cambridge.

Headlam, W., and A. D. Knox, eds. 1966. *Herodas:* The Mimes *and Fragments*. Cambridge.

Herring, E. 2007. "Daunians, Peucetians, and Messapians? Societies and Settlements in South-East Italy." In *Ancient Italy: Regions without Boundaries*, edited by G. Bradley, E. Isayev, and C. Riva, 269–94. Exeter.

Hin, S. 2008. "Counting Romans." In *People, Land, and Politics: Demographic Developments and the Transformation of Roman Italy, 300 BC–AD 14*, edited by L. de Ligt and S. J. Northwood, 187–238. Leiden.

———. 2013. *The Demography of Roman Italy: Population Dynamics in an Ancient Conquest Society, 201 BCE–14 CE*. Cambridge.

Hobbes, T. [1651] 1994. *Leviathan, with Selected Variants from the Latin Edition of 1658*. Edited by E. Curley. Indianapolis.

Hocart, A. M. [1936] 1970. *Kings and Councillors: An Essay in the Comparative Anatomy of Human Society*. Chicago.

Hodge, A. Trevor. 2002. *Roman Aqueducts and Water* Supply.[2] London.

Hoffman, P. T. 2017. "Public Economics and History: A Review of *Fiscal Regimes and the Political Economy of Premodern States*, edited by Andrew Monson and Walter Scheidel." *Journal of Economic Literature* 55, no. 4: 1556–69.

Hölkeskamp, K.-J. [1987] 2011. *Die Entstehung der Nobilität. Studien zur sozialen und politischen Geschichte der Römischen Republik im 4. Jhdt. v.Chr*[2]. Stuttgart.

———. 1993. "Conquest, Competition, and Consensus: Roman Expansion in Italy and the Rise of the *nobilitas*." *Historia* 42, no. 1: 12–39.

———. 2000. "*Fides—deditio in fidem—dextra data et accepta*: Recht, Religion, und Ritual in Rom." In *The Roman Middle Republic: Politics, Religion, and Historiography, c. 400–133 BC*, edited by C. Bruun, 223–50. Rome.

———. 2006. "History and Collective Memory in the Middle Republic." In *A Companion to the Roman Republic*, edited by N. Rosenstein and R. Morstein-Marx, 478–95. Malden.

———. 2010. *Reconstructing the Roman Republic: An Ancient Political Culture and Modern Research*. Translated by H. Heitmann-Gordon. Princeton.

———. 2011. "The Roman Republic as Theatre of Power: The Consuls as Leading Actors." In *Consuls and* res publica: *Holding High Office in the Roman Republic*, edited by H. Beck, A. Duplá, M. Jehne, and F. Pina Polo, 161–81. Cambridge.

———. 2015. "In the Web of (Hi-)stories: *Memoria*, Monuments, and Their Myth-Historical 'Interconnectedness.'" In *Memory in Ancient Rome and Early Christianity*, edited by K. Galinsky, 169–213. Oxford.

———. 2017. Libera res publica: *Die politische Kultur des antiken Rom—Positionen und Perspektiven*. Stuttgart.

———. 2018. Untitled Review: W. V. Harris, *Roman Power: A Thousand Years of Empire*. *Gnomon* 90, no. 5: 436–44.

Holland, L. L. 2008. "*Diana feminarum tutela?* The Cause of *noutrix Paperia*." *Studies in Latin Literature and Roman History* 14: 95–114.

Hollard, V. 2010. *Rituel du vote: Les assemblées romaines du peuple*. Paris.

Holliday, P. J. 2002. *The Origins of Roman Historical Commemoration in the Visual Arts*. Cambridge.

Holloway, R. R. 1994. *The Archaeology of Early Rome and Latium*. London.

Holt, J. M. 2009. "Rethinking the Ramey State: Was Cahokia the Center of a Theater State?" *American Antiquity* 74, no. 2: 231–54.

Hope, V. M. 2003. "Trophies and Tombstones: Commemorating the Roman Soldier." *World Archaeology* 35, no. 1: 79–97.

Hopkins, J. N. 2016. *The Genesis of Roman Architecture*. New Haven.

Hopkins, K. 1978. *Conquerors and Slaves*. Sociological Studies in Roman History 1. Cambridge.

———. 1983. *Death and Renewal*. Sociological Studies in Roman History 2. Cambridge.

Horden, P. 2000. "Ritual and Public Health in the Early Medieval City." In *Body and City: Histories of Urban Public Health*, edited by S. Sheard and H. Power, 17–40. Aldershot. = 2008. *Hospitals and Healing from Antiquity to the Later Middle Ages*, chap. 3. Aldershot.

Horden, P., and N. Purcell. 2000. *The Corrupting Sea: A Study of Mediterranean History*. Malden.

Hornblower, S., ed. and trans. 2015. *Lykophron:* Alexandra; *Greek Text, Translation, Commentary, and Introduction*. Oxford.

———. 2018. *Lykophron's* Alexandra, *Rome, and the Hellenistic World*. Oxford.

Horsfall, N. 2003. *The Culture of the Roman* Plebs. London.

Hoyer, D. C. 2012. "Samnite Economy and the Competitive Environment of Italy in the Fifth to Third Centuries BC." In *Processes of Integration and Identity Formation in the Roman Republic*, edited by S. Roselaar, 179–96. Leiden.

Hrychuk Kontokosta, A. 2013. "Reconsidering the Arches (*fornices*) of the Roman Republic." *JRA* 26: 7–35.

Hülsemann, M. 1987. *Theater, Kult und bürgerlicher Widerstand im antiken Rom. Die Entstehung der architektonischen Struktur des römischen Theaters im Rahmen der gesellschaftlichen Auseinandersetzung zur Zeit der Republik*. Frankfurt am Main.

Hughes, J. 2017a. " 'Souvenirs of the Self': Personal Belongings as Votive Offerings in Ancient Religion." *RRE* 3: 181–201.

———. 2017b. *Votive Body Parts in Greek and Roman Religion*. Cambridge.

Humm, M. 2005. *Appius Claudius Caecus: La République accomplie*. Rome.

———. 2014. "Espaces comitiaux et contraintes augurales à Rome pendant la période républicaine." *Ktema* 39: 315–45.

———. 2016. "Timée de Tauromenium et 'la découverte de Rome' par l'historiographie grecque des IVe et IIIe siècles." In *Les premiers temps de Rome, VIe IIIe siècles av. J.-C. La fabrique d'une histoire*, edited by B. Mineo and T. Piel, 87–110. Rennes.

Hunt, Y. 2009. "Roman Pantomime Libretti and Their Greek Themes: The Role of Augustus in the Romanization of the Greek Classics." In *New Directions in Ancient Pantomime*, edited by E. Hall and R. Wyles, 169–84. Oxford.

Huss, W. 1994. *Der makedonische König und die ägyptischen Priester. Studien zur Geschichte des ptolemaiischen Ägypten*. Stuttgart.

Hutchinson, G. O. 1988. *Hellenistic Poetry*. Oxford.

Iacobone, C. 1988. *Le stipi votive di Taranto (Scavi 1885–1934)*. Rome.

Iannaccone, L. R. 1991. "The Consequences of Religious Market Structure: Adam Smith and the Economics of Religion." *Rationality and Society* 3: 156–77.

———. 1998. "Introduction to the Economics of Religion." *Journal of Economic Literature* 36: 1465–96.

Isayev, E. 2017a. "Citizens among Outsiders in Plautus's Roman Cosmopolis: A Moment of Change." In *Citizens in the Graeco-Roman World: Aspects of Citizenship from the Archaic Period to 212 AD*, edited by L. Cecchet and A. Busetto, 135–55. Leiden.

———. 2017b. *Migration, Mobility, and Place in Ancient Italy*. Cambridge.

Itgenshorst, T. 2005. Tota illa pompa: *Der Triumph in der römischen Republik*. Göttingen.

Jackson, M. D., and C. K. Kosso. 2013. "*Scientia* in Republican Era Stone and Concrete Masonry." In *A Companion to the Archaeology of the Roman Republic*, edited by J. D. Evans, 268–84. Malden.

Jackson, M. D., F. Marra, R. L. Hay, C. Cawood, and E. M. Winkler. 2005. "The Judicious Selection and Preservation of Tuff and Travertine Building Stone in Ancient Rome." *Archaeometry* 47, no. 3: 485–510.

Jacobs, P. W., II, and D. Atnally Conlin. 2014. *Campus Martius: The Field of Mars in the Life of Ancient Rome*. Cambridge.

Jacoby, F. 1944. "ΓΕΝΕΣΙΑ. A Forgotten Festival of the Dead." CQ 38, no. 3–4: 65–75.

Jaia, A. M., and M. C. Molinari. 2012. "Il santuario di *Sol Indiges* e il sistema di controllo della costa laziale nel III sec. a.C." In *Lazio e Sabina 8. Atti del Convegno: Ottavo incontro di studi sul Lazio e la Sabina*, edited by G. Ghini and Z. Mari, 373–83.

Jannot, J.-R. 2005. *Religion in Ancient Etruria*. Translated by J. Whitehead. Madison.

Jehne, M. 2001. "Integrationsrituale in der römischen Republik. Zur einbindenden Wirkung der Volksversammlungen." In *Integrazione mescolanza rifiuto: Incontri di popoli, lingue e culture in Europa dall'antichità all'umanesimo. Atti del convegno internazionale, Cividale del Friuli, 21–23 settembre 2000*, 89–113. Rome.

———. 2006. "Römer, Latiner und Bundesgenossen im Krieg. Zu Formen und Ausmaß der Integration in der republikanischen Armee." In *Herrschaft ohne Integration? Rom und Italien in republikanischer Zeit*, edited by M. Jehne and R. Pfeilschifter, 243–67. Frankfurt.

———. 2011. "The Rise of the Consular as a Social Type in the Third and Second Centuries BC." In *Consuls and* Res Publica: *Holding High Office in the Roman Republic*, edited by H. Beck, A. Duplá, M. Jehne, and F. Pina Polo, 211–31. Cambridge.

———. 2013. "Der römische Senat als Hüter des Gemeinsinns." In *Gemeinsinn und Gemeinwohl in der römischen Antike*, edited by M. Jehne and C. Lundgreen, 23–50. Stuttgart.

Jehne, M., and R. Pfeilschifter, eds. 2006. *Herrschaft ohne Integration? Rom und Italien in republikanischer Zeit*. Frankfurt.

Jenkyns, R. 2013. *God, Space, and City in the Roman Imagination*. Oxford.

Jessen, B. 1975. "Ein neues Fragment eines *pocolom* mit Inschrift." *Hefte des archäologischen Seminars der Universität Bern* 1: 25–35.

Jew, D. In progress. *Agriculture and Carrying Capacity in Classical Athens: Modelling Historical Uncertainty*.

Jewell, E. 2019. "(Re)moving the Masses: Colonisation as Domestic Displacement in the

Roman Republic." In *Displacement and the Humanities: Manifestos from the Ancient to the Present*, edited by E. Isayev and E. Jewell. *Humanities* 8, no. 66: doi: 10.3390/h8020066.

Jocelyn, H. D., ed. 1969. *The Tragedies of Ennius: The Fragments*. Cambridge.

———. 1984. "Anti-Greek Elements in Plautus' *Menaechmi?*" *PLLS* 4: 1–25.

———. 2001. "Gods, Cult, and Cultic Language in Plautus' *Epidicus*." In *Studien zu Plautus'* Epidicus, edited by U. Auhagen, 261–96. Tübingen.

Jones, A.H.M. 1940. *The Greek City from Alexander to Justinian*. Oxford.

Jory, E. J. 1970. "Associations of Actors at Rome." *Hermes* 98, no. 2: 224–53.

Joshel, S., and L. Hackworth Petersen. 2014. *The Material Life of Roman Slaves*. New York.

Kaimio, J. 1975. "The Ousting of Etruscan by Latin in Etruria." In *Studies in the Romanization of Etruria*, edited by P. Bruun, 85–246. Rome.

Kajanto, I., U. Nyberg, and M. Steinby. 1981. "Le iscrizioni." In *L'area sacra di Largo Argentina* 1, 83–99. Rome.

Kantner, J., and K. J. Vaughn. 2012. "Pilgrimage as Costly Signal: Religiously Motivated Cooperation in Chaco and Nasca." *JAA* 31: 66–82.

Kaster, R., ed. and trans. 2011. *Macrobius*: Saturnalia. Cambridge, MA.

Kaster, R., and D. Konstan. 2016. "The Thought-World of Ancient Rome: A Delicate Balancing Act." In *The Adventure of the Human Intellect: Self, Society, and the Divine in Ancient World Cultures*, edited by K. A. Raaflaub, 149–66. Chichester.

Kay, P. 2014. *Rome's Economic Revolution*. Oxford.

Keay, S., and N. Terrenato, eds. 2001. *Italy and the West: Comparative Issues in Romanization*. Oxford.

Ker, J. 2010. "*Nundinae*: The Culture of the Roman Week." *Phoenix* 64, no. 3–4: 360–85.

Kiernan, P. 2012. "Pagan Pilgrimage in Rome's Western Provinces." *HEROM: Journal on Hellenistic and Roman Material Culture* 1: 79–106.

Killgrove, K. 2013. "Biohistory of the Roman Republic: The Potential of Isotope Analysis of Human Skeletal Remains." *European Journal of Post-Classical Archaeologies* 3: 41–62.

Kiser, E., and M. Levi. 2015. "Interpreting the Comparative History of Fiscal Regimes." In *Fiscal Regimes and the Political Economy of Premodern States*, edited by A. Monson and W. Scheidel, 557–71. Oxford.

Klar, L. S. 2006. "The Origins of the Roman *scaenae frons* and the Architecture of Triumphal Games in the Second Century BC." In *Representations of War in Ancient Rome*, edited by S. Dillon and K. E. Welch, 162–83. Cambridge.

Kleinman, B. 2018. "Scandals and Sanctions: Holding Roman Officials Accountable (202–49 BC)." PhD diss., Princeton University.

Knappett, C. 2011. *An Archaeology of Interaction: Network Perspectives on Material Culture and Society*. Oxford.

Koeppel, G., and E. Künzl. 2002. *Souvenirs und Devotionalien. Zeugnisse des geschäftlichen, religiösen und kulturellen Tourismus im antiken Römerreich*. Mainz am Rhein.

Kolb, A. 1993. *Die kaiserliche Bauverwaltung in der Stadt Rom. Geschichte und Aufbau der* cura operum publicorum *unter dem Prinzipat*. Stuttgart.

Kolb, F. 1981. *Agora und Theater: Volks- und Festversammlung*. Berlin.

Kolendo, J. 1994. "La religion des esclaves dans le *De agricultura* de Caton." In *Religion et anthro-*

pologie de l'esclavage et des formes de dépendance, edited by J. Annequin and M. Garrido-Hory, 267–74. Besançon.

Kondratieff, E. 2004. "The Column and Coinage of C. Duilius: Innovations in Iconography in Large and Small Media in the Middle Republic." *SCI* 23: 1–40.

———. 2010. "The Urban Praetor's Tribunal in the Roman Republic." In *Spaces of Justice in the Roman World*, edited by F. de Angelis, 89–126. Leiden.

Konstan, D. 1983. *Roman Comedy*. Ithaca.

Konstan, D., and S. Raval. 2018. "Comic Violence and the Citizen Body." In *Texts and Violence in the Roman World*, edited by M. R. Gale and J.H.D. Scourfield, 44–62. Cambridge.

Koolhaas, R. 1995. *S, M, L, XL*. New York.

Koput, K. W. 2010. *Social Capital: An Introduction to Managing Networks*. Cheltenham.

Kosmin, P. J. 2018. *Time and Its Adversaries in the Seleucid Empire*. Cambridge, MA.

Köster, I. 2013. "The Religious Life of Roman Plunder." Paper delivered at the Midwest Consortium on Ancient Religions, University of Michigan.

Köstner, E. 2019. "*Triumphans Romam redit*: Rom als Bühne für eine kommemorative Prozession." *Hermes* 147, no. 1: 21–41.

Kowalzig, B. 2005. "Mapping Out *Communitas*: Performances of *Theōria* in Their Sacred and Political Context." In *Pilgrimage in Graeco-Roman and Early Christian Antiquity: Seeing the Gods*, edited by J. Elsner and I. Rutherford, 41–72. Oxford.

———. 2018. "Cults, Cabotage, and Connectivity: Experimenting with Religious and Economic Networks in the Greco-Roman Mediterranean." In *Maritime Networks in the Ancient Mediterranean World*, edited by J. Leidwanger and C. Knappett, 93–131. Cambridge.

Kraemer, R. S. 1992. *Her Share of the Blessings: Women's Religions among Pagans, Jews, and Christians in the Greco-Roman World*. New York.

Krautheimer, R. 1983. *Rome, Profile of a City, 312–1308*.[2] Princeton.

Kristensen, T. M. 2012. "The Material Culture of Roman and Early Christian Pilgrimage: An Introduction." *HEROM: Journal on Hellenistic and Roman Material Culture* 1: 67–78.

———. 2018. "Mobile Situations: *Exedrae* as Stages of Gathering in Greek Sanctuaries." *World Archaeology*: https://doi.org/10.1080/00438243.2018.1488608.

Kristensen, T. M., and B. Poulsen, eds. 2012. *Ateliers and Artisans in Roman Art and Archaeology*. Portsmouth.

Kudlien, F. 1979. *Der griechische Arzt im Zeitalter des Hellenismus: Seine Stellung in Staat und Gesellschaft*. Mainz.

———. 1986. *Die Stellung des Arztes in der römischen Gesellschaft: Freigeborene Römer, Eingebürgerte, Peregrine, Sklaven, Freigelassene als Ärzte*. Stuttgart.

Kuttner, A. L. [2004] 2014. "Roman Art during the Republic." In *The Cambridge Companion to the Roman Republic*[2], edited by H. I. Flower, 348–76. Cambridge.

Lacam, J.-C. 2010. *Variations rituelles: Les pratiques religieuses en Italie centrale et méridionale au temps de la deuxième guerre punique*. Rome.

Laird, M. L. 2016. "Diversity in Architecture and Urbanism." In *A Companion to Roman Italy*, edited by A. Cooley, 181–216. Chichester.

Lambert, C., and P. Pedemonte Demeglio. 1994. "Ampolle devozioni ed itinerari di pellegrinaggio tra IV e VII secolo." *Antiquité tardive* 21: 205–31.

Lambert, M. 2001. "Gender and Religion in Theocritus, *Idyll* 15: Prattling Tourists at the *Adonia*." *Acta Classica* 44: 87–103.

Lanauro, A. 2011. *Peasants and Slaves: The Rural Population of Roman Italy (200 BC to AD 100)*. Cambridge.

Lancaster, L. C., and R. B. Ulrich. 2014. "Materials and Techniques." In *A Companion to Roman Architecture*, edited by R. B. Ulrich and C. K. Quenemoen, 157–92. Chichester.

Lancel, S. 1995. *Carthage: A History*. Translated by A. Nevill. Oxford.

Lanciani, R. A. 1893. *Pagan and Christian Rome*. Boston.

———. 1897. *The Ruins and Excavations of Ancient Rome: A Companion Book for Students and Travelers*. London.

La Penna, A. 2000. "Le *Sabinae* di Ennio e il tema della concordia nella tragedia arcaica latina." In *Identität und Alterität in der frührömischen Tragödie*, edited by G. Manuwald, 241–54. Würzburg.

La Rocca, E. 2010. "La maestà degli dèi come apparizione teatrale." In *I giorni di Roma: L'età della conquista*, edited by E. La Rocca, C. Parisi Presicce, and A. Lo Monaco, 95–114. Rome.

Laser, G. 1997. Populo et scaenae serviendum est: *Die Bedeutung der städtischen Masse in der späten römischen Republik*. Trier.

Laurence, R. 1999. *The Roads of Roman Italy: Mobility and Cultural Change*. London.

Lauter, H. 1976. "Die hellenistische Theater der Samniten und Latiner in ihrer Beziehung zur Theaterarchitektur der Griechen." In *Hellenismus in Mittelitaliens*, edited by P. Zanker, 413–25. Göttingen.

Lavan, M. 2013. *Slaves to Rome: Paradigms of Empire in Roman Culture*. Cambridge.

———. 2016. "The Spread of Roman Citizenship, 14–212 CE: Quantification in the Face of High Uncertainty." *Past and Present* 230: 3–46.

Leach, E. 2010. "Fortune's Extremities: Q. Lutatius Catulus and Largo Argentina Temple B; a Roman Consular and His Monument." *MAAR* 55: 111–34.

Le Gall, J. 1953. *Recherches sur le culte du Tibre*. Paris.

Le Guen, B., ed. 1997. *De la scène aux gradins: Théâtre et représentations dramatiques après Alexandre le Grand*. Toulouse.

Lehmler, C. 2005. *Syrakus unter Agathokles und Hieron II: Die Verbindung von Kultur und Macht in einer hellenistischen Metropole*. Frankfurt am Main.

Leigh, M. 2004. *Comedy and the Rise of Rome*. Oxford.

———. 2010. "Early Roman Epic and the Maritime Moment." *CPh* 105, no. 3: 265–80.

Lennon, J. J. 2015. "*Victimarii* in Roman Religion and Society." *PBSR* 83: 65–89.

Lepore, E. 1952. "Per la storia economico-sociale di Neapolis." *Parola del Passato* 7: 300–332.

Lerouxel, F. 2017. "L'Italie républicaine est-elle encore au centre de l'histoire économique romaine?" *REA* 119, no. 1: 197–207.

Levene, D. S. 1993. *Religion in Livy*. Leiden.

———. 2010. *Livy on the Hannibalic War*. Oxford.

Levi, M. 1988. *Of Rule and Revenue*. Berkeley.

Lewis, K., J. Kaufman, M. Gonzalez, A. Wimmer, and N. Christakis. 2008. "Tastes, Ties, and Time: A New Social Network Dataset Using Facebook.com." *Social Networks* 30: 330–42.

Lewis, M. E. 2015. "Public Spaces in Cities in the Roman and Han Empires." In *State Power in Ancient China and Rome*, edited by W. Scheidel, 204–29. Oxford.

Liebeschuetz, J.H.W.G. 2009. "The Religious Position of Livy's *History*." In *Oxford Readings in Classics: Livy*, edited by J. Chaplin and C. S. Kraus, 355–79. Oxford. = 1967. *JRS* 57, no. 1–2: 45–55.

Lightfoot, J. L. 2002. "Nothing to Do with the *Technītai* of Dionysus?" In *Greek and Roman Actors: Aspects of an Ancient Profession*, edited by P. Easterling and E. Hall, 209–24. Cambridge.

Linderski, J. 1986. "The Augural Law." *ANRW* II.16.3: 2146–312.

———. 2002. "The Pontiff and the Tribune: The Death of Tiberius Gracchus." *Athenaeum* 90: 339–66. = 2007. *Roman Questions II. Selected Papers*, 88–114. Stuttgart.

Linke, B. 2000. "*Religio* und *res publica*: Religiöser Glaube und gesellschaftliches Handeln im republikanischen Rom." In *Mos maiorum: Untersuchungen zu den Formen der Identitätstiftung und Stabilisierung in der römischen Republik*, edited by B. Linke and M. Stemmler, 269–98. Stuttgart.

———. 2013. "Die Einheit nach der Vielfalt: Die religiöse Dimension des römische Hegemonialanspruches in Latium (5.–3. Jahrhundert v. Chr.)." In *Religiöse Vielfalt und soziale Integration: Die Bedeutung der Religion für die kulturelle Identität und politische Stabilität im republikanische Italien*, edited by M. Jehne, B. Linke, and J. Rüpke, 69–94. Heidelberg.

Lintott, A. W. 1999. *The Constitution of the Roman Republic*. Oxford.

Lippolis, E. 2011. "Taranto nel IV secolo a.C." In *Krise und Wandel: Süditalien im 4. und 3. Jahrhundert v. Chr.*, edited by R. Neudecker, 121–45. Rome.

———. 2016. "La città in Italia tra modelli ellenistici e politica romana." In *E pluribus unum? L'Italie, de la diversité préromaine à l'unité augustéenne*. Vol. 2: *L'Italie centrale e la creazione di una koiné culturale? I percorsi della "romanizzazione,"* edited by M. Aberson, M. C. Biella, M. Di Fazio, P. Sánchez, and M. Wullschleger, 201–48. Bern.

Lo Monaco, A. 2016. "Wreaths, Shields, and Old Statues: Roman Magistrates in Sanctuaries of Greece." In *Hellenistic Sanctuaries: Between Greece and Rome*, edited by M. Melfi and O. Bobou, 206–27. Oxford.

Lomas, K. 1993. *Rome and the Western Greeks, 350 BC–AD 200: Conquest and Acculturation in Southern Italy*. London.

———. 2012. "The Weakest Link: Elite Social Networks in Republican Italy." In *Processes of Integration and Identity Formation in the Roman Republic*, edited by S. T. Roselaar, 197–214. Leiden.

———. 2018. *The Rise of Rome: From the Iron Age to the Punic Wars*. Cambridge, MA.

Loomis, W. T. 1998. *Wages, Welfare Costs, and Inflation in Classical Athens*. Ann Arbor.

Lott, J. B. 2004. *The Neighborhoods of Augustan Rome*. Cambridge.

Luce, T. J. 1990. "Livy, Augustus, and the Forum Augustum." In *Between Republic and Empire: Interpretations of Augustus and His Principate*, edited by K. A. Raaflaub and M. Toher, 123–38. Berkeley.

Luke, T. S . 2014. *Ushering in a New Republic: Theologies of Arrival at Rome in the First Century BCE*. Ann Arbor.

Lulof, P. S. 2014. "Reconstructing a Golden Age in Temple Construction: Temples and Roofs from the Last Tarquin to the Roman Republic (c. 530–480 B.C.) in Rome, Etruria, and Latium." In *Papers on Italian Urbanism in the First Millennium B.C.*, edited by E. C. Robinson, 113–25. Portsmouth.

Lundgreen, C. 2011. *Regelkonflikte in der römischen Republik: Geltung und Gewichtung von Normen in politischen Entscheidungsprozessen*. Stuttgart.

———, ed. 2014. *Staatlichkeit in Rom? Diskurse und Praxis (in) der römischen Republik*. Stuttgart.

Ma, J. 1999. *Antiochus III and the Cities of Asia Minor*. Oxford.

———. 2003. "Peer Polity Interaction in the Hellenistic Age." *Past and Present* 180: 9–39.

MacBain, B. 1982. *Prodigy and Expiation: A Study in Religion and Politics in Republican Rome*. Brussels.

Machiavelli, N. [1517] 1983. *Discourses on the First Ten Books of Titus Livius*. Edited by B. Crick. Translated by L. J. Walker, S.J. (rev. B. Richardson). London.

Mackey, J. 2009. "Rethinking Roman Religion: Action, Practice, and Belief." PhD diss., Princeton University.

———. 2017. "*Das Erlöschen des Glaubens*: The Fate of Belief in the Study of Roman Religion." *Phasis* 20: 83–150.

———. 2018. " 'Textualizing' Roman Religious Practices." *JRA* 31, no. 2: 618–25.

MacRae, D. 2016. *Legible Religion: Books, Gods, and Rituals in Roman Culture*. Cambridge, MA.

Malkin, I. 2011. *A Small Greek World: Networks in the Ancient Mediterranean*. Oxford.

Malkin, I., C. Constantakopoulou, and K. Panagopoulou, eds. 2009. *Greek and Roman Networks in the Mediterranean*. London.

Manconi, D., and M. C. De Angelis. 1987. "Il santuario di Ancarano di Norcia." *Dialoghi di Archeologia* 3, no. 5: 17–28.

Mann, M. [1984] 1986. "The Autonomous Power of the State: Its Origins, Mechanisms, and Results." In *States in History*, edited by J. A. Hall, 109–36. Oxford. Orig. pub. *Archives européennes de sociologie* 25: 185–213.

Manuwald, G., ed. 2000. *Identität und Alterität in der frührömischen Tragödie*. Würzburg.

———. 2011. *Roman Republican Theatre*. Cambridge.

Maras, D. 2018a. "Dancing Myths: Musical Performances with Mythological Subjects from Greece to Etruria." In *The Study of Musical Performance in Antiquity: Archaeology and Written Sources*, edited by A. Garcia-Ventura, C. Tavolieri, and L. Verderame, 137–53. Newcastle upon Tyne.

———. 2018b. "Kings and Tablemates: The Political Role of Comrade Associations in Archaic Rome and Etruria." In *Beiträge zur Sozialgeschichte der Etrusker. Akten der internationalen Tagung, Wien, 8.–10.6.2016*, edited by L. Aigner-Foresti and P. Amann, 1–108. Vienna.

Marcattili, F. 2010. "Per un'archeologia dell'Aventino: I culti della media Repubblica." *MEFRA* 124, no. 1: 109–22.

Marconi, C. 2012. "Between Performance and Identity: The Social Context of Stone Theaters in Late Classical and Hellenistic Sicily." In *Theater Outside Athens: Drama in Greek Sicily and South Italy*, edited by K. Bosher, 175–207. Cambridge.

Marmorale, E. V., ed. 1950. Naevius poeta: *Introduzione bibliografica, testo dei frammenti e commento.*[2] Florence.

Marshall, C. W. 2006. *The Stagecraft and Performance of Roman Comedy*. Cambridge.

Marsili, F. 2018. *Heaven Is Empty: A Cross-Cultural Approach to "Religion" and Empire in Ancient China*. Albany.

Martini, C. 1990. *Il deposito votivo del Tempio di Minerva Medica*. Rome.

Marzano, A. 2009. "Hercules and the Triumphal Feast for the Roman People." In *Transforming Historical Landscapes in the Ancient Empires: Proceedings of the First Workshop, December 16–19th 2007*, edited by B. Antela-Bernárdez and T. Ñaco del Hoyo, 83–97. Oxford.

Maschek, D. 2016a. "The Marble Stoa at Hierapolis: Materials, Labour Force, and Building Costs." In *Ancient Quarries and Building Sites in Asia Minor*, edited by T. Ismaelli and G. Scardozzi, 393–402. Bari.

———. 2016b. "Zwischen Stabilität und Kollaps: Mittelitalische Elitenkultur und die 'Krise' der römischen Republik." In *Elite und Krise in antiken Gesellschaften / Élites et crises dans les sociétés antiques*, edited by L. Gilhaus, S. Kirsch, I. Mossong, F. Reich, and S. Wirz, 59–81. Stuttgart.

Maskarinec, M. 2017. *City of Saints: Rebuilding Rome in the Early Middle Ages*. Philadelphia.

Massa-Pairault, F.-H. 1992. *Iconologia e politica nell'Italia antica: Roma, Lazio, Etruria dal VII a I secolo a.C.* Milan.

Massimilla, G., ed. and trans. 2010. Aitia: *Libro terzo e quarto*. Callimaco: *Introduzione, testo critico, traduzione e commento*. Pisa.

Mathé, V. 2017. "Quand un dieu s'installe: La monumentalisation du sanctuaire d'Asklépios à Épidaure (IVe–IIIe siècles av. J.-C.)." In *Quand naissent les dieux. Fondation des sanctuaires antiques: Motivations, agents, lieux*, edited by S. Agusta-Boularot, S. Huber, and W. Van Andringa, 135–49.

Mauss, M. 1923–24. "Essai sur le don: Forme et raison de l'échange dans les sociétés archaïques." *Année Sociologique* 2, no. 1.

McCarty, C., P. D. Killworth, H. R. Bernard, E. C. Johnsen, and G. A. Shelley. 2001. "Comparing Two Methods for Estimating Network Size." *Human Organization* 60, no. 1: 28–39.

McCleary, R. M., and R. J. Barro. 2019. *The Wealth of Religions: The Political Economy of Believing and Belonging*. Princeton.

McCorriston, J. 2017. "Inter-cultural Pilgrimage, Identity, and the Axial Age in the Ancient Near East." In *Excavating Pilgrimage: Archaeological Approaches to Sacred Travel and Movement in the Ancient World*, edited by T. M. Kristensen and W. Friese, 11–27. London.

McDonough, C. M. 2004. "The Christian in the Ancient Meat Market: Neglected Evidence for the Pricing of Idol Meat." *Sewanee Theological Review* 47, no. 3: 278–89 = In C. F. Konrad, ed. Augusto augurio: Rerum humanarum et divinarum commentationes in honorem Jerzy Linderski, 69–76. Stuttgart.

McGing, B. C. 2010. *Polybius' Histories*. New York.

McKenzie, J. 2007. *The Architecture of Alexandria and Egypt, c. 300 BC to AD 700*. New Haven.

Meadows, A., and J. Williams. 2001. "Moneta and the Monuments: Coinage and Politics in Republican Rome." *JRS* 91: 27–49.

Medina Quintana, S. 2017. "El trabajo de las mujeres en la Roma Antigua: Reflexiones sobre género y economía." *Dialogues d'histoire ancienne* 43, no. 2: 153–76.

Meier, L. 2012. *Die Finanzierung öffentlicher Bauten in der hellenistischen Polis*. Berlin.

Melliti, K. 2006. "Religion et hellénisme à Carthage: La politique aristocratique à l'épreuve." *Pallas* 70: 381–94.

———. 2010. "Religion, politique et hellénisme à Carthage: Approches historiques." *Semitica et Classica* 3: 91–98.

———. 2016. *Carthage: Histoire d'une métropole méditerranéenne*. Paris.

Ménard, H. 2006. "Un aspect de la *custodia templorum*: Les *aeditui*." In *Pouvoir et religion dans le monde romain*, edited by A. Vigourt, X. Loriot, A. Bérenger-Badel, and B. Klein, 231–43. Paris.

Meister, J. B. 2013. "*Adventus* und *Profectio*: Aristokratisches Prestige, Bindungswesen und Raumkonzepte im republikanischen und frühkaiserzeitlichen Rom." *MH* 70: 33–56.

Merry, S. E. 2016. *The Seductions of Quantification: Measuring Human Rights, Gender Violence, and Sex Trafficking*. Chicago.

Miano, D. 2012. "*Moneta*: Sacred Memory in Mid-Republican Rome." In *Memory and Urban Religion in the Ancient World*, edited by M. Bommas, J. Harrison, and P. Roy, 90–109. London.

———. 2015. "Spreading Virtues in Republican Italy." In *Processes of Cultural Change and Integration in the Roman World*, edited by S. Roselaar, 253–77. Leiden.

———. 2018. *Fortuna: Deity and Concept in Archaic and Republican Italy*. Oxford.

Michels, A. K. 1967. *The Calendar of the Roman Republic*. Princeton.

Migeotte, L. 1984. *L'emprunt public dans les cités grecques*. Paris.

———. 1995. "Finances et constructions publiques." In *Stadtbild und Bürgerbild im Hellenismus*, edited by M. Wörrl and P. Zanker, 79–86. Munich.

———. 2014. *Les finances des cités grecques: Aux périodes classique et hellénistique*. Paris.

Mignone, L. M. 2016. *The Republican Aventine and Rome's Social Order*. Ann Arbor.

———. "Wohnintegration im republikanischen Rom." In *Politische Kultur und soziale Struktur der römischen Republik: Bilanzen und Perspektiven*, edited by M. Haake and A.-C. Harders, 231–53. Stuttgart.

Mikalson, J. D. 1975. *The Sacred and Civil Calendar of the Athenian State*. Princeton.

Miles, R. 2011. "Hannibal and Propaganda." In *A Companion to the Punic Wars*, edited by D. Hoyos, 260–79. Malden.

Millar, F. 1998. *The Crowd of Rome in the Late Republic*. Ann Arbor.

———. 2002. *Rome, the Greek World, and the East*. Vol. 1: *The Roman Republic and the Augustan Revolution*. Edited by H. M. Cotton and G. M. Rogers. Chapel Hill.

Miller, J. F. 1982. "Callimachus and the Augustan Aetiological Elegy." *ANRW* 2.30.1: 371–417.

Miller, J. F., and J. Strauss Clay, eds. 2019. *Tracking Hermes/Pursuing Mercury*. Oxford.

Minak, F. 2006a. "Addendum sui *pocola*." In *Ariminum: Storia e archeologia*, 239–40. Rome.

———. 2006b. "In margine ai *pocola*: Una nuova testimonianza, 1." In *Ariminum: Storia e archeologia*, 41–46. Rome.

Mitchell, R. E. 1973. "The Aristocracy of the Roman Republic." In *The Rich, the Well-Born, and the Powerful: Elites and Upper Classes in History*, edited by F. C. Jaher, 27–63. Urbana.

Moatti, C. 2018. Res publica: *Histoire romaine de la chose publique*. Paris.

Mogetta, M. 2015. "A New Date for Concrete in Rome." *JRS* 105: 1–40.

Momigliano, A. 1975a. *Alien Wisdom: The Limits of Hellenization*. Cambridge.

———. 1975b. "La città antica di Fustel de Coulanges." In A. Momigliano, *Quinto contributo alla storia degli studi classici e del mondo antico*, 159–78. Rome. = 1970. *Rivista storica italiana* 82, no. 1: 81–98.

———. 1975c. "Popular Religious Beliefs and the Late Roman Historians." In A. Momigliano, *Quinto contributo alla storia degli studi classici e del mondo antico*, 73–92. Rome. = 1971. *Studies in Church History* 8: 1–18. Cambridge.

———. 1977. "Athens in the Third Century BC and the Discovery of Rome in the *Histories* of Timaeus of Tauromenium." In *Essays in Ancient and Modern Historiography,* edited by A. Momigliano, 37-66. Middletown. = 1959. "Atene nel III secolo a.C. e la scoperta di Roma." *RSI* 71: 529–56.

———. 1980. "The Social Structure of the Ancient City." In A. Momigliano, *Sesto contributo alla storia degli studi classici e del mondo antico,* 459–70. Rome. = 1974. *Annali della Scuola Normale Superiore di Pisa* ser. III.4.2: 331–49.

Mommsen, T. 1859. *Die römische Chronologie bis auf Caesar*². Berlin.

———. 1879. *Römische Forschungen*². Berlin.

———. 1885. "Die römische Anfänge von Kauf und Miethe." *ZRG* 6: 260–75.

———. 1887–88. *Römisches Staatsrecht*³. Leipzig.

Monson, A. 2015. "Hellenistic Empires." In *Fiscal Regimes and the Political Economy of Premodern States,* edited by A. Monson and W. Scheidel, 169–207. Oxford.

Monson, A., and W. Scheidel, eds. 2015. *Fiscal Regimes and the Political Eeconomy of Premodern States.* Cambridge.

Moore, T. J. 1991. "*Palliata togata*: Plautus, *Curculio* 462–86." *AJP* 112, no. 3: 343–62.

Moormann, E. M. 2011. *Divine Interiors: Mural Paintings in Greek and Roman Sanctuaries.* Amsterdam.

Moralee, J. 2018. *Rome's Holy Mountain: The Capitoline Hill in Late Antiquity.* Oxford.

Morel, J.-P. 1969. "Etudes de céramique campanienne, 1: L'atelier des petites estampilles." *Mélanges d'archéologie et d'histoire* 81: 59–117.

———. 1981. *Céramique campanienne.* 2 vols. Rome.

———. 1987. "La topographie de l'artisanat et du commerce dans la Rome antique." In *L'urbs, espace urbain et histoire (1ᵉʳ siècle av. J.-C.–IIIᵉ siècle ap. J.-C.),* 127–55. Rome.

———. 1989–90. "Aspects économiques d'un sanctuaire (Fondo Ruozzo à Teano, Campanie)." In *Anathema: Regime delle offerte e vita dei santuari nel Mediterraneo antico,* edited by G. Bartoloni et al., 507–17. Rome.

———. 1991. "La romanisation du Samnium et de la Lucanie aux IVᵉ et IIIᵉ siècles av. J.-C. d'après l'artisanat et le commerce." In *Comunità indigene e problemi della romanizzazione nell'Italia centro-meridionale: IVᵉ–IIIᵉ sec. av. C.,* edited by J. Mertens and R. Lambrechts, 124–44.

———. 2007. "Early Rome and Italy." In *The Cambridge Economic History of the Greco-Roman World,* edited by W. Scheidel, I. Morris, and R. Saller, 487–510. Cambridge.

———. 2009. "Céramiques à vernis noir et histoire." *JRA* 22: 477–88.

Morgan, M. G. 1978. "The Introduction of the Aqua Marcia into Rome, 144–140 BC." *Philologus* 122: 25–58.

———. 1990. "Politics, Religion, and the Games in Rome, 200–150 BC." *Philologus* 134, no. 1: 14–36.

Morinis, A. 1992. "Introduction: The Territory of the Anthropology of Pilgrimage." In *Sacred Journeys: The Anthropology of Pilgrimage,* edited by A. Morinis, 1–28. Westport.

Morley, N. 1996. *Metropolis and Hinterland: The City of Rome and the Italian Economy, 200 BC–AD 200.* Cambridge.

———. 2014. "Orders of Magnitude, Margins of Error." In *Quantifying the Greco-Roman Economy and Beyond,* edited by F. de Callataÿ, 29–42. Bari.

Morris, I. 2003. "Mediterraneanization." *MHR* 18, no. 2: 30–55.

———. 2009. "The Greater Athenian State." In *The Dynamics of Ancient Empires: State Power from Assyria to Byzantium*, edited by I. Morris and W. Scheidel, 99–177. New York.

———. 2015. *Foragers, Farmers, and Fossil Fuels: How Human Values Evolve*. Edited by S. Macedo. With contributions from R. Seaford, J. D. Spence, C. M. Korsgaard, and M. Atwood. Princeton.

Morstein-Marx, R. 2004. *Mass Oratory and Political Power in the Late Roman Republic*. Cambridge.

Moser, C. 2017. "Differential Preservation: The Changing Religious Landscape at the Sacred Area of the Republican Temples at Ostia." In *Ritual Matters: Material Remains and Ancient Religion*, edited by C. Moser and J. Knust, 57–72. Ann Arbor.

———. 2019a. *The Altars of Republican Rome and Latium: Sacrifice and the Materiality of Roman Religion*. Cambridge.

———. 2019b. "Sacred Outreach: The Infrastructure of Port Sanctuaries in Republican Latium." *RRE* 5: 46–82.

Mouritsen, H. 2001. Plebs *and Politics in the Late Roman Republic*. Cambridge.

———. 2006. "Caius Gracchus and the *cives sine suffragio*." *Historia* 55, no. 4: 418–25.

Muccigrosso, J. D. 1998. "Factional Competition and Monumental Construction in Mid-Republican Rome." PhD diss., University of Michigan.

Mueller, H.-F. 2002. *Roman Religion in Valerius Maximus*. London.

Mulryan, M. 2011. "The Temple of Flora or Venus by the Circus Maximus and the New Christian Topography." In *The Archaeology of Late Antique Paganism*, edited by L. Lavan and M. Mulryan, 209–27. Leiden.

Mustakallio, K. 2013. Sive deus sive dea: *La presenza della religione nello sviluppo della società romana*. Edited by D. Puliga. Pisa.

Naiden, F. S. 2012a. "Blessèd Are the Parasites." In *Greek and Roman Animal Sacrifice: Ancient Victims, Modern Observers*, edited by C. A. Faraone and F. S. Naiden, 55–83. Cambridge.

———. 2012b. *Smoke Signals for the Gods: Ancient Greek Sacrifice from the Archaic through Roman Periods*. Oxford.

Nelsestuen, G. A. 2017. "Custom, Fear, and Self-Interest in the Political Thought of Polybius." *History of Political Thought* 38, no. 2: 213–38.

Newbold, R. F. 1982. "The Reporting of Earthquakes, Fires, and Floods by Ancient Historians." *Proceedings of the African Classical Associations* 16: 28–36.

Nichols, M. F. 2010. "Contemporary Perspectives on Luxury Building in Second-Century BC Rome." *PBSR* 78: 39–61.

———. 2017. *Author and Audience in Vitruvius'* De architectura. Cambridge.

Nicolet, C. 1976a. *Le métier de citoyen dans la Rome républicaine*. Paris.

———. 1976b. *Tributum: Recherches sur la fiscalité directe sous la république romaine*. Bonn.

———. 1980. *The World of the Citizen in Republican Rome*. Translated by P. S. Falla. Berkeley.

Nielsen, I. 2007. "Cultic Theatres and Ritual Drama in Ancient Rome." In Res Bene Gestae: *Ricerche di storia urbana su Roma antica in onore di Eva Margarita Steinby*, edited by A. Leone, D. Palombi, and S. Walker, 239–53. Rome.

———. 2014. *Housing the Chosen: The Architectural Context of Mystery Groups and Religious Associations in the Ancient World*. Turnhout.

Nielsen, I., and B. Poulsen. 1992. *The Temple of Castor and Pollux*. Vol. 1. Rome.

Nonnis, D. 2010. "Le iscrizioni vascolari latine da Populonia e da contesti sacri dell'Etruria tra media e tarda repubblica." In *Materiali per Populonia* 9, edited by G. Baratti and F. Fabiani, 123–42. Pisa.

———. 2016. "Appunti sugli *ex-voto* fittili con iscrizione dall'Italia repubblicana: A proposito di una dedica medio-repubblicana da Cales." In *Vestigia: Miscellanea di studi storico-religiosi in onore di Filippo Coarelli nel suo 80° anniversario*, edited by V. Gasparini, 349–66. Stuttgart.

North, D. C., J. J. Wallis, and B. R. Weingast. 2009. *Violence and Social Orders: A Conceptual Framework for Interpreting Recorded Human History*. Cambridge.

North, J. 1967. "The Inter-relation of State Religion and Politics in Roman Public Life from the End of the Second Punic War to the Time of Sulla." DPhil diss., Oxford.

———. 1981. "The Development of Roman Imperialism." *JRS* 71: 1–9.

———. 1986. "Religion and Politics, from Republic to Principate." *JRS* 76: 251–58.

———. 1989. "Religion in Republican Rome." In *CAH* VII.2^2: 573–624.

———. 2000. *Roman Religion*. Oxford.

———. 2010. "The End of the Republic?" *JRA* 23, no. 2: 469–72.

———. 2014. "The Limits of the 'Religious' in the Late Roman Republic." *History of Religions* 53, no. 3: 225–45.

Northwood, S. 2008. "*Census* and *tributum*." In *People, Land, and Politics: Demographic Developments and the Transformation of Roman Italy, 300 BC–AD 14*, edited by L. de Ligt and S. Northwood, 257–70.

Oakley, S. P. 1997–2005. *A Commentary on Livy, Books VI–X*. 4 vols. Oxford.

Obbink, D., ed. 1996. *Philodemus: On Piety*. Part 1: *Critical Text with Commentary*. Oxford.

Ober, J. 2008. *Democracy and Knowledge: Innovation and Learning in Classical Athens*. Princeton.

———. 2010. "Wealthy Hellas." *TAPA* 140, no. 2: 241–86.

———. 2015. "Classical Athens." In *Fiscal Regimes and the Political Economy of Premodern States*, edited by A. Monson and W. Scheidel, 492–522. Oxford.

———. 2018. Introduction to *Ancient Greek History and Contemporary Social Science*, edited by M. Canevaro, A. Erskine, B. Gray, and J. Ober, 1–12. Edinburgh.

Oberhelman, S. M. 2014. "Anatomical Votive Reliefs as Evidence for Specialization at Healing Sanctuaries in the Ancient Mediterranean World." *Athens Journal of Health* 1, no. 1: 47–62.

Ogilvie, R. M. 1970. *A Commentary on Livy, Books 1–5*. Oxford.

Olcese, G. 1998. "Ceramiche a vernice nera di Roma e area romana: I risultati delle analisi di laboratorio." In *Indagini archeometriche relative alla ceramica a vernice nera: Nuovi dati sulla provenienza e la diffusione*, edited by P. Frontini and M. T. Grassi, 141–52. Como.

———. 2003. *Ceramiche comuni a Roma e in area romana: Produzione, circolazione, e tecnologia (tarda età repubblicana–prima età imperiale)*. Mantova.

Oldfield, P. 2014. *Sanctity and Pilgrimage in Medieval Southern Italy, 1000–1200*. Cambridge.

Olson, M., Jr. 1965. *The Logic of Collective Action: Public Goods and the Theory of Groups*. Cambridge, MA.

Orlin, E. M. 1997. *Temples, Religion, and Politics in the Roman Republic*. Leiden.

———. 2002. "Foreign Cults in Republican Rome: Rethinking the Pomerial Rule." *MAAR* 47: 1–18.

Orlin, E. M. 2010. *Foreign Cults in Rome: Creating a Roman Empire*. Oxford.

Osanna, M. 2011. "Siedlungsformen und Agrarlandschaft in Lukanien im 4. und 3. Jahrhundert v. Chr." In *Krise und Wandel. Süditalien im 4. und 3. Jahrhundert v. Chr.*, edited by R. Neudecker, 89–106. Rome.

Osborne, R. 1987. *Classical Landscape with Figures: The Ancient Greek City and Its Countryside*. London.

Osgood, J. 2018. *Rome and the Making of a World State, 150 BCE–20 CE*. Cambridge.

Padgett, J. F., and C. K. Ansell. 1993. "Robust Action and the Rise of the Medici, 1400–1434." *American Journal of Sociology* 98, no. 6: 1259–319.

Padilla Peralta, D. 2015. "Barbarians inside the Gate, Part 1: Fears of Immigration in Ancient Rome and Today." *Eidolon*: https://eidolon.pub/barbarians-inside-the-gate-part-i-c175057b340f.

———. 2017a. "Circulation's Thousand Connectivities." In *Rome, Empire of Plunder: The Dynamics of Cultural Appropriation*, edited by M. P. Loar, C. S. MacDonald, and D. Padilla Peralta, 261–70. Cambridge.

———. 2017b. "Italy at Knife-Point: Reading Varro *Rust.* 1.69.2–3." *CPh* 112, no. 4: 482–86.

———. 2017c. "Slave Religiosity in the Roman Middle Republic." *CA* 36, no. 2: 317–69.

———. 2018a. "An Aristocratic Dilemma: Do It Right, or Do It Better?" *Histos* 12: xxiv–xlvi.

———. 2018b. "Ecology, Epistemology, and Divination in Cic. *De div.* 1.90–94." *Arethusa* 51, no. 3. .

———. 2018c. "Hammer Time: The Publicii Malleoli between Cult and Cultural History." *CA* 37, no. 2: 267–320

———. 2019. "Monument Men: Buildings, Inscriptions, and Lexicographers in the Creation of Augustan Rome." In *The Cultural History of Augustan Rome: Texts, Monuments, and Topography*, edited by S. C. Murray, M. P. Loar, and S. Rebeggiani, 80–102. Cambridge.

———. 2020. "Gods of Trust: Ancient Delos and the Modern Economics of Religion." In *Going, Gathering, and Giving: Economies of Sacred Travel in the Ancient Mediterranean*, edited by A. Collar and T. M. Kristensen. 329–56. Leiden.

———. In progress a. "Epistemicide: The Roman Case."

———. In progress b. "An unpublished *pocolom* in the Princeton University Art Museum."

Pailler, J.-M. 1997. "La vierge et le serpent: De la trivalence à l'ambiguïté." *MEFRA* 109, no. 2: 513–75.

Pakkanen, J. 2014. "The Economics of Shipshed Complexes: Zea, a Case Study." In *Shipsheds of the Ancient Mediterranean*, edited by D. Blackman and B. Rankov, 55–76. Cambridge.

Palmer, R.E.A. 1970. *The Archaic Community of the Romans*. Cambridge.

———. 1974. *Roman Religion and Roman Empire: Five Essays*. Philadelphia.

———. 1980. "The *Vici Luccei* in the Forum Boarium and Some Lucceii in Rome." *BullCom* 85: 135–61.

———. 1990. "Cults of Hercules, Apollo Caelispex, and Fortuna in and around the Roman Cattle Market." *JRA* 3: 234–44.

———. 1997. *Rome and Carthage at Peace*. Stuttgart.

Palombi, D. 1997–98. "Compitum Acilium: La scoperta, il monumento e la tradizione medica del quartiere." *RPAA* 70: 115–35.

Panayotakis, C., ed. and trans. 2009. *Decimus Laberius: The Fragments*. Cambridge.

Panciera, S. 1995. "La produzione epigrafica di Roma in età repubblicana: Le officine lapidarie." In *Acta colloquii epigraphici latini: Helsingae 3.–6. sept. 1991 habiti*, edited by H. Solin, O. Salomies, and U.-M. Liertz, 319–42. Helsinki.

———. 2016. "*CIL* VI 8, 1. *Inscriptiones sacrae. Fragmenta*, II." In *Vestigia: Miscellanea di studi storico-religiosi in onore di Filippo Coarelli nel suo 80° anniversario*, edited by V. Gasparini, 367–80. Stuttgart.

Panella, C. 2010. "Roma, il suburbio e l'Italia in età medio- e tardo-repubblicana: Cultura materiale, territori, economie." *Facta* 4: 11–123.

Papini, M. 2015. "Republican Rome and Italic Art." In *A Companion to Roman Art*, edited by B. Borg, 95–113. Malden.

Parke, H. W. 1977. *Festivals of the Athenians*. Ithaca.

Parker, G. 2001. *The Agony of Asar: A Thesis on Slavery by the Former Slave Jacobus Elisa Johannes Capitein, 1717–1747*. Princeton.

Parker, H. N. 1999. "The Observed of All Observers: Spectacle, Applause, and Cultural Poetics in the Roman Theater Audience." In *The Art of Ancient Spectacle*, edited by B. Bergmann and C. Kondoleon, 163–79. Washington, DC.

Pascal, C. B. 1981. "October Horse." *HSCP* 85: 261–91.

Patterson, O. 1982. *Slavery and Social Death: A Comparative Study*. Cambridge, MA.

Pédech, P. 1965. "Les idées religieuses de Polybe: Étude sur la religion de l'élite gréco-romaine au IIe siècle av. J.-C." *Revue de l'histoire des religions* 167, no. 1: 35–68.

Pedley, J. G. 2007. *Greek Art and Archaeology*.[4] Upper Saddle River.

Pedroni, L. 2001. *Ceramica calena a vernice nera: Produzione e diffusione*. Città di Castello.

———. 2009. "Roma, Luna e i Liguri." *Analecta Romana* 34: 7–17.

Pegoretti, G. 1869. *Manuale pratico per l'estimazione dei lavori architettonici, stradale, idraulici, e di fortificazione, per uso degli ingegneri ed architetti*.[2] Rev. by A. Cantalupi. Milan.

Pekáry, T. 1968. *Untersuchungen zu den römischen Reichstrassen*. Bonn.

———. 2002. Imago res mortua est: *Untersuchungen zur Ablehnung der bildenden Künste in der Antike*. Stuttgart.

Pelgrom, J. 2018. "The Roman Rural Exceptionality Thesis Revisited." *MEFRA* 130, no. 1:doi: 10.4000/mefra.4770.

Pelgrom, J., and T. D. Stek. 2010. "A Landscape Archaeological Perspective on the Functioning of a Rural Cult Place in Samnium: Field Surveys around the Sanctuary of S. Giovanni in Galdo (Molise)." *Journal of Ancient Topography* 20: 41–102.

———. 2014. "Roman Colonization under the Republic: Historiographical Contextualization of a Paradigm." In *Roman Republican Colonization: New Perspectives from Archaeology and Ancient History*, edited by T. D. Stek and J. Pelgrom, 10–41. Rome.

Pensabene, P. 1979. "*Auguratorium* e tempio della Magna Mater." *Archeologia laziale* 2: 67–74.

———. 1982. "Luoghi di culto, depositi votivi e loro significato." In *Roma repubblicana fra il 509 e il 270 A.C.*, edited by I. Dondero and P. Pensabene, 77–92. Rome.

———. 1985. "Area sud-occidentale del Palatino." *Roma, Archeologia del Centro*, Lavori e studi di archeologia 6: 179–212.

———. 1988. "Scavi nell' area del Tempio della Vittoria e del Santuario della Magna Mater sul Palatino." *Archeologia laziale* 9: 54–67.

———. 1995. "Nuovi rinvenimenti nell' area sud-ouest del Palatino (1992–1993)." *Archeologia laziale* 12, no. 1: 13–28.

Pensabene, P., et al. 1980. *Terracotte votive dal Tevere*. Rome.

Peña, J. T. 2007. *Roman Pottery in the Archaeological Record*. Cambridge.

Pérez Ballester, J. 2003. *La cerámica de barniz negro del santuario de Juno en Gabii*. Rome.

Perry, M. J. 2014. *Gender, Manumission, and the Roman Freedwoman*. Cambridge.

Peruzzi, E. 1998. *Civiltà greca nel Lazio preromano*. Florence.

Petsalis-Diomidis, A. 2017. "Palimpsest and Virtual Presence: A Reading of Space and Dedications at the Amphiareion at Oropos in the Hellenistic Period." In *Excavating Pilgrimage: Archaeological Approaches to Sacred Travel and Movement in the Ancient World*, edited by T. M. Kristensen and W. Friese, 106–29. London.

Pfeiffer, R., ed. 1949–53. *Callimachus*. Oxford.

Philippides, K. 2018. "Women Chattering about a Ritual: Plautus' *Poenulus* in the Light of Theocritus (*Id.* XV), Herondas (*Mim.* IV), and Aristophanes (*Thesm.*)." *Latomus* 77: 1033–52.

Piacentin, S. 2018. "The Role of Aedilician Fines in the Making of Public Rome." *Historia* 67, no. 1: 103–26.

Pietilä-Castrén, L. 1987. Magnificentia publica: *The Victory Monuments of the Roman Generals in the Era of the Punic Wars*. Helsinki.

Pietrangeli, C. 1941. "Il Mitreo del Palazzo dei Musei di Roma." *BullCom* 19: 143–73.

Pighi, G. B. 1965. De ludis saecularibus populi Romani Quiritum libri sex^2. Amsterdam.

Pina Polo, F. 1996. Contra arma verbis: *Der Redner vor dem Volk in der späten römischen Republik*. Translated by E. Liess. Stuttgart.

———. 2011. *The Consul at Rome: The Civil Functions of the Consuls in the Roman Republic*. Cambridge.

———. 2012. "*Veteres candidati*: Losers in the Elections in Republican Rome." In Vae victis! *Perdedores en el mundo antiguo*, edited by F. Marco Simón, F. Pina Polo, and J. Remesal Rodríguez, 63–82.

Pittenger, M. R. Pelikan. 2008. *Contested Triumphs: Politics, Pageantry, and Performance in Livy's Republican Rome*. Berkeley.

Pittia, S., ed. 2005. *Denys d'Halicarnasse: Rome et la conquête de l'Italie aux I^{ve} et IIIe s. avant J.-C.* (Antiquités romaines, *livres 14–20*). With contributions from E. Caire, S. Collin Bouffier, P. Corbier, S. Crouzet, X. Lafon, and R. Robert. Paris.

Platt, V. 2018. "Double Vision: Epiphanies of the Dioscuri in Classical Antiquity." *ARG* 20, no. 1: 229–56.

Poccetti, P. 2005. "Mefitis rivisitata (vent'anni dopo . . .)." In *Italica ars: Studi in onore di Giovanni Colonna per il premio* I Sanniti, edited by D. Caiazza, 73–107. Alife.

Popkin, M. L. 2016. *The Architecture of the Roman Triumph: Monuments, Memory, and Identity*. New York.

———. 2018. "Urban Images in Glass from the Late Roman Empire: The Souvenir Flasks of Puteoli and Baiae." *AJA* 122, no. 3: 427–62.

Potter, T. W., and C. Wells. 1985. "A Republican Healing-Sanctuary at Ponte di Nona Near Rome and the Classical Tradition of Votive Medicine." *JBAA* 138: 23–47.

Potts, C. 2015. *Religious Architecture in Latium and Etruria, c. 900–500 BC*. Oxford.

Prag, J.R.W. 2014. "The Quaestorship in the Third and Second Centuries BC." In *L'imperium* Romanum *en perspective: Les saviors d'empire dans la République romaine et leur heritage dans l'Europe médiévale et moderne; Actes du colloque de Paris, 26–28 novembre 2012*, edited by J. Dubouloz, S. Pittia, and G. Sabatini, 193–209. Besançon.

Prescendi, F. 2007. *Décrire et comprendre le sacrifice*. Stuttgart.

Price, S. 1984. *Rituals and Power: The Roman Imperial Cult in Asia Minor*. Cambridge.

———. 2012. "Religious Mobility in the Roman Empire." *JRS* 102: 1–19.

Pritchard, D. M. 2012. "Costing Festivals and War: Spending Priorities of the Athenian Democracy." *Historia* 61, no. 1: 18–65.

———. 2015. *Public Spending and Democracy in Classical Athens*. Austin.

Pritchett, W. K. 1979. *The Greek State at War*. Vol. 3: *Religion*. Berkeley.

Purcell, N. 1994. "The City of Rome and the *plebs urbana* in the Late Republic." In *CAH* 4^2: 644–88.

———. 1996. "Rome and the Management of Water: Environment, Culture, and Power." In *Human Landscapes in Classical Antiquity: Environment and Culture*, edited by G. Shipley and J. Salmon, 180–212. New York.

———. 1997. Untitled Review: T. P. Wiseman, *Remus: A Roman Myth*. *BMCR* 97.5.18.

———. 2003a. "Becoming Historical: The Roman Case." In *Myth, History, and Culture in Republican Rome: Studies in Honour of T. P. Wiseman*, edited by D. Braund and C. Gill, 12–40. Exeter.

———. 2003b. "The Way We Used to Eat: Diet, Community, and History at Rome." *AJP* 124, no. 3: 329–58.

———. 2012. "Sale in Antiquity: Problems and Prospects." Lecture, Stanford University.

———. 2013. "'Romans, play on!' City of the Games." In *The Cambridge Companion to Ancient Rome*, edited by P. Erdkamp, 441–58. Cambridge.

———. 2017. "Mountain Margins: Power, Resources, and Environmental Inequality in Antiquity." In *Économie et inégalité: Ressources, échanges et pouvoir dans l'antiquité classique*, edited by P. Derron, 75–114. Vandoeuvres.

Putnam, R. D. 1993. *Making Democracy Work: Civic Traditions in Modern Italy*. Princeton.

Quillin, J. M. 2004. "Information and Fear: Domestic Fear Propaganda in Republican Rome, 200–149 BCE." *Journal of Institutional and Theoretical Economics* 160, no. 4: 765–85.

Quinn, J. C. 2018. *In Search of the Phoenicians*. Princeton.

Raboteau, A. [1978] 2004. *Slave Religion: The "Invisible Institution" in the Antebellum South*. Oxford.

Randall, R. H., Jr. 1953. "The Erechtheum Workmen." *AJA* 57, no. 3: 199–210.

Randolph, P. 1893. *From Slave Cabin to the Pulpit: The Autobiography of Rev. Peter Randolph*. Boston.

Rawson, E. 1991a. "The Antiquarian Tradition: Spoils and Representations of Foreign Armour." In *Roman Society and Culture: Collected Papers*, 582–98. Oxford. = 1990. In *Staat und Staatlichkeit in der frühen römischen Republik. Akten eines Symposiums 12.–15. Juli 1998. Freie Universität Berlin*, edited by W. Eder, 157–73. Stuttgart.

———. 1991b. "The Prodigy Lists and the Use of the *Annales Maximi*." In *Roman Culture and Society: Collected Papers*, 1–15. Oxford. = 1971. *CQ* 21: 158–69.

———. 1991c. "Theatrical Life in Republican Rome and Italy." In *Roman Culture and Society: Collected Papers*, 468–87. Oxford. = 1985. *PBSR* 53: 97–113.

Reader, I. 2014. *Pilgrimage in the Marketplace*. New York.

Reay, B. 2005. "Agriculture, Writing, and Cato's Aristocratic Self-Fashioning." *CA* 24, no. 2: 331–61.

Redfield, R., and A. Villa Rojas. 1964. *Chan Kom: A Maya Village*. Chicago.

Renberg, G. H. 2006–7. "Public and Private Places of Worship in the Cult of Asclepius at Rome." *MAAR* 51–52: 87–172.

Renfrew, C. 1986. "Introduction: Peer Polity Interaction and Socio-Political Change." In *Peer Polity Interaction and Socio-Political Change*, edited by C. Renfrew and J. F. Cherry, 1–18. Cambridge.

Rich, J. W. 2011. Untitled Review: M. Coudry and M. Humm, eds., *Praeda: Butin de guerre et société dans la Rome républicaine / Kriegsbeute und Gesellschaft im republikanischen Rom*. *BMCR* 2011.08.22.

Richard, J.-C. 2005. "Patricians and Plebeians: The Origin of a Social Dichotomy." In *Social Struggles in Archaic Rome: New Perspectives on the Conflict of the Orders*, edited by K. A. Raaflaub, 107–27. Malden.

Richardson, J. H. 2018. "Valerius Antias and the Archives." *MD* 80: 57–80.

Richardson, L., Jr. 1992. *A New Topographical Dictionary of Ancient Rome*. Baltimore.

Richardson, S. 2015. "Building Larsa: Labor-Value, Scale, and Scope-of-Economy in Ancient Mesopotamia." In *Labor in the Ancient Near East*, edited by P. Steinkeller and M. Hudson, 237–328. Dresden.

———. 2017. "Before Things Worked: A 'Low-Power' Model of Early Mesopotamia." In *Ancient States and Infrastructural Power*, edited by C. Ando and S. Richardson, 17–62. Philadelphia.

Richlin, A. 2014. "Talking to Slaves in the Plautine Audience." *CA* 33, no. 1: 174–226.

———. 2017a. "The Ones Who Paid the Butcher's Bill: Soldiers and War Captives in Roman Comedy." In *Brill's Companion to Military Defeat in Ancient Mediterranean Society*, edited by J. H. Clark and B. Turner, 213–39.

———. 2017b. "The Traffic in Shtick." In *Rome, Empire of Plunder: The Dynamics of Cultural Appropriation*, edited by M. P. Loar, C. S. MacDonald, and D. Padilla Peralta, 169–93. Cambridge.

———. 2018. *Slave Theater in the Roman Republic: Plautus and Popular Comedy*. Cambridge.

Ridgway, B. S. 1999. *Prayers in Stone: Greek Architectural Sculpture ca. 600–100 BCE*. Berkeley.

Riggsby, A. M. 2019. *Mosaics of Knowledge: Representing Information in the Roman World*. Oxford.

Rilinger, R. 2007. "Die Ausbildung von Amtswechsel und Amtsfristen als Problem zwischen Machtbesitz und Machtgebrauch in der mittleren Republik (342 bis 217 v. Chr.)." In R. Rilinger, Ordo *und* dignitas: *Beiträge zur römischen Verfassungs- und Sozialgeschichte*, edited by T. Schmitt and A. Winterling, 11–76. Stuttgart.

Rives, J. 2012. "Between Orthopraxy and Orthodoxy: Constantine and Animal Sacrifice." In *Costantino prima e dopo Costantino / Constantine before and after Constantine*, edited by G. Bonamente, N. Lenski, and R. Lizzi Testa, 153–63. Bari.

Roberts, N. 2015. *Freedom as Marronage*. Chicago.

Robinson, O. 1977. "Fire Prevention at Rome." *Revue internationale des droits de l'Antiquité* 24: 377–88.

Robinson, R. 2016. "Cult and Calendars in the Ancient Empires of Qin, Han, and Rome." PhD diss., McGill University.

Rodgers, R. H. 1982. "What the Sibyl Said: Frontinus *Aq.* 7.5." *CQ* 31: 174–77.

Rodríguez-Almeida, E. 1993. "De la *Forma Urbis Marmorea*, en torno al *Collis Capitolinus*." In *Eius virtutis studiosi: Classical and Postclassical Studies in Memory of Frank Edward Brown (1908–1988)*, edited by R. T. Scott and A. R. Scott, 31–43. Washington, DC.

Rogers, G. M. 1991. *The Sacred Identity of Ephesos: Foundation Myths of a Roman City*. London.

Roller, D. W. 2018. *A Historical and Topographical Guide to the* Geography *of Strabo*. Cambridge.

Roller, M. B. 2004. "Exemplarity in Roman Culture: The Cases of Horatius Cocles and Cloelia." *CPh* 99, no. 1: 1–56.

———. 2018. *Models from the Past in Roman Culture: A World of* Exempla. Cambridge.

Roma medio repubblicana: Aspetti culturali di Roma e del Lazio nei secoli IV e III a.c. 1977. Rome.

Rosenberger, V. 1998. *Gezähmte Götter: Das Prodigienwesen der römischen Republik*. Stuttgart.

———. 2005. "Prodigien aus Italien: Geographische Verteilung und religiöse Kommunikation." *Cahiers du Centre Gustave Glotz* 16: 235–57.

Rosenstein, N. 2004. *Rome at War: Farms, Families, and Death in the Middle Republic*. Chapel Hill.

———. 2009. "War, State Formation, and the Evolution of Military Institutions in Ancient China and Rome." In *Rome and China: Comparative Perspectives on Ancient World Empires*, edited by W. Scheidel, 24–51. Oxford.

———. 2011. "War, Wealth, and Consuls." In *Consuls and* Res Publica: *Holding High Office in the Roman Republic*, edited by H. Beck, A. Duplá, M. Jehne, and F. Pina Polo, 133–57. Cambridge.

———. 2012. *Rome and the Mediterranean, 290 to 146 BC: The Imperial Republic*. Edinburgh.

———. 2017. Untitled Review: N. Coffee, *Gift and Gain: How Money Transformed Ancient Rome*. *BMCR* 2017.11.04.

Rosivach, V. J. 1994. *The System of Public Sacrifice in Fourth-Century Athens*. Atlanta.

Roth, R. 2007. *Styling Romanisation: Pottery and Society in Central Italy*. Cambridge.

———. 2013a. "Before *sigillata*: Black Gloss Pottery and Its Cultural Dimensions." In *A Companion to the Archaeology of the Roman Republic*, edited by J. D. Evans, 81–96. Malden.

———. 2013b. "Trading Identities? Regionalism and Commerce in Mid-Republican Italy (Third to Early Second Century BC)." In *Creating Ethnicities and Identities in the Roman World*, edited by A. Gardner, E. Herring, and K. Lomas, 93–111. London.

Roth, U. 2007. *Thinking Tools: Agricultural Slavery between Evidence and Models*. London.

Rous, B. D. 2009. "No Place for Cult: The Sacred Landscape of Latium in the Late Republic." *BABESCH* 84: 53–84.

Rouveret, A. 2000. "*Captiva arma*: Guerre, butin, économie dans les cités de Grande Grèce et de Campanie du Ve siècle à l'expédition de Pyrrhus." In *Économie antique: La guerre dans les économies antiques*, edited by J. Andreau et al., 83–102. Saint-Bertrand-de-Comminges.

Rowan, C. 2013a. "Coinage as Commodity and Bullion in the Western Mediterranean, ca. 550–100 BCE." *MHR* 28, no. 2: 105–27.

———. 2013b. "The Profits of War and Cultural Capital: Silver and Society in Republican Rome." *Historia* 62, no. 3: 361–86.

Rubio-Campillo, X., M. Coto-Sarmiento, J. Pérez-Gonzalez, and J. Remesal Rodríguez. 2017. "Bayesian Analysis and Free Market Trade within the Roman Empire." *Antiquity* 91, no. 359: 1241–52.

Rucinski, S. 2003. "Le rôle du préfet des vigiles dans le maintien de l'ordre public dans la Rome impériale." *Eos* 90: 261–74.

Rüpke, J. 1990. Domi militiae: *Die religiöse Konstruktion des Krieges in Rom*. Stuttgart.

———. 1995a. *Kalender und Öffentlichkeit: Die Geschichte der Repräsentation und religiösen Qualifikation von Zeit in Rom*. Berlin.

———. 1995b. "Was kostet Religion? Quantifizierungsversuche für die Stadt Rom." In *Lokale Religionsgeschichte*, edited by H. G. Kippenberg and B. Luchesi, 273–87. Marburg.

———. 1996. "*Nundinae*: Kalendarische Koordination im republikanischen Rom." In *Kommunikation in politischen und kultischen Gemeinschaften*, edited by G. Binder and K. Ehlich, 75–98. Trier.

———. 1999. "*Collegia sacerdotum*: Religiöse Vereine in der Oberschicht." In *Religiöse Vereine in der römischen Antike: Untersuchungen zu Organisation, Ritual und Ramordnung*, edited by U. Egelhaaf-Gaiser and A. Schäfer, 41–67. Tübingen.

———. 2008. *Fasti sacerdotum: A Prosopography of Pagan, Jewish, and Christian Religious Officials in the City of Rome, 300 BC to AD 499*. Translated by D.M.B. Richardson. Oxford.

———. 2010a. "Religious Pluralism." In *The Oxford Handbook of Roman Studies*, edited by A. Barchiesi and W. Scheidel, 748–66. Oxford.

———. 2010b. "Zwischen Rationalismus und Ritualismus: Zur Entstehung des Diskurses 'Religion' in der späten römischen Republik." In *Religion und Bildung: Medien und Funktionen religiösen Wissens in der Kaiserzeit*, edited by C. Frateantonio and H. Krasser, 29–45. Stuttgart.

———. 2011. *The Roman Calendar from Numa to Constantine: Time, History, and the* Fasti. Translated by D. Richardson. Malden.

———. 2012a. "Public and Publicity." In *Greek and Roman Festivals: Content, Meaning, and Practice*, edited by J. Rasmus Brandt and J. W. Iddeng, 305–22. Oxford.

———. 2012b. *Religion in Republican Rome: Rationalization and Ritual Change*. Philadelphia.

———, ed. 2013. *The Individual in the Religions of the Ancient Mediterranean*. Oxford.

———. 2014a. *From Jupiter to Christ: On the History of Religion in the Roman Imperial Period*. Translated by D.M.B. Richardson. Oxford.

———. 2014b. "Historicizing Religion: Varro's *Antiquitates* and History of Religion in the late Roman Republic." *History of Religions* 53, no. 3: 246–68.

———. 2014c. "Roman Religion." In *The Cambridge Companion to the Roman Republic*², edited by H. I. Flower, 213–29. Cambridge.

———. 2015. "Knowledge of Religion in Valerius Maximus' *exempla*." In *Memory in Ancient Rome and Early Christianity*, edited by K. Galinsky, 89–112. Oxford.

———. 2018a. "Not Gods Alone: On the Visibility of Religion and Religious Specialists in Ancient Rome." In *Seeing the God: Image, Space, Performance, and Vision in the Religion of the Roman Empire*, edited by M. Arnhold, H. O. Maier, and J. Rüpke, 85–97. Tübingen.

———. 2018b. *Pantheon: A New History of Roman Religion*. Translated by D.M.B. Richardson. Princeton.

Ruffini, G. 2008. *Social Networks in Byzantine Egypt*. Cambridge.

———. 2012. Untitled Review: I. Malkin, *A Small Greek World: Networks in the Ancient Mediterranean*. *AHR* 117, no. 5: 1643–44.

Russell, A. 2016. *The Politics of Public Space in Republican Rome*. Cambridge.

Russell, B. 2017. "Stone Use and the Economy: Demand, Distribution, and the State." In *Trade, Commerce, and the State in the Roman world*, edited by A. Wilson and A. Bowman, 237–64. Oxford.

Rutgers, L. V. 2019. "Managing Early Christian Funerary Practice in the Catacombs of Ancient Rome: New Data and New Insights Using a Quantitative Approach." *Studies in Late Antiquity* 3, no. 2: 212–50.

Rutherford, I. 2007. "Network Theory and Theoric Networks." *MHR* 22, no. 1: 23–37.

———. 2017. "Pilgrimage and Communication." In *Mercury's Wings: Exploring Modes of Communication in the Ancient World*, edited by F. S. Naiden and R.J.A. Talbert, 195–210. Oxford.

Ryan, F. X. 1998. *Rank and Participation in the Republican Senate*. Stuttgart.

Sallares, R. 2002. *Malaria and Rome: A History of Malaria in Ancient Italy*. Oxford.

Salmon, J. 2001. "Temples the Measures of Men: Public Building in the Greek Economy." In *Economies beyond Agriculture in the Classical World*, edited by D. J. Mattingly and J. Salmon, 195–208. London.

Salzman, M. R. 1990. *On Roman Time: The Codex-Calendar of 354 and the Rhythms of Urban Life in Late Antiquity*. Berkeley.

———. 2013. "Structuring Time: Festivals, Holidays and the Calendar." In *The Cambridge Companion to Ancient Rome*, edited by P. Erdkamp, 478–96. Cambridge.

SanPietro, I. 2014. "Money, Power, Respect: Charity and the Creation of the Church." PhD diss., Columbia University.

Santangelo, F. 2011. "*Pax deorum* and Pontiffs." In *Priests and State in the Roman World*, edited by J. H. Richardson and F. Santangelo, 161–86. Stuttgart.

Satterfield, S. 2008. "Rome's Own Sibyl: The Sibylline Books in the Roman Republic and Early Empire." PhD diss., Princeton University.

———. 2012. "Livy and the Timing of Expiation in the Roman Year." *Histos* 6: 67–90.

———. 2015. "Prodigies, the *pax deum*, and the *ira deum*." *CJ* 110, no. 4: 431–45.

Sauron, G. 1987. "Le complexe pompéien du Champ de Mars: Nouveauté urbanistique à finalité idéologique." In *L'urbs, espace urbain et histoire (1er siècle av. J.-C.–IIIe siècle ap. J.-C.)*, 457–73. Rome.

Scalfari, V. A. 2009. "I *Bruttii Praesentes*: Osservazioni e considerazioni sulla *gens* in età repubblicana." In *Lazio e Sabina: Scoperte Scavi e Ricerche*. Vol. 5, edited by G. Ghini, 125–31. Rome.

Scheid, J. 1984. "Le prêtre et le magistrat." In *Des ordres à Rome*, edited by C. Nicolet, 243–80. Paris.

———. 1985a. "Numa et Jupiter, ou les dieux citoyens de Rome." *Archives de Sciences sociales des religions* 59, no. 1: 41–53.

———. 1985b. *Religion et piété à Rome*. Paris.

———. 2003. *An Introduction to Roman Religion*. Translated by J. Lloyd. Bloomington.

———. 2006. "Rome et les grands lieux de culte d'Italie." In *Pouvoir et religion dans le monde romain*, edited by A. Vigourt, X. Loriot, A. Bérenger-Badel, and B. Klein, 75–86. Paris.

———. 2012a. "Roman Animal Sacrifice and the System of Being." In *Greek and Roman Animal*

Sacrifice: Ancient Victims, Modern Observers, edited by C. A. Faraone and F. S. Naiden, 84–95. Cambridge.

Scheid, J. 2012b. *Römischen Fragen: Ein virtueller Spaziergang im Herzen des alten Rom. Plutarch*. Darmstadt.

———. 2016. *The Gods, the State, and the Individual: Reflections on Civic Religion in Rome*. Translated by C. Ando. Philadelphia.

———. 2017. "Quelques données sur les rites de fondation des temples romains." In *Quand naissent les dieux. Fondation des sanctuaires antiques; Motivations, Agents, Lieux*, edited by S. Agusta-Boularot, S. Huber, and W. Van Andringa, 239–45.

———. 2018. "La religion romaine en perspective." *Athenaeum* 106, no. 1: 189–201.

Scheidel, W. 1990. "Free-Born and Manumitted Bailiffs in the Graeco-Roman World." *CQ* 40, no. 2: 591–93.

———. 1995. "The Most Silent Women of Greece and Rome: Rural Labour and Women's Life in the Ancient World (I)." *Greece and Rome* 42, no. 2: 202–17.

———. 1996a. "Finances, Figures, and Fiction." *CQ* 46, no. 1: 222–38.

———. 1996b. "The Most Silent Women of Greece and Rome: Rural Labour and Women's Life in the Ancient World (II)." *Greece and Rome* 43, no. 1: 1–10.

———. 2004a. "Creating a Metropolis: A Comparative Demographic Perspective." In *Ancient Alexandria between Egypt and Greece*, edited by W. V. Harris and G. Ruffini, 1–31. Leiden.

———. 2004b. "Human Mobility in Roman Italy, I: The Free Population." *JRS* 94: 1–26.

———. 2005. "Real Slave Prices and the Relative Cost of Slave Labor in the Greco-Roman World." *Ancient Society* 35: 1–17.

———. 2006. "The Demography of Roman State Formation in Italy." In *Herrschaft ohne Integration? Rom und Italien in republikanischer Zeit*, edited by M. Jehne and R. Pfeilschifter, 207–26. Frankfurt.

———. 2007. "A Model of Real Income Growth in Roman Italy." *Historia* 56, no. 3: 322–46.

———. 2010a. "Real Wages in Early Economies: Evidence for Living Standards from 1800 BCE to 1300 CE." *Journal of the Economic and Social History of the Orient* 53: 425–62.

———. 2010b. Untitled Review: T. P. Wiseman, *Remembering the Roman People: Essays on Late-Republican Politics and Literature*. *AJP* 131, no. 2: 335–38.

———. 2011. "The Roman Slave Supply." In *The Cambridge World History of Slavery*. Vol. 1: *The Ancient Mediterranean World*, 287–310. Cambridge.

———. 2012. "Epigraphy and Demography: Birth, Marriage, Family, and Death." *Proceedings of the British Academy* 177: 101–29.

———. 2013. "Studying the State." In *The Oxford Handbook of the Ancient Near East and Mediterranean*, edited by P. F. Bang and W. Scheidel, 5–57. New York.

———. 2015. "The Early Roman Monarchy." In *Fiscal Regimes and the Political Economy of Premodern States*, edited by A. Monson and W. Scheidel, 229–57. Oxford.

———. 2016. "Benford's Law and Numerical Stylization of Monetary Valuations in Classical Literature." *CQ* 66, no. 2: 815–21.

———. 2018. "Building for the State: A World-Historical Perspective." In *How to Do Things with History: New Approaches to Ancient Greece*, edited by D. Allen, P. Christesen, and P. Millett, 237–59. Oxford.

———. 2019. *Escape from Rome: The Failure of Empire and the Road to Prosperity*. Princeton.

Schilling, R. 1964. "Roman Festivals and Their Significance." *Acta Classica* 7: 44–56.

———. 1979. *Rites, Cultes, Dieux de Rome*. Paris.

Schmidt, T.-M. 1990. "Studien zur Vasenkunst des Hellenismus I: Zwei 'Pocola' in der Antikensammlung und zur Bedeutung hellenistischer Eroten." *Forschungen und Berichte* 28: 71–96.

Schneider, H. 2014. "Infrastruktur und politisches System im Imperium Romanum." In *Staatlichkeit in Rom? Diskurse und Praxis (in) der römischen Republik*, edited by C. Lundgreen, 211–29. Stuttgart.

Schuhmann, E. 1977. "Hinweise und Kulthandlungen im Zusammenhang mit plautinischen Frauengestalten." *Klio* 59, no. 1: 137–47.

Schultz, C. E. 2006a. "Juno Sospita and Roman Insecurity in the Social War." In *Religion in Republican Italy*, edited by C. E. Schultz and P. Harvey Jr., 207–27. Cambridge.

———. 2006b. *Women's Religious Activity in the Roman Republic*. Chapel Hill.

———. 2010. "The Romans and Ritual Murder." *JAAR* 78: 516–41.

———. 2016. "Roman Sacrifice, Inside and Out." *JRS* 106: 58–76.

———. 2018. "*Sacrum reddere*: Sacrifice, Consecration, and Dedication in Roman Religion." *RRE* 4: 187–206.

Schulze, W. 1966. *Zur Geschichte lateinischer Eigennamen.*[2] Berlin.

Scopacasa, R. 2015a. *Ancient Samnium: Settlement, Culture, and Identity between History and Archaeology*. Oxford.

———. 2015b. "Moulding Cultural Change: A Contextual Approach to Anatomical Votive Terracottas in Central Italy, Fourth–Second Centuries BC." *PBSR* 83: 1–27.

———. 2016. "Rome's Encroachment on Italy." In *A Companion to Roman Italy*, edited by A. Cooley, 35–56. Chichester.

Scott, A. R. 2008. *Cosa: The Black Glaze Pottery* 2. Supplementary Volume 5: *Memoirs of the American Academy in Rome*. Rome.

Scott, M. 2010. *Delphi and Olympia: The Spatial Politics of Panhellenism in the Archaic and Classical Periods*. Cambridge.

Scott Ryberg, I. 1940. *An Archaeological Record of Rome from the Seventh to the Second Century BC*. London.

Scullard, H. H. 1981. *Festivals and Ceremonies of the Roman Republic*. Ithaca.

Sear, F. 2006. *Roman Theatres: An Architectural Study*. Oxford.

Segal, C. 1987. *Roman Laughter: The Comedy of Plautus.*[2] New York.

Serrati, J. 2006. "Neptune's Altars: The Treaties between Rome and Carthage (509–226 B.C.)." *CQ* 56, no. 1: 113–34.

Settipani, C. 2000. *Continuité gentilice et continuité familiale dans les familles sénatoriales romaines à l'époque impériale: Mythe et realité*. Oxford.

Sewell, J. 2010. *The Formation of Roman Urbanism, 338–200 BC: Between Contemporary Foreign Influence and Roman Tradition*. Portsmouth.

Sharrock, A. 2009. *Reading Roman Comedy: Poetics and Playfulness in Plautus and Terence*. Cambridge.

Shatzman, I. 1972. "The Roman General's Authority over Booty." *Historia* 21, no. 2: 177–205.

Shaw, B. D. 1996. "Seasons of Death: Aspects of Mortality in Imperial Rome." *JRS* 86: 100–138.

———. 1997. "Agrarian Economy and the Marriage Cycle of Roman Women." *JRA* 10: 57–76.

Shaw, B. D. 2001. "The Seasonal Birthing Cycle of Roman Women." In *Debating Roman Demography*, edited by W. Scheidel, 83–110. Leiden.

———. 2013. *Bringing in the Sheaves: Economy and Metaphor in the Roman World*. Toronto.

Sherk, R. K., ed. and trans. 1984. *Rome and the Greek East to the Death of Augustus*. Cambridge.

Sickinger, J. P. 1999. *Public Records and Archives in Classical Athens*. Chapel Hill.

Silver, N. 2012. *The Signal and the Noise: Why So Many Predictions Fail—but Some Don't*. New York.

Simon, E. 1982. *The Kurashiki Ninagawa Museum: Greek, Etruscan, and Roman Antiquities*. Mainz.

———. 1983. *Festivals of Attica*. Madison.

Simonton, M. 2017. *Classical Greek Oligarchy: A Political History*. Princeton.

Sinopoli, C. M., R. J. McIntosh, I. Morris, and A. R. Knodell. "The Distribution of Power: Hierarchy and Its Discontents." In *Early Cities in Comparative Perspective: The Cambridge World History*. Vol. 3, edited by N. Yoffee, 381–93. Cambridge.

Skinner, M. 2001. "Ladies' Day at the Art Institute: Theocritus, Herodas, and the Gendered Gaze." In *Making Silence Speak*, edited by A. Lardinois and L. McClure, 201–22. Princeton.

Slater, N. 2000. *Plautus in Performance: The Theatre of the Mind.*[2] Amsterdam.

Small, M. L. 2017. *Someone to Talk To*. New York.

Smith, C. S. 1998. "Traders and Artisans in Archaic Central Italy." In *Trade, Traders, and the Ancient City*, edited by H. Perkins and C. S. Smith, 31–50. New York.

———. 2013. "The City of Rome in the Early and Middle Republic." In *The Cambridge Ancient History: Plates to Volumes VII Part 2 and VIII; The Rise of Rome to 133 BC*, edited by C. S. Smith, 27–52. Cambridge.

———. 2015. "Performance, Communication, and Gods in Late Republican Rome." *Histos* 9: xvi–xxvi.

———. 2017. "The Fifth-Century Crisis." *Antichthon* 51: 227–50.

Smith, G.J.D. 2018. "Data Doxa: The Affective Consequences of Data Practices." *Big Data and Society* (January–June): 1–15. doi: 10.1177/2053951717751551.

Smith, M. L. 2003. "Early Walled Cities of the Indian Subcontinent as 'Small Worlds.'" In *The Social Construction of Ancient Cities*, edited by M. L. Smith, 269–89. Washington, DC.

Snodgrass, A. 1986. "Interaction by Design: The Greek City State." In *Peer Polity Interaction and Socio-Political Change*, edited by C. Renfrew and J. F. Cherry, 47–58. Cambridge.

Sobak, R. 2015. "Sokrates among the Shoemakers." *Hesperia* 84, no. 4: 669–712.

Söderlind, M. 2002. *Late Etruscan Votive Heads from Tessennano: Production, Distribution, Sociohistorical Context*. Rome.

Solin, H. 2003. *Die griechischen Personennamen in Rom: Ein Namenbuch.*[2] Berlin.

Spaeth, B. S. 1996. *The Roman Goddess Ceres*. Austin.

Spannagel, M. "Zur Vergegenwärtigung abstrakter Wertbegriffe in Kult und Kunst der römischen Republik." In Moribus antiquis res stat Romana: *Römische Werte und römische Literatur im 3. und 2. Jh. v. Chr.*, edited by M. Braun and A. Halt, 237–69. Leipzig.

Spawforth, T. 2006. *The Complete Greek Temples*. London.

Stambaugh, J. E. 1978. "The Functions of Roman Temples." *ANRW* 2.16.1: 554–608.

Stamper, J. W. 2005. *The Architecture of Roman Temples: The Republic to the Middle Empire*. Cambridge.

Stanco, E. A. 2004. "La ceramica a vernice nera della stipe di *Lucus Feroniae*, analisi preliminare." *BullCom* 105: 29–46.

———. 2009. "La seriazione cronologica della ceramica a vernice nera etrusco laziale nell'ambito dell III sec. a.c." In *Suburbium II: Il suburbium di Roma dalla fine dell età monarchica alla nascità del sistema delle ville*, edited by V. Jolivet and G. Volpe, 157–93. Rome.

Stanley, B. W., T. J. Dennehy, M. E. Smith, B. L. Stark, A. M. York, G. L. Cowgill, J. Novic, and J. Ek. 2016. "Service Access in Premodern Cities: An Exploratory Comparison of Spatial Equity." *Journal of Urban History* 42, no. 1: 121–44.

Stark, R., and R. Finke. 2000. *Acts of Faith*. Los Angeles.

Starr, C. 1980. *The Beginnings of Imperial Rome: Rome in the Mid-Republic*. Ann Arbor.

Stek, T. 2009. *Cult Places and Cultural Change in Republican Italy: A Contextual Approach to Religious Aspects of Rural Society after the Roman Conquest*. Amsterdam.

———. 2015. "Cult, Conquest, and 'Religious Romanization': The Impact of Rome on Cult Places and Religious Practices in Italy." In *The Impact of Rome on Cult Places and Religious Practices in Ancient Italy*, edited by T. D. Stek and G.-J. Burgers, 1–28. London.

———. 2016. "'Romanizzazione religiosa' tra modello poliadico e processi culturali: Dalla destrutturazione postcoloniale a nuove prospettive sull'impatto della conquista romana." In E pluribus unum? *L'Italie, de la diversité préromaine à l'unité augustéenne*. Vol. 2: *L'Italie centrale e la creazione di una koiné culturale? I percorsi della "'romanizzazione,"* edited by M. Aberson, M. C. Biella, M. Di Fazio, P. Sánchez, and M. Wullschleger, 291–306. Bern.

———. 2018. "Early Roman Colonization beyond the Romanizing Agro-Town: Village Patterns of Settlement and Highland Exploitation in Central Italy." In *The Archaeology of Imperial Landscapes: A Comparative Study of Empires in the Ancient Near East and Mediterranean World*, edited by B. S. Düring and T. D. Stek, 145–72. Cambridge.

Stern, S. 2012. *Calendars in Antiquity: Empires, States, and Societies*. Oxford.

Sternini, M., A. Baronchelli, and R. Pastor-Satorras. "Modeling Human Dynamics of Face-to-Face Interaction Networks." *Physical Review Letters* 110.168701. doi: 10.1103/PhysRevLett.110.168701.

Stopford, J. 1994. "Some Approaches to the Archaeology of Christian Pilgrimage." *World Archaeology* 26, no. 1: 57–72.

Stucchi, S. 2018. "Il regno congiunto dei due gemelli e i *Lares Grundiles* secondo Cassio Emina." *Giornale Italiano di Filologia* 70: 59–88.

Suerbaum, W., ed. 2002. *Handbuch der lateinischen Literatur der Antike. Erster Band: Die archaische Literatur. Von den Anfängen bis zu Sullas Tod. Die vorliterarische Periode und die Zeit von 240 bis 78 v. Chr*. Munich.

Susanna, F. 2016. "Basilica Emilia: Rinvenimento di uno statere aureo cartaginese." *BullCom* 117: 277–79.

Susini, G. 1970. "*Pocola* marcati: Devozione e industria." *Epigraphica* 32: 164–66.

Swift, E. 2017. *Roman Artefacts and Society: Design, Behaviour, and Experience*. Oxford.

Tacoma, L. E. 2013. "Migrant Quarters at Rome?" In *Integration in the Roman World*, edited by G. de Kleijn and S. Benoist, 127–46. Leiden.

———. 2016. *Moving Romans: Migration to Rome in the Principate*. Oxford.

Tan, J. 2015. "The Roman Republic." In *Fiscal Regimes and the Political Economy of Premodern States*, edited by A. Monson and W. Scheidel, 208–28. Oxford.

Tan, J. 2016. "The Ambitions of Scipio Nasica and the Destruction of the Stone Theatre." *Antichthon* 50: 70–79.

———. 2017. *Power and Public Finance at Rome, 264–49 BCE*. Oxford.

———. 2020. "The *dilectus-tributum* System and the Settlement of Fourth-Century Italy." In *Romans at War: Soldiers, Citizens, and Society in the Roman Republic*, edited by J. Armstrong and M. P. Fronda, 52–75. London.

Tarn, W. W. 1961. *Hellenistic Civilisation.*[3] Rev. by G. T. Griffith. New York.

Tarpin, M. 2000. "Le butin sonnant et trébuchant dans la Rome républicaine." In *Économie antique: La guerre dans les économies antiques*, edited by J. Andreau et al., 365–76. Saint-Bertrand-de-Comminges.

———. 2009. "Les *manubiae* dans la procédure d'appropriation du butin." In *Praeda: Butin de guerre et sociétee dans la Rome républicaine / Kriegsbeute und Gesellschaft im republikanischen Rom*, edited by M. Coudry and M. Humm, 81–102. Stuttgart.

Taylor, D. M. 1957. "Cosa: Black Glaze Pottery." *MAAR* 25: 65, 67–193.

Taylor, L. R. 1934. "New Light on the History of the Secular Games." *AJP* 55: 101–20.

———. 1937. "The Opportunities for Dramatic Performances in the Time of Plautus and Terence." *TAPA* 68: 284–304.

———. 1960. *The Voting Districts of the Roman Republic*. Rome.

———. 1966. *Roman Voting Assemblies from the Hannibalic War to the Dictatorship of Caesar*. Ann Arbor.

Taylor, L. R., and R. T. Scott. 1969. "Seating Space in the Roman Senate and the *senatores pedarii*." *TAPA* 100: 529–82.

Taylor, M. 2017. "State Finance in the Roman Middle Republic: A Reevaluation." *AJP* 138, no. 1: 143–80.

———. 2018. "The Election of Centurions during the Republican Period." *Ancient Society* 48: 147–67.

Taylor, R. 2000. "Watching the Skies: Janus, Auspication, and the Shrine in the Roman Forum." *MAAR* 45: 1–40.

———. 2003. *Roman Builders: A Study in Architectural Process*. Cambridge.

———. 2014. "Labor Force and Execution." In *A Companion to Roman Architecture*, edited by R. B. Ulrich and C. K. Quenemoen, 193–206. Chichester.

Taylor, R., K. Wentworth Rinne, and S. Kostof. 2016. *Rome: An Urban History from Antiquity to the Present*. Cambridge.

Termeer, M. K. 2016. "Votives in Latin Colonies: A Perspective beyond 'Religious romanization.'" In *Orte der Forschung, Orte des Glaubens: Neue Perspektiven für Heiligtümer in Italien von der Archaik bis zur Späten Republik. Akten der internationalen Tagung in Darmstadt am 19. und 20. Juli 2013*, edited by M. Bolder-Boos and D. Maschek, 117–27. Bonn.

Terrenato, N. 2012. "The Enigma of 'Catonian' Villas: The *De agri cultura* in the Context of Second-Century BC Italian Architecture." In *Roman Republican Villas: Architecture, Context, and Ideology*, edited by J. A. Becker and N. Terrenato, 69–93. Ann Arbor.

———. 2013. "Patterns of Cultural Change in Roman Italy: Non-elite Religion and the Defense of Cultural Self-Consistency." In *Religiöse Vielfalt und soziale Integration. Die Bedeutung der Religion für die kulturelle Identität und politische Stabilität im republikanische Italien*, edited by M. Jehne, B. Linke and J. Rüpke, 25–42. Heidelberg.

———. 2014. "Private *vis*, public *virtus*: Family Agendas during the Early Roman Expansion." In *Roman Republican Colonization: New Perspectives from Archaeology and Ancient History*, edited by T. D. Stek and J. Pelgrom, 45–59. Rome.

———. 2015. "The Archetypal Imperial City: Rome and the Burdens of Empire." In *Early Cities in Comparative Perspective: The Cambridge World History*. Vol. 3, edited by N. Yoffee, 513–31. Cambridge.

———. 2016. "The Romanization of Rome: Between Cultural Change and Elite Tastes." Lecture, Princeton University.

———. 2019. *The Early Roman Expansion into Italy: Elite Negotiation and Family Agendas*. Cambridge.

Thompson, G. L. 2005. "Constantius II and the First Removal of the Altar of Victory." In *A Tall Order: Writing the Social History of the Ancient World; Essays in Honor of William V. Harris*, edited by J.-J. Aubert and Z. Várhelyi, 85–106. Munich.

Tilly, C. 1985. "War Making and State Making as Organized Crime." In *Bringing the State Back In*, edited by P. Evans, D. Rueschemeyer, and T. Skocpol, 169–86. Cambridge.

———. 1990. *Coercion, Capital, and European States, AD 990–1992*. Malden.

———. 2005. *Trust and Rule*. Cambridge.

———. 2010. "Cities, States, and Trust Networks: Chapter 1 of *Cities and States in World History*." *Theory and Society* 39: 265–80.

Toliver, H. M. 1952. "Plautus and the State Gods of Rome." *CJ* 48, no. 2: 49–57.

Tommasi, C. O. 2014. "Il nome segreto di Roma tra antiquaria ed esoterismo: Una riconsiderazione delle fonti." *Studi Classici e Orientali* 60: 187–219.

Toner, J. 2013. *Roman Disasters*. Cambridge.

Torelli, M. 1995. *Studies in the Romanization of Italy*. Edmonton.

———. 1997. "Appius Alce: La gemma fiorentina con rito saliare e la presenza dei Claudii in Etruria." *Studi Etruschi* 63: 227–55.

———. 1999. *Tota Italia: Essays in the Cultural Formation of Roman Italy*. Oxford.

———. 2006. "The Topography and Archaeology of Republican Rome." In *A Companion to the Roman Republic*, edited by R. Morstein-Marx and N. Rosenstein, 81–101. Malden.

———. 2014. "Genucilia: Épigraphie et fonction, quelques considérations." In *Les potiers d'Étrurie et leur monde: Contacts, Échanges, Transfers; Hommages à Mario A. Del Chiaro*, edited by L. Ambrosini and V. Jolivet, 415–28. Paris.

Trypanis, C. A., ed. and trans. 1958. *Callimachus*: Aetia, Iambi, *Lyric Poems*, Hecale, *Minor Epic and Elegiac Poems, Fragments of Epigrams, Fragments of Uncertain Location*. Cambridge, MA.

Tucci, P. L. 1997. "Dov'erano il tempio di Nettuno e la nave di Enea?" *BullCom* 98: 15–42.

———. 2018. "A Funerary Monument on the Capitoline: Architecture and Painting in Mid-Republican Rome, between Etruria and Greece." *JRA* 31: 30–52.

Turcan, R. 1982. Untitled Review: *Mercure romain: Le culte public de Mercure et la fonction mercantile à Rome de la République archaïque à l'époque augustéenne; Revue de l'histoire des religions* 199, no. 3: 320–23.

Turfa, J. M. 2004. "Anatomical Votives." In *Thesaurus cultus et rituum antiquorum* (ThesCRA). Vol. 1: *Processions, Sacrifices, Libations, Fumigations, Dedications*, 359–67. Los Angeles.

———. 2006a. "Etruscan Religion at the Watershed: Before and After the Fourth Century

BCE." In *Religion in Republican Italy*, edited by C. E. Schultz and P. Harvey Jr., 62–89. Cambridge.

Turfa, J. M. 2006b. "Was There Room for Healing in the Healing Sanctuaries?" *ARG* 8: 63–80.

Ulrich, R. B. 1994. *The Roman Orator and the Sacred Stage: The Roman* templum rostratum. Brussels.

Urquhart, L. 2010. "Colonial Religion and Indigenous Society in the Archaic West Mediterranean: c. 750–400 BCE." PhD diss., Stanford University.

Uslaner, E. M. 2002. *The Moral Foundations of Trust*. Cambridge.

Vaahtera, J. E. 2000. "Roman Religion and the Polybian *politeia*." In *The Roman Middle Republic: Politics, Religion, and Historiography, c. 400–133 BC*, edited by C. Bruun, 251–64. Rome.

Van Beek, B. 2017. *The Archive of the* architektones *Kleon and Theodoros* (P. Petrie Kleon). Leuven.

Van der Ploeg, G. 2018. *The Impact of the Roman Empire on the Cult of Asclepius*. Leiden.

Van Hooff, A.J.L. 1977. "Polybius' Reason and Religion: The Relations between Polybius' Casual Thinking and His Attitude towards Religion in the *Studies of History*." *Klio* 59, no. 1: 101–28.

Van Hoorn, G. 1951. *Choes and Anthesteria*. Leiden.

Várhelyi, Z. 2007. "The Specters of Roman Imperialism: The Live Burials of Greeks and Gauls at Rome." *CA* 26: 277–304.

Vassallo, S. 2012. "The Theater of Montagna dei Cavalli-Hippana." In *Theater outside Athens: Drama in Greek Sicily and South Italy*, edited by K. Bosher, 208–25. Cambridge.

Veal, R. 2017. "The Politics and Economics of Ancient Forests: Timber and Fuel as Levers of Greco-Roman Control." In *Économie et inégalité: Ressources, échanges et pouvoir dans l'antiquité classique*, edited by P. Derron, 317–57. Geneva.

Vella, C. 2016. "Constructions of Consensus: Monument Building and the Fourth to First Millennium BC in the Central Mediterranean Islands." *Journal of Mediterranean Archaeology* 29, no. 2: 225–45.

Virlouvet, C. 1987. "La topographie des distributions frumentaires avant la création de la *Porticus Minucia Frumentaria*." In *L'urbs: Espace urbain et histoire, Ier siècle avant. J.C.–IIIer siècle après J.C.*, 175–89. Rome.

Vogliano, A., ed. [1937] 1966. *Papiri della R. Università di Milano* 1. Milan.

Vogt, E. Z. 1969. *Zinacantan*. Cambridge, MA.

Volk, K. 2015. "Roman Pythagoras." In *Roman Reflections: Studies in Latin Philosophy*, edited by G. D. Williams and K. Volk, 33–49. Oxford.

Volkmann, H. 1990. *Die Massenversklavungen der Einwohner eroberter Städte in der hellenistisch-römischen Zeit.*[2] Stuttgart.

Von Domaszewski, A. [1909] 1975. *Abhandlungen zur römischen Religion*. New York.

Von Reden, S. 2007. "Classical Greece: Consumption." In *The Cambridge Economic History of the Greco-Roman World*, edited by W. Scheidel, I. Morris, and R. Saller, 385–406. Cambridge.

———. 2010. *Money in Classical Antiquity*. Cambridge.

Von Staden, H. 1996. "Liminal Perils: Early Roman Receptions of Greek Medicine." In *Tradition, Transmission, Transformation: Proceedings of Two Conferences on Pre-modern Science Held at the University of Oklahoma*, edited by F. J. Ragep, S. P. Ragep, and S. J. Livesey, 369–418. Leiden.

Von Ungern-Sternberg, J. 2006. "Die *gens Claudia*: Adelsstolz und Republik." In *Erinnerungsorte der Antike: Die römische Welt*, edited by E. Stein-Hölkeskamp and K.-J. Hölkeskamp, 290–99. Munich.

Vottero, D., ed. *Lucio Anneo Seneca: I frammenti*. Bologna.

Wachter, R. 1987. *Altlateinische Inschriften: Sprachliche und epigraphische Untersuchungen zu den Dokumenten bis etwa 150 v. Chr.* Berlin.

Wahlberg, S. E. 2008. "Ovid's Fasti and the Tradition of Callimachus' Aetia in Rome." PhD diss., University of Pennsylvania.

Walbank, F. W. 1957–79. *A Historical Commentary on Polybius*. 3 vols. Oxford.

Wallace, R. W. 1990. "Hellenization and Roman Society in the Late Fourth Century B.C.: A Methodological Critique." In *Staat und Staatlichkeit in der frühen römischen Republik. Akten eines Symposiums 12.–15. Juli 1998. Freie Universität Berlin*, edited by W. Eder, 278–302. Stuttgart.

Walsh, K., P. Attema, and T. de Haas. 2014. "The Pontine Marshes (Central Italy): A Case Study in Wetland Historical Ecology." *BABESCH* 89: 27–46.

Walsh, P. G. 1961. *Livy: His Historical Aims and Methods*. Cambridge.

Walter, U. 1998. "Der Begriff des Staates in der griechischen und römischen Geschichte." In *Althistorisches Kolloquium aus Anlaß des 70. Geburtstages von Jochen Bleicken*, edited by T. Hantos and G. A. Lehmann, 9–27. Stuttgart.

———. 2004. Memoria *und* res publica: *Zur Geschichskultur im republikanischen Rom*. Frankfurt am Main.

———. 2014. "Ordnungszersetzung: Der Fall der späten römischen Republik." In *Aufruhr—Katastrophe—Konkurrenz—Zerfall. Bedrohte Ordnungen als Thema der Kulturwissenschaften*, edited by E. Frie and M. Meier, 83–115. Tübingen.

———. 2017. "Patrizier und Plebeier in der römischen Historiographie." *MH* 74, no. 2: 172–99.

Ward, L. 1990. "Roman Population, Territory, Tribe, City, and Army Size from the Republic's Founding to the Veientane War, 509 BC–400 BC." *AJP* 111, no.1 : 5–39.

Warde Fowler, W. 1899. *The Religious Experience of the Roman People*. London.

Way, M. 2000. "Violence and the Performance of Class in Plautus' *Casina*." *Helios* 27, no. 2: 187–206.

Wazer, C. 2016. "Between Public Health and Popular Medicine: Senatorial and Popular Responses to Epidemic Disease in the Roman Republic." In *Popular Medicine in Graeco-Roman Antiquity: Explorations*, edited by W. V. Harris, 126–46. Leiden.

Webb, R. 2008. *Demons and Dancers: Performance in Late Antiquity*. Cambridge, MA.

Weigel, R. 1986. "Meetings of the Roman Senate on the Capitoline." *L'Antiquité Classique* 55: 333–40.

———. 1998. "Roman Generals and the Vowing of Temples, 500–100 BC." *Classica et Mediaevalia* 49: 119–42.

Weinstock, S. 1957. "Victor and Invictus." *HTR* 50, no. 3: 211–47.

Weissenborn, W., and H. J. Müller, eds. 1880. T. Livi Ab urbe condita libri. Berlin.

Welch, K. E. 2007. *The Roman Amphitheatre: From Its Origins to the Colosseum*. Cambridge.

Welch, M. R., D. Sikkink, E. Sartain, and C. Bond. 2004. "Trust in God and Trust in Man: The Ambivalent Role of Religion in Shaping Dimensions of Social Trust." *Journal for the Scientific Study of Religion* 43, no. 3: 317–43.

Welch, M. R., D. Sikkink, and M. T . Loveland. 2007. "The Radius of Trust: Religion, Social Embeddedness and Trust in Strangers." *Social Forces* 86, no. 1: 23–46.

Welch, M. R., R.E.N. Rivera, B. P. Conway, J. Yonkoski, P. M. Lupton, and R. Giancola. 2005. "Determinants and Consequences of Social Trust." *Sociological Inquiry* 75, no. 4: 453–73.

Wellman, B. 2012. "Is Dunbar's Number Up?" *British Journal of Psychology* 103: 174–76.

Welsh, J. T. 2011. "Accius, Porcius Licinus, and the Beginning of Latin Literature." *JRS* 101: 31–50.

Welwei, K.-W. 2000. Sub corona vendere: *Quellenkritische Studien zu Kriegsgefangenschaft und Sklaverei in Rom bis zum Ende des Hannibalkrieges*. Stuttgart.

West, S. 1984. "Lycophron Italicised." *JHS* 104: 127–51.

Whitley, J. 2001. *The Archaeology of Ancient Greece*. Cambridge.

Williams, J.H.C. 2001. *Beyond the Rubicon: Romans and Gauls in Republican Italy*. Oxford.

Wilson, P. 2008. "Costing the Dionysia." In *Performance, Iconography, Reception: Studies in Honour of Oliver Taplin*, edited by M. Revermann and P. Wilson, 88–127. Oxford.

Wilson, R.J.A. 2013. "Hellenistic Sicily, *c.* 270–100 BC." In *The Hellenistic West: Rethinking the Ancient Mediterranean*, edited by J.R.W. Prag and J. Crawley Quinn, 79–119. Cambridge.

Wilson Jones, M. 2000. *Principles of Roman Architecture*. New Haven.

Winter, F. E. 1993. "The Role of Royal Patronage in the Development of Hellenistic Architecture." *EMC* 12: 251–81.

———. 2006. *Studies in Hellenistic Architecture*. Toronto.

Wiseman, T. P. 1994. *Historiography and Imagination: Eight Essays on Roman Culture*. Exeter.

———. 1998. *Roman Drama and Roman History*. Exeter.

———. 2008. *Unwritten Rome*. Exeter.

———. 2009. "'Mime' and 'Pantomime': Some Problematic Texts." In *New Directions in Ancient Pantomime*, edited by E. Hall and R. Wyles, 146–53. Oxford.

———. 2015. *The Roman Audience: Classical Literature as Social History*. Oxford.

———. 2016. "Maecenas and the Stage." *PBSR* 84: 131–55.

Wissowa, G. 1912. *Religion und Kultus der Römer*.[2] Munich.

Witham, L. 2010. *The Marketplace of the Gods: How Economics Explains Religion*. Oxford.

Wolf, D., and C. Lorber. 2011. "The 'Galatian Shield without Σ' series of Ptolemaic Bronze Coins." *NC* 171: 7–53.

Wonnacott, T. H., and R. J. Wonnacott. 1990. *Introductory Statistics*.[5] New York.

Woolf, G. 2005. "A Sea of Faith?" In *Mediterranean Paradigms and Classical Antiquity*, edited by I. Malkin, 126–43. London.

Wuthnow, R. 2002. "Religious Involvement and Status-Bridging Social Capital." *Journal for the Scientific Study of Religion* 41, no. 4: 669–84.

Xie, L., S. L. Kuhn, G. Sun, J. W. Olsen, Y. Zheng, P. Ding, and Y. Zhao. 2015. "Labor Costs for Prehistoric Earthwork Construction: Experimental and Archaeological Insights from the Lower Yangzi Basin, China." *American Antiquity* 80, no. 1: 67–88.

Yap, A. J., A. S. Wazlawek, B. J. Lucas, A.J.C. Cuddy, and D. R. Carney. 2013. "The Ergonomics of Dishonesty: The Effect of Incidental Posture on Stealing, Cheating, and Traffic Violations." *Psychological Science*: doi: 10.1177/0956797613492425.

Yoffee, N., ed. 2015. *Early Cities in Comparative Perspective: The Cambridge World History*, vol. 3. Cambridge.

Yoffee, N., with N. Terrenato. 2015. "Introduction: A History of the Study of Early Cities." In *Early Cities in Comparative Perspective: The Cambridge World History*. Vol. 3, edited by N. Yoffee, 1–24. Cambridge.

Zavaroni, A. 2006. "Le *iuvilas* di Capua, Anna Perenna e gli *Argei* romani." *DHA* 32, no. 2: 43–58.

Zeggio, S. 1996. "Il deposito votivo." In *Meta Sudans I: Un'area sacra in Palatio e la valle del Colosseo prima e dopo Nerone*, edited by C. Panella, 95–113. Rome.

———. 2016. "Riflessioni per una terminologia dei contesti votivi di Roma." In *Le regole del gioco: Tracce, archeologi, racconti; Studi in onore di Clementina Panella*, edited by A. F. Ferrandes and G. Pardini, 147–75. Rome.

Zink, S. 2015. "The Palatine Sanctuary of Apollo: The Site and Its Development, 6th to 1st c. B.C." *JRA* 28: 358–70.

Ziolkowski, A. 1986. "Les temples A et C du Largo Argentina: Quelques considérations." *MEFRA* 98, no. 2: 623–41.

———. 1992. *The Temples of Mid-Republican Rome and Their Historical and Topographical Context*. Rome.

INDEX

Page numbers in *italics* indicate illustrations, tables, and figures.

A NOTE ON THE TYPE

This book has been composed in Arno, an Old-style serif typeface in the classic Venetian tradition, designed by Robert Slimbach at Adobe.